THE U.S.S.R. AND THE MIDDLE EAST

TEL AVIV UNIVERSITY

The Russian and East European Research Center
and
The Shiloah Center for Middle Eastern
and African Studies

THE U.S.S.R.
AND THE MIDDLE EAST

Edited by
Michael Confino and Shimon Shamir

A HALSTED PRESS BOOK

JOHN WILEY & SONS, New York · Toronto
ISRAEL UNIVERSITIES PRESS, Jerusalem

Library of Congress Cataloging in Publication Data
Main entry under title:

The U.S.S.R. and the Middle East.

"A Halsted Press book."
1. Russia—Foreign relations—Near East. 2. Near
East—Foreign relations—Russia.
I. Confino, Michael, 1926–   ed. II. Shamir, Shimon, ed.
DS63.2.R9U19   1973   327.47'056   73-2735
ISBN 0-470-16832-3

IUP Cat. No. 36084

Composed, printed and bound by Keter Press, Jerusalem
PRINTED IN ISRAEL

INTRODUCTION

This book is the product of a Conference on the Soviet Union and the Middle East, held at Tel Aviv University under the auspices of the School of History. The Conference was organized by the Shiloah Center for Middle Eastern and African Studies and the Russian and East European Research Center. Thirty-six European, American, and Israeli scholars, specialists in Middle Eastern and Soviet studies, participated (see list on p. 439). The Conference conducted seven sessions between 26 and 30 December, 1971.

* * *

At the time of the Conference, a principal phase of the Soviet Middle Eastern venture appeared to be nearing a successful completion. After a decade and a half of circumspective but constant penetration, the Soviet Union had now become a Mediterranean power with recognized interests in the Middle East where it regulated economic investments, exercised political influence, and operated military bases. The Soviets had recently formalized their status in Egypt, the leading Arab state, by concluding a treaty of friendship and cooperation, and to many it was reminiscent of the treaties on which the British dominant position in the area had rested in the past. Shortly afterwards, the Soviet Union's Middle Eastern positions had been utilized for the airlift of arms to the Indian subcontinent, thus enabling Soviet-backed India to triumph over the Pakistanis who were favored by both the U.S. and China. This seemed, therefore, an appropriate moment to pause and reflect on the Soviet entrenchment in the Middle East: How were Soviet policies made and operated? What were their long-range objectives? How did they affect political systems and societies in the Middle East? How deeply were the Soviets committed in the Middle Eastern conflict? And, finally, to what extent was their involvement constrained by superpower polarities?

ix

To set the ground for its deliberations, the Conference started off by probing into the making of Soviet policy. Following an opening session in which Professor Pipes presented a paper on the operational principles of the Soviets' foreign policy and Professor Morgenthau—on the dynamics of their Middle Eastern policy, the first working session of the Conference took up the question of the relative weight of the various factors that affected Soviet policy-making. The opening papers dealt with three such factors: the domestic forces (Professor Dallin), the economic burden (Dr. Ofer) and the ideological dimension (Dr. Eran).

In the discussion which ensued, Professor Pipes said he did not see indications to support the view that Moscow's domestic concerns now had priority over its foreign ones. Professor Hurewitz pointed to the large investment of bureaucratic organizational interests and institutional prestige, mainly of the military establishment and its sub-components, as a factor occupying a prominent place among the driving forces of Soviet Middle Eastern policy. Professor Laqueur expressed skepticism about the practical implications of the post-Stalin changes in the Soviet decision-making process and about the significance of differences detected in the writings of experts in various Soviet institutions. Following in the same vein, Professor Dinerstein agreed that Soviet decision-makers were not much influenced by the writings of experts, but nevertheless, he claimed, detailed information revealed that these writings offered insight into many related problems. Professor Shamir questioned the applicability of what was called the Party-orientation in Soviet policy-making to a country like Egypt and doubted the realism of that trend. Dr. Pinchuk commented that it would be unjustified to belittle the role of Party-orientation in Soviet policies for, as long as the Soviet Union bids for leadership in the world Communist movement, it must show regard to the reactions of Communist parties. Dr. Berner pointed out indications of the existence of a group which regarded Marxist-Leninist revolution as the vehicle for stabilizing Soviet influence in the area and sought, for example, to change the Egyptian regime. Professor Lewis raised the question of the possible effects of the Soviet Union's attitude toward its Jewish minority on its Middle Eastern policy, in a manner somewhat parallel to the way its attitudes toward its Turkish and Armenian elements had influenced its dealings with Turkey and Iran.

The last discussant in that session, Professor Löwenthal, challenged the conception of Soviet policy as being motivated by a sense of abiding conflict with the non-Communist world. He said that while it was true that the Soviet leadership might need a sense of struggle for their legitimation, it was doubtful whether they were capable of conducting foreign policy, over a long period, as a consistent offensive, concentrating all efforts at each particular time on a particular enemy of their choice.

> On the whole, Soviet foreign policy has to take place in a world in which a very large element is not foreseeable and, of course, one of the least foreseeable elements is developments within the Communist bloc, or within what once was the Communist bloc. The new conflict with China . . . is a conflict which is part of these unforeseen developments in which the Soviet Union suddenly finds itself on the operational and strategic defensive. . . .
> Even the old rivalry, the superpower rivalry with the United States, cannot be conceived in terms of a one-sided offensive by the Soviet Union. There is on both sides, at the present time, a desire for stability of one's own power sphere, and at the same time an inability to confine oneself to the defensive because it is in the nature of world-power rivalry that any neutral area, any power vacuum, is something that one has to fill or else the other fills it.

Professor Löwenthal proposed that the Soviet Union operated in a world system where it was again and again faced with priority decisions with which it had to react. These, he said, were, above all, of three types: allocation of resources between foreign and domestic needs; priorities between the conflict with China and the conflict with the West; and, in its strategy in the Third World, preference for existing regimes or the more radical forces beyond them. At any rate, the decisions of Soviet foreign policy did not spring from a preconceived operational plan but from the necessities of changing situations, both external and domestic.

The Soviet Union's overall strategy in the Middle East was discussed in the second session of that day, following a paper by Dr. Pinchuk which had set it in historical perspective and an opening statement by Professor Kolkowicz which had established its basic patterns. (Dr. Becker's paper on the Soviet policy toward the Persian Gulf and oil had also been distributed for that session.) The first participant in the discussion, Dr. Altug, said that one of the basic traits of the Soviet Union's strategy was in fact a continuation of that of czarist Russia, namely lending support, in a very selective way, to movements of national

liberation in the areas which they wished to penetrate. Several discussants
held the view that the Soviet Union was primarily concerned with China
and hence its southward thrust was aimed at the encirclement of that
adversary. Professor Churba, on the other hand, pointed to the theory
that Soviet activities in the area were directed, in the first phase, at the
neutralization of the U.S. Sixth Fleet and the outflanking of NATO
forces in the Mediterranean and Western Europe; having accomplished
that they would turn against China. Professor Morgenthau expressed
the opinion that the Soviets, like the British in the past, have neither a
"grand design" nor a clear-cut hierarchy of objectives: they were
expanding simultaneously, using different methods for different purposes,
and "where there is an opportunity which fits into their interests, they
will seize it." Mr. Allon pointed out that while it was true that in military
terms the Soviets were trying to avoid a two-front confrontation,
nevertheless, short of risking war, and wherever they sensed weakness
of will in their opponents, they would seize any opportunity to extend
their influence. Employing a new version of gun-boat policy, now based
on missile-equipped fleets, they operated on more than one front. It is
a fact, he said, that they challenged the West both in the Mediterranean
and Indian Ocean, both in the Middle East and Indian subcontinent.

Professor Lewis suggested that "the emergence of a Soviet empire
on the Indian Ocean, of the type which flourished in centuries past,"
was not improbable. He noted that there existed

... a parallel between the present growth of the Russian empire in
Asia and the growth and flowering of the British Empire in Asia at
an earlier stage. Two changes seem to be taking place in the nature
of Russian interests in the Middle East. One is the gradual transformation of Russia from the intrusive power interested in making
trouble, to the established power interested in enjoying its position,
making use of its position. The other is the shift of Russian interest
from the western half of the Middle East to the eastern half of the
Middle East, to, in fact, the traditional Imperial road to India.

In India, Russia is still, shall we say, at the East India Company
stage; Clive has not yet emerged. But already there exists a problem
which British India faced for so long, not of the northwest frontier
but of the northeast frontier. If Russia is replacing Britain, China is
replacing Russia as the power threatening the subcontinent. And
there too there is a parallel in the intrusive Chinese activities in the
Middle East, and the kind in which the Russians engaged when they

could, and as and where they could, at an earlier stage. The Russians
are obviously greatly alarmed by Chinese activities in the Horn of
Africa, in Southern Arabia, in Tanzania, and so on.

Accepting the validity of the analogy between today's Soviets and the
British empire-builders, Professor Dinerstein nevertheless pointed out
that the Soviets in this case were not going to be rewarded by lucrative
colonies but burdened with demanding clients, and it may be correct
to suppose that their venture at empire-building will be abandoned.
However, he warned, for those who are at the present in the way of
this venture, it would make all the difference in the world whether this
took place sooner or later. Professor Binder, drawing attention to the
striking adaptability which the Soviet policy had shown in its dealings
with a great variety of political regimes and leaderships in the area,
suggested that the idea of *Pax Sovietica,* as a goal, would perhaps lend
coherence to the diversified Soviet activities in the Middle East better
than the idea of a Soviet empire. Professor Laqueur assessed that
physical occupation by Soviet forces was highly unlikely beyond Eastern
Europe. The expansion of the Soviet sphere of influence was possible,
"but influence is not necessarily domination."

The second day of the discussions was devoted to the Soviet Union's
impact on the Middle Eastern countries, either by virtue of its own
presence and activities or through those of the overwhelmingly Soviet-
oriented local Communist movements. This issue had already been raised
on the previous day in connection with Dr. Eran's paper and in a paper
presented by Professor Halpern on "Soviet Powerlessness in the Transformation of Arab Society." Examining the problem through the lenses
of a theory which articulated eight basic ways of human encounter and
suggested a new perception of power and modernization, Professor
Halpern had observed:

> The Soviet contribution has greatly affected the clash of incoherent
> power elements within and among Middle Eastern states but it has
> not enhanced Arab capacity for modernization. . . .
> Though many intelligence operatives, policy-makers, journalists, and
> scholars earn a living by worrying about the possibility of a positive
> correlation between Soviet influence and Communist influence in
> the Middle East, I have always held that the negative correlation

which has in fact obtained for so long ought to be taken seriously. I should like to mention only one especially neglected reason for this negative correlation. Navies, however big, whether in the Mediterranean or the Persian Gulf, whether Soviet or American, together with their armies and airforces, are powerless directly or indirectly to transform those human relations which alone can sustain *any* Arab government of *any* political persuasion long enough to overcome domestic incoherence. . . .

You cannot build a modernizing society on this foundation. There is not enough sustained discipline and cooperation here to construct and then support with the threat of Soviet occupation even the equivalence of the current Czechoslovak regime. Nasser amply proved the limits of what even a fellow-Arab can do for other Arabs. Bourguiba, more successful in modernizing than any other Arab leader, has also been most able to contain foreign influence. . . .

The greater likelihood, already much in evidence, is a Soviet contribution to the deformation rather than the transformation of Arab society. Soviet military assistance, by its weight and emphasis, encourages Arab society to take the training of pilots much more seriously than the training of scientists. It helps to exaggerate the political influence of the military and the domestic security apparatus without being able to prevent them from being discredited by their defeats, yet does little or nothing to help those Arabs concerned with genuine modernization. Soviet economic assistance tends to confuse the difference between electrification and socialist collaboration. The Soviet view of its own interests in the world encourages the Arabs in their own tendency to locate the main cause of troubles in external rather than domestic problems.

Professor Halpern cautioned that growing weakness and incoherence among the Arabs would tend to lead to fanatic violence, probably practised by small Arab groups, without a concern for rational calculation or likely success.

Commenting on Professor Halpern's paper, Dr. Gitelman questioned whether the Soviet Union was at all interested, at the present stage, in the transformation of Egyptian or, for that matter, any other society. He expressed the view, supported by several other speakers, that beyond Eastern Europe, the Soviets had abandoned the attempt to transform, in the light of Marxism-Leninism, the social base and the value structure of client states and preferred to conduct itself in the area as a world superpower.

All the papers presented on the second day dealt with the local scene. Professor Vatikiotis assessed the Soviet impact on Egypt while Professor Kedourie analyzed Egyptian resentment of Communism and the Soviets emanating from basically Islamic roots. Several papers gave detailed historical accounts of Communism in selected Arab countries (Dr. Dann—Iraq; Dr. Levy and Dr. Rabinovich—Syria; Dr. Cohen—Jordan; Professor Shamir—Egypt; Dr. Shaked, Dr. Warburg, and Miss Souery—Sudan); all but one were written by associates of the Shiloah Center utilizing, among other sources, the Center's extensive documentation system.

In the discussion, Professor Löwenthal elaborated on the concept of "licensed infiltration" by which he had explained the entrance of Communists into the single-party structures of Soviet-sponsored nationalist regimes. The intention, he explained, was not to act as a subversive opposition from within but to gain influence over the regime itself, "possibly turning Nasser into a Castro." This strategy, however, has apparently failed. Dr. Eran pointed out that actually the Egyptian Communists had not been forced by the Soviets to join the A.S.U. While the Soviets certainly wished them to do so, they nevertheless preferred this to come about through a decision adopted by the Egyptian Communists themselves, so as not to bear responsibility, before the world Communist movement, for the dissolution of a Communist Party. Dr. Berner drew a comparison between "licensed infiltration" in Egypt and in Algeria and concluded that in Egypt the weakness of the Communists and the insignificance of their leaders have decided the fate of this venture. He pointed out, however, that in the hypothetical case of a Soviet seizure of control, even a meager Communist nucleus could rapidly grow to become a big ruling party—witness the experience of Eastern Europe. Professor Binder said that while the Communists did not have any considerable influence in Egypt and "licensed infiltration" had ceased to be a meaningful policy, it would be an exaggeration to speak of the impenetrability of Egyptian society. Some factions might emerge which would present themselves to the Soviets as allies preferable to the present regime.

Ideology, however, was not considered to be an effective vehicle. Ideologies, said Professor Vatikiotis, are formulated by the persons in power and the "scribblers pervade them to the population and among themselves." Turning to the case of Syria, Professor Lewis demonstrated that "in conditions of chronic insecurity and endemic disloyalty, people will tend to rely for political action on more traditional, and therefore more reliable, solidarities—on those of kinship, of region, and of sect." This was reiterated by Dr. Rabinovich who showed that in Syria both the Communist Party and the Ba'th Party could be regarded, to a large extent, as a response to the unique problem of the minorities.

Professor Kedourie suggested that in view of all this perhaps all Communist parties in the Arab world, with the exception of that of Iraq, might be regarded as "paper tigers." Professor Baer dwelt on the inherent weakness of the Communist movement in Egypt, which had expressed itself in the past in the fact that the movement had often been split into several factions; even absorption into the nationalist movement had precedents in the past. He stressed that the deep roots of Islam in Egyptian society and the strong anti-Communist and anti-Soviet sentiments they fed should not be seen as irrelevant to the power struggle in that country. Dr. Levi specified that in his evaluation an intensification of anti-Soviet popular currents could definitely be expected and that it might eventually bear resemblance to the anti-Imperialism that had shaped Arab policies in the last two decades and before.

The location of the Conference in Israel allowed the participants to gain firsthand impressions of two aspects of the Soviet position in the Middle East: the problems of Zionism and Jewish emigration in Soviet policy, and the implications for Israel of the Soviet involvement in the Arab-Israeli conflict. Accordingly, the Conference participants met, for discussion of the first question, with Jewish intellectuals recently arrived from the Soviet Union, and for discussing the second—with Israeli leaders. Among the latter was Deputy Prime Minister Yigal Allon who participated actively in the Conference—not as a representative of official policy but as a prominent Israeli thinker on questions of regional politics and strategy and the author of several books in that field.

The first question was discussed in the first session of the last day of the Conference. The session was opened by Mr. Ro'i's paper on Soviet-Israeli relations during the Stalin period and in the year following Stalin's death. The paper was supplemented by an analysis of Soviet policy on Jewish emigration in later years, presented by Israeli M.K. Arie Eliav, an expert on this particular subject. Eliav listed the numerous considerations in Soviet thinking, working in favor or against allowing Jewish emigration. He showed that Soviet decisions were made through struggle between opposing trends and contradictory interests. This called, he concluded, for a flexible policy on the part of Israel so as to find a common language with the pragmatist elements in Soviet policy-making.

Following along the same lines, the discussants joined efforts to provide an explanation for the Soviet policy toward Jews and Jewish emigration. Professor Pipes suggested that some high Russian officials, regarding the Jew as the primary carrier of the liberal germ, might have reached the conclusion that there was no room for Jews in the Soviet Union. He recalled that the similarly motivated drive of the Warsaw regime to make Poland *Judenfrei* had probably been undertaken with Soviet consent. Several speakers pointed to the Soviet Union's endemic minorities problem as the key to understanding its Jewish policies. Professor Dinerstein said that unlike in the Stalin period, when Jews were isolated and helpless, at the present time their protest has found resonance among other awakening national minorities and in international politics. The attitude of other nationalities of the Soviet Union was particularly alarming for the Soviet leaders who must be aware of the fact that within a few years the non-Russian nationalities will exceed the Russian population. This fear, cautioned Professor Dinerstein, may turn in either direction. Professor Laqueur, assessing that the Soviet Union was moving to a certain form of national socialism, agreed that the Jewish question, and the national question in general, was going to become a most acute domestic issue in the years to come. This, however, did not mean that Jewish emigration could not be turned off, from one day to the next, in the very same way it had been turned on, he concluded.

Professor Löwenthal pursued the line of thought earlier suggested by Professor Lewis, concerning the link between Moscow's attitude to minorities and its policy toward the respective nationalist centers outside the borders of the Soviet Union (see above). He pointed to possible implications of Soviet anxieties about the existence of such centers for the policy toward the State of Israel. The discovery of Jewish attachment to Israel, he said, had had a great deal to do with Stalin's turning against the Israeli state. Similarly, he warned, if the Soviet Union was made to feel that each of the three million Soviet Jews was regarded a candidate for emigration and hence potentially disloyal, this would increase the dangers of Soviet hostility to the State of Israel. Professor Lewis, on the other hand, qualifying his own analogy, pointed out that while aspirations of the other minorities could be satisfied only by dismemberment of the Soviet Union, the aspirations of the Jews could be satisfied by emigration. As other possible motives for allowing Jewish emigration, he proposed that, in the absence of diplomatic relations with Israel, the Soviets might have felt the need to maintain another type of contact and to have some leverage on Israel. Perhaps, he suggested as a tentative thought, they were also interested in letting out the most nationally minded Jews so that the resumption of diplomatic contacts with Israel would not stir up too active enthusiasm among the Jewish population. Professor Confino questioned the notion of a direct linkage between the Soviet domestic policy toward the Jews and their policy toward Israel. Historically, he said, these two were inversely related, which suggested the possibility that they were regarded by Moscow as belonging to two entirely different areas. He also suggested that in Soviet opposition to Zionism, ideology was a less important factor than it had generally been assumed.

To explain the anti-Jewish attitude of the Soviet authorities, Professor Morgenthau noted that the Jews, traditionally believers in a higher law and a higher source of truth, were always suspect of disloyalty. "There is an existential incompatibility between the Soviet Jews and the Soviet government, which goes even beyond the incompatibility of other religious minorities," he concluded.

The second subject of that day was the Soviet involvement in the Middle Eastern conflict, on both the plane of the competing superpowers and that of the local contenders. Papers were read on the Soviet involvement in the Arab-Israeli conflict (Mr. Allon), the relation of superpower rivalry to the conflict (Professor Hurewitz), and the transformation of the local subordinate system (Professor Binder). The broader aspects of the problem were analyzed in the last paper, dealing with Soviet dilemmas in the Middle East (Professor Laqueur).

The discussion which followed centered on some problems that were of great relevance to the Israelis' position vis-à-vis the Soviet-Arab coalition. It started off with the question: To what extent did Israeli moves make any difference to Soviet policy in the area? Professor Dinerstein challenged the popular Israeli notion that it did not. Without attempting to decide the issue of the Soviet response in 1970 to the Israeli deep-penetration bombing in Egypt, he affirmed that major decisions were usually made by the Soviets not according to some long-range plan but in response to immediate situations, and there were no grounds to suppose that this was not so where Israel was concerned. Professor Confino stated that, on the other hand, at least in the case of the 1955 arms deal with Egypt—responsibility for which had so often been attributed to the Israeli raid on Gaza—there existed evidence which predated the initiation of the deal several weeks prior to the raid. The Soviet maneuvers on the eve of the Six-Day War, which according to one version were based on "the straw-man gambit" and emanated from a preconceived scenario, could also be seen as indicative of the Soviet *modus operandi*. Professor Kolkowicz suggested that the Middle East was the first region where the Soviet Union acted without being under the pressure of a threat to its own vital interests. Accordingly, he said, Israel did have the capacity to influence Soviet calculation through its political behavior and the signals it transmitted.

What was the likelihood of a Soviet intervention to support the Arab side against Israel? Professor Lewis pointed out that as far as the Soviet-Egyptian treaty of friendship and cooperation was concerned, the Soviets stopped short of making any military commitment. The inference was that the Soviets kept their options open in Egypt, "including the right to let the Egyptians down again if this seems to be in other respects expedient." Professor Horelick maintained that the involvement of patrons in a war started by one of the clients against the will of the former should not be excluded. It all depended on the circumstances:

> For the purposes of projecting into the future, I think we have to distinguish between different levels of conflict, different strategies and tactics that might be adopted by the combatants. For example, renewed fighting on the Egyptian side that involved the need to maximize the sanctuary status that the Egyptians felt their interior enjoyed would present one kind of a problem. A renewal of fighting which took the form of artillery shelling—a different kind of problem. Equally, the strategies and tactics adopted by the Israeli side in responding to the Egyptian ones would determine whether or not the disinclination of the Soviet Union to become involved would override the strong disinclination not to see its clients defeated again.

Professor Löwenthal said that the situation should be analyzed in the light of global bipolarity which, in his opinion, even if changing, remained an established fact. He warned that the relationship of the United States to its allies and protégés could no longer be taken for granted and because of this the non-intervention of the Soviet Union could not be taken for granted either. Therefore, it had become absolutely vital for exposed countries like Israel to constantly make their points of view and political aims understandable and convincing to the U.S. For this purpose a positive effect on public opinion was of primary importance. Professor Morgenthau maintained that while objectively the importance that the Soviets attached to the Middle East was a limited one, under certain circumstances their position in the area could become an issue to which they would subjectively attribute excessive importance. In his opinion, the U.S. position, which was crucial in this situation, had not changed in any decisive way nor had the reliability of its support been diminished. He affirmed that U.S. deterrence was inherent in the bipolarity of nuclear power, which had not been affected by recent developments. Professor Morgenthau, too, stressed the importance of public opinion for upholding a positive attitude on the part of U.S. policy-makers to the problems of Israel.

Replying to the two last speakers, Mr. Allon said that with all the importance Israel attached to world public opinion, it sometimes found itself in a position where this had to be superseded by considerations of Israel's vital interests, such as the need to establish secure borders. The U.S. posture vis-à-vis the Soviets, however, was determined to a larger extent by the view of its interests, which in this part of the world often happened to coincide with those of Israel. The position of the U.S. in this area, he suggested, was stronger than was generally believed and the Soviet attempts to extend their influence were facing increasing difficulties and risks. In these circumstances, he concluded, the Soviets, who usually became very cautious when faced with serious opposition, would not find it easy to take a decision to intervene directly.

Thus, the question of Soviet intentions, which had become the main theme of the deliberations of the Conference, was also the one with which it concluded its last session. It may be noted that the conclusion of the Conference coincided with the expiry of President Sadat's "year of decision," and while nobody was expecting a prompt renewal of the Middle Eastern war, the question whether the Soviet Union would allow itself to be drawn into taking an active role in a war initiated by its Egyptian clients, or perhaps even yield to their pressure and signal consent to the resumption of hostilities, was very much in the air. The crucial question, as Professor Confino pointed out in his concluding remarks, was whether the Soviet Union was going to upgrade its objectives in the Middle East or whether this area now represented for it a diminishing priority.

The year that has elapsed since the Conference seems to have borne out the participants who held that Soviet policy in the Middle East operated within limits determined by the constraints of global bipolarity. Not only has this been reasserted at the Moscow summit meeting in May 1972, but it was also dramatically demonstrated in Egypt in July when the Soviets preferred to incur the humiliation and losses of withdrawing their military personnel rather than yield over an issue which, they felt, involved a risk of confrontation. The Soviets have had to put up with other setbacks in the area, such as the overtures made by Arab governments, notably the Sudan and Yemen, to the U.S.

However, this year's trends of developments can by no means be seen as unilinear, for the very same year witnessed also the intensification of Soviet efforts to establish their influence and presence in the oil-rich and strategically located areas of the eastern part of the Middle East, namely Iraq, the Persian Gulf and the Indian Ocean's western coasts. This may, perhaps, imply a significant realignment of Soviet interests in the Middle East, but then it may also reflect the downgrading of Soviet objectives in the area. The rhythm of a great power's expansion and recession, of course, is hardly susceptible to the fluctuations of a single year. It is rather through the perspective of decades that the import of these developments, as well as that of others discussed in this book, will emerge for all to see.

There is, indeed, some uneasiness in the thought that while the statements of the contributors to this book are immutably recorded here, its readers will continue to grow wiser on the same questions with which it has dealt. It remains only to be hoped that, from that vantage point, they will not view too unkindly these efforts to grasp the components of an immensely complex reality and to discern the course of the rapidly whirling wheels of change.

*   *   *

The papers presented in this volume comprise most of those read at the Conference. It was found impractical to reproduce also the proceedings of the deliberations beyond the synopsis presented above. The brief summaries of the contributions of the discussants have undoubtedly done them injustice but the limitations of space made it impossible to represent more faithfully their level of articulation. For the same reason, I did not follow the usage of many editors of similar collections of papers to include summaries of the papers themselves, hoping for the indulgence of the readers who in some cases may have to refer to the texts of the papers in order to discern the crux of the argument. Copies of the full transcript of the Conference have been filed at the Shiloah and Russian Centers.

For the convenience of the users of this book, I have not arranged the papers in the volume in the order of their presentation, but according to subject-matter, grouping the papers which deal primarily with the Soviet Union separately from those which concentrate on the Middle Eastern states. The original order of presentation is indicated above in the synopsis of the discussions.

The usual post-conference revisions were made by the authors in the first half of 1972. A number of papers, mainly those presenting hard factual data, were updated at the proofreading stage in autumn 1972. Beyond that, the editing policy was to modify the manuscripts as little as possible, thus preserving the individual style and characteristics of each paper.

Spelling and transliteration have been unified but here, too, various exceptions were allowed. For example, the strict system of transliteration from Arabic (which is that employed by the Shiloah Center) was not applied in the papers of the Sovietologists.

The two Centers wish to express their gratitude to all those who assisted in organizing the Conference and publishing this volume; they are too many to be listed here by name. Above all, our thanks are given to the scholars who participated in the Conference and shared with us their knowledge and insight.

December 1972

SHIMON SHAMIR

PART ONE
THE SOVIET THRUST

1. THE MAKING OF SOVIET FOREIGN POLICY

RICHARD PIPES

SOME OPERATIONAL PRINCIPLES OF SOVIET FOREIGN POLICY

Perhaps the best way to define the scope of this essay is negatively, by stating what it is not. Our purpose is not to lay bare the motives of Soviet foreign policy or its ultimate aspirations. These topics lie at the heart of the matter, of course, and cannot be entirely ignored; but, belonging as they do to the realm of national and elite psychology, they are best set aside for separate treatment.[1]

Nor will our concern be with the narrower subject of Soviet techniques of negotiation. Although diplomats trained in the traditional school have good reason to look upon Russian (or, more precisely, Communist) methods of negotiating as in a class of their own, it is doubtful whether such methods actually exist.[2] Frustrations experienced in negotiating with Communists derive from the fact that the latter often engage in talks in order not to reach an agreement but to attain some other, incidental objective, such as ascertaining how strong is their opponents' determination on a given issue, splitting hostile alliances, or influencing world opinion. When they intend to use negotiations in this manner, Communist diplomats indeed display an intransigence which can be mollified only by full acceptance of their terms, that is, by surrender of the principle of compromise which is the quintessence of negotiation.

However, whenever they happen to be interested in a settlement, Communist diplomats act in a traditional manner, efficiently and undeterred by difficulties. One need only recall the speed with which in 1939 the Soviet Union concluded its non-aggression treaty with Germany, or the relative ease with which the Communist bloc settled its outstanding difficulties with the West immediately after Stalin's death, once the new party leadership in Russia had concluded that a detente was in order. Responding to Eisenhower's "deeds not words" speech of April 16, 1953, in which the President called for a resolution of several major problems, among them Korea, Vietnam, and Austria, Communist diplomats negotiated in reasonable time mutually agreeable terms on issues which only a short time earlier had seemed to defy all solution. As a result, in July 1953 there was an armistice in Korea, in June 1954 an armistice in Indochina, and in May 1955 a long overdue treaty with Austria. It certainly is no coincidence that shortly after President Nixon had announced he intended to pay a state visit to China, hoary disagreements affecting the status of West Berlin melted away and a workable draft of a four-power agreement could be hammered out. All of which suggests that if the West often faces excruciating difficulties negotiating with the Communists the fault lies not in different negotiating techniques. The Communists employ distinct methods of diplomatic intercourse only when they have in mind objectives other than negotiation and agreement.

One way to describe what we will be talking about is to borrow terms from the vocabulary of military science. The language of Soviet politics is permeated with militarisms: even the most pacific spheres of government activity become "fronts" which have to be "stormed," all-out "offensives" are launched to conquer internal difficulties, and even peace itself becomes the object of a "struggle." The martial language is appropriate, for, as will be noted shortly, Soviet theory does not distinguish sharply between military and political forms of activity, regarding both as variant ways of waging conflict which it regards as the essence of history. "Strategy" and "tactics" are useful in this connection, and have been employed. But even more accurate is a third term from the vocabulary of Soviet military theory, "the art of operations" (*operativnoe isskustvo*). Its origin apparently goes back to the 1890s, but it acquired special relevance in the 1920s, when Soviet experts, analyzing the record of World War I and of the Russian Civil War, concluded that neither "strategy" nor "tactics" adequately described warfare waged with mass armies under industrial conditions. They then created the concept "art of operations" to bridge the two. Since that time this concept has occupied an honored place in Soviet military thinking, and, indeed, some Soviet authorities credit Russian victories in World War II to its systematic application. If tactics describes the employment of troops on the battlefield, and strategy the overall disposition of all of one's forces, "the art of operations" denotes the fluid and dynamic element in military planning by virtue of which individual tactical moves are coordinated over a period of time to promote the ultimate strategic objective, defeat of the enemy.

According to Soviet theorists, under conditions of prolonged modern warfare, victory requires a succession of interdependent operations, based on solid logistic support and synchronized to produce on the enemy mounting pressure which, attaining unbearable levels, eventually causes him to collapse. In the literature on the subject, there are just enough hints to indicate that "the art of operations" is derived mainly from analysis of the campaigns waged in World War I by General Ludendorff, whose masterful conduct of "total" war seems to have exercised a greater influence on Communist political practices than the writings of Karl Marx and Friedrich Engels combined. "The purpose of operations is the destruction, the complete annihilation of the vital forces of the enemy," states a recent Soviet handbook on the subject, paraphrasing an authority of the 1920s, "its method is the uninterrupted attack; its means, prolonged operational pursuit, which avoids pauses and stops, and is attained by a succession of consecutive operations, each of which serves as the transitional link toward the ultimate goal, accomplished in the final, closing operation."[3] The whole concept, with its stress on coordinated, uninterrupted assault intended to bring mounting pressure on the enemy, admirably describes what is probably the most characteristic feature of Soviet foreign policy.

The subject is of great importance and deserves the kind of careful study given to Soviet military practices. Soviet foreign policy involves a great deal more than diplomacy: diplomacy is one of its minor instrumentalities and Soviet diplomats resemble more the bearers of white flags sent to cross combat lines than the staff officers or the combatants. But it is also more than mere military bluster. One cannot isolate from the total arsenal of Soviet foreign policy any one weapon and by neutralizing its sting hope to parry its thrust. To understand this policy one must understand its mode of operations.

THE ART OF OPERATIONS

In an essay on creativity, Arthur Koestler observed that seminal ideas are born from bringing two premises belonging to two different mental fields to bear upon each other.[4] Using this approach, Marxism may be said to owe its influence to a successful fusion of sociology with economics, and Freudianism to the grafting of medicine onto psychology. With this definition in mind, we may ascribe the significance of Leninism as an ideological force in the 20th century to an innovative linking of politics with warfare—in other words, to the militarization of politics, which Lenin was the first statesman to accomplish.

For psychological reasons which need not be gone into here, Lenin was most attracted in the writings of Marx and Engels not by the liberal and democratic spirit strongly in evidence there, but by the idea of class war. Peter Struve, who knew him well in his early political career, says that Lenin took to Marx's theory mainly because he found in it "the doctrine of class war, relentless and thoroughgoing, aiming at the final destruction and extermination of the enemy."[5] Class war, of course, was and remains the common property of all socialist and anarchist movements of modern times. But to Lenin, more than to any other prominent radical of his period, it was a real, tangible thing: a daily, hourly struggle pitting the exploited against the exploiters and (after November 1917) what he defined as the "camp of socialism" against that of "capitalism" or "imperialism." What to Marx and Engels was a means, became for him an end. His preoccupation as theorist was always with the methods of waging political warfare: anything that did not in some way bear on that subject, he regarded as harmful, or at best, as useless. All his thinking was militant. He was the first public figure to view politics entirely in terms of warfare, and to pursue this conception to its inexorable conclusion. Lenin read Clausewitz rather late in life (1915), but he immediately found him a most congenial writer. He referred to him often, praising him as a thinker whose ideas, as he once put it, have become "the indispensable acquisition of every thinking man."[6] As one might expect, he especially admired Clausewitz' insistence that war and politics were not antithetical means of conducting relations among states but alternatives, chosen according to what the situation required. On one occasion, Lenin told a friend that "political tactics and military tactics represent that which the Germans call *Grenzgebiet* [adjoining areas]," and urged Communist party workers to study Clausewitz to learn the applications of this principle.[7]

These historical and biographical facts require mention because the Soviet leadership in power since November 1917 has been thoroughly imbued with the spirit of Leninist politics. The reason lies not in the innate force of Lenin's ideas or the ability of any idea to be bequeathed intact from one generation to another. It lies in the fact that the Soviet leadership of today finds itself in a situation in all essential respects identical with the one Lenin had left on his death, that is, devoid of a popular mandate or any other kind of legitimacy to justify its monopoly of political power except the alleged exigencies of class war. The regime is locked in; and even if it wanted to extricate itself from its predicament by democratizing, it could not do so because of the staunch opposition of the bureaucratic establishment to genuine political reform. The closed character of Russia's ruling elite, its insulation from the inflow of fresh human types and ideas by means of the principle of co-optation, assures a high degree of ideological and psychological' continuity. In this respect, the Soviet elite resembles a self-perpetuating religious order rather than what one ordinarily thinks of as a governing class. The growth of productivity, the rise in living standards, the spread of education, and the sundry other factors which some Western observers count on in time to liberalize the Soviet system have no bearing either on the internal position of the ruling elite or on its political outlook. Only a major upheaval—such as a prolonged and unsuccessful war, or a prolonged and unresolved feud among the leaders—could alter the situation.

The Soviet government conducts a "total" foreign policy which draws no principal distinction between diplomatic, economic, psychological, or military means of operation. It also does not differentiate in any fundamental respect between domestic and foreign relations. This accounts for the virtual absence in the Soviet Union of a literature devoted to the theory of foreign relations. Every policy decision, after all, is made in the Politburo of the party. As a rule, the Soviet Minister of Foreign Affairs (the incumbent, Andrei Gromyko, included) is not a member of the Politburo—a fact which suggests what importance attaches to his office. The Soviet Union maintains a Ministry of Foreign Affairs with its diplomatic corps because other countries with which it deals happen to do so. It does not, however, charge the Ministry with the formulation of foreign policy. All important foreign policy decisions are made in the Politburo and often even carried out by its own departments. The role of the Ministry is further whittled down by the practice increasingly to entrust foreign policy matters to organs of the police and intelligence. The KGB, through its "Foreign Directorate" (First Main Administration), and with the assistance of organs of military intelligence (GRU), may well have a greater voice in Soviet foreign policy, especially as it concerns the so-called Third World, than the Ministry of Foreign Affairs. Alexander Kaznacheev, a one-time Soviet diplomat stationed in Rangoon, states that among his hundred or more colleagues in the embassy, fewer than one-fifth actually worked for the Ministry and were responsible to the Ambassador; the remainder was employed by other agencies, mostly engaged in intelligence activities and reporting directly to Moscow.[8] In contending with a foreign policy of such an unorthodox kind, the United States has had to charge its own Central Intelligence Agency with a variety of responsibilities exceeding its formal mandate. These activities have recently been restrained, to the visible relief of the KGB and other operational intelligence agencies of the Soviet Union, which prefer to have this particular field all to themselves. The steady shift of the epicenter of US foreign policy management from the Department of State to the White House is probably part of the same process which earlier had led to the broadening of the CIA's functions, namely the need somehow to counter "total" Soviet policy with a "total" policy of one's own.

THE CORRELATION OF FORCES

When we say that Soviet policy is inherently militant we do not mean to imply it is necessarily belligerent. In the context of an ideology which regards armed conflict as only one of several instruments at the politician's disposal, militancy can assume a great variety of expressions. If those who take a "soft" line in regard to Soviet Russia tend to err in their estimate of Soviet motives and aims by making them appear more reasonable than they in fact are, the "hard" liners err only a little less seriously in their judgment of Soviet procedures, overestimating the role of warfare and neglecting other means of waging battle which Russia employs. In the decade that followed the end of World War II, American policy toward the Soviet Union, anchored as it was in the "hard" position, concentrated so exclusively on the Soviet military threat that when in 1954–55 Russian strategy changed and "peaceful coexistence" replaced the head-on assault attempted under Stalin, American policy was thrown into a confusion from which it still has to recover.

Militancy rather means maintaining one's citizenry in the state of constant war-like mobilization, and exerting relentless pressure outside Russia's borders. The means used differ, depending on the circumstances.

One of the basic ingredients in the formulation of Soviet foreign policy is what Russian theoreticians call the "correlation of forces" (*sootnoshenie sil*). By this term is meant the actual capability of the contending parties to inflict harm on each other, knowledge of which allows one to decide in any given situation whether to act more aggressively or less, and which of the various means available to employ. The concept is used in the analysis of the internal conditions of a foreign country in which Russia has an interest (in which case it refers to the power relationship of social classes), as well as to international affairs where the parties are sovereign states or multinational blocs. Analyses of the "correlation of forces" are by no means an academic exercise. Under Khrushchev, when rivalry with the United States assumed new and dangerous forms, Soviet publications were filled with learned inquiries into the power balance between the Western and Eastern blocs, and there is every reason to believe that then, as now, such studies seriously influence policy. "Force," of course, is a vague and relative concept, and Russian analysts almost always overestimate quantity (e.g., land, population, and productivity figures) at the expense of quality (e.g., fighting spirit, cultural factors, or the caliber of leadership). Still, mindful of the Russian proverb: "If you don't know the ford, don't step into the river," they do not plunge into contests blindly; they rarely gamble, unless they feel the odds are overwhelmingly in their favor.

Russian leaders regard military force as a weapon to be used only in extreme contingencies when there is no alternative and the risks involved appear minimal. There are many reasons to account for this caution, the main one probably being lack of confidence in their own troops, especially when engaged outside Soviet borders. They much prefer to use military force as a means of blackmail. The reluctance to commit their military forces abroad distinguishes Soviet expansionism from the German, and it would be a mistake to hope to contain it by excessive reliance on methods which might indeed have stopped Hitler in the 1930s.

The militancy of Soviet foreign policy rests on the unspoken assumption that the Soviet Union can assail the enemy at a time and a place, and in a manner of its own choosing. It is so strongly permeated with the offensive spirit that contingency plans in the event of failure and enemy counter-attack seem rarely to be drawn up, if only because even to contemplate retreat opens one to accusation of defeatism. The Russians are quite prepared to pull back when resistance on any one sector of the enemy front turns out to be stronger than anticipated: there are always other sectors which are less staunchly defended and where one's force can be applied to better advantage. But when the opponent chooses to strike back, they are surprisingly vulnerable. The inability of the Russians, in the summer of 1941, to stop Hitler from penetrating deep into their country was in no small measure due to a failure to prepare for defensive war. In the Cuban missile imbroglio of 1962, the response in Moscow to decisive American counter-measures was panic. (How embarrassing to the Soviet government may be judged from the fact that Khrushchev's famous cable of October 26 to President Kennedy still has not been released. Considering that much more embarrassing revelations concerning the US government have been made public in recent years, such solicitude for Russian feelings seems out of place.) Nor did the Soviet leadership seem to have anticipated the outbreak of the Israeli-Arab war of 1967, which its own actions had done a great deal to provoke. If, so far, the government of Soviet Russia has not been required to pay a heavier price for the failure to anticipate blows, it is only because their opponents usually have been content with a reversion to the *status quo ante* and did not press their advantage.

Militancy is so deeply entrenched in the mentality of the Soviet elite, it follows so naturally from the character of its personnel and its relationship to the population at large, that it is doubtful whether the best way to ease East-West tensions is by attempting a piecemeal resolution of specific disagreements. Those who urge so in the name of pragmatism are in fact motivated by impatience. In the case of East-West tension, specific disagreements are not the cause but the consequence. The Second World War, too, after all, was not fought over Danzig.

THE USES OF THREAT

On February 23, 1942, on the occasion of the 25th anniversary of the founding of the Red Army, Stalin issued an Order of the Day in which he listed five "constant principles" that win wars. They were, in order of importance, first and foremost "stability of the home front," followed by second, morale of the armed forces, third, the quantity and quality of the divisions, fourth, military equipment, and fifth, ability of the commanders.[9] That Stalin should have attached such significance to morale, and in particular to the morale of the civilian population, is not surprising considering that the Bolsheviks came to power in Russia because the "home front," unable to withstand the strains of war, had collapsed. Given his admiration for Hitler, Stalin might even have come to believe that German defeat in World War I, too, had been caused by the failure of the civilian population to support the front-line troops. In this pronouncement, we have a valuable clue to that element in military and political operations which the maker of Soviet Russia and his heirs regard as crucial.

It has long been an axiom of military theory that the ideal battle is won before a single shot has been fired, by the victor depriving the enemy of the will to resist. Demoralization has been practiced with particular success by Napoleon, and German military theorists, following the example he has set, have striven with great determination to duplicate his feats. For all their admiration for the German military and willingness to learn from them, the Russians, however, have been slow to apply this particular principle to politics. The foreign policy of the Soviet Union in the first quarter of a century of its existence was ponderous and unimaginative. Soviet leaders seem first to have learned how to unnerve the opponent without actually fighting (or as a prelude to fighting) from observing the brazen manner in which Hitler, alternating threats with inducements, had managed to paralyze England and France. The effect on colonial peoples of Axis victories has often been noted; but it was probably no smaller on Soviet Russia which shared with the colonial nations a sense of awe toward the great powers of the West. Stalin has expressed on a number of occasions respect for Nazi methods, but always with one reservation: Hitler was overconfident, he underestimated the enemy, he did not know when to stop. The Cold War which he himself launched in 1946 represented, in effect, a replay of Hitler's game but with careful attention to the "correlation of powers."

The quality common to Nazi and post-1946 Soviet methods of waging political warfare is the practice of making limited, piecemeal encroachments on Western positions to the accompaniment of threats entirely out of proportion to the losses the West is asked to bear. The threats are coupled with all kinds of inducements which make non-acquiescence even more absurd. The Soviet Juridical Dictionary, in its definition of threat as a criminal offense, inadvertently provides a useful description of its uses as a political weapon: Threat (*ugroza*), it says, is a "distinct type of psychic influence on the victim for the purpose of compelling him to commit one action or another, or to refrain from committing them, in the interest of the threatener. . . . Such threats . . . can serve to paralyze the victim's will . . . ."[10] In the case of international politics, the primary target of threats is public opinion. Their function is to disorient it to the point where it refuses to follow the national leadership and by passive or active resistance forces the government to make one concession after another.

Threats can be of a direct and an indirect kind. Khrushchev specialized in the former, cultivating the public stance of a violent and unpredictable man whom it would be unwise to provoke—a ploy of which Hitler was the first to make masterful use. Sometimes Khrushchev liked to drop hints what Russia would do if thwarted—hints so vaguely worded as to be open to differing interpretations. At other times he spelled out his threats with brutal frankness, as for example, when he spoke of "country-busting." The present Soviet administration, though not immodest in making its capacity at punishing adversaries clear, prefers to appear as a mature world power, aware what awesome responsibility possession of nuclear weapons imposes on it. But it is not averse to taking advantage of the "irresponsibility" ploy by shifting blame on its friends and allies, which it occasionally depicts as wildly emotional, hoping, by this device, to enlist Western support for its policies. This gambit has been used repeatedly in recent years in the Middle East. A recent dispatch from London by United Press International, for example (and it is one of many), credits anonymous East European diplomatic sources with the intelligence that the Soviet Union fears Egypt could involve it in a Middle Eastern war against its wishes. Russia—so the dispatch continues—is, of course, doing all it can to restrain President Sadat, but since its own prestige is at stake "precipitate Egyptian war action could drag Moscow into hostilities despite Russian intentions."[11] The implied conclusion is that the United States in order to avoid general war in which it might have to confront the Soviet Union, should compel Israel to comply with Egyptian terms. Such "leaks," reported by the Western press as if they were news, have for Soviet Russia the same value as direct threats but they cost it even less, allowing it to blackmail in the name of third parties.

Until it had the bomb and the means of delivering it across continents, the Soviet Union was unable credibly to threaten military action as Hitler had done in 1933–39 and therefore could not wage global Cold War in an effective manner. Stalin had ordered the manufacture of atomic and hydrogen bombs but without having a clear understanding of their uses: he probably thought he had to have them to be able to face the United States as an equal. His attempts at paralyzing the West into submission were ultimately a failure because his threats carried no conviction. The benefits to be derived from nuclear blackmail were first grasped by Khrushchev and the military who had helped him unseat the more cautious Malenkov. Almost immediately upon coming to power, Khrushchev instigated a major deception intended to convince the United States that he had at his disposal more nuclear weapons and better means of delivering them than in fact was the case. First came Aviation Day of July 1955 when small units of Bisons, apparently flying in circles over Moscow, suggested to Western observers that Russia already had a respectable fleet of strategic bombers. Two years later came the Sputnik, and an even more incredible deception concerning the number of Soviet ICBM's.[12] These strategems helped undermine the traditional sense of invulnerability to external attack of the United States and persuade it that the only viable alternative to mutual nuclear destruction was accommodation with the Soviet Union. This proposition was not explicitly stated but hinted at. It was President Eisenhower and his advisors who first spelled out the principles that there was "no alternative to peace," that "war had become unthinkable," and that, therefore, negotiation was the only feasible way of settling all disagreements with the Soviet Union. The Geneva Conference of 1955 and the Camp David meeting of 1959 formalized this understanding. Since, as will be pointed out, the Soviet Union enjoys great advantages in negotiations with Western powers, the acceptance by the West of these principles represented a considerable Russian victory. It set the rules for the conduct of operations against the West in a fashion favorable to the Soviet side.

In one sense, the policy of threats initiated by Khrushchev has not worked: even nuclear blackmail has not made the United States and its allies give up their principal positions, such as NATO and West Germany's membership in it. But the policy has had considerable effect on Western public opinion. Ever since the Soviet Union has acquired the ability to inflict heavy punishment on Western countries a paralysis of the will has set in. The leadership stands firm but it can no longer wholly depend on the citizenry, and this condition sooner or later must reflect itself in national policies. While encouraging these tendencies toward isolationism and *embourgeoisement* in the West, the Soviet leadership in its internal policies seeks to steel the Soviet population and by depriving it of the good things of life to keep it lean, hungry, and alert.[13]

APPEALS TO FOREIGN GROUPS

In seeking to influence foreign opinion, Soviet leaders rely on sociological methods of analysis to differentiate the various social and ethnic groupings and determine where each is most vulnerable. We are dealing here with a practical application of political sociology learned from Marx, with which the founders of the Soviet state had gained experience while still in the underground. The method is certainly not infallible: it serves better to spot weaknesses than strengths. Even so, it is vastly superior to that rather amateurish manner with which some Western powers approach foreign affairs. Five years ago, when the United States committed half a million men to fight a ground war in Vietnam, not a single American university had a chair devoted to Vietnamese history. (There still is none at the time of writing, for that matter.) It is simply unthinkable that the Soviet Union would ever plunge into a major foreign intervention without acquiring beforehand a solid store of historical, economic, political, social, and cultural information on the country in question, and from it obtain at least some idea who are its potential friends and who its enemies there, and how to deal with them. A large part of the research in Soviet institutes devoted to the social sciences and of academic and cultural exchanges is intended to provide the government with such information. Although Russians enjoy a reputation for abstract theorizing and Americans for pragmatism, in the formulation of foreign policy the reverse holds true. The Russians are not likely to undertake any action on the basis of highly generalized assumptions; they usually arrive at decisions on the basis of concrete, factual data in which everything bearing on the "correlation of forces" is given the most careful scrutiny.

Before World War II, Soviet propaganda was aimed primarily at the same underprivileged groups which traditionally had been the object of socialist attention: the working class and colonial peoples, above all, followed by other discriminated or deprived groups. Since World War II, the appeal to the underprivileged has been gradually muted and the Soviet leadership has been increasingly courting the established and the aspiring. Why this change occurred it is difficult to say. Perhaps the lower classes had not justified the high hopes placed in them, revealing an unsuspected penchant for nationalism. Perhaps the Russians were impressed by the success which Hitler had had in manipulating the upper and middle classes in England and France.

Finally, perhaps as the ruling class of Russia has itself turned into a privileged order it has come to feel greater affinity for its counterparts abroad. Whichever explanation is the correct one, there can be no doubt that in recent years Russian Communists have courted with greater vigor and success the upper third of the social strata than the bottom.

In Western countries, the appeal is to the moneyed and managerial elite. In recent years, Soviet theorists have become increasingly sophisticated in their analyses of "capitalist" societies, recognizing the existence of various interest groups within what under Stalin had been considered a homogeneous "ruling class."[14] This information enables the Soviet government to direct appeals calculated to sway influential groups in favor of its policies and through them to apply political pressure on foreign governments. In addition, individual persons, valuable because of their connections or their influence on public opinion, are won over by appeals to their greed or vanity. A considerable effort is mounted to this end, an effort of whose dimensions the general public—and often its very victims—have little inkling. In the underdeveloped countries, much of the effort is aimed at the aspiring lower middle class, which is lured by the prospect of secure office jobs in the enlarged bureaucracy which would come into being under a one-party system and a centralized economy.

In this connection a few words must be said about the function of foreign Communist parties, which is often misunderstood. Communist parties are not used for purposes of subversion except in the most backward areas of the world because, being open to penetration by police agents, they cannot provide the necessary security. KGB agents who have been uncovered in the West not only had no connection with local Communists but sought to appear very conventional. Nor are these parties thought of as alternate governments to take over after the existing governments have been overthrown. When, after World War II, the Soviet Union occupied Eastern Europe it did not put into positions of power local Communists but Communists schooled in Moscow. Once the East European client states had been solidified, the local Communists were purged as thoroughly and with even greater vindictiveness than adherents of the so-called "bourgeois" political parties.

The principal role assigned Communist parties abroad seems to lie in the realm of legitimate political activities and opinion molding. Where they enjoy enough voter support to form significant parliamentary blocks—as in France or Italy—they can be used to tip the legislative scales in a manner favorable to the USSR: for example, by opposing NATO or the Common Market. Where they are not strong enough to do so, they can still provide vigorous opposition to the groups in power and to some extent intimidate them. Public demonstrations are particularly useful. These are never spontaneous but they appear as such and always receive public notice. A well-organized demonstration can create a completely false impression of the actual state of opinion in a given country and sway fence-sitters. In October 1968, while a crowd of 6,000 protested on Grosvenor Square against American intervention in Vietnam, only seven demonstrators showed up in front of the Soviet Embassy to protest the invasion of Czechoslovakia. In Tokyo, the masses roam the streets to protest the terms on which Okinawa is to be transferred to Japan; there is no news of demonstrations against Soviet refusal even to discuss the transfer to Japan of the Kurile Islands. In countries with a low level of literacy, the Communist press is also often used to spread the most outrageous lies aimed at discrediting individuals, parties, and states unfriendly to Soviet interests and prepared by the "disinformation" branch of the KGB. Last but not least, foreign Communist organizations are valuable to the Soviet Union for internal purposes. On any issue, the Soviet press can always cite resolutions of foreign Communist parties to convey to the Soviet public an impression of solid support abroad for Russian policies. Useful as they are, one must not overestimate the importance which the Soviet leadership attaches to foreign Communist parties. It much prefers to establish working relations with the foreign elites; and there is enough evidence on hand to indicate that when the interests of the Soviet Union require it, foreign Communist parties are readily sacrificed. They are only one element in the calculation of forces, and not the most weighty one at that.

SOME DIPLOMATIC PROPAGANDA TECHNIQUES

In addition to appealing to specific opinion and interest groups abroad, the Soviet Union also engages in major propaganda moves on issues which it regards as of major international importance, the purpose of which is to attain concrete political advantages. These are never launched haphazardly: they are deliberate, projected over the long term, and pressed with great vigor.

The most important of those has been the cause of peace. There is no need to go into the history of the various peace campaigns initiated by Stalin and perpetuated by his successors. What merits attention is the adroit use made of the peace slogan for the benefit of Soviet foreign policy. Inside Russia, the Communist regime has succeeded for a long time in establishing the principle that any opposition to it is, *ipso facto* and, as it were, by definition, counter-revolutionary. Once that principle has been established, the Soviet government need not examine any claims made against itself or engage in self-justification. It may admit, in retrospect, that errors have been committed; but while the policies which might lead to these errors are in effect, no questioning is allowed, since to do so is tantamount to giving aid and comfort to the class enemy. From the time it has acquired nuclear weapons the Soviet Union has succeeded to a surprising extent in persuading foreign opinion that insofar as any conflict between the major powers creates the danger of world destruction, all hostility to the Soviet government and its ideology or any thwarting of its will is *ipso facto* and by definition tantamount to war-mongering. By this logic, "anti-Communism" is equated with "anti-humanism." Like so many weapons of political warfare, this device is double-edged; but it so happens that the other edge is never bared.

To maintain its reputation as *defensor pacis,* the Soviet Union frequently concocts imaginary threats to world peace, which it then takes credit for dissipating. Soviet histories of foreign policy are filled with such incidents: for example, an alleged Turkish threat to Syria in 1957, alleged United States plots against Iraq in 1958 and 1962, and alleged Western designs against the Congo in 1960 and Cyprus in 1964. By foiling such nefarious designs of its own invention, the Soviet Union gains much credit at small expense and minimum risk. In the spring of 1967 this time-tested device backfired when an alleged Israeli plot against Syria, put forward by Soviet intelligence, for once was not quietly resolved but led to war.

An interesting and often successful technique employed by Moscow is to turn the tables on the opponent by confusing the real issues at stake. A classic example is Soviet propaganda in the present Israeli-Egyptian dispute. To understand how this technique works it is best to abstract from the specific issues of the Israeli-Egyptian conflict and approach it in a generalized manner. Two powers—let us call them A and B—are at odds. War breaks out, the country B defeats A, occupying in the process A's territory. At this juncture, in normal international practice, sooner or later negotiations begin. In the peace settlement which results, the defeated party usually has to make some concessions to the victor, among them, possibly, territorial ones. If for the defeated party A we substitute, say, France in 1870–71 or Finland in 1939–40, and for the victorious party B, respectively, Prussia and the Soviet Union, the pattern becomes clear. In both instances, the victor secured from the vanquished some territory and returned the remainder. Such too, according to the dictates of logic, precedent, and interest of the countries involved, ought to be the outcome of the 1967 War. That it is not is due, in the first place, to the unwillingness of Egypt to recognize the existence of Israel as a sovereign state. In this refusal Egypt is supported by the Soviet Union. The peculiar feature of this conflict is that whereas the real issue at stake is negotiation between the belligerents, Soviet propaganda has managed to make the main issue appear Israeli withdrawal from territories occupied in the course of the war. Thus, a matter which should be part of the final settlement of the conflict becomes a precondition of negotiations leading to a settlement. Whatever one's feelings about the substance of the Israeli-Egyptian dispute, one cannot but admire the adroit use of an intellectual confidence trick to turn the tables on an opponent and shift the burden of recalcitrance from oneself to the other party.

SOVIET ESTIMATE OF THE AMERICAN PSYCHE

In dealing with the United States in particular, the Russians have worked out over the past thirty years an interesting set of approaches based on certain assumptions about American ways of thinking and feeling.

When discussing relations between America and Russia, one cannot emphasize strongly enough the effect which their disparate economic traditions have had on their political conduct. A country like the United States, whose preoccupation is commercial, is inherently predisposed toward compromise: each trading transaction, after all, must hold some profit for both parties; negotiation is over the division of profits, not over the principle of mutual benefit. On the other hand, a country which makes its living primarily from the production and consumption of goods—never mind whether agricultural, extractive, or industrial—is equally predisposed toward exclusive possession and the denial of the principle of compromise.

This factor has had immense influence on the conduct of international relations of the two countries. When the United States makes a proposal to the Soviet Union, it invariably includes in it provisions designed to make it palatable to the other party; in other words, it makes concessions in advance of actual negotiations, assuming the other party will do likewise. But where the other party is a country like the Soviet Union, without a great commercial tradition and further-more impelled by ideology toward intransigence, this assumption does not hold. The Russian position always represents the actual expectations of the Soviet government, weighted down with additional unrealistic de-mands to be given up in exchange for the other side's concessions. In this sense, the Russians always enjoy an immense advantage in negotiating with a country like the United States. Any compromise works in their favor insofar as the American preliminary position already includes some concessions which need not be fought for at all. Occa-sionally, in diplomatic talks, Russian negotiators work out with their opposite numbers from the West a compromise formula which is then sent to Moscow as representing the Western position. Clearly, when Moscow sends back its counterproposals, the Russians come out the winners. This technique of "splitting the half" theoretically gives the Russians three-quarters of the gain in any compromise solution.

Equally important though more difficult to define is the Russian play on certain elements in the American psyche. A strong residue of Protestant ethics causes Americans to regard all hostility to them as being at least in some measure brought about by their own faults. That one can be hated for what one is rather than for what one does (to use Mr. George Kennan's formula) is difficult to reconcile with the liberal Protestant ethic which still dominates American culture. It is quite possible to exploit this tendency to self-accusation by setting into motion a steady barrage of hostile actions accompanied by expressions of hatred. The natural reaction of the victims, if they are Americans, can be and often is bewilderment, followed by guilt. Thus is created an atmosphere conducive to concessions whose purpose it is to propitiate the allegedly injured party. The roots of English appeasement of the 1930s probably lay in these psychological factors common, in some measure, to peoples of Anglo-Saxon culture; and the Russians, imitating the Nazis, have had much success in exploiting similar methods. One need only recall the uses made of so-called American "intervention" in the Russian Civil War, as a counterpart of the Versailles *Diktat,* to see the parallel.

Finally, mention must be made of the American predilection for "getting things done": impatience with discussions which seem to lead nowhere because the other party refuses to be drawn in and recrimination over acts (defaulting on debts excepted) which, as it were, have been sanctified by the passage of time. This forward-looking psychology causes Americans to seek as speedily as possible a common ground with a diplomatic adversary. The Russians often take advantage of this trait, urging American diplomats, in the name of "realism," to accept the *status quo* where it happens to benefit the Soviet Union, and proceed from there to "constructive" solutions of problems still outstanding, i.e., problems which happen to affect adversely the Soviet Union. It is in the name of such "realism," for example, that Soviet diplomacy is demanding the recognition of the Soviet occupation of East Germany or Czechoslovakia by the Western powers as a *fait accompli* and a starting point for moves leading toward a general détente. Needless to say, no such pragmatism is shown by Soviet diplomats where the realities of the situation are not in their favor, as in the case of the Israeli occupation of Arab territories taken in the 1967 war. A good historical memory and endless patience—neither of them typically American traits—are essential to neutralize this diplomatic technique.

ADHERENCE TO PRIORITIES

The militant spirit of the Soviet leadership, its refusal to separate sharply either peace from war or internal politics from external ones, and the participation in the making of foreign policy of several organizations, among which the Ministry of Foreign Affairs occupies a place of subordinate importance—all this creates a foreign policy which tends to be undisciplined and overactive to the point of frenzy. Soviet foreign policy consists, in the first instance, of an interminable succession of probings, which like military reconnaissance, are meant to draw enemy fire and reveal his capabilities, dispositions, and intentions. Much attention is paid in Moscow to these responses. The Soviet government undoubtedly likes the arrangement with the White House established in the 1960s, by virtue of which the two parties signal to one another some of their intentions: it saves Moscow a great deal of guesswork and permits it to make appropriate dispositions of its own forces. In the past it has not always correctly interpreted American responses: overly sophisticated signals bewilder Russian leaders and can mislead them. There can be little doubt that Stalin interpreted

Dean Acheson's statement that Korea was not within the American "defense perimeter" to mean just what it said. Acheson's attempt to deflect from himself responsibility for some blame in the Communist attack on South Korea is not convincing. For although it may be true, as he says, that other statesmen and military figures had made the same point before him, his voice, as that of the Secretary of State and President Truman's confidant, was in Russian eyes the authoritative one.[15] Brilliant and successful as he generally was in dealing with them, in this one instance Acheson inadvertently gave the Russians the wrong signal. President Kennedy's careful distinction between "defensive" and "offensive" weapons in response to Soviet arms shipments to Cuba, could well have suggested to Moscow lack of resolution, and encouraged it to send missiles there. In principle, it does not pay to be too clever with Russian politicians: they are inclined to interpret ambiguity as equivocation, equivocation as weakness, and weakness as a signal to act.

Although uncommonly activist, Soviet foreign policy is not haphazard and without direction. The record indicates that it tends at any one time to concentrate on only one major task.

The very first objective of Soviet foreign policy is to make certain that all the territory which at any time has come under Russian or Communist rule remains so: in other words, that whatever changes occur in the world map affect the holdings of the other camp. The reason why this should matter so much is complicated and only partly explainable by the need to appear to be always advancing and never retreating imposed on its adherents by historical materialism. Another and perhaps the major part of the explanation lies in the historical experience of Russia, namely in the manner by which the centralized Russian state originally came into being. The national state of Western Europe typically emerged from the suppression by the monarchy of the feudal nobility and clergy, and the concentration in its own hands of all public authority. While this process also occurred in Russia, there another factor came into play as well. The rulers of Moscow, aspiring to become masters of the whole country, had first to subjugate the numerous rival principalities born from the collapse of the Kievan state in the 12th and 13th centuries. To do so, they had to conquer territory and incorporate it into the Muscovite domain. From the earliest, seizing land, uprooting from it all vestiges of self-government, and holding on to it, has assumed for the rulers of Russia an extraordinary importance, becoming in their mind the essential attribute of sovereignty. Stalin carried this preoccupation to the lengths of an obsession: he not only made certain to recover territories (Eastern Poland, the Baltic states, and Bessarabia) which he had first obtained by virtue of his nefarious deal with Hitler, but he also insisted on recovering all the lands lost by the tsars. Sometimes the cost of holding on to conquered land is unreasonably high, as in the case of the Kurile Islands, whose retention mars Russia's relations with Japan.

Russian Communists consider the status of lands and peoples presently under their control entirely beyond discussion. In this respect, Soviet foreign policy adheres consistently to the principle "what is mine is mine, what is yours is negotiable." For evidence we need look only at Berlin. The status of Berlin after World War II was regulated by agreements made among the four Allies. Hence, any unilateral change in its status by one of the four occupying powers was illegitimate, and at the very least should have been accompanied by similar changes in the status of the other parts. Now in 1958 the Soviet Union decided to recognize East Germany as a sovereign state and gradually transferred East Berlin to its control. The Western powers both refused to recognize this act as legitimate and to follow suit by transferring sovereignty over West Berlin to the Federal Republic. The Russians for their part have not allowed the status of East Berlin to be placed on the agenda of any of the summit meetings or conferences concerning the fate of the two Germanys since 1958. At the same time, however, by applying intermittent pressure on West Berlin, and in particular by hindering its communications with West Germany, they have transformed what in fact is a problem of Berlin as a whole into a "West Berlin problem" which threatens peace and as such requires a negotiated settlement. In the recently concluded four-power agreement, the Federal Republic apparently secured better terms on Berlin than it had expected. Still, the cold fact remains that neither the Federal Republic nor the Western powers secured in it any concessions whatever on East Berlin because East Berlin was not even on the agenda. Under these conditions, the Russians have nothing to lose and always something to gain from negotiations, which helps explain their penchant for summit meetings, security conferences, and other big power encounters.

Closely connected with the insistence on holding on to land, is the quest for foreign diplomatic recognition. The importance attached to securing international legitimacy became evident from the instant

Communists had seized power in Russia. Lenin's policy, which led to the signing of the Brest-Litovsk Treaty in March 1918, rested on the premise that every price was worth paying as long as in return the Central Powers would recognize his regime was the legitimate government of Russia. Lenin's conduct on this occasion is regarded by Communist theoreticians as a textbook model. The implicit recognition of East Germany contained in the recently concluded four-power agreement probably outweighs in the eyes of both Russian and East German Communists the value of all the concessions which they had to make to secure it: the more so that they had no right to the things they traded in the first place. It may also be noted that the Russians find genuine satisfaction in the fact that from what otherwise was a thoroughly humiliating experience—the Cuban missile episode of 1962—they had managed to retrieve implicit American recognition of the Castro government.

The defensive element in the Soviet foreign policy is unmistakably clear: the sanctity of Communist authority, once established, is inviolate; violation means war. The West has accepted this equation, allowing the Soviet government to concentrate on offensive operations.

Since the end of World War II, the Soviet offensive effort has concentrated on three consecutive targets. Between 1946 and 1953 it was Europe, where the aim was to eliminate American influence and to transform the entire area into a Soviet dependency. This attempt having failed, due to resolute American opposition, the priorities changed. In 1954–55, Stalin's successors launched a flanking movement against the United States and Western Europe aimed at detaching the so-called Third World. The policy of what became known as "peaceful coexistence," put into effect concurrently and coupled with nuclear blackmail, was designed to keep the United States at bay while it was being contained and isolated. A brilliant success, this gambit may well have borne even more spectacular results were it not that the Chinese Communists refused to go along with it. In the 1960s, the conflict with China has increasingly attracted Russia's principal attention. In the past several years, the previous strategy of containing and isolating the United States has been replaced by one stressing the containment and isolation of Communist China.

While pursuing the primary objective of the moment, the Soviet Union does not neglect other opportunities; but by and large, mindful of the principle of "correlation of forces," its leaders maintain a clear distinction between the primary thrust and diversionary actions. The quiet manner in which they have in the 1960s liquidated their political interests in such areas of tertiary bearing on their conflict with China as West Africa and Latin America, and are presently pursuing a détente in Europe, illustrates this fact. Anyone who deals with Soviet foreign policy must also know how to distinguish the central from the incidental, and not allow himself to be misled by noisy but nonessential diversions.

ROLE OF INTELLIGENCE SERVICES

Not even the most cursory survey of the subject can avoid some mention of the influence which intelligence organs exercise on the formulation and execution of Soviet foreign policy. Russians are very proud of their intelligence services, being confident of their ability to penetrate the highest echelons of political and military establishments abroad. Their pride and confidence are justified. Sir William Hayter, one-time British Ambassador to Moscow, concedes that probably no important secrets are hidden from Soviet intelligence. But the uses to which information obtained by these services is put is another matter. Sir William goes on to say:

> [Soviet diplomatic agents] seem only able to gather information by underhand intelligence means and to be incapable of picking up the kind of information that any normal foreigner can acquire by using his eyes and ears. Partly this is due to the distrust with which they are trained to regard all non-Communist phenomena. Partly it is due to their distrust of each other, which makes normal contact with foreigners, and normal reactions to such contacts, suspect in the eyes of the numerous agents who are watching each other in the embassies. For whatever reasons, one has the impression that Soviet embassies have much information about, but little real knowledge of, the countries in which they are working.[16]

These generalizations can be broadened to include not only the Soviet embassies but that whole vast realm of foreign policy where the intelligence services play a major part. Intelligence organs are constitutionally unsuited to judge broader issues of public policy and in particular to understand public opinion. The Soviet intelligence apparatus is even less suited for work of this kind than the others, because, accustomed as it is to operating with virtual impunity at home, it instinctively treats all politics as a subject of manipulation pure and simple. There is much indication to suggest that some of the outstanding fiascoes of Soviet foreign policy in the Third World have been caused by overconfident and ill-informed intelligence operatives.

Even more risky have been Soviet experiences with the device of "disinformation" so dear to the heart of the KGB because so successful in the hermetically sealed environment of Soviet Russia. On the face of it, the grand deception perpetrated on the United States in the 1950s concerning the number of Soviet bombers and ICBM's was an outstanding success. It succeeded in that it caused the United States to give up the idea of "massive deterrence" and freed the Russians to engage in all kinds of adventures in the Third World. But in the end the deception brought the Soviet Union more harm than good because the authors ignored its political implications. For one, it spurred the United States to enlarge its rocket arsenal. Secondly, it confused and angered the Chinese government which, apparently uninitiated into the secret, took Soviet boasts at face value and interpreted Russia's failure to press its alleged advantage over the United States as cowardice, collusion, or both.

THE EFFECTS OF THE SINO-SOVIET CONFLICT

Soviet foreign policy since the end of World War II has been predicated on the assumption that the United States, Russia's principal rival, does not covet anything that belongs to the Soviet Union and therefore will not pursue offensive operations. This conviction must first have been planted in the mind of Soviet leaders by America's refusal in the late 1940s to take advantage of its nuclear monopoly in face of rising Soviet challenges and provocations. If there were any doubts about its validity, they should have been dispelled by the hollowness of John Foster Dulles' "rollback" threat. With this assurance, the Soviet Union could launch with relative impunity the offensive operations whose outlines we have sketched. In such a contest, time clearly was on Soviet Russia's side. Its offensive operations carried out on many levels assured that it could lose nothing and gain much, while Western public opinion could be expected to exert increasing pressure on their governments to seek accommodation as an alternative to nuclear holocaust.

Today much of this policy lies in shambles. The conflict with China is a calamity of the first order for the Soviet Union, with the profoundest consequences for the conduct of its external relations. That Russian leaders and theorists do not talk much about these implications only serves to underline the gravity with which they view the matter, because, as a rule, the Soviet hierarchy is least inclined to discuss in public issues which concern it the most. The calamity derives not only in incurring the enmity of a country regarded as a trusted ally responsible for guarding Russia's eastern flank. Rather, it derives from the nature of the Chinese Communist regime and the kind of political warfare it is likely to wage against the Soviet Union. Henceforth, the comfortable premises which had permitted the Soviet Union to carry out long-term offensive operations will no longer apply. China does not recognize the inviolability of Russian possessions: indeed, it makes active territorial claims on the USSR. It cannot be intimidated by nuclear blackmail, because its population is held as firmly in the regime's grip as is the Soviet. On all issues, it does not seek the middle ground, but full satisfaction of its interests. In the Third World, it appeals to much the same constituencies, in short, it enjoys the same advantages vis-à-vis the Soviet Union that the Soviet Union for the past quarter of a century has enjoyed vis-à-vis the West.

As the tricks which have worked so well with the prudent commercial nations of the West prove unavailing against another Communist regime, Soviet Russia may well throw caution to the wind and rely increasingly on brute force. Under these conditions, militancy can indeed come to mean belligerency. The immense and uninterrupted growth of the Soviet military establishment in all its branches suggests that such a shift may already have taken place. In the perspective of history, the Indo-Pakistani war can appear as the opening round of a trial of physical strength, since behind Russia's puzzling concern for the self-determination of Bangladesh seems to lie the desire to eliminate Pakistan, China's ally on the subcontinent.

Psychologically speaking, the Soviet Union may be at that point in its history which Germany had reached around 1890: a point at which it feels predisposed to throw aside cautious probing based on the weighing of the "correlation of forces," in order to engage in "world politics" in which power is pursued for its own sake. If that happens, other operative principles in the conduct of foreign relations will have to be worked out.

NOTES

[1] I have attempted to deal with this matter briefly in "Russia's Mission, America's Destiny: The Premises of U.S. and Soviet Foreign Policy," *Encounter*, October, 1970.

[2] This subject is treated by a group of experienced negotiators in Raymond Dennett and Joseph E. Johnson, eds., *Negotiating with the Russians* (Boston 1951), and in an amusing chapter in Heinz Pächter's *Weltmacht Russland* (Oldenburg-Hamburg 1968), pp. 372–377.

[3] *Voprosy strategii i operativnogo isskustva v sovetskikh voennykh trudakh, 1917–1940 gg.* (Moscow 1965), p. 13.

[4] *Insight and Outlook* (New York 1949), especially Chapter XVIII, "The Eureka Process."

[5] Cited in my book, *Struve, Liberal on the Left, 1870–1905* (Cambridge, Mass. 1970), p. 134.

[6] V.I. Lenin, *Sochineniya*, 3rd ed., (Moscow 1926–1937), XXX, 333pp. Admiration for Clausewitz is something the Bolsheviks and the Nazis have in common.

[7] V.Sorin, "Marksizm, taktika, Lenin." *Pravda*, No. 1 (January 3, 1923), 5. On another occasion, Lenin wrote: "To have an overwhelming superiority of forces at a decisive moment in a decisive place—this 'law' of military success is also the law of political success . . . " Lenin, *Sochineniya*, XXIV, 635. Lenin's copious notes on Clausewitz are reprinted in *Leninskii sbornik*, XII (1931), pp. 387–452.

[8] Cited in Sir William Hayter, *Russia and the World* (London 1970), pp. 18, 19.

[9] Cited in J.M. Mackintosh, *The Strategy and Tactics of Soviet Foreign Policy* (London 1962), pp. 90, 91.

[10] P.I. Kudriavtsev, ed., *Iuridicheskii slovar'*, 2nd ed., II (Moscow 1956), p. 550.

[11] *The Boston Evening Globe*, November 10, 1971, p. 15.

[12] This fascinating story is described by Arnold L. Horelick and Myron Rush, *Strategic Power and Soviet Foreign Policy* (Chicago 1966). I owe these two authors the reference cited above in Note 10.

[13] It is interesting to observe that whereas in the era of "peaceful coexistence" with the West, the Soviet government goes out of its way to maintain in Russia the spirit of ideological militancy toward the West, during the period of amity with Nazi Germany (1939–41) it was equally anxious in its internal propaganda to give no offense to the government of Hitler.

29

[14] H. William Zimmerman, *Soviet Perspectives on International Relations, 1956–1967* (Princeton, N.J. 1969), pp. 214–218.

[15] Dean Acheson, *Present at the Creation* (New York 1969), pp. 357–358.

[16] Hayter, *Russia and the World.* p. 24.

ALEXANDER DALLIN

DOMESTIC FACTORS INFLUENCING SOVIET FOREIGN POLICY*

Soviet foreign policy, like so much else, is a product of both heredity and environment. Over the years, foreign observers have paid considerable attention to the role of the Russian heritage. Similarly, there has been ample discussion of the extent to which the outside world prompts Soviet initiatives and responses on the international scene. But until recently far less weight has been attached to the domestic environment as a determinant of foreign policy. Yet it has become increasingly clear that this "linkage" is an essential dimension to consider for an understanding of Soviet foreign policy, particularly in the years since Stalin's death.[1]

INDIVIDUALS, FACTIONS, AND GROUPS

Despite all ideological and organizational taboos, conflicts and "factionalism" have been endemic in the Soviet leadership throughout its history. At times repressed and barely detectable, at others virtually overt, divergences over political strategy and tactics among the leaders have been a (poor) substitute for public debate or at least discussion within the elite. Inevitably, differences have arisen on foreign policy as well. A few examples may suffice to illustrate the nature of the issues:

1918—over the wisdom of the Treaty of Brest-Litovsk with the Germans, and by implication, between principled purity and expedient adaptation; 1928—over the propriety of signing the Kellogg-Briand Pact, and by implication, over fundamental alternatives in political alliance strategy; 1938—over the implications of the Munich agreement and the looming choice between a "Western" and a "Nazi" orientation in Soviet policy;

* The author would like to express his gratitude to several institutions which have supported or facilitated the work on which in varying degrees the present paper is based: the National Endowment for the Humanities, the Russian Institute of Columbia University, and the Hoover Institution on War, Revolution and Peace.

31

1948—the Zhdanov/Malenkov dispute, essentially between a militant forward policy and a more inward-oriented. "Russia-first" policy; 1958—over the desirability and feasibility of a *détente* with the United States and its reciprocal consequences for the Sino-Soviet relationship; 1968—over the necessity of armed intervention in Czechoslovakia, and over the possibility of strategic arms limitation agreements with the U.S.

Time and again, from the early days of the Soviet regime when peace abroad was recognized as a precondition for survival at home, to the ludicrous charges of treason against leading Bolsheviks in the purge trials of the 'thirties, to the post-Stalin realignment of "revisionists" and "dogmatists," modernists and traditionalists, basic policy orientations in Moscow either have been explicitly concerned with foreign policy or have had inescapable foreign policy implications. This suggests a central point in our argument: an inner logic that links a "revisionist" attitude in foreign affairs to "revisionism" at home and in doctrine, and similarly translates "sectarianism," or Stalinism, or conservatism into a totality of interlocking views on both internal and external affairs. In this light, Soviet politics may be seen in significant measure as a contest among such orientations.

It is true that foreign affairs have generally been of lesser saliency than domestic problems in the consciousness of Soviet officialdom. Indeed, it has been a common fallacy of foreign observers to attribute excessive importance to foreign-policy issues, e.g., in seeking to explain changes in the Soviet leadership. But, without thereby abandoning the *Primat der Innenpolitik*, since Stalin's death the prominence of foreign-policy issues has increased substantially; in the 1960s they came to figure frequently on the agendas of Central Committee sessions (and no doubt the closed policy sessions of the "collective leadership" since the ouster of Khrushchev).

In the meanwhile Soviet politics had of course undergone significant changes, which have been amply examined in recent studies. A few pertinent trends may be singled out.

(1) Given the command nature of the Stalin system in politics and economics, there was no basis for tolerating the assertion of divergent priorities, inasmuch as the country was committed to the achievement of a single set of overriding objectives, to which all else must be subordinated. Once after Stalin this total mobilization orientation was abandoned—and once the terror abated in the wake of Stalin's own

demise—it was only natural that diverse demands and priorities should be voiced within the leadership, which thus faced a range of options reflecting different preferences and values, but without any mechanism for adjudicating such divergences.[2]

(2) In the meanwhile Soviet society had experienced the gradual and inescapable (albeit unintended) process of functional differentiation, with a crystallization of different attitudes, which tends to accompany the modernization of society everywhere. Members of the elite have thus tended to become informal spokesmen for various groupings or causes— in effect, incipient interest or opinion groups. While (except for the military) these have not been institutionalized and are often cleft among themselves (as indeed is the Party, too), these groups strive for better access to and a greater influence on the decision-makers; over time, they seem to acquire a measure of self-conscious identity. It is natural that their priorities in regard to public policy should often differ, and should do so with important implications for foreign affairs.[3]

(3) Soviet politics has been marked by a multitude of contradictions, zigzags, and ambiguities. But, whatever one's overall assessment of its significance, clearly there has taken place a real, albeit limited, pluralization of political life (and, as its counterpart, an even more far-reaching fragmentation of international Communism). The result has been an existential acceptance of political negotiating, bargaining, and coalition-building within the leadership and the political elites, in varying constellations expressing contests not only of competing power groups, personalities, and patronage networks, but also of rival policies. It is sound to argue that Soviet politics is not merely a struggle for brute power but rather the interaction of power *and* policy. As an astute "Kremlinologist" writes,

> . . . policy conflicts, personal rivalries, and personnel shifts at the top levels bear on [the Soviet leader's] continuing effort to sustain or expand his dominance. . . . He inevitably offends some political forces and pleases others in pressing his policies, thereby generating conflict within the regime. . . . In fact, it is the way [an] issue is defined by the leader or faction in power that gives shape and tone to all the tensions and contentions within the present regime.[4]

Political alignments and cleavages have been too varied to be comprehended by any simple formulae. But there is evidence of correlation between political postures and (1) the functional requisites of a political actor's job, (2) jurisdictional bureaucratic competition, and (3) informal membership in particular patronage networks. A famous *Pravda* cartoon in 1923 showed Foreign Commissar Chicherin tearing his hair while Zinoviev, as head of the Comintern, was declaiming an inflammatory revolutionary manifesto.[5] Men professionally identified with foreign trade and aid (including its top executives, from Leonid Krasin and Anastas Mikoyan to the current crop of Soviet foreign-aid officials) have typically been more favorable to an accommodation abroad than Party bureaucrats, who (as Brzezinski has suggested) tend to fear the domestic consequences of a weakened sense of the enemy and of weakening "vigilance" and controls at home. In the last analysis (Ploss, among others, has correctly argued) the whole giant effort of building up Soviet war and heavy industry has been justified first and foremost by reference to an external threat. Some significant correlation may also be found between political attitudes and age groups. Thus, willing belief in the official dogma seems greatest among the bureaucratic beneficiaries of the Stalin era—those who were upwardly mobile in the era of the first three five-year plans. On the other hand, the demand for open communications, free contacts, and opportunity to travel abroad appears to be much the strongest in the youngest age group of Soviet adults. Or, to provide a more speculative example, ground-force commanders in the Soviet army may be assumed to take more implacable and rigid positions of hostility toward the outside world than do, say, academics and poets.[6]

It should be added, however, that one must guard against inferring individual attitudes from such group characteristics.[7] Moreover—as Khrushchev himself exemplified but appears later to have forgotten—individuals do not necessarily remain wedded to the same political orientation or to the same political patrons in the dynamics of Soviet political strife.

The general pluralization of Soviet political life may be taken to be a necessary, though not a sufficient, condition for the aggregation of divergent political priorities bearing on foreign affairs at a level below the top leadership. Meanwhile, the very existence of a "collective" leadership structurally imparts its own characteristics to the political process.

The possibility of losing on policy issues without losing one's job (let alone one's head) in itself prompts greater candor in expressing divergent views. The frequent inability of the collective to reach a consensus dovetails with the mood of stabilization reacting against Khrushchev's erratic improvizations, to make it an informal rule of thumb that when views diverge hopelessly the first impulse in the leadership is to do nothing at all. And when there is such divergence, the tendency is to give greater weight to the opinion of outsiders and to make greater use of expert consultants. While differences now tend to be kept quiet more effectively than under the ebullient Khrushchev, there is an inherent element of instability in the absence of any mechanism for institutionalizing this limited pluralism in the Soviet elite.

LIMITED PLURALISM AND FOREIGN AFFAIRS

Against this background it is possible to develop typologies distinguishing among ways in which the domestic political environment impinges on foreign policymaking.

The Extreme Cases

Conditions under which the domestic impact is minimal comprise, first and foremost, periods of relative routine and continuity of policy, when implementation is left to the specialized bureaucracy responsible for it. The other pole which similarly minimizes political interplay is policymaking at moments of especial crisis or requiring exceptional surprise. The Soviet decision to dispatch nuclear missiles to Cuba, in 1962, as well as the handling of the subsequent crisis were apparently in the hands of literally five or six people.[8] (This in itself, however, is not so unusual, as analogous decisions in other countries would illustrate.) Yet the immunity from political pressures which the decision-makers claim under such conditions is short-lived indeed. Even in a system lacking formal accountability by the leadership, its conduct is subject to scrutiny once the crisis has passed. And even if Khrushchev at the time survived the trauma, he found himself much on the defensive after both the Hungarian crisis of 1956 and the Cuban crisis of 1962—as it were, on probation before his peers, inasmuch as the events made manifest some miscalculation or malfunction. Characteristically, in the winter of both 1956–57 and 1962–63 Khrushchev was obliged to soft-pedal his own policies not only in the area directly related to the crisis but across the board (and, in fact, sought to pre-empt some of the anticipated attacks by compromising with his rivals' priorities).

Still, these are rather exceptional circumstances. It is in the intermediate band, somewhere between routine and crisis, that the impact of contending forces, factions, lobbies, and arguments on the home front tends to be greatest on Soviet foreign affairs.

Systemic Dissent

At this point one may introduce the analytical distinction between "systemic" and "marginalist" dissent from official policy. If we take the systemic critic to be fundamentally at odds with the premises and broad purposes (rather than with particular elements or with techniques of achieving shared goals), a Soviet official could not expect to survive in office while articulating a systemic critique. Indeed, among the few examples of this type we find the only "insiders" at the time of or after their forced retirement. This is true of both prime specimens—Maxim Litvinov, at one end of the spectrum, and Viacheslav Molotov, at the other.[9]

The closest analogue to Litvinov's systemic dissent from Soviet foreign policy in the post-Stalin era must be sought among the alienated intelligentsia or, more particularly, in the twilight zone of reluctantly tolerated dissent by individual specialists—notably, scientists—needed by the regime. It is understandable that in the voluminous *samizdat* literature and the corpus of petitions submitted to the Soviet authorities, foreign affairs play a very subordinate role. Moreover, in the post-Stalin years the poignancy and drama of foreign policy moves productive of alienation have been lacking, except for individual actions such as the Hungarian and Czechoslovak interventions (both of which did indeed stimulate memorable protests inside the U.S.S.R.).

While there are occasional references to foreign policy in documents from the so-called democratic opposition in the Soviet Union, the single most striking and influential discussion is contained in academician Andrei Sakharov's essay published abroad under the title, *Progress, Peaceful Coexistence, and Intellectual Freedom*. Its tenor is suggested by one of its opening paragraphs:

The division of mankind threatens it with destruction. Civilization is imperiled by a universal thermonuclear war, catastrophic hunger for most of mankind, stupefaction from the narcotic of "mass culture" and bureaucratized dogmatism, a spreading of mass myths that put entire peoples and continents under the power of cruel and treacherous demagogues, and destruction or degeneration from the unforeseeable consequences of swift changes in the conditions of life on our planet. In the face of these perils, any action increasing the division of mankind, any preaching of the incompatibility of world ideologies and nations is madness and a crime.

Without dwelling on the proposals contained in his essay, one may point out that it, too, characteristically links domestic and foreign visions, both the nightmare and the alternative of progress. Men all over the world, writes Sakharov, "despise oppression, dogmatism, and demagogy—and their more extreme manifestations: racism, fascism, Stalinism, and Maoism. They believe in progress based on the use, under conditions of social justice and intellectual freedom, of all the positive experience accumulated by mankind."

It is in no sense to belittle either the intellectual quality or the civic courage of its author to suggest that even this essay is bound to have been of marginal impact, at best—perhaps a thorn in the leaders' flesh but, among the multitude of pressures exerted upon them, no more than a reminder of uncertain magnitude.

There is no comparable document from the other end of the political spectrum, presenting a coherent neo-Stalinist or Maoist world view. The closest known approximations are the (unpublished) article submitted by former premier and foreign minister Viacheslav Molotov to the Party's leading journal, *Kommunist,* in April 1960, and his letter to the XXII Congress in October 1961. What is known of his orientation leaves little doubt about his policy preferences. Yet it is likely that, among the various strands of Stalinism, foreign policy finds few spokesmen eager to rehabilitate or return to the characteristics of the Stalin era. Even though arguments such as Molotov's may fall on some receptive ground in the older bureaucracy, they are likely to carry little weight with Soviet policy-makers.

One group which, by contrast, has had the opportunity to cause some mischief—and thereby hope to influence official behavior—by conducting a limited "foreign policy" of its own, is the Soviet security apparatus. Under Lavrenti Beria there was of course a good deal more of this than in recent years; indeed, one could identify the comings and goings of "his" men and his factional enemies—e.g., Semionov and Tiul'panov in East Germany—with the ups and downs in the Kremlin in the years from 1946 to 1952. While those days are gone, there are grounds for believing that an autonomous police initiative (perhaps with some backing from on high) was responsible for the series of incidents in 1963–64, which included the arrest of Professor Frederick C. Barghoorn and the harrassment of other visitors from abroad, and of Soviet intellectuals hospitable to Western scholars—and presumably receptive to "bourgeois" values.[10] Even this kind of initiative appears to have been stopped in the last several years (though an outsider cannot determine to what extent variations in Soviet practice, e.g., in granting exit visas or arresting foreign visitors, are explicable in terms of such rival orientations).

In general, the concern among Western scholars with decision-making may well have contributed to a neglect of the extent to which a policy can be subverted in the process of its implementation. But here foreign affairs constitute something of an exception, for, unlike internal policy, foreign policy execution tends to be removed from the public and to have no tangible consequences for it (short of war). Moreover, the relative isolation of the Soviet Union from the outside world in terms of "transactions"—such as trade, investment, tourism, even transnational organizations, and mail—as well as the coercive discouragement of any divided values or loyalties shared with the outside world (to the detriment of Soviet policy) makes for the relative weakness, if not virtual absence, of other "linkage groups" or alternative foreign policy elites with contacts or experience abroad.

Opportunists and Foreign Policy

Another subtype to consider is the opportunist espousal of foreign-policy issues by men engaged in a power struggle and seeking additional pawns to throw at their opponents. In practice this type turns out to be surprisingly hard to identify. The best example of the post-Stalin years may be Khrushchev's own alignment with the "hardliners" and the military in his contest with Georgii Malenkov in 1953–55. As his later posture so totally contradicted this stance in the initial post-Stalin phase, the observer is left to wonder whether he was engaging in a clever series of tactical maneuvers (which, to be sure, had to be credible to his allies), or whether his strikingly contrasting later policy reflected an intervening learning process and genuine conversion. The point is of particular interest since we are here dealing with an alignment over what was to become the recurrent, classic complex of issues spanning both domestic and foreign affairs—the prospects of war, the relative priority of consumer goods and heavy industry, the magnitude of the military budget, and the needs of Soviet agriculture.

The difficulty encountered in identifying recent examples to fit this rubric reinforces the general conclusion that the instrumental use of foreign policy issues in factional jockeying has tended to become increasingly rare. For one thing, policy failure no longer need mean personal failure for its advocate; hence there is now less to be gained by adding further, contrived issues to a dispute. And secondly, foreign policy issues have little "clout" in Soviet elite circles, given the recognition of their complexity and the absence of influential foreign policy elites.

Such a hypothesis, if true, would reinforce our disposition to consider differences relating to foreign affairs, as they appear in Soviet esoteric pronouncements, as genuine rather than manipulative. (Indeed, it is likely that, because of the limits on legitimate dissent in Soviet politics, such public hints often substantially understate the scope of differences, since it is mandatory to couch differences in terms of technical objections on the grounds of feasibility, scope, timing, or cost, rather than substance.[11])

Elite Politics and Derivative Conflict

The single most pervasive and persistent political cleavage, throughout the Communist world, has been the dichotomy into what is often called the "left" and "right." These admittedly unsatisfactory labels continue to have a distinct meaning in Communist parlance, as they describe—in their more extreme manifestations—profoundly divergent attitudes, values, and political moods; not so much ideological differences as contrasting political strategies. Conceptually (though not always in practice) there has indeed been a logical congruence among "left" domestic, foreign, and doctrinal attitudes, and a similar congruence on the Communist "right." Indeed, it is remarkable to what extent shifts in Soviet domestic and foreign strategies have tended to go hand in hand.[12]

The dichotomy comprises a variety of distinct but intrinsically linked problem-areas and attitudes, including some which bear directly on foreign affairs. Quite schematically, the contrasting and admittedly oversimplified political preferences of "left" and "right" may be taken to include an option in favor of "transformation" on the left, in favor of "stabilization" on the right; for mobilization on the left, for normalcy on the right; for tension-management on the left, for consensus-building on the right; a willingness to resort to militancy and if need be violence, on the left, as against a preference for incrementalism on the right. The "Red vs. expert" dichotomy fits the left/right cleavage—partisanship and the priority of politics on the left; rationality and the priority of economics (or, more generally, science) on the right. Finally, the priority of heavy industry, on the left, as against the more vigorous development of consumer goods and agricultural priorities, on the right, likewise proves congruent with this overall cleavage.

In practice, individual political actors have not always consistently expressed these opposing tempers and priorities, nor of course always chosen their extreme formulation. Still, these and cognate elements help us understand the underlying connexity, e.g., of a distinctive "left" perception of opportunities abroad—be it by a Zinoviev in the early 1920s, or a Zhdanov after World War II, or a Mao after 1957—with a predilection for drastic action and a concomitant disposition to tighten controls and discipline at home. They also help explain the logical linkage, in recent years, of divergent Soviet views of American intentions, with political arguments over resource allocation and arms control. Thus the linkage of détente-and-welfare priorities as against preparedness-vigilance-"forward" foreign policy also fits plausibly into this dichotomy. "Welfare Communism" and "warfare Communism" are oversimplified, polarized, and rather inadequate but not entirely inappropriate labels for these orientations.

In a relatively few cases—such as the differences over American intentions—the split among Soviet specialists and politicians concerns *directly* their perceptions of the outside world and the resulting Soviet opportunities. Most frequently, however, what is involved is a foreign policy posture derivative from—or a function of—but consistent with, positions taken on domestic affairs. This phenomenon could be illustrated by a great many examples such as the way strategic considerations, economic priorities, welfare advocacy, self-serving propaganda on behalf of the "military-industrial" complex, perception of Soviet strength or weakness, personalities of leaders, and other variables combine, as in a parallelogram of forces, to produce a congruent arms-control posture, or agricultural policy, or space program.[13]

Why should there be such a tendency for proponents of this or that policy option to extend their position to congruent arguments in the foreign policy field? Two answers suggest themselves: (1) the psychological-ideological compulsion of totalism—especially pronounced in Leninism; that is, the need to provide a homogeneous analytical framework to the entire domain of public policy; and (2) the structural connexity of seemingly discrete dimensions of policy in a system of total central control but limited resources. Manifestly, decisions regarding the production of chemical fertilizer, or housing, or steel are bound to have reciprocal implications for foreign aid, ICBM's, and generally the country's posture in foreign as well as domestic affairs.

Though it is perhaps too soon to be sure, it is likely that the traditional Leninist compulsion to totalism is withering. (There is, in this regard, an interesting change in the domestic consequences of the Sino-Soviet split: while under Khrushchev a deterioration in Soviet-Chinese relations typically strengthened "revisionist" tendencies in Soviet internal policies as well, since Khrushchev's ouster Sino-Soviet relations appear not to have had such a domestic corollary effect.) Even if this is indeed so, there are good reasons to think that the second, structural source of this linkage is nonetheless here to stay for the indefinite future.

ISSUES AND INCIDENTS

A fuller analysis might at this point dwell in detail on the shifting political configurations at the apex of the Soviet pyramid and seek to isolate their foreign-policy components. In the present paper some of the possible lines of inquiry can be merely suggested briefly.

The congruence of political orientations at home and abroad can be simply illustrated by selecting some representative spokesmen for them—for instance, in the early days, Leon Trotsky or Nikolai Bukharin; in the Stalin era, Andrei Zhdanov or Viacheslav Molotov; most recently Frol Kozlov and Mikhail Suslov. In each instance one would be able to distill from their pronouncements and writings a characteristic and fairly consistent clustering of views. For the "hardliner" a (somewhat synthetic) syndrome might include a linkage such as this:

No retreat abroad;
No let-up of controls or discipline at home;

Larger defense spending and military forces-in-being;
Inevitability of war;
Image of the United States as aggressive and plotting against the Soviet
  Union;
Faster growth rate for heavy industry than for light and food industries.

Khrushchev himself perhaps best exemplifies the centrality of the
détente-cum-reform syndrome but also the frequency of vacillations,
hesitations, and tactical shifts of policy positions. Still, the linkage
of the suggested issues is apparent, whether one examines his stand in
July 1955, in the Central Committee confrontation with Molotov;
or in 1959, when he linked his stand on China with the advocacy of a
troop cut, the exploration of improved relations with the United States,
the "virgin lands" project, and a sequence of "liberalizing" gestures
at home; or in 1963, at the time of the Nuclear Test Ban Treaty, when
the linkage was epitomized by his remark to a visiting American delegation that "We shall reduce expenditures on defense, and this money
shall be directed to the production of chemical fertilizer."[14]

A more exhaustive examination of the problem would also need
to dwell on the complex of resource allocation, the most persistent and
periodically the most visible arena of contention in Soviet politics.
This is where one sees, among other tensions, a sequence of collisions
between the advocates of change and the defenders of the *status quo;*
of welfare and of defense priorities; of consumer goods and agriculture
against those in heavy industry. Indeed, unlike other policies, resource
allocation cannot be postponed: this is one reason why budgetary and
resource decisions reveal the changes in the relative influence of different
societal groups and political factions better than most other issues do.

It may be commonly underestimated how convincing a picture has
been provided by the best available foreign studies for certain periods
of the recent Soviet past, reconstructing the dialogue among Soviet
leaders, factions, and elites month after month, year after year—in
effect, decoding their esoteric references (and silences) and relating
changes in argumentation and influence to developments in the "real
world." To give but one salient example, there is considerable and detailed documentation of the prolonged argument, in the early 1960s,
between Kozlov, Suslov, and the spokesmen for the "military-industrial"
complex (both military and managerial)—the alignment its enemies liked
to refer to as the "metal-eaters"—against Khrushchev and his fellow-

advocates of what *their* enemies referred to as "goulash Communism." Almost invariably the zigzags in resource allocation can be correlated with clearcut and congruent changes in foreign policy, be it relations with Tito, polemics with China, or incidents on the road to Berlin.

No less convincing have been the most sophisticated studies of the Soviet military—including the differences among various branches of the service and cliques of commanders, the evolving civil-military tug-of-war, and the range of politico-military assumptions and doctrinal conceptions current in the Soviet elite.[15] One instance of linkages deserves to be singled out in this connection: the political confrontation, in 1959–61, of the pro-Khrushchev coalition, including the advocates of a *détente* with the United States, the agricultural lobby, the "modernizers" among the senior military and in particular those prepared to rely on a nuclear deterrent and the new rocket command, the proponents of arms-control agreements, and the consumer goods advocates, on the one hand; and, on the other, the defense-industry spokesmen, the World War II generation of marshals and generals whose experience was largely with conventional forces, and an array of Stalinoid party and state bureaucrats.[16]

Similarly, it has proved possible to trace the changing "mix" of various political inputs in the zigzags of Soviet disarmament and arms-control policy over the years. This, too, turns out to be an issue which by its very nature highlights the changing balances of economic, political, and military priorities.[17]

Many of the above references are to the Khrushchev era—essentially, the years from 1956 to 1964, when such interactions and linkages were particularly visible to the outside world. Though it has again become harder to identify them in the years since Khrushchev's ouster—in part, because there is now some consensus on the rules of the game of politics, including keeping such differences quiet—all standard indicators suggest an essential continuity of issues, cleavages, and arguments. In this connection it is worth focusing particularly on the latest (XXIV) Communist Party Congress, in the spring of 1971. Along with a mood of smug bureaucratic incumbency, there was a tendency to sweep controversial questions under the rug, and in general for the insiders to have and to hold their privileges of status, authority, and creature comforts. What was new was the evidence of Brezhnev's espousal of a "pro-agriculture" policy and his legitimation of the demand for "consumer goods now," at least on the level of words and slogans. Clearly on the defensive, probably having been charged with betrayal by his "hardline" associates, Brezhnev wound up rebuking the heavy-industry lobby and more generally those who continued to oppose greater stress on consumer demands. As he warned,

> What was explicable and natural in the past when other tasks were in the foreground, is unacceptable, comrades, in present conditions. And if some comrades do not take this into account, the Party has the right to see in such attitudes either a failure to understand the essence of its policy . . . or a desire to justify their own inactivity.[18]

Others, to be sure, continued at and after the Congress to press for the priority of heavy industry in the new five-year plan. In all likelihood, this is the complex of issues that caused first the postponement of the Congress by nine months and then further delay in the publication of the new economic plan.

The XXIV Congress thus revealed a substantial and costly commitment to a sustained effort on behalf of Soviet agriculture— ironically, the very issue which successively Malenkov and Khrushchev also identified as the Achilles' heel of the system and over which they stumbled; as well as (for the first time) a slightly faster growth rate for light than for heavy industry.

In the broadest sense, the whole set of priorities in the new five-year plan implies a reading of the world scene, which assumes that no showdown, with either the United States or China, is likely in the next several years. The most obvious corollary of this orientation is the fact that the overt military budget did not go up—significant at the very least as a signal to Soviet officialdom. Whether, given American and Chinese policies, such a decision is wise continues to arouse deep disagreement within the Soviet elite; and it is interesting that the issue is still alluded to in terms virtually identical with those which Premier Nikita Khrushchev and Marshal Rodion Malinovsky used, some 10 years earlier, in arguing about both the nature of American intentions and the combat readiness or adequacy of the Soviet armed forces.

Thus, from about 1960 on, the moderates—including Khrushchev and Mikoyan—spoke of the Soviet Union as having attained the needed level of defensive and deterrent might and, given such sufficiency, stressed economic growth as vital in the peaceful competition with imperialism; whereas the militants—including Kozlov, Suslov, and Konev—continued to stress the necessity to "strengthen the defensive capability" of the Soviet Union. In this light, the exchanges of 1971 become particularly revealing, for Brezhnev now declared (while acknowledging the importance of heavy industry for a high defense potential) that "today the Soviet Army is assured of all types of modern military equipment," adding that of course "the future development of the defense industry and the concrete program of its activities will to a great extent depend on the international situation." By contrast, Marshal Grechko, writing immediately prior to the Congress, stressed the commitment to "making possible that the world of socialism is stronger today than it was yesterday, and that it be stronger tomorrow than it is today."[19]

This is, after all, but a new installment of a familiar story. As Khrushchev was later to recall,

> I know from experience that the leaders of the armed forces can be very persistent in claiming their share when it comes time to allocate funds. . . . Unfortunately there is a tendency for people who run the armed forces to be greedy and self-seeking.

And he went on to relate the same anecdote which he had told reporters during his stay in New York in 1960, commenting on the similarity of tensions in Washington and Moscow, on the basis of President Eisenhower's observations:

> It's just the same. Some people from our military . . . come and say, "Comrade Khrushchev, look at this! The Americans are developing such and such a system. We could develop the same system, but it would cost such and such." I tell them there's no money, it's all been allocated already. So they say, "If we don't get it, . . . the enemy will have superiority over us." So we discuss it some more, and I end up by giving them the money they ask for.[20]

The continuing tug-of-war is also illustrated by the (symbolic and by no means random) changes in the composition of the Central Committee. Whereas the informal representation of various interest groups has remained fairly stable, the military hardliners (along with the Shelepin clique) lost some ground at the XXIV Congress. No less significant than the changes in numbers is the fact that the one military man promoted to full membership in the Central Committee is Colonel General Nikolai Ogarkov, deputy chief of the Soviet delegation to the Strategic Arms Limitation Talks. The complementary facet of this personnel policy was the promotion of men identified with a moderate (or even "dovish") posture toward the United States: Ambassador Dobrynin (promoted from candidate to full member of the Central Committee); Georgii Arbatov, director of the Academy's U.S.A. Institute and probably the most influential "America expert" consulted by the top Soviet leadership; and Nikolai Inozemtsev, the "realist" director of the Institute of World Economy and International Relations. This was a novel kind of expert to put on the Central Committee, and their inclusion evidently reflected the outcome of a prior backstage debate over American prospects and intentions—an issue over which there continue to be conflicting judgments in Moscow.

Ever since the 1940s there have been differences among the Soviet elite over the U.S. Some have insisted that the imperialist beast cannot change its spots, that by its very nature the United States is bound to be essentially aggressive and hostile to the U.S.S.R., and that American policy cannot but mirror the predatory inclinations of the ruling monopolies. Others have, on the contrary, emphasized the changes in American capitalism since World War II, the divisions among dominant economic interests and public opinion, and the "sobering" impact of nuclear weapons and Soviet might: these have tended to be the spokesmen for the belief that there are in Washington at least two major tendencies—what Khrushchev chose to call "men of reason" and "madmen" (a dichotomy he similarly applied to the Communist camp in the era of the Sino-Soviet split).

It is significant that the differences between these two outlooks have tended to fit the political perceptions and preconceptions of particular actors with regard to other problem areas.[21] While the debate has remained unresolved, the Vietnam war evidently played into the hands of the diehards, who cited it as evidence of the unchanging nature of U.S. intentions. But—perhaps because of the seriousness with which the Chinese challenge was perceived after 1965–66—Soviet leaders resisted a return to the old line of unalterable hostility. For all intents and purposes, the question of American intentions remained open; as one Soviet official privately quipped, "We cannot decide as yet whether the United States is evil or stupid."

In this light, Soviet pronouncements in 1970–72 suggest a new preponderance of the moderates and their continued alliance with the consumer-goods and agricultural lobbies. Foreign Minister Gromyko declared at the XXIV Congress, for instance, that Soviet foreign policy has the Leninist task of "insuring the most favorable possible conditions for the building of Socialism and Communism and of averting the danger of a new world war." But he also made clear that this approach was not universally accepted in Moscow, though he implied that the carping should be dismissed as Chinese-inspired.

The point is apparent from another authoritative and less polemical pronouncement published at the time the Soviet Union agreed to the SALT negotiations:

> . . . Experience has shown [it stated] that only under conditions of a relaxation of tensions is it possible to concentrate a maximum of resources on accomplishing the plans for the building of Communism.[22]

All this connotes neither a Soviet eagerness to yield on issues of substance nor any irreversible option in favor of a serious *détente*. But it does suggest a renewal of the tacit alliance in the Soviet elite among the "welfare" spokesmen, the proponents of arms control, and the senescent bureaucrats less and less inclined to take dangerous risks abroad. It also permits speculating that the advocates of gross strategic parity with the United States have carried the day over those pushing for a serious try to achieve strategic superiority—and have done so for a combination of prudential, political, and economic reasons.

THE HOME FRONT AND THE MIDDLE EAST

How, if at all, does the foregoing bear on recent Soviet policy in the Middle East? It should be clear that, at the level of generalization at which the whole problem has been sketched here, and with the relative paucity of current information, what emerges has only very limited applied (let alone predictive) uses insofar as specific situations are concerned. Moreover, our discussion is not meant to suggest that every Soviet move abroad becomes a subject of elite disputes or that for every foreign policy posture there need be, so to speak, a domestic isostere. Even if correct, our line of analysis deals with broad tendencies—and even overwhelming tendencies cannot be assumed to be operative in every specific instance. This is particularly true of Soviet policy in the Middle East inasmuch as there are certain unprecedented aspects to this particular setting, which make the prediction of Soviet behavior foolhardy if not foolish.

There is no evidence that Soviet behavior in this area is currently animated by a consciousness of, let alone a commitment to, Russian "historical" objectives. In its early days Soviet foreign policy explicitly repudiated tsarist goals, here as elsewhere; and in more recent years the relevance of traditional objectives may be assumed to have been attenuated, as it typically does everywhere, as a by-product of modernization, which brings about changes in both the objective and the perceived needs of the state. Surely it is neither the Straits nor the Holy Places which today are the prizes for which the Soviet Union exerts itself in the Middle East.

Nor has Soviet behavior here amounted to the implementation of a timetable with specified targets. The leadership is only too keenly aware of the fact that, wherever in the past it set itself territorial targets of penetration, it invariably failed. Where it has succeeded in gaining a measure of influence, this has been in pursuit of targets of opportunity and not prior design—opportunity, one might add, created as often as not by the failures of other powers (notably, the U.K. and the U.S.) to provide or maintain alternative options or support for for the local authorities or societies.

Seen from the vantage point of the Kremlin and its "academic" consultants, Soviet policy in the Third World has been marked by a succession of misconceptions—from Stalin's failure to differentiate imperialist from national-revolutionary forces, to Khrushchev's over-optimism about the natural propinquity of Communist and non-Communist interests in the "Zone of Peace." Moscow has watched with dismay the ouster or alienation of its erstwhile friends and clients—Chiang, Qassem, Ben Bella, Nkrumah, Sukarno, Sékou Touré, to mention just a few. Moreover, in none of the countries involved has there developed an indigenous political base that might be relied upon; in fact, in none has the Communist Party been even legally kept alive.[23]

The Soviet decision-makers are thus caught in a strange but not entirely novel tension between the temptation to capitalize on a power vacuum which has led, step by step, to increasing Soviet involvement in the area, and the strong impulse not to get more deeply involved in a situation which Moscow may not be able to control and which could, if fighting resumed, confront the Soviet leadership with the unpalatable alternatives of risking a showdown with the United States or letting down its expensive clients. Reflecting as it does their perception of an American mood of retrenchment fed by the Vietnam experience, and newly acquired Soviet global capabilities, especially in naval power, Soviet policy has already "paid off" in making the U.S.S.R. a major factor in the Eastern Mediterranean and the Middle East. But one may speculate that none of the alternatives even vaguely entertained in Moscow can seem satisfactory, for in essence total control must be recognized to be illusory, withdrawal unacceptable, and anything short of full control risky at best.

Under such conditions Moscow has, no doubt intentionally, kept a modicum of room for maneuver in a variety of ways, at least one of which has a distinctly domestic component. The relative reticence of Soviet mass media regarding the extent of Soviet military presence and commitments in the Middle East permits the leadership in this instance to shape policy with a fairly free hand insofar as "public opinion" is concerned. There is assuredly no effort to build up the situation as a potential *casus belli*.

By the same token, on other than a tactical level alternative policy preferences are likely to be articulated only by those oblivious to the realities of the local scene in the Middle East and extrapolating from domestic considerations, or else by ideologically committed zealots prepared to ignore the specifics of the area.

It is likely that Soviet "doves" have urged greater restraint on policy-makers. The considerable sensitivity of official and unofficial spokesmen to the description of the U.S.S.R.'s role in Egypt as a Soviet Vietnam suggests that there has been intense discussion and criticism along the lines of military risk-taking; the consumer-goods school, on its part, is also likely to have argued that—on the basis of precedent and priorities—aid to Egypt amounted to money and equipment down the drain, which could more urgently and profitably be used at home. But the dominant orientation in the leadership has resisted such arguments inasmuch as yielding to them would be tantamount to acknowledging a severe political setback.

It is certain that there have also been Soviet "hawks" pressing for a more vigorous (not to say adventurous) Soviet policy. Most dramatic perhaps is the case of Nikolai Yegorychev, until the Six-Day War of 1967 First Secretary of the Moscow City Committee of the CPSU—a key political position. While there is some uncertainty about the circumstances and issues that led to his ouster, it is clear that far more was involved than a factional power struggle. Yegorychev did, it is true, belong to the clique of what might loosely be labeled the young fascists à la Shelepin, Semichastnyi, and Pavlov, who had opposed Brezhnev, who in turn managed step by step to eliminate them from positions of responsibility. But if his position was in jeopardy—and he was aware of it—all the more reason for Yegorychev not to espouse foreign-policy causes certain to attract only very limited support among his comrades on the Central Committee or even higher up, unless he genuinely believed in the policies he stuck up for.

A greater commitment of support on the Arab side, in the setting of 1967, would appear to be quite congruent with what is known of Yegorychev's public pronouncements prior to that time— a (strong but not unambiguous) record of anti-intellectualism, intolerance of dissent, xenophobia and intense hostility toward the West. Coupled with his official visit to Cairo earlier in 1967, which must have led him to expectations and psychological commitments rooted in personal experience, this record suggests the plausibility of his advocating deeper Soviet involvement in the Middle East, a position which evidently led him to depict Soviet policy during the crisis as a sell-out of the Arab clients (and perhaps to advocate support of guerrillas and Communist detachments in the Arab world). His ouster may have been as much an indication of the impermissibility of challenging the wisdom of official policy in such a fashion as the product of an opportunity welcomed by the Brezhnev clique to get rid of him. It need not have prejudged subsequent Soviet policy in the area. But it illustrates both the existence and the failure of more "hawkish" critiques of official conduct.[24] It is hard to see, however, how such hardline views can carry the day inasmuch as even the Soviet naval and air force militants were apparently eager to avoid incidents with Israeli forces and *a fortiori* to forestall anything that might bring the U.S. more actively into the picture.[25]

No doubt, there is also a temptation to step up Soviet activity so as to undercut Chinese efforts in the region. But on balance the Soviet estimate of the Chinese challenge in this area must be rather low, compared to the potential trouble resulting from Chinese endeavors further east and to the likely priorities of Chinese engagement. Indeed, if anything, the increasing complexities of superpower jockeying are likely to impose greater, rather than lesser, restraint on Soviet policy here, too.

There is assuredly no evidence—surmises to the contrary notwithstanding—that Soviet policy in the Middle East is being made, in Moscow or on the spot, by the military. If the military have been successful in establishing a stronger presence here than anywhere else outside the Communist world, they have thereby also increased the risks of conflict. The resulting dilemmas leave open a range of options to Soviet policy-makers, which only a better knowledge of internal detail could circumscribe any further.[26]

PERCEPTIONS, PERSPECTIVES, PERPLEXITIES

There is so much more in this complex interrelationship that we are ignorant of that it would be naive or irresponsible to suggest finite answers to impossible questions. Who structures the options that are placed before the Soviet leaders? Who decides what issues they handle and what policies are in effect set by bureaucratic fiat? What is the role of the staff of the Central Committee? To what extent are individuals perceived as spokesmen for interest or opinion groups, and does such identification enhance or hinder their performance? These are but a few of the many blank spaces on the vast map of Soviet elite politics.

Over the years, Soviet policy and policy-making have undergone substantial changes. Yet it scarcely proves easier now to strike a balance than it was in earlier days. For each dilemma dismissed there appears to be a new conundrum; for each challenge weathered, another faces the leadership. While there is now less faith in Moscow in the inevitable operation of the laws of history, there is also among the leaders a far greater consciousness of their newly gained power. The constraints previously imposed on the conduct of foreign policy by a keen awareness of potential dissidence at times of crisis, have largely been dissipated; but the system has meanwhile generated unintended forces which amount to an impressive and growing array of in-system critics and watchdogs. Whereas the possession and awareness of nuclear power have engendered a commitment to avoid "confrontations" that could lead to the use of the ultimate weapon, there is also likely to be an instinctive tendency—

now that gross strategic parity with the United States seems to have been attained—to take somewhat greater gambles in the pursuit of Soviet objectives. On the one hand, the Sino-Soviet conflict has struck a fatal blow to the dominant and time-honored "two-camp" perception of the world and its assumed division into friends and foes, and has led to substantial disorientation and cognitive dissonance; on the other hand, the setbacks and confusions of purpose among other powers —first and foremost, the United States—and the perception of (real or potential or imaginary) power vacuums tend to stimulate a new appetite for initiatives to take advantage of such opportunities.

The primacy of Soviet interests and objectives remains overwhelmingly domestic; and the many needs and shortcomings—in economy, technology, administration, planning, recruitment and socialization, and management—are perhaps more realistically perceived in Moscow than they have ever been before. But there is also little doubt that the temptation has increased to escape the dilemmas of politics, the stalemates and frustrations, the doubts and drab routines of bureaucratic intrigues, and the persistent pressures to solve the insoluble, precisely by reaching abroad, by seeking to translate overwhelming power into tangible packages of success—something that has thus far eluded the Soviet leaders, a fact which itself has in turn added to the sum total of their frustration and insecurity in the midst of massive might.

On the one hand, the increase in gross national product has reduced the tautness of the budget and the pains of choosing among alternatives none of which seemed to satisfy all the effective needs. On the other hand, making more guns *and* more butter, more tanks and trucks *and* more textiles, toys and television sets also generates new pressures of rising expectations and consumer demands at home.

While the limited broadening of the circle of decision-makers and the increased access for spokesmen for some interest groups—as well as the greater consultation of experts—all imply elements of responsiveness, this process also encourages a greater catering to instincts for drama and showmanship, political upstaging, chauvinism and sensationalism, especially in a setting in which there is no other mechanism for rival factions to mobilize broader support.

If the tendency to make better use of specialists has made for greater competence and improved information—that is, has made for greater rationality—the contending pressures of narrower self-interest expressed by occupational groups tend to make politics, on the contrary, a more irrational product of these rival forces.

Thus Moscow is caught between temptation and restraint, commitment and frustration. It is vital then not to oversimplify or ignore the total setting of pulls and pushes in which the Soviet leaders find themselves. There remain old phobias, the memory of old traumas, instincts and deeply ingrained habits, along with the new power, new perceptions, and new perplexities.

NOTES

[1] This paper also omits any discussion of the constraints and pressures of economic development, natural resources, geography, and demography, as well as the regime's perception of public opinion at large. The term "linkage" has come into general use in this connection largely thanks to the work of James N. Rosenau. See in particular Rosenau, ed., *Linkage Politics* (Free Press 1969), and Rosenau, "Pre-Theories and Theories of Foreign Policy," in Barry Farrell, ed., *Approaches to Comparative and International Politics* (Northwestern University Press 1966). See also Wolfram Hanrieder, "Compatability and Consensus," *American Political Science Review*, LXI:4 (1967).

While these approaches are stimulating, original, and often suggestive to students of Soviet policy, the categories used therein prove frequently to be less than adequate for our purposes; and in the few instances in which a self-conscious effort has been made to apply them to the Soviet scene, these have turned out to be the most strained parts of the studies in question. Moreover, the Soviet case (unlike many others) does not involve the contentious issue of the increasing interpenetration of national and international systems.

For earlier discussions of the entire problem, see in particular Vernon V. Aspaturian, "Internal Politics and Foreign Policy in the Soviet System," in Farrell, *op. cit.;* Sidney Ploss, "Studying the Domestic Determinants of Soviet Foreign Policy," *Canadian Slavic Studies,* I:1 (Spring 1967); and this writer's "Soviet Foreign Policy and Domestic Politics," in *Journal of International Affairs,* XXIII:2 (1969). For the contrary argument, denying the importance of domestic political pressures and constraints, see, e.g., Richard Pipes, "Domestic Politics and Foreign Affairs," in Ivo J. Lederer, ed., *Russian Foreign Policy* (Yale University Press 1962); also, for a rather different approach, John A. Armstrong, "The Domestic Roots of Soviet Foreign Policy," *International Affairs* (London), LXI:1 (1965).

[2] See Chalmers Johnson, ed., *Change in Communist Systems* (Stanford University Press 1970).

[3] See H. Gordon Skilling and Franklyn Griffiths, eds., *Interest Groups in Soviet Politics* (Princeton University Press 1971); also Zbigniew Brzezinski and Samuel Huntington, *Political Power USA/USSR* (Viking 1967).

[4] Carl A. Linden, *Khrushchev and the Soviet Leadership 1957–1964* (Johns

54

Hopkins Press 1966), pp. 5, 15. For other reliable (though by no means infallible) guides to the specific sequences of conflicts within the Soviet leadership, see also Robert Conquest, *Power and Policy in the USSR* (St. Martin's 1954); Ploss, ed., *The Soviet Political Process* (Ginn 1971); Michel Tatu, *Power in the Kremlin* (Viking 1968); and Michael Gehlen, *The Politics of Coexistence* (Indiana 1967).

[5] Reproduced in Alexander Dallin and Alan F. Westin, eds., *Politics in the Soviet Union: Seven Cases* (Harcourt, Brace 1966), p. 33.

[6] There is even quantitative evidence that in the post-Stalin period different professions and occupations have acquired distinctive and characteristic patterns of outlook and preferences, which may be identified from official publications of these subgroups. Thus, Milton Lodge, in his *Soviet Elite Attitudes Since Stalin* (Merrill 1969), shows on the basis of content analysis how the economic, legal, and military elites have increasingly developed distinct profiles of political attitudes—each distinct from the others and all subtly but significantly differentiated from that of the Party elite. (Changes in the composition of the Central Committee of the Party and of the Supreme Soviet, incidentally, illustrate important trends indicative of changes in elite recruitment patterns.) While particular techniques and findings can be challenged, the thrust of Lodge's findings fully corroborates those arrived at by more intuitive or anecdotal means.

[7] Lewis J. Edinger and Donald D. Searing, "Social Background in Elite Analysis," *American Political Science Review*, 61:2 (June 1967).

[8] "Khrushchev made the decision to withdraw Soviet offensive weapons from Cuba in consultation apparently with Mikoyan . . . , Kosygin, Suslov, Brezhnev, and . . . Kozlov. These men appear to form a kind of 'presidium within a presidium' . . . " (United States Senate, Committee on Government Operations, *Staffing Procedures and Problems in the Soviet Union*, 1963, p. 25).

[9] In Litvinov's case we are dealing with one of the few surviving "old Bolsheviks" who had known and in many ways admired the West. In Soviet foreign policy he symbolized the "Western" alternative, both to the Nazi-Soviet Pact of 1939 and to the "two-camp" perspective of the Cold War, to which Stalin, Molotov, and Zhdanov subscribed. The latter reassertion of the dichotomic vision of the world in the context of 1944–46 amounted to the victory of the "diehards" over men who had come to accept at face value some of the wartime professions of Allied concord and who neither took for granted the inevitable return to an adversary relationship between East and West, nor interpreted every new development as evidence further validating the incompatibility between the "socialist" and "capitalist" worlds.

When an American correspondent happened upon Litvinov just as he was being retired from the Soviet foreign ministry in mid-1946, Litvinov candidly volunteered: "As far as I am concerned, the root cause is the ideological conception prevailing here that conflict between the Communist and capitalist worlds is inevitable." (Richard C. Hottelet released this report only after Litvinov's death. See *New York World Telegram,* January 28, 1952.) Other statements by Litvinov fully bear out this orientation. In May 1943, on the eve of his departure for Moscow, he had told U.S. Undersecretary Welles that Stalin was completely isolated from all those seeking to convey some sense of reality about the West; that all those sharing Litvinov's own orientation had in effect been eliminated from the foreign office; and that he had no confidence that he himself could do any good once he was back in Moscow—"the trouble in Russia today was that everything centered in one individual, namely, Stalin himself." (Notes by Sumner Welles, May 7, 1943, in *U.S. Foreign Relations . . . 1943,* III:522–23.) A similarly blunt picture emerges from Edgar Snow, *Journey to the Beginning* (Random House 1958, ch. 17, "Warning from Litvinov"); and from Alexander Werth, *Russia at War 1941–1945* (Dutton 1964), p. 938:

> Perhaps the most diehard 'softy' was Litvinov, who remained one even as late as 1947. I had a conversation with him at the reception given by Molotov on Red Army Day in February 1947. . . . He said he was extremely unhappy about the way the Cold War was getting worse and worse every day. By the end of the war, he said, Russia had had the choice of two policies: one was to "cash in on the good-will she had accumulated during the war in Britain and the United States." But they (meaning Stalin and Molotov) had unfortunately chosen the other policy. Not believing that "goodwill" could consti-tute the lasting basis for any kind of policy, they had decided that "security" was what mattered most of all, and they had therefore grabbed all they could. . . .

It is worth noting that in the Stalin days Litvinov's concern was limited to the field of foreign relations—his proper *resort.* Nor was Litvinov foolhardy enough to publicize his views to a broader audience. He was not a contender for power nor even a rival for a subalternship which so often conferred some elbow-room in the conduct of policy. He bowed out, bitter and broken. If after 1946 there remained "little Litvinovs" in the Soviet bureaucracy, as is likely, they were studiedly silent (or, more likely, sought to demonstrate their loyalty by extravagant hyperbolae in praise of the senescent Stalin), and after 1948 even esoteric references to alternative images of the West (as revealed in the Varga controversy) tended to be suppressed.

[10] See the chapter by Frederick C. Barghoorn, in H. Gordon Skilling and Franklyn Griffiths, eds., *Interest Groups in Soviet Politics* (Princeton University Press 1971), esp. at pp. 114, 122ff.; and Michel Tatu, *Power in the Kremlin,* pp. 198–200.

[11] This point has been made, in other connections, by Professors William Zimmerman and Franklyn Griffiths.

[12] Suffice it to think of such turning points as 1921, 1946, and 1956. For a fuller discussion of this question, see Dallin, "Soviet Foreign Policy and Domestic Politics." This use of "left" and "right" follows the Communist usage of these terms and not the very different content given them, e.g., by Zbigniew Brzezinski. (See his "The Soviet Political System: Transformation or Degeneration?" in Brzezinski, ed., *Dilemmas of Change in Soviet Politics* [Columbia 1969].)

[13] A recent study has carefully collated the evidence that during the crisis over Czechoslovakia in 1968 the party leadership in Soviet Ukraine, being particularly concerned about the attitudes of its own population, turned out to be among the first to press for Soviet armed intervention in Czechoslovakia. See Grey Hodnett and Peter J. Potichnyi, *The Ukraine and the Czechoslovak Crisis* (Australian National University 1970).

[14] Khrushchev, *Stroitel'stvo kommunizma v SSSR . . .,* VIII (Moscow 1964), p. 51. In more general terms, the same connexity is already indicated in the 1961 CPSU Program.

[15] See, e.g., Roman Kolkowicz, *The Soviet Military and the Communist Party* (Princeton 1967); Thomas W. Wolfe, *Soviet Strategy at the Crossroads* (Harvard 1964); and John Erickson, "The 'Military Factor' in Soviet Policy," *International Affairs* (London), April 1963.

[16] See especially Wolfe, *op. cit.,* ch. 2–3.

[17] See F.J.C. Griffiths, "Inner Tensions in the Soviet Approach to Disarmament," *International Journal* (Toronto), Autumn 1967; Walter Clemens, Jr., "Underlying Factors in Soviet Arms Control Policy," Peace Research Society, *Papers,* VI (1966); Roman Kolkowicz, ed., *The Soviet Union and Arms Control* (Johns Hopkins 1970); Thomas B. Larson, *The Soviet Union and Disarmament* (Prentice-Hall 1969).

[18] Leonid Brezhnev, Central Committee Report to the XXIV CPSU Congress, March 30, 1971.

[19] *Kommunist* (Moscow), 1971, No. 4, p. 38.

[20] *Khrushchev Remembers* (Little, Brown 1971), pp. 519–20.

[21] A thorough treatment of Soviet differences over the United States is to be found in the doctoral dissertation of Franklyn C. Griffiths (Columbia University 1972).

[22] K. P. Ivanov, *Leninskie osnovy vneshnei politiki SSSR* (Moscow 1969), p. 50; cited in Sidney Ploss, "Politics in the Kremlin," *Problems of Communism,* May-June 1970, p. 8.

[23] See papers in Part II.

[24] See Tatu, *op. cit.,* pp. 532ff., and especially Christian Duevel, "The Political

Credo of N. G. Yegorychev," Radio Liberty Research Paper, No. 17 (1967).

[25] The hypothesis implied in the foregoing discussion is reinforced by an interesting study which became available after the present paper was completed (Ilana Dimant, "PRAVDA and TRUD—Divergent Attitudes Towards the Middle East," Hebrew University of Jerusalem, Soviet and East European Research Center, Research Paper No. 3, June 1972). Concluding (as the present author does) that "the Soviet attitude towards the complex of Middle East issues is not monolithic," it finds that *Trud*, the Soviet trade union paper, had followed "a more uncompromising, 'dogmatic' line towards the United States as well as towards the Arab regimes," and has urged a "more revolutionary, 'party-oriented' approach" toward the Arab world, implying a greater willingness to disengage the Soviet Union from firm commitments to the Arab elites. It further concludes that *Pravda*, by contrast, faithfully reflects the Brezhnev line. Finally, it advances the hypothesis that the *Trud* orientation reflects the views of A.N. Shelepin and his associates, a view which is plausible and which fits in with the interpretation given above, but for which the evidence remains admittedly speculative and, at best, indirect (pp. 60–69).

[26] Other interesting facets of domestic politics relevant here but in neither case controlling insofar as Soviet behavior in the Middle East is concerned are the policy regarding the emigration of Jews to Israel and the attitude of Muslim and Turkic groups within the U.S.S.R. While by no means decisive in regard to specific political moves, the coalition of economic, regional, and political interests in the Soviet elite expressing concern about looming energy shortages is also certain to have heightened Soviet awareness of and interest in Middle Eastern oil resources.

2. THE SOVIET POSTURE IN THE MIDDLE EAST: POLICY, STRATEGY, AND IDEOLOGY

BEN-CION PINCHUK

SOVIET PENETRATION INTO THE MIDDLE EAST IN HISTORICAL PERSPECTIVE

In 1972, the Soviet Union appears to some observers as the dominant power in the Middle East. Even a casual summary of Soviet assets in the area presents an impressive list of achievements. The Kremlin holds a predominant position in Egypt, Syria, and Iraq; it wields strong influence in Algeria, South Yemen, and Somalia, and to a lesser degree its presence is felt in other countries in the Middle East and North Africa. The Kremlin, after many years of mutual hostility, has succeeded in establishing friendly relations with Turkey and Iran. Symbolic of the recently acquired status is the impressive Red Fleet which cruises the waters of the Mediterranean. It seems as though Brezhnev and Kosygin have succeeded in realizing the goals of Peter I, Catherine II, and some of the 19th-century Imperial statesmen. It is also possible that the present Soviet penetration into the Middle East constitutes a new phase and a new form of Russian and Soviet expansion—a phase that departs substantially from the established patterns of Russian expansion and confronts the Soviet leadership with a new set of problems and dilemmas.

One of the distinctive features of Russian imperialism throughout history has been its expansion into territories contiguous to former Russian areas. The result was the creation of a territorially compact empire. The determining factor for the continued existence of the empire was Russian physical presence. The presence of Russian settlers and soldiers determined to a large extent the borders of the Russian Empire.

In several respects, Soviet expansion has continued in the pattern of its predecessor. Territorial contiguity coupled with actual Soviet military presence has remained a distinctive feature of the new and expanded Russian Empire in Eastern Europe even though there has been no formal incorporation. Basic social and political reconstruction characterizes Russian expansion in the Soviet era. Until the mid-fifties of the present century, Soviet expansion was limited to areas adjoining the Soviet Union. No claim is being made here that the motivation

61

and ultimate goals of Imperial Russia and of the Soviet Union are similar. They certainly differ in form and substance. One is nevertheless justified in attributing the same geographical pattern, as well as the same form of physical presence, as the determining factors holding together the pre-and post-1917 empires. In this sense there is a striking continuity in pattern from the time of Imperial Russia until the death of Stalin.

The Russian-Soviet drive into the Middle East until the mid-sixties of the present century followed the same scheme of attempted expansion or political dominance which one finds in other regions. Almost until the end of the 18th century Russia's drive in the direction of the Middle East coincided with the problem of establishing a stable southern border. It was not only a question of geography, but to a greater extent a problem of coming to terms with the political power on the other side of the border. The annexation of the Ukraine, after the peace of Andrussovo in 1667, brought Russia into more direct contact with the Ottoman Empire, the major Middle Eastern power, and its Crimean vassal. In the course of nearly a century and a half, Russia pushed forward its southern border on the European side of the Black Sea to the Pruth, and on its eastern side it annexed Georgia and large portions of Armenia. The border with Iran in the Caucasus and on the eastern shore of the Caspian Sea has been relatively stable since 1828. Using a rather broad generalization, one might say that the combined interests of various European powers, Great Britain being the strongest and most consistent, held the Russian frontier with the Middle East with only minor changes for a century and a half.[1]

Since the first quarter of the 19th century, with the stabilization of Russia's Middle Eastern border, unfulfilled designs and futile attempts replaced actual expansion. Russia's three wars in the 19th century against the Ottoman Empire resulted in rather minor adjustments of its southern border. Yet even the unrealized plans reflect the attitude of Russian policy-makers. Plans for the annexation of territories or the creation of spheres of influence, with the exception of Constantinople, always encompassed areas adjacent to Russian territory, whereby the Russians were able to establish their physical presence. This pattern had previously been discernible in Catherine's famous Greek Project. According to that plan, she intended to annex the area between the Bug and the Dniester to establish a vassal state in present-day Rumania and revive the "Greek Empire," perhaps with her grandson Constantine as ruler. Characteristically, areas not adjacent to Russian territory were assigned to other powers; Serbia and Dalmatia to the Habsburg Empire; Morea, Crete, and Cyprus to Venice; Syria and Egypt would have gone to France.[2] The pattern is rather clear: areas that could not be reached directly by Russian power did not constitute part of the expansion plan.

Russia's negotiations with Great Britain in 1844 and in the years immediately preceding the outbreak of the Crimean War, show yet another pattern of its policy toward its southern neighbor. According to Nesselrode's Memorandum of 1844, it was Russia's firm desire to keep the Ottoman Empire intact as long as possible. Russia's policy-makers considered an early disintegration of the Ottoman Empire a "catastrophe" and therefore were eager to prepare for such an eventuality by entering into a series of agreements with the interested European powers in order to prevent a general European war.[3] It is clear that Russia preferred a weak Ottoman Empire that could be easily manipulated, to a general partition that would bring strong neighbors to its southern frontier. Russia was reluctant to replace the power vacuum of the Ottoman Empire by a new balance of power (that would be created by the dissolution of that empire and that might result in the eventual decrease of Russia's influence in the area).

The Crimean War of 1854–6 and the Congress of Berlin in 1878 proved that Russia was confronted on its southern frontier by a European coalition (whose actual composition differed from time to time), which would prevent Russia from creating a power vacuum on its southern border. During the Crimean War and the Great Eastern Crisis of 1875–8, Russian policy was strongly influenced by, and made use of, although not for the first time, religious and social feelings and ideology. Great Britain, at that time, was the main power that thwarted Russian designs in the Middle East. Yet toward the end of the 19th century, British statesmen had second thoughts about their attitude to a further southward expansion of Russian power. Persia was divided in 1907 between Great Britain and Russia into two spheres of influence: the southern part British, and the northern part Russian. A neutral zone separated the British and Russian areas. Here again we can recognize the pattern of Russian expansion into neighboring areas. Great Britain, Russia's ally in World War I, agreed in March 1915 to the acquisition by Russia of Constantinople, the western shore of the Straits, and part of the Asiatic shore. The planned expansion of Russian power southward was prevented by the Bolshevik Revolution of 1917.

The rise to power of a new regime in 1917 had not changed the geographical pattern of Russian designs in the Middle East. Yet an obvious change took place on the ideological level. Communism, a universal ideology, replaced Panslavism and Christianity as the ideological basis of Russian expansion. Manifestos were published calling "all 'Eastern' people to see the new light emanating from Moscow," and Communist parties were organized wherever possible. Yet the only real effort to expand Soviet rule in the area was made in a region bordering on Soviet territory, namely, northern Iran. This attempt failed through the combined efforts of the Iranian government supported by Britain, and because of the basic weakness of the Soviet state at the time.[4] For all practical purposes the Soviet Union ceased to exercise an important role in the destinies of the region until the eve of World War II.

Indicative of Soviet thinking as pertaining to the Middle East during World War II were the plans brought forth by the Soviet leadership concerning division of the areas into spheres of influence. In November 1950 Molotov, then serving as the Chairman of the Council of Commissars and Foreign Commissars, conducted a series of conversations in Berlin on the future of Soviet-German collaboration. During those talks various plans to partition the "bankrupt British Empire" were discussed. Even on that occasion the Soviet statesman did not go beyond the established territorial mode of Russian expansion: he demanded as Russia's share in the spoils an area contiguous to the Caucasus extending to the Persian Gulf.[5]

When World War II was approaching its final phase, the Soviet leaders presented a series of demands concerning the Middle East. At Yalta, in February 1945, Stalin demanded the establishment of Soviet bases in the Straits and the return of the provinces of Kars and Ardahan which Russia had yielded to Turkey in 1921. The Soviet demands were refused by the Western allies.[6] Raised again in 1946, they were accompanied this time by military and naval "maneuvers" along the Soviet-Turkish frontier and in the Black Sea. Only the strong American backing given to the Turks convinced Stalin to forego his demand.

Iran was another case of a Soviet attempt to penetrate an area contiguous to their territory, following World War II. Northern Iran had been occupied by Soviet troops, with the agreement of Great Britain, in order to keep open the supply line to Russia. Both powers agreed to withdraw their forces six months after the war. Yet even during the war's final phases, Soviet activity indicated that the Russians had long-term plans for expanding their influence in Iran. They strengthened the Communist-dominated Tudeh Party, kept the central government in Tehran out of the northern area, and—most important of all—supported the separatist movement in Azerbaijan and among the Kurds. In December 1945, they sponsored the establishment of the Autonomous Republic of Azerbaijan and the Kurdish Peoples' Republic. The Iranian government appealed to the U.N., protesting Soviet interference in its internal affairs. What actually convinced the Soviets to retreat was the manifest American support of the Iranian government. America's involvement was in turn facilitated by the fact that Great Britain's influence in Iran, while definitely on the wane, was still quite considerable.[7]

A new pattern of Soviet designs for influence and expansion begins to emerge in the years immediately following Stalin's death in 1953. World War II signaled the collapse of the British and French empires. Great Britain and France lacked the resources and will to defend their imperial spheres of influence, their retreat being more often than not encouraged by the United States. The result was the creation of a power vacuum that provided tempting opportunities for the extension of Soviet influence. The emergence of the so-called neutralist countries had not changed Stalin's basically negative attitude toward the national liberation movements and their leaders. The prevailing "two camps" concept of the international situation, dominant in the minds of Soviet policy-makers until Stalin's death, made it difficult for the Soviet Union to cooperate with the countries that had only recently acquired independence from their Western masters. Stalin's rigid categorization held that any non-Communist country was capitalist or capitalist-controlled. This attitude prevented the Kremlin from exploiting the opportunities arising from the disintegration of the Western empires.

The years 1953–5 saw a perceptible change in Soviet attitudes toward various leaders of the Third World, a change that eventually developed into a clear departure of Soviet policy from previously established patterns. The indications that change was taking place were many and varied. For the first time India and Burma were mentioned in a favorable context in one of Malenkov's speeches in August 1953.[8] In September of the same year, the Soviets signed a five-year trade agreement with India. The favorable and positive attitude toward neutralist countries, their national movements, and leaders that one detects in Soviet publications during 1955 indicates that a basic change was taking place in Soviet policy.[9] The Kremlin's enthusiastic support of the Bandung Conference in April 1955 as well as the Khrushchev-Bulganin trip to India, Burma, and Afghanistan signified the political emergence of a new line.[10] Khrushchev developed a new ideological approach toward the underdeveloped world at the 20th Congress of the Soviet Communist Party in February 1956. He replaced the concept of the "two camps" by the concept of the "two zones"—the "War Zone" composed of the capitalist-imperialist West, and the "Peace Zone" that included the Socialist and non-Socialist "peace-loving" countries. Thus was formulated the ideology that enabled the Soviet Union to develop new forms of relations, influence, and expansion in areas beyond the immediate proximity of Soviet territory.[11] What facilitated the implementation of the new ideological formulation and the exploitation of the opportunities offered by the collapse of the old empires was the new sense of power with which the Soviet leadership was imbued.

By the mid-fifties, the Soviet Union had developed a thermonuclear and I.C.B.M. delivery capacity that gave the Soviet leaders a new sense of strength and parity with the West. The Soviet Union was becoming a global power, involved in shaping the destinies of countries and people far away from its territory. The mid-fifties saw the gradual emergence of a new pattern of Soviet expansion. It should be emphasized that the development of the new pattern of what might be called "global expansionism" was a slow process conditioned by the improvement of Soviet global capabilities, such as its missile forces, navy, strategic air forces, etc. It also developed and gathered momentum in response to the relative weakening of its opponents.

The Arab Middle East became one of the first and major areas in which the new pattern of Soviet expansion developed. Here the departure was most dramatic and far-reaching in its consequences. Turkey and Iran, traditional areas of Russian expansionist designs, were left alone. They constituted part of the "Northern Tier"—a link in the West's global defense system. Nasser's Egypt provided the Soviet Union with its initial foothold in the Arab world. The first arms deal between the Soviet Union and Egypt was made public in September 1955. Soviet policy-makers exhibited extreme caution; the Soviet Union was not officially participating in the deal—it was rather Czechoslovakia that actually supplied the arms. Soviet sources described it as an ordinary commercial exchange.[12] In retrospect, it is clear that the arms deal was the beginning of a major breakthrough of Soviet influence into the Arab countries, and the Third World in general. Egypt became the major base of Soviet operations in the Arab world as well as a showcase of its achievements in the Third World. Soviet influence in the Arab world has increased since 1955 not so much as a result of Soviet planning and initiative as through its skillful exploitation of internal developments in the region and the blunders of its opponents. Thus, in 1956–7, during the Suez Crisis, Arab public opinion credited the Soviet Union as the outside power most instrumental in rescuing Egypt, despite the fact that the Kremlin played only a secondary role, as compared with the U.S., in forcing the retreat of the allies from Egyptian land.[13] The Soviet Union emerged from this crisis as a recognized Middle Eastern power playing the role of protector of Arab nationalism.[14]

Despite friction and setbacks, Soviet investments, influence, and involvement in the Middle East from 1955 to the present have increased and broadened. Since the Six-Day War the Soviet Union has considerably increased its physical military presence in the region. It had in 1971 air and naval bases in several Arab countries as well as a sizeable concentration of Soviet military personnel in Egypt. The latter became a major operational base for Soviet air and naval units as well as a stepping stone for operations into other regions. Only recently, in January 1971, Egypt served as a transfer base for Soviet equipment to India. At the same time, one can detect a systematic Soviet effort to build up a more reliable political base to secure its influence and huge investments in the Arab world. This effort was particularly strong in Egypt, where Soviet influence was behind some of the purges in the Egyptian army following the June 1967 defeat. One can also detect a serious attempt to influence Egypt's ruling party, the Arab Socialist Union. The May 28, 1971 "Friendship and Collaboration Agreement" between Egypt and the Soviet Union can be considered as part of the Kremlin's effort to institutionalize and stabilize its influence in the region. It is important to note that in this sphere Soviet efforts have been less successful than in establishing its military presence.[15]

Soviet influence and presence in the Middle East constitute a clear departure from the geographical pattern as well as from the actual implementation of Russian expansion in the past. In spite of the impressive achievements in the region, the Soviet Union has not yet reached a stable form of relations, influence, and presence in any of the countries of the Middle East.

The massive expulsion of Soviet personnel and advisers from Egypt in July 1972 should have a sobering effect on Moscow's policy-makers. The most striking aspect of this expulsion is the fact that after almost 17 years of exertion, and huge investments in material and prestige, the Kremlin failed to establish a firm and reliable support in Egypt, a country that was almost totally dependent on Soviet military supplies and political backing. It became obvious that the Soviet Union had maneuvered itself into an awkward position: while having great obligations and commitments it lacked the power to manipulate the developments in the region in its favor. The deterioration of the Soviet position in Egypt raises serious doubts as to the soundness of the Kremlin's gains in other parts of the Middle East and in the Third World in general. One is tempted to go even further and doubt the wisdom of any of the great powers who attempt to secure a firm base in the Afro-Asian and Latin American countries in an era that is still much governed by the impact of liberation from imperialism. While departing from the traditional pattern of expansion, Soviet policy-makers have not yet developed a clear concept of the goals of Soviet global expansion. While still speaking in terms of complete social transformation as the final goal, it is doubtful whether actual Soviet policy is being determined by such considerations. Yet it would be erroneous to speak about Soviet imperialism, with traditional empires in mind. In the second half of the 20th century this type of imperialism is rather an anachronism. Some of the problems and setbacks of Soviet policy in the Middle East are the result of the search of Soviet policy-makers for appropriate means of control and influence as well as their attachment to antiquated patterns and concepts. We are in the midst of attempts to create some kind of new Russian empire which will be different in form from the Russian-Soviet model as well as from other imperial forms known from the past. It is rather doubtful whether these attempts will succeed.

NOTES

1 Cyril E. Black, "The Pattern of Russian Objectives," in Ivo J. Lederer (ed.), *Russian Foreign Policy* (Yale University Press 1962).

2 M. S. Anderson, *The Eastern Question* (London 1966), pp. 8–9.

3 J. C. Hurewitz, *Diplomacy in the Near and Middle East, A Documentary Record 1535/1914*, Vol. 1 (Princeton 1956), pp. 130–132.

4 Firuz Kazemzadeh, "Russia and the Middle East," in Ivo J. Lederer, *op. cit.*

5 Raymond James Sontag and James Stuart Beddie (eds.), *Nazi-Soviet Relations 1939–1941* (New York 1948), pp. 217–259.

6 Herbert Feis, *Churchill, Roosevelt, Stalin. The War They Waged and the Peace They Sought* (Princeton 1970), pp. 441–489.

7 George Lenczowsky, *Russia and the West in Iran, 1918–1948* (Cornell 1949), p. 216 *et passim*.

8 Richard F. Roser, *An Introduction to Soviet Foreign Policy* (Prentice Hall 1969), p. 291.

9 David J. Dallin, *Soviet Foreign Policy After Stalin* (London 1962), p. 291.

10 *Ibid.*, pp. 291–321.

11 Roser, *op. cit.*, pp. 293–295.

12 *Ibid*, pp. 391–398.

13 Walter Z. Laqueur, *The Soviet Union and the Middle East* (London 1959), p. 239.

14 Dallin, *op. cit.*, pp. 406–421.

15 Oded Eran and Jerome E. Singer, "Soviet Policy towards the Arab World 1955–1971," *Survey* No. 4, 1961, pp. 24–29.

Hans Morgenthau

THE IDEOLOGICAL AND POLITICAL DYNAMICS OF THE MIDDLE EASTERN POLICY OF THE SOVIET UNION

The interaction between ideology and politics in the Soviet Union is intimately connected with the topic of this paper; for it is precisely the interaction between ideology and foreign policy which makes the foreign policy of the Soviet Union so difficult to predict, so complicated, and also, if one may say so, so interesting. If one looks at the history of Soviet foreign policy from the viewpoint of this interaction between ideology and foreign policy, one can distinguish four separate periods differing in the interplay between those two elements.

Obviously the first period—the Leninist period—is dominated by dedication to the principles of Marx and Lenin. This revolutionary period is perhaps best defined by Trotsky's statement, before he left for the Peace Conference at Brest-Litovsk, that he would make a revolutionary proclamation that would be the end of Soviet foreign policy.

However, the objective facts of history very rapidly intruded in this simple-minded conception of a world revolution which was to follow automatically the revolution in Russia and thereby render a Soviet foreign policy superfluous. Let us recall the debate in the Politbureau in January 1918, when the question arose as to whether or not to conclude a peace treaty with Germany, whose armies were advancing deep into Russia. The majority was of the opinion that a peace treaty was unnecessary, since revolution in Germany was both inevitable and imminent and once it had come about, the German proletarians would embrace their Russian comrades and foreign policy would then be unnecessary. It is characteristic of the political genius of Lenin, who was in the minority, that he combined the belief in the inevitability of the world revolution with a correct assessment of the political realities of the hour. He said that, naturally, the revolution in Germany is inevitable, but nobody knows when it will come. Tomorrow, next week, next month, next year. We can't wait, so we must make a compromise, we must deal with the German Government, we must conclude a peace treaty, without abolishing our belief in the inevitability of the world revolution.

71

One could analyze this same development from other examples, since it is typical whenever a religious or pseudo-religious system of beliefs comes in contact with a recalcitrant reality. One can discern the same development in the combination of the belief in the inevitability, let me say, of salvation, or of the Second Coming of Christ or the Messiah, with the facts of life which have not yet produced this ultimate state of history. Thus, one maintains one's belief in the inevitability of the ultimate denouement of the historic process in combination with a realistic assessment of the actual historic situation and the need for action within the context of such a situation.

It was Stalin who drew the extreme conclusions from this conflict between ideology and reality by proclaiming socialism in one country; for he realized, especially after the failure of the revolutions in Germany, Hungary, and Poland, that the Soviet Union could no more wait for the coming of the revolution which would save it, than it could wait in January 1918 for the proletarian revolution in Germany. It had to establish socialism in one country, failing which there would be no socialism in any country.

Stalin thus pursued a foreign policy which followed the classic tsarist lines of expansion. I have always found the self-characterization of Stalin in a discussion with Eden during World War II illuminating. He said to Eden: "The trouble with Hitler is that he does not know where to stop. I know where to stop." It is true that the containment policies of the West in the aftermath of World War II greatly strengthened his tendency to stop at a certain point. However, I have no doubt that Stalin's aims were very much in the tradition of tsarism: expansion in Eastern Europe, as far as this was feasible, considering the risks involved; expansion into the Mediterranean and the Persian Gulf. These were the classic roads of expansion of the Russian Empire.

One of the fundamental errors of Western and, more particularly, of American statesmanship was the misunderstanding of those limited, traditional objectives of Stalinist foreign policy. We looked at Stalin as though he were Trotsky. We confounded Stalin with Trotsky, the spokesman for the uncompromising original Marxist-Leninist foreign policy, stimulating and supporting world revolution as the only answer to the needs of the Soviet Union.

It should also be mentioned that Stalin used Communist ideology, Communist subversion, and Communist parties and governments not for their own sake but for the purposes of the Russian State, which took precedence over ideological considerations. I recall a discussion I had in the late 1940s with an ambassador accredited to Moscow, who told me with what disdain Stalin had referred to the Eastern European Communists, who allowed themselves to be used by the Soviet Government for the purposes of the Russian State.

When we come to Khrushchev, we encounter a different mixture of ideology and traditional foreign policy. In one sense one can say that Khrushchev revived the Leninist-Marxist conception of the ultimate triumph of Communism, not so much through revolution, but through the impact the example of the Soviet State, especially after the spectacular achievement of the Sputniks, would have upon the world. It was indeed the belief of Khrushchev that with this model of development before them, the nations of the Third World would rally to the Soviet Union, would adopt her methods, and would become her allies and clients. And thus the United States and the West would be isolated, and finally, as Khrushchev put it, "we shall bury you."

Obviously this policy failed as it was expressed by Khrushchev in capricious moves on the chessboard of foreign policy. Certainly Stalin would never have dreamt of transforming Cuba into a military and political outpost of the Soviet Union. And while this outpost is today an established fact, it costs the U.S.S.R. about four hundred million dollars a year, with benefits which can hardly be regarded as of paramount importance for her vital interests.

It is at this point that one must consider the relationship between this general development of Russian foreign policy and Soviet policies in the Middle East; for it is during this Khrushchevian period that the Soviet Union appears as an active and increasingly important agent in the Middle East. When I speak here of the Middle East, I am not referring to the traditional interests of the Soviet Union in Turkey and Persia. Those were indeed the traditional interests of Russia, which have their roots in tsarist policy. But the attempt to transform Egypt into a client of the Soviet Union is an entirely different matter.

It is true that a little over 200 years ago the Russians controlled the coastline from Latakiya to Alexandria for a brief period—really by an accident of history which had nothing to do with the vital interests of Russia. But what happened in 1955 was something radically different: the beginnings of the deep involvement of the Soviet Union in territories not adjacent to her own and not legitimized by the traditional desire of the U.S.S.R. to gain access to the Mediterranean and the Persian Gulf. This intrusion into the Middle East, in the form of an ever closer relationship with Egypt, Syria, and Iraq, opens a new chapter in the foreign policy of the Soviet Union.

On the one hand, if one looks at the situation from the Soviet point of view, one can justify this intrusion into the Middle East in Stalinist terms; for the close military and political relations which were established in the mid-fifties between Egypt and the Soviet Union were a response to the attempt on the part of the United States to extend the policy of containment to the Middle East in the form of the Eisenhower doctrine and the Baghdad (now called C.E.N.T.O.) Pact. These two moves in foreign policy were to fail completely for reasons which are somehow related to the interaction between ideology and foreign policy. Here ideology got the better of, and misled, foreign policy. For the Soviet Union simply jumped over the ideological barrier which the Baghdad Pact was supposed to have erected in the Middle East.

This is, you may say, the Stalinist interpretation of the new relations between the Soviet Union and the Middle East. The other interpretation, the second factor in this situation, is the Khrushchevian capriciousness which grabbed at any kind of foothold anywhere. Cuba is one example, and Egypt is another.

With the end of the Khrushchevian period, we enter into a new phase of Soviet foreign policy, which is characterized by a methodical geopolitical expansion of the Soviet Empire into the empty spaces which were left by the liquidation of the British and French empires. A glance at the map shows us how everywhere from the Eastern Mediterranean and the Middle East, through the Persian Gulf, the Red Sea, South Asia, and the Western Pacific in general, the Soviet Union advances step by step into territories contiguous or close to her own.

The Soviet Union has embarked upon a worldwide expansionist policy, which uses in particular the sea as the vehicle for advancement. For that policy, Egypt became a strong point, which the present rulers of the Soviet Union inherited from Krushchev and which was supposed to become one of the anchors keeping the expansion of the Soviet Union into North Africa and Asia on an even keel.

The concrete relations between the Soviet Union and Egypt took on yet another aspect, which is unique in the relations between the Soviet Union and the client states outside Eastern Europe, i.e., the treaty of 27 May, 1971, creates as close a political and military relationship between the Soviet Union and Egypt as that existing between the U.S.S.R. and the other members of the Warsaw Pact. In other words, the U.S.S.R. established a relationship with Egypt, a country geographically removed from the Soviet Union, which is similar to that which developed almost naturally between her and the neighboring nations of Eastern Europe. Thus, Egypt became a client of the Soviet Union, and the latter invested the former with an importance, especially in terms of Soviet prestige, which was bound to lead to certain assumptions concerning the future of Soviet-Egyptian relations and the general policies of the Soviet Union in the Middle East.

It is no exaggeration to say that the presence of about 20,000 Russian military personnel in Egypt, as long as it lasted, with the complete integration of their functions with those of the Egyptian armed forces, created for the Soviet Union a stake in Egypt, in terms of Soviet prestige, which is not dissimilar to the stake which the United States had in South Vietnam in 1964. And I would say that the Soviet Union could during that period no more have tolerated a defeat of Egypt, especially after the model of the defeat of 1967, than the United States thought it could accept a defeat of Vietnam in 1964–65. In other words, the prestige of the Soviet Union was so closely engaged in Egypt that a defeat of Egypt would have been tantamount to a defeat of the Soviet Union. The limits within which the Soviet policy in the Middle East operates today are dictated primarily by the risks which the U.S.S.R. anticipates if she pursues a certain policy—in much the same way as the fear of a direct military conflagration with the Soviet Union or China, or both, has restrained the United States in Vietnam. Thus the fear of a similar confrontation with the United States holds back the Soviet Union. The degree of that restraint is bound to be commensurate with the degree of the Soviet Union's fear of such a confrontation. In turn, a measure of that fear is the determination with which the United States makes it clear to the U.S.S.R. that she runs considerable risks of confrontation if she pursues a certain political and military policy in the Middle East.

It is, of course, difficult to say with any degree of assurance what the aims of the Soviet Union in the Middle East actually are, for they are to a very great extent not aims of a substantive character—aside from naval facilities—but are essentially in the nature of prestige in-to intrude into the Third World and which has for this reason revived terests. The U.S.S.R., which has suffered a number of defeats in attempts the ideological commitment to foreign Communists on the occasion of the abortive *coup* in Sudan, is bound to encounter great difficulties in reconciling herself to additional defeats. Here we come back to the interaction between ideology and foreign policy. The Soviet Government is in the most uncomfortable position of having to govern in the name of an ideology—Marxism-Leninism—which has lost most of its creditibility in the Soviet Union and elsewhere. It has been reduced essentially to a mechanical ritual in whose truth very few people in the Soviet Union actually believe. Thus the Soviet leaders cannot, when they are faced with failure, fall back upon an unquestioned, objective system of beliefs which justifies their rule. They must have success, or they must at least minimize failure and make it appear as a success, in order to be able to legitimize their rule. In other words, in the absence of a plausible ideological foundation for their rule, they are driven back upon a minimal pragmatic justification, i.e., success or at least the avoidance of failure.

This is an additional element which would make it very difficult for the Soviet Union to stand idly by while the Arab states are defeated again. It is for this reason that it is extremely unlikely that the Soviet Union is interested in the resumption of hostilities. On the contrary, it is very likely that the U.S.S.R. does everything in her power to prevent it. But she is in this respect in the same position in which the United States has found herself time and again vis-à-vis dependent and weak clients: it is the client who can force the hand of the powerful protector. If an Arab leader gives the order to attack tomorrow, whatever the preferences of the Soviet Union with regard to this particular action are, her hand might be forced.

Let me say again in conclusion that the limits within which the Soviet Union is willing to operate in this complicated and dangerous context are determined by the counteraction she can expect.

If the U.S.S.R. anticipates a weak or non-existent counteraction, she will go as far as she deems necessary to protect and promote her interests. On the other hand, if she forsees a counteraction which entails enormous risks for herself, she will do everything in her power to limit her involvement in a new military confrontation in the Middle East. Soviet policy in the Middle East is predominantly determined by the prestige interests which have accrued to the Soviet Union over the years. The extent to which the Soviet Union will pursue these prestige interests will depend upon her assessment of the risks entailed.

Roman Kolkowicz

THE SOVIET POLICY IN THE MIDDLE EAST

Most of the papers presented to this Conference fall into three categories, or more specifically, adopt three approaches to the question: "Why did the Soviet Union enter the Middle East?" Some authors responded with "Why not?" explaining recent Soviet involvement in the Middle East as largely a continuation of traditional Russian historical and geopolitical interests in the area. Other analysts responded with "Why at all?"—implying that the costly and rather complex nature of Soviet commitments in the Middle East seem irrational and unpromising in terms of potential results. And still others responded with "Why now?", suggesting the need for a better understanding of some recent international and regional developments as a way to a sharper perception of objectives and political calculations in Soviet policy toward the Middle East. This paper falls into the latter category, and will attempt to relate Soviet objectives and actions in the Middle East to a broader spectrum of Soviet political and military interests.

DYNAMICS OF SOVIET FOREIGN POLICY

An examination of Soviet foreign policy of recent decades yields certain patterns of dynamics and objectives of Moscow's politics. The essential dynamics of Soviet foreign policy are expansionistic and the patterns of this expansionism may be described in terms of a triad: expand-consolidate-hold. The first major phase of Soviet expansionism resulting from their victory over Germany in World War II bears witness to this expansionistic pattern; the second phase of Soviet expansionism, in the Middle East, bears the marks of the same pattern. And although the Soviets do not seek territorial conquest in the Middle East, the pattern of expand-consolidate-hold applies here as well.

A second aspect of Soviet foreign policy is its close relationship to Soviet security concerns, their general military capabilities, and the levels of their strategic capabilities relative to those of the West. Briefly,

77

the expansionist momentum of Soviet policy seems to be closely related to Soviet perceptions of their military strength, their ability to support regional diplomatic political overtures with the requisite manpower and military technology, and their assessment of the strategic ratios as a "global balancer" of super relationships. Thus, Stalin's conventional military and strategic capabilities and doctrines were essentially regionally-continentally oriented. Stalin's foreign policy remained largely regional-continental.

Khrushchev's foreign policy was characterized by an unprecedented activism and "optimism," leading to massive, though unsystematic and "harebrained" expansion of Soviet diplomatic and economic activity around the globe. At the same time, however, Khrushchev's conventional and strategic capabilities remained inferior to those of the West. It is therefore not too surprising that when Soviet threats to some important Western interests were challenged, he chose not to resist, but instead to cut his losses and yield. Khrushchev's foreign policy sought to cover up Soviet military inferiority with a blustering, militant pose and verbal overkill. When his bluff was called, however, he drew the correct conclusions and reverted to the traditional patterns of Soviet foreign policy.

The Brezhnev leadership in the Kremlin has finally succeeded where previous Soviet leaders failed: their strategic power is equal to that of the West; Soviet conventional forces are comparable to those of the West; Soviet strategic doctrines are now globally oriented and Soviet foreign policy reflects these important changes in the political calculus of the Kremlin.

A third aspect of Soviet foreign policy lies in the quality of "orchestration," i.e., the balancing of many interests and problems around the globe so that their various components can be brought to bear on any particular foreign policy issue that is relevant. This principle of policy orchestration also suggests a Soviet concept of priorities and hierarchy of interests and objectives, with the presumed subordination of lesser objectives to the larger and more vital interests of the political elites. This is particularly relevant in the analyses of patron-client relations involving the Soviet Union.

A fourth aspect of Soviet foreign policy lies in its relationship to perceived strengths and weaknesses of their major adversaries. Thus, the Soviets tend to initiate venturesome foreign policy moves during periods of assumed Western weakness, preoccupation with domestic or internal political concerns, during periods of psychological stress or in other calculated propitious circumstances.

To summarize, Soviet foreign policy appears to be essentially expansionistic; this expansionism is influenced by the balance of military forces and technologies vis-à-vis the West; it is an orchestrated policy, whose tactical variants relate to perceived opportunities and calculated risk-costs. It is a policy that pursues political expansion in a careful and calculated manner, a policy that seeks to avoid frontal assaults on areas of presumed vital interests to the West.

SOVIET POLICY TOWARD THE THIRD WORLD

Soviet foreign and military policy had since World War II concentrated largely on the West. Soviet strategic policy and doctrine remained Western-oriented, or, more properly, U.S./NATO-oriented, for the past two decades. Major Soviet policy moves since the war clearly support this assumption: the rejection of the Marshall plan and the creation of the Comecon; the creation of the Warsaw Pact as a reaction to NATO; Soviet arms production and deployment programs (MRBM, IRBM, ICBM systems) were largely Western-oriented, as were Khrushchev's missile diplomacy, his gamble to emplace offensive missiles in Cuba, and policies toward Germany and Berlin.

The Third World remained a region of marginal interests to the Soviets, at least until the middle-late 1950s. Stalin had considered the leaders of the former colonial areas as undependable bourgeois of marginal utility in the zero-sum game of international politics. Khrushchev's assumption of full powers in the C.P.S.U. and the government in the late 1950s did not materially change this Soviet attitude. To be sure, Khrushchev embarked on an active policy of penetration of the former colonial areas. However, this was "a shot-gun" approach of rather indiscriminating broadcasting of Soviet support and resources to any willing recipient in the Third World. In distinction to Stalin's "pessimistic" assessments of policy opportunities in the regions of the former colonial areas, Khrushchev seemed to pursue a policy premised on "optimistic" assessments of their political utility. However, after the initial enthusiasm waned and certain bitter realities materialized about the reliability and controllability of the Nassers, Sukarnos, Castros, and others—the Soviet leadership began to reassess their policies in the Third World. By then a new leadership had taken power in the

C.P.S.U. and they based their policy preferences on a different calculus.

The Brezhnev regime seems to have assessed Khrushchev's policies in the Third World negatively and, abandoning the "optimistic" premises of that policy, seeks to follow a policy of "realism." This implies a more careful, orderly and prudent assessment of the costs/gains involved in the economic, military, and political initiatives in the Third World. It suggests a policy that is at once tougher as well as more prudent. It is a policy that concentrates on Third World areas of more immediate consequence and potential payoff to current Soviet policy concerns. It is a policy that concentrates on areas of greater logistical accessibility; it is a policy that implies greater commitment to protect and defend their investments of prestige, economic and military resources against regional or Western challenges.

NEW SOVIET GRAND DESIGN:
POLICY OF HOLD-AND-EXPLORE

Soviet foreign policy since World War II has been, as suggested above, largely Western-oriented. However, the Soviet leaders who succeeded Khrushchev have in recent years attempted to realign Soviet foreign policy in a different direction. Briefly, this emerging new foreign policy seems to move from a predominantly Western to an Eastern and Southern orientation. The likely motivations for this new foreign policy line stem from Soviet concerns with their future relations with China as well as from perceived opportunities in the region south of Russia.

This new Soviet political orientation is described here as a policy of hold-and-explore. Thus, Soviet leaders are vitally interested in holding and stabilizing their political, military, and economic relations with the West, in order to gain a greater freedom of action in future dealings with China, as well as a greater political flexibility for the exploration of perceived policy opportunities in the Middle East, North Africa, and Indian Ocean areas.

This emerging Soviet policy line is substantiated by several political initiatives emanating from the Kremlin, e.g., Soviet proposals for a European Security Conference, Soviet interest in normalizing their relations with West Germany, Soviet interests in arms control schemes, and Soviet low-key reactions to recent U.S. military moves in South East Asia; these and other Soviet initiatives and actions indicate their preference for a normalization of relations with the West or for a stabilization of their western flank. At the same time, the Soviet Union has continued its efforts to strengthen its borders with China and to prepare for future contingencies in that area. Moreover, the Soviet leaders have indicated their growing interests in the regions of the Middle East and Indian Ocean, including the unprecedented signing of treaties with the United Arab Republic and India.

The policy of hold-and-explore suggests a Soviet appreciation of the changing political and military realities in international politics. First, it suggests that the current leadership in the Soviet Union consider the past main line of Soviet foreign policy (mainly anti-Western) as a policy of high cost, high risk, and low payoff. On the other hand, the new policy direction seems to be one of relatively low cost, low risk, and potentially of high payoff. More specifically, a continued arms race with the West would be very expensive and would result in a likely Western over-reaction that would match any Soviet arms increments. Thus, a stabilization of the strategic arms race at mutually acceptable levels would ensure the Soviets for the first time of strategic and therefore political equality with the United States, a dearly sought goal of several generations of Soviet leaders. Secondly, the Soviets have given up hope for any further gains in central and western Europe. Thirdly, the Soviets seem to assume that a stabilized general European situation would also stabilize the tensions and stresses prevalent in eastern Europe and would at the same time increase the flow of trade and modern technologies across the ideological boundaries, which would redund to Soviet interests.

The new hold-and-explore policy direction seems to indicate a new phase of Soviet expansionism. Having attained strategic equality with the West, and having set their East European areas into some kind of order, the Soviets are becoming better prepared for increasing low-level pressure in the vulnerable regions south of Russia, while at the same time being more capable of dealing with their China problem. What is argued here is that an indispensable basis for Soviet penetration of the southern regions and for a more resolute treatment of China is the stabilization of their western flank. Without that assurance, the Soviets would be potentially facing a two-front confrontation, one in the East and one in the West. This is a nightmare possibility which the Soviet leaders would seek to avoid at any cost. Thus, recent Soviet "peaceful and reasonable" overtures toward the West seem to be in the nature of tactical adjustments necessary for their new expansionist phase of foreign policy.

THE SOVIET UNION IN THE MIDDLE EAST

Soviet entry into the Middle East can be explained in terms of a rational calculus on the part of Soviet leaders as well as by fortuitous circumstances and accidents of history. Soviet presence in the Middle East may be seen as resulting from: the failure of U.S. containment policies; the peculiar "optimism" of Khrushchev regarding policy opportunities in the Third World; the petulance of nationalist Arab leaders in dealings with Western governments. Whatever the initial reasons for Moscow's gaining a foothold in the region, they have now become historical data of greatest interest to historians and political scientists. Of more immediate relevance, however, is the problem of the heightened current Soviet interest in the region and the reasons for their willingness to strengthen and formalize their commitments to their allies.

The Arab countries in the Middle East seem to represent a classic area for Soviet penetration. It is a region of unstable governments, unstable societies, great economic backwardness, inequality of wealth, and virulent anti-Western hatred and passions; an area of relative proximity to the borders of the Soviet Union; a region that is undergoing major socio-political transformations. Moreover, whatever the tensions and disunities that separate Arab from Arab and prevent a concerted approach to their various socio-economic and political problems, they are largely united in their vehement hostility toward Israel and thus by proxy toward the United States. Indeed, the Arab Middle East would appear to be ripe for Soviet manipulations and penetration.

In addition to the intra-regional considerations, we ought to consider the exogenous factors that would even further enhance Soviet interests in the area. Several developments in the relations of the super-powers during the latter half of the 1960s seem to have enhanced Soviet interests in the Middle East: U.S. preoccupation with a seemingly endless conflict in South East Asia served to deflect American interest from Europe and its peripheries; the outburst of urban unrest in the United States has diminished the popular support for future commit-ment of American forces or political support to "remote areas" of the globe; the rising domestic pressures on the American president for the reordering of national objectives and for allocation of resources has further reduced the credibility of U.S. resolve to become involved in new political-military gambles short of those considered to be vital; the preoccupation of the United States with Vietnam resulted in the erosion of NATO's vitality and credibility, in addition to the damage done to it by General De Gaulle. Thus, as the Soviet Union was turning away from its past anti-U.S. policy stance, so was the United States becoming preoccupied with a non-Soviet-centered conflict in Asia.

Moreover, while the United States was expending large sums of money and manpower in the regional conflict in Asia and thus neglecting the upkeep of its strategic forces (which were deemed "sufficient" and as having reached designed "ceilings"), the Soviet Union was embarked on a massive arms program that was to eventually catch up with and outdistance the United States. The Soviets were also rapidly increasing their naval capabilities and modernizing their conventional forces.

Given this state of affairs, and in the light of the above-suggested dynamics and patterns of Soviet foreign policy, it is clear that the Soviets would quickly recoup their losses after the unexpected outcome of the Six-Day War and continue to press their interests and objectives in the Middle East. Thus, the newly grown, vast Soviet military power, in a rather advantageous international setting, is looking for a purpose. The way this particular purpose will be defined will depend on several constraints of the political rules of the game:

a) One of these rules of the game would be to avoid direct confrontation with the other superpower. This is probably among the highest of Soviet priorities.

b) Avoid the formal commitment of Soviet forces to the region, short of some critical situation in which the Soviet presence in the Middle East is threatened.

c) Avoid two-front confrontations, i.e., simultaneous military challenge from the East and the West, or from the South and the West.

Within these constraints of the rules of the game, there is, however, plenty of maneuvering room for the pursuit of Soviet policy and military objectives in the Middle East. The Soviets are becoming deeply entrenched in the Middle East and any serious attempt to oust them from the region would represent a political setback for the sponsors of Soviet Middle East policy in the Party and would be likely to bring forth resistance from the Soviet military establishment to any potential accomodating overtures by their political leaders. The Soviet military had in the past been forced by their Party leaders to bear the brunt for defeats engineered by civilians. The Cuban missile crisis and its humiliating consequences still rankle the marshals and generals. Since the Soviet military has grown in institutional and political strength in recent years and since they consider the Middle East a desirable area for expansion, for both strategic and testing purposes, they are not likely to let go of it without a struggle.

However, while Soviet presence in the Middle East does not seem to be acutely threatened, further penetration of the region will very likely proceed in an uneventful, non-provocative and gradual, aggregative manner. The reasons for this assumption rest on considerations of the patron-client relationship between the Soviet Union and its Arab clients in general, and Soviet relations with Egypt in particular.

In pursuing their political and military objectives in the Middle East, the Soviet leaders must juggle several conflicting interests simultaneously; Soviet interests and constraints at the superpower level; Soviet interests and constraints at the intra-bloc level; and finally their interests and constraints at the regional Middle Eastern level. Now, as with other patron-client relations, the Soviet-Arab relations are characterized by a divergence of primary objectives, by a dissimilarity of focus, and by a sense of profound mutual suspicion. The leaders of the client state perceive the utility of the relationship mainly in terms of their own, narrow, national interests, with minimal concern for the global problems of their patron. On the other hand, the Great-Power patron perceives the interests of the client state largely in terms of their utility to the larger objectives of its own policy. Thus, while the Arab policies are largely linear, in the direction of obtaining their national interests, the Soviet policies are more complex and hierarchical. While the Arab clients are relatively unencumbered by extra-regional considerations, Soviet leaders must maintain a sense of balance between the regional interests and the broader interests of a superpower. This game of balances motivates the Soviet Union to undertake policy initiatives which create disaffection among the Arabs. For in going along with Arab militancy the Soviets are likely to provoke critical situations that might involve the United States. A constant resistance to Arab demands and their frustrations may critically erode Soviet credibility and utility among the Arabs. The Soviets will therefore continue to navigate between the two extremes of policy choices, and seek to ensure that their restless clients do not force the situation into a fait accompli, which may necessitate an undesirable response by Moscow.

In the light of the above considerations, it would appear that a preferable middle-range policy for the Soviets in the Middle East is one of prolonged stalemate, a policy of neither war nor peace. An outbreak of renewed hostilities with Israel is likely to create catalytic conditions which may prevent the localization of the war and could bring in the United States in some capacity. This is a highly undesirable policy choice for the Soviets, since it would endanger a carefully orchestrated policy of global normalization and stabilization of relations with the West. At the same time, a peaceful settlement of the Middle Eastern situation would erode the rationale for Soviet presence and would diminish Arab dependence on their Moscow patron. This is equally an undesirable choice. Thus, the Trotsky formula of "no peace-no war" seems to fulfill current Soviet policy needs. Moreover, this formula, for varying reasons, seems acceptable to the two other interested parties in the Middle Eastern situation, that is the United States and Israel. The Egyptians, however, have found the "no peace-no war" formula unacceptable, and have remonstrated their dissatisfaction by the ouster of Soviet "specialists" from their country. The Egyptian position was authoritatively examined by a Sadat confidant, M. Haykal, in the pages of his newspaper *al-Ahram* in June and July 1972:

> There is definitely a point of view in the Arab world which says that the Soviet Union is interested in the state of no peace-no war prevailing in the area. . . . Continuation of the state of no peace-no war makes the area more dependent on the Soviet Union. . . . The Soviet presence can increase under these circumstances . . . it makes it easier to deal with the Arab world from several angles.
>
> The Soviet Union wants to settle the crises in which it is interested one after another. . . . It is better for the Middle East to wait its turn, so it does not confound Soviet calculations. A miscalculated motivation in the Arab-Israeli conflict at this time might impose war, and war—because of the U.S. commitment to Israel—might produce a confrontation.

Haykal concludes therefore that "Egypt is the only one among the four main parties involved in the Middle East crisis which has no interest in the continuation of this state of no peace-no war." He even took the Soviet President Podgorny to task for publicly rebuking the Egyptians on this issue. Podgorny said on July 6, 1972: "Those saying that the Soviet Union benefits from the state of no peace-no war are repeating imperialist propaganda against us." Haykal accuses Podgorny of "misconstruing what I had said more than it can bear."

It would be rather optimistic to assume that the recent cooling of Soviet-Egyptian relations signifies a major, final reversal of the pattern of Middle East politics. The Soviets have made some tactical adjustments in the Middle East, but their long-range political and strategic interests remain steadfast: to penetrate the region politically, to exploit Arab weakness, divisiveness and frustrations, and thus wait for proper targets of opportunity.

CONCLUDING REMARKS

It was the purpose of this brief paper to explain recent Soviet political involvement in the affairs of the Middle East as a logical and predictable outcome of the dynamics of Soviet foreign policy. The dynamics of that policy are those of a vast imperial power that has been contained within its borders for decades by its military inferiority and by formal containment policies of the West. Once these constraints have become eroded, once the military might of the Soviet Union had become equal to that of the West, Soviet leaders began to look for targets of opportunity in which to employ their considerable economic, military, and technological power. Having experimented for a while with quasi-revolutionary, spoiler-type, anti-Western policies in the "soft" areas of the world, the ruling elites in Moscow perceived the essential disutility of such an approach, and have turned instead to a policy which is more closely attuned to their immediate political and military objectives.

Soviet expansionism (a term that may seem anachronistic in the nuclear era) may be explained in terms of strategic needs, economic opportunities, or even ideological imperatives. However, a close scrutiny of Soviet actions and rationalizations fails to support the argument for a "rational" explanation of their expansionism. Soviet security is adequately assured by their domestic and subsurface strategic weapons; Soviet foreign involvements are very costly and hardly of economic benefit; even the ideological rationale fails to be credible. Thus, one must conclude that Soviet expansionism is largely one of momentum, a case of enormous power looking for a purpose. Or, it may be explained in terms of "settling a score" with the United States. For one may construe the first two decades of the post-war period as one of *Pax Americana,* with the Soviet Union remaining largely contained and inferior throughout the period. Now that the last remnants of *Pax Americana* have been shattered in the quagmire of Vietnam and in the disrupted urban areas of America, the Soviets may see themselves as the inheritors of that role, and dream of a Pax Sovietica.

Soviet expansionism into the regions of the Middle East and Indian Ocean is to be viewed with great concern. As the traditional superpower tensions and confrontations abate, the Soviets will see themselves less constrained to probe for soft spots in these regions. Their new policy style is reasonable, accommodating, and pragmatic. Yet, their vision seems clear and their actions persistent and purposeful.

In the Middle East, the Soviets will continue to penetrate the several receptive countries in a capillary manner, seeking to establish a sounder foundation from which to explore even further in a region they consider to be their future sphere of influence. Thus, in playing for time and seeking to prevent collision with the other superpower, the Soviets are likely to pursue a low-profile policy in the Middle East. Their view of their allies and client states in the region is clearly instrumental and utilitarian.

If there is one lesson to be learned by small allies of great powers, both those of the West and East, it is that when the larger designs of the patron clash with those of the client, the latter can easily become expendable. Even recent history contains striking examples of such a cavalier attitude of great powers toward their past close and loyal allies. Thus, it would seem in the best interests of small states in a regional conflict to keep their powerful patrons at a distance and to seek to settle their differences within a regional context. Otherwise, they may invite their own demise as the pawns in a global game of superpower *Kriegspiel.*

WALTER Z. LAQUEUR

SOVIET DILEMMAS IN THE MIDDLE EAST

It is the object of this paper to define Soviet expectations and intentions in the Middle East with particular reference to the Arab world and to outline the main problems confronting Soviet policy at this time. It is not my intention to provide an historical account of Soviet policy in the Middle East; the developments that have led to the present stage are described and analyzed in two books of mine: *The Soviet Union and the Middle East* (1958), and *The Struggle for the Middle East* (1969 and 1971). The interest of the Soviet Union in the Middle East is that of a superpower (which, unlike the United States, is not, or at any rate, not yet, a *status quo* power) in an adjacent area that offers good prospects for extending its political and military influence. Several circumstances have favored these designs. The area is militarily weak, politically unstable and divided, and economically, with a few exceptions, underdeveloped. Unlike Western Europe, the Middle East—with the exception of Turkey—is not part of the Western defense system. The risks the Soviet Union is likely to incur in its forward policy in the area are therefore infinitely less than those in Europe, or indeed in many other parts of the world. Having said this I ought to add immediately that I do not consider direct Soviet military involvement in the area at present is very likely; at any rate, not substantially in excess of what there is already. While the Chinese danger is uppermost in Soviet minds, Moscow has other more urgent preoccupations: to neutralize Western Europe, on the basis of the *status quo,* to pursue an active role in the Indian subcontinent, to bring about the withdrawal of American forces from Europe and other parts of the world.

This is not to say that the Middle East no longer enjoys high priority in Soviet strategy. It simply means that the Soviet leaders want at present no more than controlled tension in the area. It seems to be clear that direct Soviet military involvement in the area, quite apart from the risk of a wider conflagration, would defeat some of their designs elsewhere, such as the European Security Conference to which they attribute at present greater importance. The Soviet leaders seem to have realized

89

that it is impossible to combine a *détente,* even in the limited sense (as they interpret it), with a war involving Soviet forces in the Middle East.

But I ought to add two *caveats* to this seemingly reassuring perspective. Once the Soviet Union will be under less pressure from China, once it has made more progress in Europe, once it has restored "order" as far as the unruly satellites are concerned, it will no doubt pursue a more determined policy in the Middle East, involving higher risks. The second *caveat* is this: I have spoken so far about Soviet intentions and policies, about the controlled tension, which seems best to serve its purposes. But the Soviet Union is not in full control in the Middle East, as recent events have again demonstrated. The tension may get out of control; one can envisage more than one such scenario in the context. In this case, and if things should go badly for its allies, the Soviet Union may well find itself drawn into a direct military engagement despite the fact that this would be contraindicated as far as other, more important Soviet interests are concerned.

The attractions of the Middle East as far as the Soviet Union is concerned can be easily defined. Geographically proximity is an obvious factor. Ten years ago, or even five, I would not have mentioned oil in this context, for until recently the Soviet Union was self-sufficient in this respect. But Soviet (and Eastern European) consumption is now outstripping production, and there is little doubt that toward the end of the present decade Middle Eastern oil will figure as a major factor in Soviet strategy. But more important than economic and even military factors (such as bases in Egypt and elsewhere) are political considerations, even if these may appear at first sight somewhat abstract and intangible. Expansion in a southward direction has been one of the constant factors in Russian foreign policy for more than 200 years. Furthermore, and more concretely, if the Middle East became an exclusive Soviet sphere of influence this would have far-reaching repercussions on the situation in Europe as well as in Africa and Asia. It would constitute, in fact, a radical change in the global balance of power. It is not my assignment here to describe in detail the probable consequences: they are all too obvious.

Soviet policy in the Middle East at present aims, very briefly, at the neutralization of Turkey and Iran and at the installation in the Arab world of regimes on which it can rely for close collaboration on the pattern established under President Nasser. The general assumption behind this policy was that power in the Arab countries is bound to pass gradually into the hands of people even more closely identified with Soviet policies. It was generally expected that there would be ups and downs in this process and occasional setbacks. But about the general trend of development there is (or to be precise: was—until recently) little doubt in Moscow. There is no denying that events in Egypt, Syria, Algeria, and other countries in the 1960s seemed to bear out Soviet expectations. There was a progressive radicalization in domestic affairs in these countries, as well as growing identification with Soviet policies: factories and banks were nationalized, important sections of the state apparatus were revamped according to the Soviet model, etc. But beyond a certain point the Soviet Union has so far failed to make progress, and therefore more sober thoughts have prevailed in Moscow about the rate of political progress not only in the Middle East but in the Third World in general.

To amplify what I mean I have to refer in some detail to the circumstances which have favored, and still favor, the Soviet advance in the Middle East, and to the factors that impede it. I have already mentioned the intrinsic weakness of the area—political, military, and economic. To this one should add the shortsightedness and political inexperience of some of its leaders. These are no doubt absolutely genuine in their frequent professions of unswerving devotion to national independence. But the result of the policies they have pursued has not been to strengthen their independence; on the contrary, they have become dependent on the Soviet Union to a growing degree. True enough, there have been growing misgivings in the Arab world—not only since the recent events in the Sudan. But to assuage these misgivings it is usually argued that the Soviet Union is a disinterested country which, in contrast to the Western imperialists, has no desire to interfere in internal Arab affairs. The simple geopolitical facts of political life have not yet been fully accepted in the Arab world. The mistaken idea still persists that the Soviet Union is not only a benevolent, but also a geographically distant country. (The distance between the Egypt and Soviet border—not to mention Iraq and Syria—is in actual fact less than that between Cairo and Khartoum or between Cairo and Tripoli). The countries of the Middle East have been sidetracked by their internal quarrels to such an extent that the question whether victory over Israel would be worthwhile, if it could be achieved only at the price of independence, is brushed aside as irrelevant in Baghdad and Damascus if not in Cairo. Whatever Arab feelings about Israel, this state does not constitute a serious threat to the independence and sovereignty of the Arab countries, for the simple reason that a small country is not a big power and that moreover there is no "Israeli party" in Cairo, Damascus, and Baghdad, which could seize power from within. There is, on the other hand, a "Russian party" which as recent events have shown is a strong contender for leadership. Yet in most Arab eyes Israel is still the main and not the lesser danger. Somehow, it is argued, they will get rid of the Russians once Israel is defeated, and the Arab world will then regain its full independence and freedom of action. It is a striking example of what some Marxist philosophers call "false consciousness" and it helps one understand why Soviet policy has so far encountered a most favorable psychological climate.

But the more deeply the Soviet Union has become involved in the Middle East, the more complicated its position. To a certain extent this was an inevitable process. While the West was "in," and the Soviet Union "out" in the Middle East, Moscow did not have to take sides—just as it could be on friendly terms with both India and Pakistan, to give an example from another part of the world. The West had the monopoly of committing mistakes, whereas the Soviet Union could do no wrong. Progressive involvement in Arab affairs meant that Moscow has had to choose, to join sides in the many existing conflicts. The existence of Communist parties and pro-Russian factions in the Arab world is the main bone of contention but by no means the only one. The Soviet Union cannot at one and the same time support General Numeiri and those who want to overthrow his regime; it can be tried—but the attempt is bound to fail. If the Soviet Union were just a big power the dilemmas facing it would be less acute. But since it is also the head of the world Communist movement, its position has become even more difficult. It cannot opt out entirely from its commitments to its local followers without causing fatal damage to the legitimacy of its claims for leadership—and this at a time when its authority as the leader of the Communist camp is in dispute anyway.

Soviet policy-makers have become reconciled to the fact that political power in the Arab world—certainly in the so-called "progressive countries"—will remain for a long time to come in the hands of military juntas, rather than political parties supporting Moscow. This, from the Soviet point of view, is not *per se* a major disaster. Since the Communist bloc lost its monolithic character, the Soviet Union can no longer count on the automatic support of other Communist parties, unless it also happens to be in physical domination of the country concerned. Albania is Communist and Finland is not, but there is little doubt that Soviet policy-makers vastly prefer the Helsinki over the Tirana government. To give another example: Many Communist parties dissented from the Soviet invasion of Czechoslovakia in 1968, whereas the military governments of Egypt, Syria, and Algeria supported it without reservation. The Soviet leaders may therefore be forgiven for reaching the conclusion that in a critical situation they can rely more on clients than on purely ideologically motivated supporters. The advantages of having to deal with non-Marxist rulers are obvious. Consideration of "proletarian internationalism," of "social humanism," etc. are not likely to enter the picture. The clients can be relied upon to support Soviet policy, because they need Soviet help.

And yet, there is a basic element of uncertainty with regard to the political orientation of these military regimes, and the situation is by no means satisfactory from the Soviet viewpoint. Ten years ago Soviet policy-makers were far more optimistic than at present about the intentions and political prospects of the military dictatorships in the Third World. The reasoning at the time was briefly this: Military leaders such as Nasser were "radical democrats in uniform." Even though their outlook was as yet beclouded by certain petty bourgeois prejudices, it was assumed that the "objective logic" of events would carry them into much closer collaboration with the Communists and the Soviet Union than they had originally envisaged and intended. For they were not acting in a political vacuum; once the means of production had been nationalized and capitalism was on the way out, the ruling officers, needing a political mass basis, were bound to turn to "scientific Socialism," i.e., to the Communists. For only these could provide the doctrine and the political know-how needed for the mobilization of the masses.

In recent years it has been realized that this appraisal has been overoptimistic. Communism found it difficult at the time to understand fascism because economic factors were not sufficient to explain Hitler's and Mussolini's policy. In a similar way Communists now begin to realize—though they are still far from a full understanding—that their previous notions about the situation in the Middle East were at best half true. Economic changes do not necessarily have the expected political results; military leaders can turn with equal ease "left" and "right" in rapid succession, to apply terms of classification which should be used as sparingly as possible with reference to Middle Eastern politics.

As a result there is now scarcely veiled disappointment in Moscow about the agonizingly slow progress made by Communism in parts of the Third World, about the "complicated state of affairs," about the fact that army officers may be power-hungry or "career motivated," even if they constantly use the anti-imperialist political rhetoric which should endear them to the Communist camp. These shortcomings and "inconsistencies" of the junta are more frequently explained with reference to the "petty bourgeois background" of the military rulers. But it is doubtful whether such explanations take one much further. There is nothing "petty bourgeois" about a man like Colonel Kadhafi who was born in a Bedouin tent and now disposes of billions of dollars. The real explanation for the apparent "inconsistencies" is much easier. In the struggle for power between rival officers' groups ideological considerations usually play a secondary role. Nationalization of industries and banks, and agrarian reform by no means lead to socialism or Communism; the ideological climate prevailing in the Arab world is populist, nationalist-socialist, as it is, *mutatis mutandis,* in China and the Soviet Union. The decisive issue in the Third World, including the Arab countries, is not whether the state has the monopoly of foreign trade, but in whose hands political power has come to rest; who is running the state.

In this context, Soviet policy in the Middle East has to face three contradictions which it cannot shirk and to which so far it has not been able to find a satisfactory answer. The first has already been hinted at. According to the Soviet blueprint, the progressive military rulers were gradually to "democratize political life," i.e., hand over power to the avantgarde—the Communists. But in fact the Colonels and the Majors have not shown the slightest intention to do so. They have dealt ruthlessly with those challenging their power. According to Soviet expectations, the military were to be politicized, i.e., made to share power with civilian leaders. In fact, the opposite has happened; political life has been militarized, with Syria as a striking example (the take-over of the Neo-Ba'th by the Syrian army command). It could be argued with some justification that since the ruling juntas do not constitute a political homogeneous body, it may still be possible for pro-Communist or pro-Russian elements among them to effect a take-over and to oust their rivals. This possibility does exist. In view of the weakness of political structures in the Arab world, a handful of determined people stand a good chance of making a successful bid for power, provided, of course, they are in control of army units or the political police. And, with a little luck, they may keep it.

But a pro-Communist or pro-Russian *coup* in one country is bound to provoke with almost mathematical certainty suspicion and antagonism in others and to give rise to counterforces. Victory in one country will mean defeat elsewhere. In other words, unless the pro-Russian forces make steady and even progress in all the key countries of the Arab world, the overall balance as far as the Soviet Union is concerned may be negative.

The Arab-Israeli dispute has become increasingly problematic from the Soviet point of view. Earlier on it undoubtedly facilitated the Soviet advance in the Middle East. It was not the only, nor even the most important factor. The forces supporting the Soviet Union have made their greatest strides in those parts of the Middle East least affected by the Arab-Israeli dispute, such as the Sudan. But in recent years the conflict has become a major obstacle as far as the further progress of Communism is concerned. While the conflict lasts, the overriding aim of defeating the common enemy (Israel) narrowly circumscribes Communist action or tends altogether to prevent it. For the Communists cannot afford to ignore the appeals for national solidarity and for a truce both inside the Arab countries and between them. Soviet observers assume, not perhaps altogether wrongly, that but for the continuation of the Arab-Israeli conflict, power in the Arab capitals may well have passed from the "bourgeois nationalist elements" into the hands of the "radical democrats" if not the Communists. Certainly the Arab world would be in a state of far greater internal turmoil but for the struggle against Israel, which acts as a stabilizing factor. Soviet leaders could have instructed their followers according to the basic tenets of Leninist strategy to transform the war against Israel into a "revolutionary war." They have not done so, partly, because the Communists are too weak, given the present balance of power in the Arab world, and partly because such a course of action, if successful, would result in a state of anarchy which may well benefit the pro-Chinese rather than the pro-Soviet elements among the radicals in the Arab world.

These are some of the sources of conflict facing the Soviet Union in its policy vis-à-vis the Arab countries. There is every reason to assume that these contradictions will loom even larger in the years ahead. But what are the options open to Soviet policy? Developments in Algeria over the last few years have been disappointing from the Soviet viewpoint. Kadhafi's regime in Libya and Numeiri's in the Sudan are at present openly anti-Communist, and Sadat's rule constitutes a retreat in comparison with Nasser's. Soviet policy-makers cannot possibly be very happy about the new Arab federation, since its political significance, if any, will be that of a reactionary "Holy Alliance" preventing revolutionary uprisings in its components parts. It is the Arab version of the Brezhnev doctrine—stood on its head. The fact that it might be applied against Jordan, for instance, does not offer much comfort. Events in the Sudan earlier this year have foreshadowed the shape of things to come. Soviet expectations that military dictatorships *tout court* cannot hold on to power for long, because they lack political know-how and a mass basis, have not so far been borne out by the course of events. These assumptions may still be correct in the long run; Nasser, too, had his quarrels with the Communists and the Soviet Union but mended his ways toward the end of his rule. But Sadat has been more difficult to deal with and if the Iraqi and the Syrian rulers have been willing to appoint a few Communist ministers the situation in Cairo is certainly unsatisfactory from the Soviet point of view. If the Soviet Union should decide to support the opposition to the military regimes, they will be inviting open conflict, risking their past gains in the area, and even a restoration of closer relations between these leaders and the West. For despite the vituperation heaped on the West, it cannot be excluded that the help of the West will be sought by military dictators facing defeat at the hands of the Communists. If, on the other hand, the Soviet Union and its supporters in the Arab countries should prefer a policy of wait-and-see, on the assumption that the political constellation will be more auspicious at some future date (after another lost war against Israel, or some major economic setback, or the growth of popular discontent for yet other reasons), they will be in danger of being outflanked from the left by more extreme factions.

It seems, nevertheless, that Soviet policy is most likely to follow a cautious course of action. Provided that there will be no reconciliation with China or that for other reasons a decisive shift in the global balance will not take place in the near future, it is clearly in the Soviet interest to "freeze" the situation. Sadat's regime may be highly unsatisfactory as a guarantee for the Soviet investment (political, military, and economic) in the Middle East, but at the moment there may be no alternative. It follows that Soviet policy in the short run is likely to be defensive, to aim at consolidating its gains rather than attempting to make further advances. Any gamble would be dangerous in the present constellation, for it could result in a further setback which might have undesirable repercussions within the Soviet Union. It would provide ammunition for a faction inside the Kremlin, which challenges the present leadership. Personal changes in the Soviet leadership are almost certainly bound to take place in the next few years, and since such *revirements* usually take place against the background of a struggle for power, the present leadership will probably opt for the least risky policy in order not to expose itself to attacks by its opponents.

Nevertheless, it cannot be stressed too often that since the Soviet Union is not in full control as far as events in the Middle East are concerned, not even over the actions of their followers and clients, there is always a very considerable element of uncertainty. It would be foolish for this, as well as for other reasons, to assume that the Soviet leadership will automatically pursue a cautious policy simply because this is at the present moment in its best interest. Moreover, "freezing" in the Middle East context means the continuation of "controlled tension"—but there is no guarantee that tension will not get out of control. "Consolidation" does by no means imply that the Soviet Union will be condemned to prolonged inactivity. The treaty of friendship between the Soviet Union and the U.A.R. concluded in May 1971 meant much less than many observers thought at the time. But if the Soviet Union suffered a setback, temporary or lasting, in Egypt, they certainly made progress in Iraq and Syria in 1971/2. At present the main aim of Soviet policy in the Middle East remains, to summarize, the consolidation of its gains, and at the same time the creation of a political climate in which the replacement of the present rulers by others more closely identified with Soviet ambitions in the area will be possible with a minimum of friction. The more distant aim is the transformation of the military regimes into political coalitions dominated (or at least guided) by the Communists. But this remains for the time being a fairly remote prospect inasmuch as the key countries in the Arab world are concerned Soviet policy toward Israel will not undergo any basic change, though it is quite possible, and indeed likely, that there will be occasional friendly gestures toward Jerusalem in order to impress the Arabs that they must not take Soviet assistance for granted in all circumstances.

Altogether, the Middle East is an area in world politics to which Soviet commentators apply the term "slozhni" (complicated) more and more frequently. Ten years ago they were more confident than now of having all the answers.

SECOND THOUGHTS ON THE THIRD WORLD:
A NOTE

Writing on the dilemmas facing the Soviet Union in the Third World, I noted on a recent occasion that the decisive issue was not whether the banks had been nationalized, or a foreign-trade monopoly established, but in whose hands political power had come to rest, or who, in other words, was running the state . . . . Very shortly thereafter I came across a programmatic article by a leading Soviet author, which to my surprise (and gratification) made exactly the same point: "Few people today will question the fact that non-capitalist development is still not socialism . . . the paramount question is that of power . . . the problem of the new leadership."[1] This is certainly a far cry from the optimism of Soviet commentators of the late 1950s and especially the early 60s when, in the words of one of them, the stormy break-up of the colonial system and the anti-capitalist slogans of many leaders of the national liberation movement created the illusion that in a very short period the overwhelming majority of the former colonies would go over, if not to the socialist, then to the non-capitalist road of development. It was thought that the impossibility of solving the basic problems of the developing countries on the lines of capitalism would inevitably compel the leaders of the new states to choose socialism for their future.[2]

"Socialism" in this context, needless to say, means not democratic socialism but the Soviet model. Today more sober counsels prevail in Moscow; the Soviet leaders and their experts are sadder and wiser men. The process of disenchantment began around 1965; it is usually explained with reference to the overthrow of Sukarno, Ben Bella, Modibo Keita, Qassem, and Nkrumah, all of whom disappeared within a short time, almost without a struggle. Another factor which no doubt also played a very important role was the growing conflict with China. For if relations with a Communist country could go so terribly wrong, disappointment in the Third World was not really such a surprise. This sobering process has been described ably and in detail in a series of articles by David Morison[3]; I do not intend to retrace his steps or to update his survey but to concentrate on some of the ideological implications of the "second

98

thoughts" with particular reference to the Middle East. It ought to be stated in advance that the writings of these commentators do not necessarily provide a key to the understanding of Soviet policy, nor do they automatically reflect the views of the leaders, who being politicians act with a good deal of pragmatism, if not opportunism. The Soviet political analyst and commentator is not the scout who moves in advance of the column and provides ideological guidance for those following him; he is more often to be found in the rearguard and his task is the often unenviable one of rationalizing unexpected developments in Leninist terms, of squaring them with official Soviet ideology. His assignment, in short, is less similar to that of the prophet than to the lawyer who has to think of explanations and justifications. Nevertheless, even if there are occasional differences between them, these experts cannot possibly stray too far from the column and their views reflect therefore, *grosso modo,* the conflicting ideas and moods prevailing in the leadership.

That the Soviet commentators should react sharply to the events in the Sudan goes without saying. What is more interesting is the growing criticism of the countries in which there has been no such dramatic setback. To give but a few examples: one author writing about Algeria concludes sadly that agrarian production had stagnated if not declined, that the agrarian reform of 1966 has largely remained on paper, that the political activity of the peasantry is weak if not non-existent.[4] Ulyanovksi, whom I have already quoted once, goes one step further and claims that the peasants will not bring socialism anyway, that any attempt to harness them immediately to the anti-capitalist struggle will only evoke distrust, and that there is therefore no scope for far-reaching political aims in the framework of a predominantly peasant movement.[5] Popov complains that public life has not been democratized even in countries such as Syria, Egypt, and Algeria, and that the slogans about handing over power to workers and peasants remain on paper.[6] Yet another writer notes the slipshod ideology of these regimes, the weak links with the masses, and the fact that the creation of "vanguard parties of socialist orientation" has turned out to be a far more complicated matter than was earlier supposed.[7] The same complaint was made previously in a symposium on political parties in Africa, edited by Solodovnikov. Finally, there are complaints that habits of systematic work have as yet to be inculcated in these countries, and that there is no automatic obligation of a rich (socialist) country to help a poor one.[8]

In other words, the developing countries should stand on their own feet and develop their own resources instead of taking it for granted that the Soviet Union will give them an unlimited amount of economic aid. This point has been made by countless Soviet authors, including L. Zevin and V. M. Kollontai, and in detail in S. L. Tiulpanov's book *Ocherki politicheskoi ekonomiki,* published in 1969, which deals specifically with the problems of developing countries.

Some of these complaints, while reflecting various stresses and strains in Soviet relations with the Third World, are tactical in character, others go much deeper, and it is with these that I am mainly concerned in the present paper. One of the main issues at stake is that of nationalism. This has been traditionally one of the weakest points of Marxism-Leninism; the Soviet Communists misunderstood the powerful appeal of nationalism not only in Europe in the 1920s and 1930s; they made similar mistakes in their own empire after the World War II, resulting first in Tito's defection and subsequently in the partial break-up of the Communist monolith. According to Soviet doctrine, nationalism is a transitory phenomenon—a statement which is no doubt correct *sub specie aeternitatis* but which is of no great help in analyzing concrete situations in the present-day world. Furthermore, according to the traditional tenets, "bourgeois nationalism" is reactionary in the developed countries of the West, at any rate, whereas the nationalism of an oppressed people is progressive. In this respect events during the last decade have compelled Soviet authors to modify views:

> The dialectics of the national-liberation movement are such that the nationalism of an oppressed nation, which is a powerful uniting force while that nation is fighting for its political independence, may in certain conditions work to weaken its anti-imperialist unity. The revolutionary forces that use the nationalism of oppressed nations for their purposes, historically justified as its use may be, have to face the consequences.

This is a somewhat cryptical statement (especially the "have to face the consequences"), but it is made a little clearer by the same author when he adds that the growing nationalist fervor is successfully used by ruling circles "to dull class consciousness among the working people so that no discordant notes should sound in the general nationalist chorus. The concept of national unity as such is sometimes used . . . to veil class contradictions and push them back out of sight."[9]

The Arab world is certainly one part of the globe in which national-ism has been a factor of paramount importance, and Soviet authors who have regarded it for many years as a harmless aberration to be viewed with friendly tolerance, to which no offence should be caused, have begun to re-examine this phenomenon. "Arab nationalism," writes G. Mirsky, "is a particularly strong ideology which bases itself on history, tradition, the whole course of the political struggle, which makes use of the Palestinian question which is singularly urgent and painful for the Arabs."[10] This ideology, an admixture of nationalist and religious motives, creates a negative attitude toward Communism, which is regarded as basically internationalist and atheistic in character. According to Mirsky, even the "revolutionary democrats" ruling Egypt and Syria, let alone Iraq, are "prisoners" of this ideology; "only a few, the brightest, ideologically most advanced people" have so far been able to escape the pernicious consequences of this ideology. How is one to explain the singularly strong impact of nationalist ideology in the Arab countries and elsewhere in the Third World? Even Mirsky—certainly one of the "brightest and most advanced" Soviet commentators—falls back on the time-honored theory according to which it is all the fault of "petty bourgeois elements." He adds, but only as an afterthought, that it may have to do also with the general level of development—cultural, social, and political—of the country and the broadness of the outlook of the ruling army officers, the ability to put general above group interests. Putting the blame on the "petty bourgeois elements" is not even a half truth, since almost the entire leadership of all national-revolutionary movements (and one should add, also the Communist parties) has been of petty-bourgeois origin—unless of course it came from a higher-up social class. It has been shown time and time again that these elites can with equal ease turn to left and to right; that inasmuch as there has been a turn toward socialism in the Third World, it has been toward national rather than international socialism, if not toward populism, and that a similar process, *mutatis mutandis,* has taken place inside the Soviet Union, which is therefore not in a good position to invoke prole-tarian "internationalism" against the "nationalist deviationists."

The question of power in the Third World is of course closely connected with the thorny problem of military dictatorship. Nowhere is this issue more acute than in the Middle East, for all "progressive" countries in this area are now ruled by such regimes. It will be recalled that in the early 1950s Soviet commentators experienced difficulties in adjusting themselves to this new phenomenon; even Nasser was attacked at first as a fascist adventurer.[11] Gradually, however, the attitude changed and the approach became far more positive. A great many reasons were adduced to demonstrate that the military intelligentsia was playing a progressive role in the Third World: imperialism had kept the native officers in an underprivileged position and they had therefore become an agent of the patriotic resistance against foreign domination. These officers hailed mainly from petty-bourgeois families, urban and rural, i.e., from social strata much nearer to the working people than to the upper-crust bourgeoisie. Therefore (to pursue the same line of argument) they were usually anti-capitalist, and not just anti-imperialist in inspiration. Furthermore, they were among the most enlightened and dynamic forces in the social life of the Third World, an agent of modernization very much in contrast to developed societies, where the officer corps is said to represent inertia and reaction; the officers in the Third World were compelled to acquaint themselves with modern methods of production and organization.

Since in many of these countries "political parties were structurally too vague to take charge," the officer corps was propelled into the position of leadership. Mirsky, who has investigated the problem of the "military intelligentsia" in greater depth than most of his colleagues, adds a number of other fairly obvious reasons to strengthen his argument: the officer corps is the only group, however small, to have power in its hand—and does not hesitate to apply it; it has arms and knows how to use them.[12] Mirsky also mentions in this context the resentment felt by the army officer stationed in the provinces against society in the capital, and his contempt vis-à-vis bourgeois parliamentarianism. He also makes great play of the close connection between the military and the radical intelligentsia on the one hand and the "simple people" on the other, reaching in the end the manifestly wrong conclusion that in the underdeveloped countries there is no abyss (as there is in the West) between the officer corps and the masses of soldiers.[13] Mirsky, who was one of the first to draw attention to the "progressive role" of the officer corps, did, however, clearly delineate the limitations of this group in the socio-political process and thus safeguard himself against disappointments and the reproaches of those of his colleagues who warned all along against overrating the role of the army, its dictatorial leadership, and the glorification of individual heroes.[14]

Mirsky subdivided the military rulers into six categories, and only one of them in this scheme, "revoliutsionni demokrat v pogonach" (revolutionary democrats with epaulettes),[15] was more or less reliable from the Soviet point of view. He specifically named Nasser, Boumedienne, and Syrian leaders in this context; it ought to be mentioned that up to Nasser's death the U.A.R. was always regarded as the model country in which everything had (gradually) gone right in extending the "national-democratic revolution," broadening its basis, and the "consistent development of an increasingly definite, explicit program of social construction," a "serious shift in the political thinking of the U.A.R. leadership."[16] The other, less progressive categories need not interest us here; suffice it to say that according to Soviet authors writing in the late 1960s there were on the one hand the Careerists: "(Sometimes (!)) the leaders of a military *coup d'état* are motivated less by political considerations than by a purely career-inspired desire to seize power," and on the other the "progressives" who, having come to power, had realized that the army was no substitute for a society's democratic institutions, that it lacked a definite political and ideological platform. They were inexperienced in the sphere of political organization and realized that they had to secure the active participation of the working people and its most progressive elements—meaning the Communists.[17] Even Mirsky with his sympathy for the "revolutionary democrat with epaulettes" reached the conclusion that the psychologic mold of the young revolutionary officer corps was not favorable for developing the qualities needed for political work and organizational activity on the highest level:

> The professional officer can, at best, be a capable administrator, on the lower or medium level. Patriotism, devotion to duty, will power, resolve, discipline, organization—this is not sufficient when the task is not just to keep order but the complex, accurate and patient work essential for the radical reconstruction of social relations.[18]

So far it is difficult not to agree with Mirsky, but in the next step of his reasoning he went manifestly wrong, as events in recent years have shown. Arguing that "purely military regimes cannot last long in the present-day world," he maintained that the revolutionary military leadership in the U.A.R., Algeria, Syria, etc. aims at mobilizing the masses and at establishing an avant-garde political party: "Such regimes cease in fact to be military in character."[19] This appraisal was based on the assumption that the political development in Egypt under Nasser was more or less irreversible and that many other Third World countries would follow the Egyptian example. Mirsky was aware of the ideological weakness of the socialist conception of the "revolutionary democrats," its eclectic and inconsistent character. But he expected, on the basis of the Egyptian example, that practical experience would guide the U.A.R. leadership the right way; his motto was like Spengler's: "Volentem fata ducunt, nolentum trahunt." For was it not true that in the U.A.R. revolutionary practice had led the military leaders further than they had intended to go, that the "logic of the class struggle" had compelled them to attack those sectors of the society which they originally had not wanted to touch?[20]

Soviet commentators will no doubt provide in due time a Leninist explanation for the recent setbacks in the Arab world. It should not be too difficult to find plausible reasons. Mirsky can argue that he has always argued that the developing countries need some form of N.E.P. but that any such policy involves considerable political risks; for unlike the situation in Russia in the 1920s the countries concerned are not ruled by Communist parties. However, more interesting than such exercises are the ideas of Soviet authors concerning the political future of the Third World, especially the countries previously believed to be most advanced on the road toward "socialism." One of the likely consequences of the setbacks in the Arab world will be the upgrading, at best on the theoretical level, of the local Communist parties. Until recently, to give but one example, it was fashionable to blame the Egyptian and Algerian Communists for their "sectarian" mistakes, for not supporting Nasser and Boumedienne once it had become clear that Egypt and Algeria had chosen the non-capitalist path. The Central Committee of the Egyptian party was criticized for seeing in the Egyptian reforms of 1961 nothing more than a manifestation of monopoly state capitalism "thus threatening the further development of the revolution."[21] Such an argument amounts to justifying Nasser's action banning the Communist Party. It is unlikely that similar harsh judgments will be passed in future. On the contrary, the present tendency is to put the blame for the "prejudices, distrusts, and errors that persist to this day in Syria, Iraq, and the Sudan" squarely on the "right-wing national democrats."[22]

But giving theoretical support to the Communists in the Arab world is one thing, providing open political assistance another, far more risky business. On the theoretical level the present trend is a reversal toward the emphasis of the leading role of the working class and its "avant-garde party." Mirsky stressed even in his earlier book that the creation of a progressive avant-garde party devoted to building socialism was a *conditio sine qua non* on the road to socialism. Writing two years later, Ulyanovski stressed that "it is the working class in the 'Third World' countries that has objectively been assigned the role of the vanguard of the socialist forces, and no other class can replace it in that historic function."[23] This sounds very radical and dogmatic, but in practice it may lead toward "revisionist" policy recommendations. For since a strong working class does not yet exist in the Third World, time is obviously not yet ripe for pressing far-reaching political changes. On another occasion the same author has suggested that the transformation of a revolutionary-democratic dictatorship into the dictatorship of the proletariat could be effected by means of the "international dictatorship of the proletariat in the person of the world socialist system."[24] What the author means is not absolutely clear, unless he has in mind the political and if necessary the military intervention by other Communist regimes. But in the article I quoted in the very beginning, Ulyanovski stated *expressis verbis* that present-day non-capitalist development is *not* a repetition of the experience of Outer Mongolia or of the Soviet Central Asian republics, because the direct leadership of Marxist-Leninist parties is missing. True enough, he returns later on in his article to the Mongolian and Central Asian experience but only to claim that it shows that the revolutionary process will continue for several decades and that the transitional stage cannot be measured in terms of months or even years.[25] This is clearly a *non-sequitur*, for if the situation in the Third World differs in essential respects from the state of affairs in Mongolia and Central Asia, no predictions could or should be made with regard to the length of the "revolutionary process."

I would like to take leave at this point from the Soviet analysts of the Third World scene. One ought to add in fairness that a great many sensible observations have been made by Soviet commentators on specific economic and social problems in the Third World—about industrialization and agrarian reform, about foreign aid and fair terms of trade, about the impact of the scientific and technological revolution and economic growth. But as far as the political problems of the Third World are concerned the general picture is one of confusion. The commentators all agree that the revolutionary process will take much longer than originally expected. But where will it lead to? The tacit assumption seems to be that the non-Communist military leaders will be unable to solve their countries' problems and that, as a result, they will have in the end to accept the Communist model—or be overthrown. Furthermore, it seems to be postulated that the political influence and the military might of the Soviet Union will grow in the years and decades to come, that there will be a decisive shift in the global balance of power, and that as a result the Soviet Union will be in a position—unlike today—to exert direct pressure and thus be able to give decisive help to its followers in Third World countries. These assumptions take a great deal for granted and they ignore equally many factors such as the Sino-Soviet conflict and the internal disarray in the Communist world. Short of direct intervention it is difficult to see in what way the Soviet Union will be able to instal a leadership in Third World countries, which will have the minimum qualifications (from the Soviet point of view) for making the transition to the "dictatorship of the proletariat." The most they can hope for in the foreseeable future are military regimes which pursue a foreign policy more or less in line with the Soviet Union because they are, to a varying degree, dependent on Soviet help. To this the Soviet leaders seem apparently reconciled, but events during the last few years have taught them that there will be many ups and downs in this respect in the years to come. Unless the Communist parties will be made legal and have freedom of action in the Arab world and other Third World countries, the "vanguard party" on which the Soviet leaders continue to put their hopes will simply not come into existence, quite irrespective of the progress of industrialization and the numerical growth of the working class.

Perhaps the Soviet commentators will reach one day the conclusion sections of the New Left have drawn years ago, namely, that a vanguard party is not really necessary and that a few determined people will be able to act as agents of the wave of the future—and carry out the revolution from above—provided they are in control of the levers of state power. This would mean that the ideological pendulum has swung back to various doctrines of the pre-Marxist era. But even that would not get to the core of the problem, namely that the Soviet Union is no longer the model for other Communist regimes and that the installation of a Communist regime is not necessarily synonymous with one friendly disposed toward the Soviet Union. Looking back after a quarter of a century it seems that more worries have been caused to the Soviet Union by the victory of Communism in countries over which it has no direct control than by the survival of non-Communist regimes. It is unlikely that future developments in the Third World will redress the balance, even though the Soviet leadership will no doubt go on trying and may have local successes in extending its sphere of influence.

NOTES

[1] R. Ulyanovski, "The 'third world'—Problems of Socialist Orientation," *International Life*, 9, 1971, p. 21.

[2] V. Tyagunenko, "Some Problems of National Liberation Revolutions in the Light of Leninism," *Mirovaia Ekonomika i Mezhdunarodniie otnosheniia*, (MEMO) 5, 1970.

[3] "The USSR and the Third World," *Mizan*, October–December 1970.

[4] Potekhin in *Pravda*, June 21, 1971, and in MEMO 3, 1971.

[5] MEMO 6, 1971.

[6] *Aziiali Afrika Sevodnia*, 11, 1970.

[7] *Kiva in Aziia i Afrika Sevodnia*, 3, 1971.

[8] V. Smirnov, *Vneshnaia Torgovlia*, 3, 1971.

[9] A. Iskenderov, *The Third World* (eds. Y. Zhukov et al.), (Moscow 1970). pp. 229–230.

[10] G. Mirsky, *Armiia i Politika v Stranakh Azii i Afriki*, Moscow, 1970, p. 160.

[11] This adjustment was for doctrinal reasons not altogether easy, for according to Leninist tenets the state is an instrument of class rule, and the army and the police its main tools. This could be circumvented only by arguing that class differentiation in the Third World had not proceeded very far and that the army was therefore a relatively independent force (Mirsky and Pokatayeva, MEMO 3, 1966).

[12] Iskenderov, *loc. cit.*, pp. 193–196; Mirsky, *loc. cit.*, pp. 193–196.

[13] Mirsky, *ibid.*, p. 19.

[14] For instance A. Kaufman, *Narodi Azii i Afriki*, 4, 1968.

[15] Mirsky, *loc. cit.*, p. 302.

[16] Zhukov, *loc. cit.*, p. 54.

[17] Iskenderov, *loc. cit.*, pp. 196–197.

[18] Mirsky, *loc. cit.*, p. 307.

[19] Mirsky, *loc. cit.*, p. 309.

[20] Mirsky, *loc. cit.*, p. 318.

[21] Solodovnikov, p. 201.

[22] Ulyanovski, p. 33.

[23] *Loc. cit.*, p. 31.

[24] *Kommunist*, 4, 1968.

[25] Ulyanovski, pp. 29, 34.

Oded Eran

SOVIET PERCEPTION OF ARAB COMMUNISM AND ITS POLITICAL ROLE

The main purpose of this paper is to report on the divergences in Soviet writing concerned with the role of the Arab Communists in client Arab states, particularly Egypt. I will attempt also to identify some of the political and institutional sources of the differing viewpoints.

The Soviet change of attitude in the mid-fifties toward the Arab "national bourgeois" regimes occurred at a time when many people in the Kremlin entertained hopes with regard to the political prospects of the Arab Communist parties. Since a "dual policy," in the sense of preserving good working relations with the Arab governments while simultaneously seeking to subvert them, was not feasible, the problem of the relations between the Communist parties and the incumbent regimes became crucial.

It apears that since 1956, despite several attempts to define the principles of Communist strategy in the "national liberation movement," there has been no consensus inside the Kremlin regarding this question. More specifically, in Soviet writing, two opposing dispositions toward organized Communist activity inside radical anti-Western regimes have manifested themselves, one of which can be labeled *non-party oriented* and the other *party oriented*. The first, belittling the role and significance of a distinct Communist organization, has conceptualized Soviet interest and Communist behavior mainly in terms of harmonious relations with the ruling Arab elites; the second, regarding the independence of the Arab Communist parties as important for Soviet policy, visualized dialectical relations between the Communists and the incumbent regimes.

The apparent similarity between these two contrasting orientations and the historical disagreement between Lenin and Roy or Stalin and Trotsky on Communist strategy in the East is superficial because the issue under debate since the 20th Congress of the C.P.S.U. has been whether tnere is a *raison d'être* at all for an independent Communist organization within a radical regime. The debate has been conducted particularly, though not exclusively, in reference to countries, such as Egypt, where domestic Communism has not been strikingly successful.

The question of the relationship between the Communist Party and the national government has not been limited to the Arab world. Nonetheless, due to the continuous conflict between Arab nationalists and Communists, the Arab case has been uppermost in the debate and has had a strong impact on its development. In fact, the evolution of the debate since 1956, between adherents of the *party orientation* and of the *non-party orientation*, can be very clearly related to the crests and troughs in the endemic antagonism between Arab nationalism and Communism.

* * *

Prior to 1962 there had been no open attempt to articulate a *non-party orientation* and it expressed itself in the press only by implication. It could be identified by the scant attention that the press had given to the Arab Communist parties; before 1959, a considerable number of Soviet publications either avoided any discussion of the Arab Communist parties or referred to them only very infrequently.[1] Furthermore, the incumbent regimes quite often had been described as popular regimes, supported by the masses,[2] in a deliberate attempt to de-emphasize any sort of internal class conflict. Already in the late fifties, on several occasions one could detect a tendency to elevate the revolutionary role of the military in the Arab countries and to put it above the role of the Communist Party.[3] These trends were precursors of the theory, first propounded in 1962 and later developed more fully, of the "revolutionary democracy."

The tendency to belittle the role of the Communist parties was by no means universal in Soviet literature pertinent to the subject. Optimistic assessments regarding the immediate political prospects of Arab Communism continued to appear occasionally in Soviet publications.[4] Nevertheless, between the 20th Congress and late 1958, such an approach was rare.

Against the background of the persecution of Communists in the U.A.R., the Nasser-Qassem rivalry, and the subsequent anti-Communist policies of Qassem himself, the *party-oriented* disposition appeared more often and the debate between the two orientations intensified. The lessons of the events in the Arab world were ambiguous. On the one hand, intensification of anti-Communist policies furnished a strong argument in support of a more antagonistic attitude on the part of the Communists toward the governments. On the other hand, the abrupt termination of Communist influence in Syria in 1958 and in Iraq in 1959 demonstrated the folly of Communist "activism" inside client states. [5]

*   *   *

Differences along these lines had been apparent in the Soviet and Communist sources between the 21st and 22nd Party Congresses. In the first place, the statement of the 81 Communist parties of November 1960 and the new program of the C.P.S.U. adopted by the 22nd Congress, which introduced the concept of the "national democratic state," differed in their conception of Communist tactics inside the national states. The statement suggested a *dual strategy,* namely, giving full support to the progressive foreign policy espoused by Third World regimes, while mobilizing opposition to the anti-democratic tendencies of these same regimes. The party program, for its part, avoided any dialectic conception of the proper relationship between the Communists and their collaborators. These differences can be explained by the fact that the statement was the product of a Sino-Soviet compromise, while the program reflected the Soviet position only. However, a considerable number of Soviet sources preferred to emphasize the conflict-oriented conception of Communist strategy prescribed by the statement. [6] A few Soviet sources even went so far as to suggest that proletarian hegemony was a requirement for the "national democratic state." [7]

The co-existence of the two conceptions was particularly evident in the Soviet writing on Iraq during the same period. Although none of the Soviet sources ever justified the Kirkuk uprising or any attempt to overthrow Qassem, there was no universal agreement as to the guiding principles of Communist behavior inside the regime, and while some publications visualized harmonious relations with the government, others placed the emphasis on "non-antagonistic" contradictions. [8]

From 1962 on, the *non-party orientation* became more articulate and the debate pertaining to the role of the Communists more open. The chief spokesman for the *non-party orientation* was G. Mirskii, an expert on Arab affairs, whose main preoccupation was Egypt and, to a lesser extent, Algeria and some sub-Saharan states. The essence of the new theory, which he developed in a series of articles, was that in underdeveloped countries, where the proletariat and the bourgeoisie were still weak and premature classes, petit-bourgeois elements such as the lower-ranking military officers and the intelligentsia could constitute a true "revolutionary democratic" force capable of leading their countries to socialism.[9] On several occasions the role of the military was described by Mirskii in terms identical to those used by Marxist theory with regard to the proletariat itself: "avant-garde carrier of the historical mission" . . . "classless force" . . . "symbolizing the goals of the nation."[10] In such a case, the historical mission of the Communist Party was practically transferred to "elements close to the working class"[11] and the *raison d'être* of an *independent* Communist organization became questionable.

An interesting fact is that the *party-oriented* criticism of these ideas emerged, in full force, shortly after the *coups* of February and March 1963 in Iraq and Syria and the repressive measures taken in these countries against the Communists. It was against this background that the exponents of the *non-party orientation* were reminded that it had been a departure from Marxism-Leninism "to put aside the Communists and to opt instead for politically unstable strata."[12] The *party-oriented* sources accepted the concept of the "revolutionary democratic" parties but insisted that some form of an alliance between them and the Communist Party as such was a necessity.[13] Evidently, according to this conception, the Nasser regime could *not* be categorized as a "revolutionary democratic" government leading its country to socialism.

* * *

The quasi-scholarly debate between *party orientation* and *non-party orientation* had a specific political and institutional background. On the surface, it had been conducted from 1959 to 1964, between two research institutes of the U.S.S.R. Academy of Sciences: the Institute of the Peoples of Asia, as a spokesman for the *party orientation,* and the Institute of World Economics and International Relations, as a spokesman for the *non-party orientation.* Though neither institute was really monolithic in its approach, a dominant trend was recognizable in each of them.

At the time of the 21st Party Congress, the Institute of the Peoples of Asia reoriented and reorganized its research program, shifting the focus of interest from the "national bourgeoisie" to the "working class" and criticizing the state of research in this field.[14] Until 1964 most of the *party-oriented* material which emphasized militancy on the part of the Communist parties originated with this institute and its journals. Through a special series of books and periodic reports the institute cultivated an optimism regarding the immediate prospects of Communism, particularly in the Arab world.[15] The Institute of World Economics and International Relations for its part became the sponsor of less optimistic evaluations of the political strength and class consciousness of the Afro-Asian proletariat.[16] It was at the academic conferences organized by this institute in the years 1962, 1963, and 1964 that some of its scholars elaborated the *non-party-oriented* ideas.

The two institutes reflected fundamental disagreements which had developed within the Kremlin. According to the report of an Israeli Communist source, throughout most of the Khrushchev period the Praesidium was divided between "the class approach" and the "big power approach," as he termed it.[17] According to the same source, M. Suslov was the Soviet leader who represented the class approach. He argued that Khrushchev's policies had practically abandoned the Communist parties, and insisted on more Soviet support for the persecuted Arab parties. Suslov's opposition to Khrushchev had a bureaucratic background. The shift of focus from the level of the Communist movement to the level of governmental relations minimized the role of the International Department of the Central Committee, of which Suslov and his associate Ponomarev were in charge. Another Israeli Communist source reports that the International Department became an institutional source of opposition to the policies of the First Secretary: "Ponomarev's opposition to Khrushchev was departmental, this was his job."[18] The Institute of the Peoples of Asia would appear to have been under the influence of the International Department, with at least two members of its faculty being on the staff of the department: B. Gafurov, the director of the institute,[19] and R. Ulianovskii, currently the deputy director of the International Department in charge of its activities in the Third World.

The bureaucratic sources of the *non-party orientation* were less evident. Thus one can only speculate, taking into account the emphasis placed on normal diplomatic relations and on the role of the military. In any case, Khrushchev, on a visit to Egypt in May 1964, described it as a country building socialism and thereby identified himself as a sponsor of Mirskii's ideas. At the time of his ouster, Khrushchev was reportedly accused, among many other things, of pursuing policies toward Egypt, Algieria, and other Arab countries, which had led to the disorientation and degeneration of the local Communist parties.[20] Without mentioning names, similar accusations were made by some Soviet and Communist publications both immediately before, as well as immediately after, Khrushchev's downfall.[21]

Against this background, it appears somewhat strange that the *non-party orientation* did not suffer any setback as a result of Khrushchev's removal. On the contrary, after October 1964 a consensus seems to have developed within the Kremlin, around the Khrushchevist approach, viz., that the old principle of the independent Communist Party had lost its universality and that it had become an admissible option in countries such as Egypt and Algeria (where strong Communist parties had never materialized) to dissolve the party and thus enable individual Communists to join the ruling party.

Undoubtedly, the admission of the Algerian Communists into the F.L.N. already during Khrushchev's rule, the entrance of the Egyptian Communists into the Arab Socialist Union in 1965, and the coming to power of the Marxist-oriented wing of the Syrian Ba'th in 1966 helped to close much of the gap between the two orientations. Nonetheless, the approach adopted by the post-Khrushchev regime was closer to the *non-party orientation* and differed from it only in the greater emphasis placed on the role of the individual Communists in persuading the leadership of the ruling party to follow the Soviet model of party-state relations and "go over to positions of the working class." At the same time it was a real departure from the *party orientation* as priority was given, in the case of some countries, to the C.P.S.U. relations with the ruling parties of client regimes over and above relations with the national Communist parties.

The consensus of the post-Khrushchev regime brought new assignments to the International Department. It assumed responsibility for a most significant and sensitive area of Soviet-Arab relations, viz. inter-party relations. Ironically, the International Department became the main executor of the ideas which it had so severely criticized during Khrushchev's rule. No wonder that shortly after Khrushchev's disappearance his critics in the department became ardent supporters of the conceptions which he had promoted. R. Ulianovskii wrote several articles, in reference to the Arab Socialist Union and the F.L.N., in which he expressed the idea that these parties eventually would be transformed into Marxist-Leninist parties, practising scientific social-ism.[22] The Soviet breakthrough on the level of relations with the A.S.U. dates back to this period. Another major breakthrough occurred after the Six-Day War. From that date onwards there is an evident Soviet effort to emphasize that relations with Egypt and other radical regimes are being conducted on both governmental *and* party levels: Egyptian delegations to Moscow are labeled "party-state" delegations, a term usually reserved for delegations from bloc countries. Egyptian officials are referred to by both their state and party positions. The participation in state visits to Egypt of Soviet officials associated with the International Department has been on the increase since then.[23]

Nonetheless internal criticism of the enthusiasm for the "revolu-tionary democratic" parties has not ceased in the Soviet Union since Khrushchev's fall. As a matter of fact, almost any Soviet setback in a radical regime in Africa or Asia created fertile ground for questioning the wisdom of the official line. Such was the case last summer with the removal of the Sabri-Gomaa group in Cairo and the repression of the Sudanese Communist Party. Interesting, however, is the fact that the current criticism of the official line *does not* come from the same institutional sources which had been critical of Khrushchev. On the contrary, the leaders of the International Department are now so closely associated with the official line that *they* are being criticized and called to account with those same arguments that they themselves had used against Khrushchev. Recently, Ulianovskii was criticized for promoting the "incorrect" idea that the A.S.U. would become a Marxist-Leninist party, and for neglecting to cultivate a truly independent Marxist organization in Egypt.[24] On the other hand, Ponomarev, who in 1961 had called for opposition to regimes which persecuted Communists,[25] reminded the Communist parties last October in *Kommunist* to behave themselves and not to alienate the incumbent national governments.[26] There was an implied reprimand to the Sudanese Communists in this reminder.

CONCLUSIONS

The switch of the International Department from a *party-oriented* position to a *non-party-oriented* one is indicative of the real nature of that particular debate within the Kremlin. It was in fact a *political issue* rather than a *policy issue*: the *party orientation*, which has been a minority disposition since 1956, did not offer any real alternative to Soviet policies in the Arab world. This was true in 1959, and it is true today, with regard to the serious troubles which the Soviet government is having with the Sadat regime. The option of relying heavily on the activity of a local Communist Party and running a permanent risk of alienating the incumbent regime is not an admissible option as far as Soviet policy is concerned. Seeking some form of arrangement between the Communists and the client governments has been, and will remain in the forseeable future, a necessity for Soviet policy. I believe that the Soviet government is much more comfortable with individual Communists inside a ruling party than with a well-organized, influential Communist Party, permanently requiring justification for its independent existence. The *party orientation* should be understood, therefore, as an attempt to make political profit out of an emotional issue which no longer has operative meaning. It is likely, therefore, to remain a minority approach.

Furthermore, the consensus in the Kremlin with regard to the basic principles of policy toward the Arab world seems to be far wider today than it was under Khrushchev. I was not able to identify any distinct group with a strong organizational base behind this criticism of the official line, as had been the case in 1965. It appears, therefore, that the Brezhnev-Kosygin regime has managed to unite a broad coalition, far broader than in Khrushchev's period, behind the policy on this issue. This unity has been achieved through a more reasonable division of labor between the relevant bureaucracies, making them all responsible for the policy.

NOTES

[1] See for example Iu. Basistov and I. Ianovskii, *Strany Blizhnevo and Srednevo Vostoka,* Tashkent 1958. The Communist parties of Egypt and Syria were hardly mentioned while the Iraqi Communist Party and its ongoing struggle against Nuri Said were widely discussed.

[2] See "XX Sezd Kommunisticheskoi Partii Sovetskovo Soiuza i Zadachi Izucheniia Sovremennovo Vostoka," *Sovetskoe Vostokovedenie* No. 1, 1956, pp. 8–9.

[3] See Podpolkovnik E.I. Dolgopolov, *Natsionalno-Osvoboditelnie Voiny v Sovremennuiu Epokhu,* Ministerstvo Oborony SSSR (Moscow 1960); I. Milovanov and F. Seiful Muliukov, *Irak Vchera i Sevodnia,* GosIzdat, (Moscow 1959).

[4] See for instance L. N. Vatolina and E. A. Belyaev, *Araby v Borbe za Nezavisimost,* Institut Vostokovedeniia, Akademiia Nauk SSSR, 1957.

[5] For the self-criticism exercised by the Iraqi Communists after the Kirkuk uprising see "Iz Materialov Plenuma Ts.K. Kommunisticheskoi Partii Iraka," *Kommunist* No. 12, August 1959. For the militant approach see V.Li, "O Nekapitalisticheskom Puti Razvitiia," *Aziia i Afrika Sevodnia* No. 11, Nov. 1961, and B. Ponomarev, "O Gosudarstve Natsionalnoi Demokratii," *Kommunist* No. 8, May 1961.

[6] See L.N. Chernov, "Kommunisty Stran Azii i Afriki v Avangarde Borby Za Svobodu i Natsionalnuiu Nezavisimost," *Narody Azii i Afriki* No. 5, 1961; see also V. Pavlov, "Soiuz Rabochevo Klassa i Krestianstva i Sotsialnie Preobrazovania Na Vostoke," *Aziia i Afrika Sevodnia* No. 10, Oct. 1961.

[7] See A. Yermolaev, "Programma Deiatelnosti Kommunisticheskikh i Rabochikh Partii," *Partinaiia Zhizn Kazakhstana* No. 1, Jan. 1961; V.P. Agafonov, "Leninskoe Uchenie O Vozmozhnosti Nekapitalisticheskovo Razvitiia Kolonialnykh i Zavisimykh Stran i Yevo Znacheniie Dlia Sovremennosti," *Nauchnyye Doklady Vysshei Shkoly* (Fil. Nauki) No. 3, 1962; N.G. Pospelova, "Ekonomicheskie, Klassovye i Politicheskie Osnovy Gosudarstva Natsionalnoi Demokratii i Yevo Funktsii," *Vestnik Leningradskovo Universiteta* No. 23 (E-Fil-Prav), Vypusk 4, 1962; V.I. Pavlov and I.B. Redko, "Gosudarstvo Natsionalnoi Demokratti i Perekhod k Nekapitalisticheskomu Razvitiiu," *Narody Azii i Afriki* No. 1, 1963.

[8] The non-dialectical conception was manifest in I. Milovanov and F. Seiful Muliukov, *op. cit.,* while the dialectical conception showed up in B.M.

117

Dansig, *Irak v Proshlom i Nastoiashchem*, Institut Narodov Azii, Akademiia Nauk SSSR (Moscow 1960). The two approaches were evident in Khrushchev's report to the 21st Congress.

9 See G. Mirskii, "The UAR Reforms," *New Times* No. 4, Jan. 24, 1962; R. Avokov and G. Mirskii, "O Klassovoy Strukture v Slaborazvitykh Stranakh," *MEiMO* No. 4, April 1962; G.I. Mirskii, "O Putiakh Nekapitalisticheskovo Razvitiia Osvobodivshikhsia Stran," *Nauchnyye Doklady Vysshei Shkoly* (Fil. Nauk) No. 6, 1962; G. Mirskii, "Tvorcheskii Marxism i Problemy Natsionalno Osvoboditelnykh Revolutsii," *MEiMO* No. 2, Feb. 1963, and other.

10 G. Mirskii and T. Pokataiva, "Klassy i Klassovaia Borba v Razvivaiushchikhsia Stranakh," *MEiMO* No. 3, 1966.

11 See report on a scholarly conference in *MEiMO* No. 6, 1964, and G. Mirskii, "The Proletariat and National Liberation," *New Times* No. 18, 1964.

12 R. Avakov and L. Stepanov, "Sotsialnie Problemy Natsionalno Osvoboditelnoi Revolutsii," *MEiMO* No. 5, 1963.

13 See Ulianovskii's speech at the 1964 *IMEiMO* conference as well as Akopian's speech on the same occasion; see also Suslov's speech before the Plenum of the Central Committee in Feb. 1964 (*Plenum Ts. K KPSS* Moscow, Feb. 1964).

14 See N.S. Pavlov, "Obsuzhdenie Itogov Raboty Institutov Vostokovedeniia i Kitavedeniia Akademiia Nauk SSSR za 1958g," *Voprosy Istorii* No. 4, 1959. It was R. Ulianovskii, acting director of the Institute of Oriental Studies, who presented the report on the state of the research; see also "XXI Sezd KPSS i Zadachi Vostokovedeniia," *Problemy Vostokovedeniia* No. I, 1959.

15 For optimistic assessments of the immediate chances of Arab Communism, see V. Kiselev, "Arabskii Proletariat Nabiraet Sily," *Aziia i Afrika Sevodnia*; V.N. Kiselev, "Formirovanie Rabochevo Klassa v Stranakh Arabskovo Vostoka," *Polozhenie Rabochevo Klassa i Rabochee Dvizhenie v Stranakh Azii i Afriki 1959–1961*, Institut Narodov Azii Akademiia Nauk SSSR (Moscow 1962). The book is one of a series on the subject.

16 Two sections of these institutes became particularly identified as parties to this debate: the Section for the Workers' Movement of the Institute of the Peoples of Asia and the Section for the International Workers' Movement of the Institute of World Economics and International Relations. These two sections published in April and August 1962, respectively, two contradictory reports on the current situation of the Workers' Movement in the Third World. The April 1962 report ("Podem Rabochevo Dvizheniia v Stranakh Azii i Afriki," *Kommunist* No. 6, April 1962, prepared by the section of the Institute of the Peoples of Asia) offered an optimistic picture of a growing Communist influence, while the August report ("Klassovaia

Borba Trudiashchikhsia v Stranakh Kapitala," *MEiMO* No. 8, August 1962, prepared by the section of the *IMEiMO*) was much less optimistic on this point.

[17] Interview with S. Mikunis, Secretary-General of the Israeli Communist Party, Tel Aviv, July 29, and August 11, 1969.

[18] Interview with M. Sneh, a member of the Politbureau of the Israeli Communist Party, Tel Aviv, June 18, 1969.

[19] See U.S. Congress, Senate Committee on the Judiciary, *Soviet Intelligence in Asia, Testimony of Alexander Kaznacheev*, 86th Congress, First Session, Dec. 14, 1959, p. 13.

[20] Interview with M. Sneh, *ibid.*

[21] See Khaled Bagdasch in *World Marxist Review* No. 8, 9, 1964; G. Kim, "Natsionalnaia Nezavisimost i Sotsialnyi Progress," *Aziia i Afrika Sevodnia* No. 10, Oct. 1964.

[22] R. Ulianovskii, "Nekotorie Voprosy Nekapitalisticheskovo Razvitiia Osvobodivshikhsia Stran," *Kommunist* No. 1, Jan. 1966.

[23] Ponomarev, and, to a lesser extent, Ulianovskii are frequent visitors to Egypt since 1964.

[24] V.F. Volianskii, "Rol Subektivnovo Faktora v Borbe za Sotsialisticheskuiu Orientatsiu Razvivaiushchikhsia Stran Afriki," *Vestnik Moskovskovo Universiteta* No. 3, 1971.

[25] B. Ponomarev, "O Gosudarstve Natsionalnoi Demokratii," *Kommunist* No. 8, May 1961.

[26] B. Ponomarev, "Aktualnye Problemy Teorii Mirovovo Revolutsionnovo Protsessa," *Kommunist* No. 15, 1971. See also R. Ulianovskii in "Tribuna Obmena Mneniami," *Problemy Mira i Sotsialisma* No. 9, 1971.

3. THE SOVIET UNION, ISRAEL AND THE ARAB-ISRAEL CONFLICT

Yaacov Ro'i

SOVIET-ISRAELI RELATIONS, 1947–1954

Despite its traditional anti-Zionist outlook, the Soviet Union began to take cognizance of the Jewish *yishuv* (community) in Palestine soon after the German invasion of Soviet territory in mid-1941. In 1941, and early in 1942, Soviet ambassadors and representatives in a number of capitals (Washington, London, Ankara, and Teheran) received Zionist and Palestinian Jewish leaders who tried to gain Soviet support for Jewish aims in Palestine. In the summer of 1942, two Soviet diplomats were sent from Ankara to Palestine to tour the *yishuv*, on the occasion of the establishment of a countrywide League for Friendly Relations with the U.S.S.R.[1]

In the latter part of 1943, the Soviets themselves began to initiate contacts and to manifest an active interest in the Jewish cause in Palestine within the framework of preparations toward a general peace settlement. By the time of the visit of Ivan Maiskii to Palestine early in October 1943,[2] the Soviets were apparently working on the dual assumption that the Jewish question would be an urgent international issue at the end of the war and that they, as one of three major world powers, must be prepared to adopt a definite stand on this issue, as on all others requiring an international solution during the course of peace negotiations.

In July 1944, Stalin informed Emil Somerstein, a member of the Provisional Polish Government set up in that month, that the Soviet Union would support an international solution of the Jewish problem at the end of the war,[3] while Malenkov was said to have declared on the same occasion that the Jewish people must receive satisfaction of its territorial claims in Palestine.[4] At Yalta in February 1945, Stalin, Roosevelt, and Churchill agreed to the consolidation of the Jewish national home in Palestine and to the opening of that country's doors to Jewish immigration in the immediate future.[5] In the same month, in London, the Soviet delegation at the founding conference of the World Federation of Trade Unions supported a resolution to enable the Jewish people to continue the building up of Palestine as their national home.[6]

123

The British decision, announced by Churchill at the end of February 1945, to refrain from bringing up the Palestinian question for discussion in the international forum, deprived Soviet support of the Jewish national home in Palestine of practical meaning. The Soviet stand had been taken in the context of a presumed cooperation on the part of the three allied powers, for in fact they had no means of intervening in Palestine except as a great power within the framework of a general worldwide peace settlement. Although the Soviets attempted to force Britain's hand at the founding conference of the United Nations in San Francisco in May 1945,[7] Britain continued in her refusal to raise the question of her Palestinian mandate in an international forum until Ernest Bevin's announcement of February 1947, that the British Government had decided to refer the issue to the United Nations.

During this period—early summer 1945 to the spring of 1947—the Soviets held back from issuing any official statement of their stand on Palestine's political future. Yet, while their diplomats in the Arab countries and a number of Soviet pamphlets, newspapers, articles, and broadcasts indicated that the U.S.S.R. was favorably disposed toward a Palestine settlement within the general lines demanded by the Arabs,[8] the Soviets were in fact taking a number of practical steps designed to further the Jewish cause. In particular, they aided and abetted emigration from Eastern Europe, notably Poland, to the Western Occupation Zones of Austria and Germany, with the full knowledge that the emigrants intended to make their homes in Palestine. The significance of this assistance to the Jews was in no way mitigated by the fact that it was apparently motivated by Soviet interests in the realm of great power politics, and not by any desire to help the Jews or the *yishuv*. The Soviets' primary intention was presumably to create a situation in which the occupation authorities, and ultimately, their respective governments, would be faced with a situation in which the DP camps would be a source of permanent unrest in Germany and Austria. It might also create trouble at home, especially in the U.S., and thus give Washington and London a direct interest in changing the *status quo* in Palestine in contradiction to declared British policy. The Soviet communications media showed constant awareness of the political implications of the British and American dilemma on the question of Jewish emigration from Europe to Palestine, and of American pressures on the British Government brought to light by the published Truman-Attlee correspondence of August-September 1945.[9] Nor did the Soviets disguise their very negative reaction to American-British cooperation over Palestine as manifested in the Anglo-American Committee of Inquiry on Palestine, which was clearly intended by Britain to commit the United States to her policies and to prevent any possibility of Soviet intervention in Palestine and the Middle East.[10] The Soviet press made much of Bartley Crum's revelations on this score in 1947, when he published his book on the Committee and its mission.[11]

At the same time, the Soviets were showing a direct interest in the Near Eastern scene itself. Having established diplomatic missions in Cairo, Baghdad, and Beirut in 1943–4, the Soviets were engaging in considerable political activity in the "Arab East." They maintained contact with a great variety of social and political groupings, including such Arab Muslim parties and leaders as the Muslim Brethren and the Mufti of Jerusalem, Ḥajj Amīn al-Ḥusaynī (who was in Egypt from June 1946),[12] but their main emphasis was on the national and religious minorities in which the area abounded. This concentration on the minorities, however, was not the consequence of choice but of circumstances. While giving moral support to the Syrian and Lebanese demand for the withdrawal of French and British troops from the Levant countries in 1945–6,[13] and to the Egyptian demand for a British withdrawal from Egypt in 1946–7,[14] the Soviet Union was in fact in no position to offer substantial political or other support for the national demands of the Muslim Arab majority in a Western-monopolized political arena. Moreover, the Soviets found themselves impeded and frustrated by the Arab governments, the British-orientated Arab League, and the vested interests of leading Arab circles in existing Arab regimes and the social and political traditions they represented.[15] The minorities, on the other hand, were more easily accommodated, some of them, indeed, being specifically oriented toward the Soviet Union. Thus many Armenians were "repatriated" to Soviet Armenia in the years 1945–8, and a number of Orthodox Christians in this period called on the Arabs to look to the U.S.S.R. for help (for example, 'Īsā al-'Īsā, owner of the daily newspaper Filasṭīn).[16]

Such a minority-oriented policy might logically indicate Soviet support for the Palestinian Jewish yishuv as a means of furthering their influence and establishing their position as a power and a factor in the politics of the Arab East. Yet the Soviets were in an obvious dilemma here, since support of the yishuv would mean opposing Arab demands; in contrast to this, the support they gave other minorities, whose aims in no way clashed with those of the Arabs, involved no friction with the Muslim Arab majority.

The Soviets, therefore, refrained from committing themselves to either the Arabs or the Jews as long as the Palestinian issue was not on the international agenda as a matter demanding a practical solution, but they seemed to tend toward the Arabs. From February 1947, however, the situation changed as it became clear that some decision would soon be demanded of all powers, including the U.S.S.R.

Nevertheless, there is little to indicate that the Soviet leadership had reached a decision by May 1947, when Deputy Foreign Minister Andrei Gromyko made his well-known speech at the First Special Session of the United Nations General Assembly. On 14 May, 1947, Gromyko declared that the U.S.S.R. would support neither an all-Arab nor an all-Jewish Palestine, since it recognized the past and present rights of both peoples in Palestine. His government, therefore, favored a federal Arab-Jewish state. Should this prove unworkable, the U.S.S.R. would support the establishment in Palestine of two independent states, one Arab and one Jewish.[17] The Jewish reaction to this was for the most part enthusiastic, since in 1946 the Zionist Organization had substituted partition for the Biltmore demand for all of Palestine west of the Jordan as its program (the Jewish Agency Executive in August 1946 and the Zionist Congress in December).[18] Nevertheless, Gromyko's speech was in fact highly qualified support of partition, and the Soviets were careful from May to September 1947 to make no further commitment concerning their ideas on Palestine's political future.

There seem to have been two or three main reasons for this ambivalence in the Soviet stand, even at this late stage. In the first place, it was not clear how the majority of states would vote, and the Soviets were apparently not prepared to make any statements, as they had in 1945, only to find themselves supporting a lost cause. Secondly, the British were planning at this stage to evacuate Egypt and not Palestine; they were, in fact, transferring supplies and equipment from Egypt to El-Arish.[19] (The British assumption at this time was that the United Nations would be unable to reach any decision on the Palestine question, and would therefore reaffirm the British Palestine mandate: while an American-Soviet agreement seemed out of the question—as Bevin's Middle Eastern adviser Harold Beeley explained in a private conversation—no such agreement having as yet been achieved at the United Nations, no other arrangement would enlist the support of the two-thirds majority necessary for effecting any change in the *status quo*.[20]) Finally, the Egyptian Government had decided to present to the United Nations a demand for a revision of the Anglo-Egyptian Treaty of 1936 and the evacuation of British troops from the Canal Zone. As long as the Egyptian demand was before the Security Council, and it was possible that Britain might in fact quit Egypt, there was no sense in insisting first and foremost on a British departure from Palestine.

In September, the circumstances changed. Firstly, on 3 September the U.N. Secretariat published the report of the Special Committee on Palestine (U.N.S.C.O.P.). The 11 members of the committee unanimously called for an end to the British mandate, and although divided as to the preferable solution, the majority advocated the country's partition into two independent states with economic union.[21] Secondly, on 10 September the Egyptian demand was removed from the Security Council agenda, having been rejected by all members of the Council except for the U.S.S.R. and Poland.[22] Finally, on 26 September the British decided—presumably as a result of the above developments—to evacuate Palestine and remain in Egypt.[23]

Thus, although it cannot be excluded that the Soviet leadership provided for such a contingency some time between late February and early May 1947, it was only after these events, and two days after the American statement of support for partition (made by Hershel Johnson in the Ad Hoc Committee of the Second Regular Session of the U.N. General Assembly), that the Soviets announced their decision to support partition. The statement to this effect, issued on 13 October by Semen Tsarapkin,[24] ushered in several weeks of intense cooperation between Soviet and American representatives in a subcommittee of the Ad Hoc Committee, which was set up to elaborate details of the partition plan to be implemented by the parties concerned under the aegis of the United Nations.[25]

This cooperation calls attention to another significant aspect of the Soviet support of the establishment of a Jewish state in Palestine, namely, its relevance to the politics of the East-West conflict. It will be recalled that in April 1947, Stalin had maintained (in a conversation with Harold Stassen[26]) that there was no reason why states with different regimes and economic systems, such as the U.S.A. and the U.S.S.R., should not cooperate. In September 1947, however, at the founding conference of the Cominform, Andrei Zhdanov and Georgii Malenkov had proclaimed the doctrine of the division of the world into two hostile camps. Yet the division was not to be determined by geography, for while the two opposing trends were represented and led by the U.S.A. and the U.S.S.R., respectively, the latter had recognized kindred forces in imperialist countries, whose task it was to promote the national interest under the leadership of the working class, viz. the local Communist Party, while neutralizing the anti-Soviet line adopted by their respective governments. It is apparently in this context that we must view the emphasis placed by the Soviets in their communications media—and especially in their Yiddish broadcasts to North America, which they had doubled in quantity in the winter of 1946–7—on Soviet support for the Jewish cause in Palestine and on the enthusiastic Jewish response to the Soviet stand. It seems that until late 1948, after the United States presidential elections of November, the Soviets intended their support of the Jewish cause in Palestine to increase the sympathy for the Soviet Union in the U.S.A. both among Jews and non-Jews, especially as the Soviets recognized the Jews as a traditionally radical and non-conformist group and estimated very highly their political influence in the American domestic arena.

Having reached and announced their decision in favor of partition and having voted for it on 29 November, 1947, the Soviets persisted in their support for the General Assembly resolution in the months preceding and following the establishment of the Jewish state. This support consisted in the main of political backing in the international arena and aid of a practical nature behind the scenes. The Soviets were active in thwarting and overcoming British, and later American, reservations as regards partition, notably after the United States called in March 1948 for the establishment of a provisional international trusteeship for Palestine[27]; for this purpose a second special session of the United Nations General Assembly was convened in mid-April. (This session was still under way when the State of Israel was proclaimed on 14 May, 1948, an event that made its purpose irrelevant.) At the same time the Soviets were providing material aid to the Jews in Palestine in the form of Czechoslovak arms,[28] the first consignment of which reached Palestine in late March 1948.[29] It will be recalled that Jewish-Arab fighting had broken out in Palestine on the day following the passage of the partition resolution, and that although the United States had announced an embargo on arms supplies to Jews and Arabs, the British were in fact supplying arms to the Arab side.[30]

The practical aspect of Soviet aid entered a new phase with the invasion of Israel by the armies of the Arab states on 15 May, 1948. In the same way as they had hitherto prepared an official apologia for the supply of Czechoslovak arms by constant reference to British violation of the embargo on arms to the Middle East, so now the Soviets emphasized the role played by British officers in the Arab armies in order to provide justification for the emigration from Eastern Europe to Israel of Jews of military age, notwithstanding the Security Council resolution of 29 May, 1948. This resolution called on "all governments and authorities concerned" to refrain from introducing fighting personnel and war matériel into the Middle East.[31]

One further factor that was an essential ingredient of Soviet policy on Palestine was the attempt to legitimize the Soviet Union's direct role, together with the other major powers, in deciding Palestine's future. This involved a consistent line of calling for the participation of the permanent members of the Security Council in all bodies and commissions established by the United Nations in the period when Palestine was a major issue on the international agenda—from May 1947 to December 1948—and for maximum control of events in Palestine by the Security Council itself. This stand was no less consistently opposed by the United States, notably in her refusal in the early months of 1948 to establish the international force called for in February 1948 by the Palestine Commission which had been set up by the partition resolution to supervize the transition from the mandatory regime to the establishment of the two independent states. The American attitude was based on the knowledge that if U.S. personnel were included in such a force the Soviets could not be excluded from it. The Soviet position on the issue of a token military presence found its most blatant exposition in June 1948, when ledge that if U.S. personnel were included in such a force the Soviets representation—Gromyko said the U.S.S.R. wanted to send no more than five persons—on the staff of military observers required by the United Nations mediator on Palestine, Folke Bernadotte.[32]

While the Soviet Union did not achieve its aim of gaining a recognized political, if not military, foothold in Palestine, its specific strategic purpose in Palestine was in fact attained, namely the ousting of Britain from the country and the inclusion of most of Palestine's major bases and strategic positions in the independent Jewish state. These bases and positions included both the port of Haifa and the Lydda airfield and, most important, the Negev. Any other arrangement for the Negev would have afforded the British a land bridge between their forces and bases in Egypt on the one hand and Transjordan and Iraq on the other. As the Israel Foreign Minister Moshe Shertok (Sharett) reported on returning from Paris, where the United Nations was discussing the Palestine question in the autumn of 1948, the Soviets were acting as if they represented the Israeli case.[33]

Although Soviet support for Israel in the international arena was unstinting until the General Assembly accepted Israel as a member of the United Nations in May 1949, the Soviets were beginning to display doubts about Israel in their own communications media during the second half of 1948. While these reservations appear to have had practical consequences in the sphere of Soviet-Israeli relations beginning only in December 1948 or January 1949, the first signs of a change were visible early in September 1948.[34]

The reasons for the change do not seem to have been directly related to developments in Israel. They were apparently the result of the intensive anti-Jewish campaign in the U.S.S.R. in the latter part of 1948 and the effect on Soviet Jewry of the establishment of the State of Israel. The first of these factors, in turn, appears to have been a by-product of two separate manifestations: a specifically anti-Jewish policy adopted in the winter of 1947–8[35]; and the intensified attack on "bourgeois nationalism" combined with the greater emphasis on Soviet isolationism after the open break with Tito in June 1948. The Jewish minority, hitherto treated as all other Soviet national minorities, was henceforth—until the end of Stalin's rule—excluded from the list of recognized minorities. Even as individuals the Jews became the object of increasing suspicion in view of their personal connections with the capitalist world, and virtually all their remaining institutions in the Soviet Union were closed down in the last three months of 1948,[36] while their leading public figures and cultural representatives were imprisoned, deported, and executed. In the period from December 1948 to March-April 1949, the Soviet authorities also conducted an intense and much-publicized anti-cosmopolitan campaign—cosmopolitanism was said to be the obverse side of bourgeois nationalism—whose apparent purpose was to display the disloyalty to the Soviet Union of Jews in general and Jewish intellectuals and members of the liberal professions in particular.

The repression of Jewish culture and the anti-Semitism revealed in the anti-cosmopolitan campaign, as well as the repression of Zionist organizations and institutions still existing in the People's Democracies of Eastern Europe, seem to have been implemented without any connection with Israel, and need not, perhaps, have had any repercussions on Soviet-Israeli relations. However, the enthusiasm aroused among Soviet Jewry by the establishment of the Jewish state, moreover with Soviet support, was a factor of quite a different order. On 8 May, 1947, a few days before his above-mentioned speech, Gromyko had told the First Committee of the United Nations General Assembly that Soviet Jewry was not interested in emigration to Palestine.[37] Events, however, proved otherwise, for several thousand young Jewish men understood the Soviet support of the war of national liberation of Palestinian Jewry—one Soviet source actually compared the Palestinian war with the Civil War in Spain[38]—to imply the possibility of their own participation in it.

In addition, a number of spontaneous demonstrations greeted the establishment of the State of Israel, including a special service in Moscow's main synagogue in June or July of 1948. To these were added the tumultuous welcome given to Golda Meyerson (Meir), Israel's first envoy to the U.S.S.R., in October 1948 (despite Ilya Ehrenburg's warning, published in *Pravda* in September), and a number of contacts which Soviet Jews established with the Israeli legation in Moscow from the time of its arrival early in September 1948. The Soviet authorities could clearly not be expected to remain indifferent to these manifestations. Within days of the demonstrations on the High Holy Days at the Moscow synagogue in honor of Mrs. Meyerson, arrests began.[39]

Until February 1949 the steps taken by the Soviets to prevent contacts between their own Jewish citizens and the Israeli diplomats were initiated by the security police, without any representations to the Israeli legation. The latter received its first intimation of trouble when Deputy Foreign Minister Valerian Zorin informed Mrs. Meyerson that his government would not tolerate these contacts.[40] In fact, however, although actual contacts were virtually stopped, Soviet Jewry, and particularly those of its elements which were directly affected by anti-Semitism or anti-Jewish restrictions, such as the *numerus clausus* introduced in the universities and the increasing dismissals of Jews from a number of professions, began to show an increasing interest in Israel and even identification with the Jewish state. The national awakening which Soviet Jewry, like most Soviet national minorities, had experienced during World War II and the national consciousness evoked by the Holocaust found their only outlet, after the liquidation of the last Jewish cultural institutions, in an emotional, if not physical, connection with Israel. Although the Soviet policy of assimilating its Jewish minority had been successful to a large degree, the anti-Jewish atmosphere and restrictions, the Soviet classification of Jews as such in their passports and papers, combined with the elimination of everything Jewish and of the very word "Jewish" from official and public life, prevented the Jews from losing their identity completely.

Both these factors gathered momentum in the remaining years of Stalin's life. On the one hand the Soviet authorities continued their anti-Jewish discrimination, and on the other Soviet Jews—and particularly students, intellectuals, and members of the liberal professions— began to develop an increasingly personal interest in the State of Israel. While the latter trend found very little opportunity for expression, official Soviet anti-Jewish policy had some very far-reaching practical consequences, attaining its peak in the trial of Slansky's conspiratorial "center" in Czechoslovakia in November 1952 and in the Doctors' Plot, "revealed" by the Soviets in January 1953. The Czechoslovak political trials were the result of a Soviet-inspired and Soviet-directed policy and in these show trials as well as in the Doctors' Plot the Jewish character of most of the accused was explicitly indicated. Moreover, in contrast to earlier anti-Jewish campaigns, the Jewish defendants were officially charged with being connected with Israel and accused of complicity in her pro-imperialist policies. In this way Israel—represented at the Slansky Trial by the two witnesses Mordekhai Oren and Shim'on Orenstein—was openly linked with world Jewry as partners in a plot against the U.S.S.R. and the People's Democracies.[41] The Doctors' Plot and its concomitants actually led directly to the severance of relations with Israel in February 1953. Although the intensified anti-Jewish campaign was apparently primarily a cover for political purges of non-Jews (of whom Lavrentyi Beriia was to have been the chief victim),[42] it had acquired a momentum of its own, especially within the framework of international relations, which were dominated by the extreme anti-American tendencies of the Soviet leadership in the last six months of Stalin's rule.[43]

The connection of the State of Israel, and more particularly its government, with American imperialism had become a recurrent theme in the Soviet press from 1949. The first indication of criticism of Israel, apart from an isolated article in *New Times*, early in September 1948, appeared in a pamphlet by Izrail' Genin in December 1948.[44] (It was characteristic of Soviet propaganda practice that a Jew was chosen to announce a change for the worse in the Soviet appreciation of the Jewish state.) The change, however, cannot apparently be attributed to any act of the Israelis themselves. Thus, although the Soviets reacted very sharply, for example, to the loan received by the Israeli Government from the American Export-Import Bank in February 1949, there is no reason to believe that this affected the Soviet attitude to the State of Israel in any substantial way. This is borne out by the fact that when Israeli diplomats in Moscow approached Andrei Vishinskii, shortly after he became Foreign Minister in March 1949, with a request for a similar loan from the U.S.S.R., the latter promised to give the matter careful consideration.[45]

Nor can it be reasonably argued that the change was the result of any disappointment with the domestic and/or foreign policies of the Israeli Government. The Soviets had no illusions, even several years before the establishment of the State, about the "Right Socialist" tendencies of Mapai and its American sympathies. It is possible that the Soviets were hopeful that the merger of Aḥdut Ha'avoda and Hashomer Haẓa'ir in the new party of Mapam in January 1948 would strengthen the groups which were oriented toward the socialist camp and the world of tomorrow as represented by the Soviet Union, and thus give them a more solid representation in the country's legislature and government. They were also aware of the strength of Mapam in the Israel armed forces. This may have motivated in part the military and political aid given to Israel by the Soviet Union and the People's Democracies in 1948, and it certainly gave this aid a rationale that was convincing within the Soviet bloc. However, even if some quarters placed their hopes in progressive groups in Israel, these expectations were clearly not to be weighed against the Soviet domestic problems raised by the aforementioned Soviet Jewish aspects of the situation. Thus, the first signs of the change in the attitude to Israel preceded the elections to the first Knesset on 25 January, 1949, and the formation of the new Israeli Government, without Mapam, early in March.

If, then, we assume—as it seems we must—that the deterioration in the Soviet official appraisal of Israel was unrelated to any policies of or actions taken by Israel, and if, in particular, we take into account the fact that in practice the Soviets continued, until May 1949, their unmitigated support of Israel in the international arena, we are obliged to seek other reasons for the change in late 1948. It might be tempting to attribute it to the Soviet attitude toward the Arab states, but there is no supporting evidence for any such supposition. Another possibility is that the role that support of Israel might have played in winning American Jewish sympathy for the U.S.S.R. had lost its practical significance. Firstly, American Jewry was becoming increasingly critical of the U.S.S.R.; secondly, after the presidential elections of November 1948—in which, however, New York accounted for more than half the votes received by Henry Wallace—and with the intensification of the cold war, Soviet hopes of influencing the U.S. domestic scene must necessarily have diminished. Yet it does not seem that this could have been the sole or even chief motive for a shift to a policy that was inconsistent with the support shown Israel by the Soviet Union at the United Nations well into 1949. Such a contradiction can only have been the outcome of an intrinsically more vital issue, which, in view of the developments mentioned above, must almost certainly have been the reaction of Soviet Jewry to the establishment of the State of Israel and its support by the U.S.S.R.

The question of national security, always a vital issue, was especially weighty in the Soviet Union in late 1948. Moreover, at that time the Jews were being publicly accused of disloyalty to their Soviet motherland and of connections—ideological and actual—with their brethren in the main imperialist states. (One of the charges brought against active figures of the Jewish Anti-Fascist Committee who were arrested late in 1948 or early in 1949 was that in 1944 they proposed the establishment of a Jewish autonomous region in Crimea.[46]) In these circumstances, it was but a short step to include Soviet Jewry's active interest in Israel in the general anti-Jewish campaign. As to the claim that only a very small segment of Soviet Jewry felt any identification with Israel and events there in 1948, it must be counter-argued that while this interest was publicly manifested by only several thousands of Jews, their demonstrations came at a time when every individual who dared openly express his interest presumably represented many more who were understandably apprehensive of doing so. This assumption has been borne out by a number of Soviet Jews who have since been able to bear witness to their own doings in this period.[47] In any event, in Stalin's last years the association even of a few members of a group with disloyalty was sufficient reason for repressive measures against the group as a whole.

Although the disparagement of Israel by the Soviet communications media could logically be expected to have affected Soviet-Israeli bilateral relations, and undoubtedly mirrored a policy change, day-to-day relations remained comparatively unchanged. The acceptance of

Israel as a member of the United Nations in May 1949, and the Armistice Agreements concluded by Israel and her four Arab neighbors with the mediation of Ralph Bunche between February and July 1949, placed Israel irrevocably on the international map and automatically ended the need for the political support given her by the U.S.S.R. in 1948. To all appearances it was thus objective circumstances that dictated the change, for there no longer existed a vital common cause—for Israel a matter of life and death, and for the U.S.S.R. an important strategic interest—namely, the establishment of the State of Israel within the frontiers determined by the partition resolution of November 1947. In these conditions of a necessarily lesser commitment, the Soviet Union continued to maintain the appearances of normal and even friendly relations with Israel until very shortly before the severance of diplomatic ties in February 1953.

In the period from 1949 until the death of Stalin in March 1953, the Soviets continued their efforts to create opportunities for the extension of their influence in the Arab East. The focal point, however, of Soviet activity in this period was no longer to be found among minority groups, but within the Muslim Arab majority. Increasing unrest and anti-British activity in the Arab world on the one hand, and growing Soviet consciousness of the potential of the upsurge of nationalism in the colonial world as a whole on the other, led the Soviets to divert their main attention to the Arab states. It was also, apparently, a Soviet contention that the State of Israel with its technical progress and democratic regime would act as a catalyst for reform throughout the region. It is not clear whether this was to come about as a result of the Arab-Israel conflict, which would bring home to the Arabs both the fact of their own backwardness and the need for a change that might enable them to alter the balance of power in the region, or simply by the salutary example provided by Israel. The existence of the contention itself, however, can hardly be doubted.

Throughout the discussion of the Palestinian question at the United Nations in 1947 and 1948, the Soviets, while limited by their basic attitude, had stressed that their stand was in no way intended to be anti-Arab. Their support of the *yishuv*, their U.N. delegation explained, was part and parcel of their foreign policy, one of the principles of which was the right to self-determination of every people. The Soviets had been at pains to stress that the Arabs would not lose by the establishment of the Jewish state, and Gromyko assured them that the day would come when they would look to the U.S.S.R. for assistance.[48] Yet by mid-1949 the Soviets were freer. They had gained what they could from the establishment, and existence, of the State of Israel and were showing signs of the change of emphasis in their own orientation. The Soviet orientalist Vladimir Lutskii, at a symposium of experts held in Moscow in June 1949 jointly by the Institute of Economics and the Pacific Institute of the Academy of Sciences of the U.S.S.R., said that Israel had not fulfilled the conditions imposed on the Jewish state. The partition resolution of November 1947, he explained, had called for "the establishment of an independent, democratic Jewish state." Yet Israel was being built up as "a Zionist bourgeois state." She opened her gates to foreign capital, accepted a loan from the Export-Import Bank on conditions inconsistent with state sovereignty, and expressed her readiness "to join the aggressive Mediterranean bloc knocked together by the Anglo-American imperialists." Israel's leaders, Lutskii went on, opposed the World Peace Congress (held in April 1949), demanded that the Israeli trade unions leave the World Federation of Trade Unions, and were truckling to the Anglo-American bloc at the United Nations.

Having explained the official reasons for the U.S.S.R.'s change of policy toward Israel—again a Jew was chosen for the task of announcing the worsening in attitude—Lutskii justified Soviet support of Israel in the Palestine war by pointing out that war's contribution to the political change for the better throughout the Arab East. "The Palestinian war," according to Lutskii, "sharpened the crisis of the colonial system in the Near East, demonstrated to the Arab popular masses all the rottenness and the reactionary nature of the ruling cliques of the Arab countries, and exposed their intimate ties with English and American imperialism." Moreover, the Palestine war had brought "the already difficult economic position of the Arab peoples to the verge of catastrophe."

Lutskii's most important statement, however, was that "all the objective conditions for a new upsurge of the national-liberation struggle are currently prevalent in the Arab countries."[49] Yet the Soviet recognition of a new Arab role in the struggle against imperialism, notably in Iraq and Egypt, remained for a considerable time to come a unilateral manifestation, unrelated to international developments. Thus, while the Soviets were preparing the theoretical background for a change in their attitude toward the Arabs, and apparently buttressing this by suggestions in late 1949 and early 1950 for some economic aid, the Arabs were not, on the whole, ready to respond to Soviet advances. The Arabs' first serious misgivings about their Western links and entertainment of the possibility of shaking off some of them were given expression in April 1950 when Ma'rūf ad-Dawālībī, the Syrian Minister of National Economy, called for a non-aggression pact with the U.S.S.R.[50] Similar ideas were expressed in the Syrian Parliament by Muṣṭafā as-Ṣibā'ī of the Muslim Socialist Front and by a Muslim Brethren deputy who supported a proposal for the establishment of political, military, and economic relations with the U.S.S.R. in order to put an end to the difficulties being placed in the way of the Arabs by the U.S.A. and Britain.[51] Simultaneously, the Egyptian Foreign Minister Muhammad Salāh ad-Dīn was saying that he had "almost decided" to make a statement that would be a "moderate version" of Dawālībī's.[52] When the United States, Britain, and France made their Tripartite Declaration of 25 May, 1950, the acceptance of which by most states of the area virtually imposed a *Pax Occidentala* on the "Arab East," the Soviets considered themselves virtually excluded from effective influence in an area they were just beginning to penetrate.

Further opportunities for cooperation with the Arab states against the West soon presented themselves, first in the international arena and then in a regional context. With the outbreak of the Korean War on 25 June, 1950, most of the Arab states adopted a stand that was firmly opposed to the American line in Korea, and with the creation of a neutralist bloc in the United Nations in December 1950, in which the Arabs played an important role, the Soviets found themselves practically aligned with the Arab states.[53]

The next important development came almost a year later, in October 1951, when Egypt prevented the formation of the Middle East Command, of which she was to have been a founder-member, by rejecting the invitation extended to her by the U.S.A., Britain, France, and Turkey. The Soviet Government, which was jolted into intense diplomatic activity as a result of the project—the major Soviet apprehension vis-à-vis the Middle East had for a number of years been the possibility of the creation in the area of a regional military alliance under Western auspices—was more than appreciative of the Egyptian stand, and began to take an active interest in the Egyptian struggle against the British presence.[54]

Yet until Stalin's death the Soviet-Arab *rapprochement*, insofar as it existed, was based only on a common negative interest and the awareness of a common adversary; it was one of fits and starts, never growing beyond embryonic stages. Perhaps the best evidence of this, and certainly the most relevant from the point of view of Soviet-Israel relations, was the Soviet stand on the Arab-Israel conflict. With the exception of their vote on the internationalization of Jerusalem in December 1949, which does not seem to have been intended against Israel[55] and which they officially renounced in April 1950,[56] the Soviets at no stage voted with the Arabs against Israel. Their delegation maintained an almost unbroken record of abstentions which were intended to express reservations concerning motions that were mostly Western initiatives and designed, at least from the Soviet standpoint, to further the continued Western supervision of the armistice machinery.[57]

However, a substantive change in Soviet-Israel and Soviet-Arab relations came about in the year following Stalin's death. While it was apparently Lavrentyi Beriia, as Minister of the Interior, who was responsible for the speedy liberation of the doctors,[58] the case against whom had been mounted as part of an extensive purge of which Beriia himself was to have been the chief victim, all the new leaders seem to have been agreed on the need for a normalization of international relations. This involved both a modification of the extreme anti-American stance of Stalin's last months and the rectification of a number of issues where it was felt that Stalin had done harm to Soviet interests by exceeding rational limits. It was not surprising that within this framework the Soviets began, as early as April, to put out feelers concerning the resumption of diplomatic relations with Israel.[59] In July the Soviets announced their resumption,[60] and the return of the Israeli Minister to Moscow in November as well as the presentation of his credentials to President Kliment Voroshilov were given wide publicity in the Soviet press and other information media.[61]

Appearances notwithstanding, there is no evidence that the new Soviet leadership, or any element within it, conceived of friendly relations with Israel. This may have been the result of a latent anti-Semitism with which some of them, notably First Secretary Nikita Khrushchev, were known to have been tainted, but it was more probably due to objective conditions. Israel was not only no longer a center of anti-imperialist struggle and activity, but was apparently not even taken into account by the West in its new plans for a Middle East military alliance. (Secretary of State John Foster Dulles, on returning to the U.S.A. after a tour of the Middle East in the spring of 1953, mentioned only the Arab states and the "northern tier" in his report on the possibilities of establishing a regional defense organization, omitting all reference to Israel.[62])

On the other hand, the new leadership was very definitely entertaining designs for a *rapprochement* with Egypt early in 1954, and perhaps even earlier. It is not clear to what extent the Free Officers' *coup* of July 1952 played a role in influencing Soviet plans. The *coup* aroused Soviet suspicions as being United States-oriented and was at first negatively viewed in the U.S.S.R.[63] Nor do the policy and views of the new Egyptian leadership seem to have given the Soviets any reason for changing their attitude throughout 1953. However, in January 1954 an Egyptian "economic delegation" headed by Deputy Minister of War Ḥasan Rajab arrived in the U.S.S.R. for a visit of nearly two months[64]; it will be recalled in this connection that the Soviets insisted in late 1955 that their arms deal with Egypt was a purely commercial transaction. At the same time, Egyptian Minister of National Guidance Ṣalāḥ Sālim announced that the Soviets had offered to help Egypt in her development program and would in fact probably undertake a number of development projects in Egypt.[65]

Moreover, in January 1954 the Soviets, for the first time, used their right of veto in the Security Council to demonstrate their support of the Arabs in the Arab-Israel dispute. On 22 January they vetoed a Western draft resolution which, they said, was intended to further the United States' economic penetration and domination of the Arab countries.[66] (The issue under debate was an Israeli plan for digging a canal in the demilitarized zone on the Syrian-Israeli border for the diversion of part of the River Jordan's waters. President Eisenhower had sent a special representative, Eric Johnston, to negotiate with Israel and the Arab states in an attempt to elaborate a joint plan for the use of these waters.) In March 1954 the Soviets used their veto again, this time against a draft resolution that called upon Egypt to open the Suez Canal to Israeli shipping and cargoes and to ships and cargoes sailing from and bound for Israeli ports.[67] In September 1951 the Soviet delegation at the United Nations had abstained on a similar resolution, presumably because of the lack of any substantive Soviet-Egyptian relations at the time. Yet early in 1954 the Soviets seemed to be entertaining hopes of using their stand on the Arab-Israel conflict—combined with their new relationship with Egypt—to effect the long-sought political presence in the Middle East.

It was apparently this same aim that guided the U.S.S.R. in her relations with Israel. From this period until well into 1956,[68] it seems that the Soviet Union contemplated filling a mediator's role in the Arab-Israel conflict. This necessitated the maintenance of appearances of an Egyptian-Israeli equilibrium, which, in fact, the Soviets went to considerable pains to keep up. In April 1954, for example, the Soviet and Egyptian legations in Cairo and Moscow were raised to the level of embassies and in August the Soviet and Israeli legations in Tel Aviv and Moscow were similarly raised. (The discerning reader of the two announcements could, however, note a difference in attitude: while the Soviets talked of mutual agreement and equality between the two sides in the instance of Egypt,[69] they stressed the fact of the Israeli approach to the U.S.S.R. as justification for the change in the case of Israel.[70]) Trade agreements with Egypt and Israel in 1954 provided for the export to both of Soviet oil, and so on. (Again the nature of the two agreements was basically different, the one with Egypt containing far preferable conditions for the other side.[71])

The development of Soviet-Israel relations beyond 1954 exceeds the limits of this paper, the purpose of which has been to indicate the fact of the change in the first year or so after Stalin's death both in the criteria which served as guidelines for Soviet policy toward Israel and in Soviet tactics under the new leadership.[72]

* * *

In conclusion, it may be claimed that Soviet-Israel relations throughout the period under discussion were governed by a series of considerations that were in fact almost entirely extraneous to the bilateral relations of the two states. It is true that the first stage of these relations was characterized by a common interest—the expulsion of British troops from Palestine and the establishment of a strong Jewish state that would defend its independence and its frontiers against the Arab protégés of Great Britain—but the Soviets, as their representatives stressed in the United Nations, had no direct positive interest in Palestine. Once Israel was established and her existence consolidated, the Soviets still found themselves effectively and, in part intentionally, excluded from any influence, let alone presence, in the area. Israel was basically Western—and, particularly, U.S.A.—oriented, and the United Nations bodies responsible for the implementation of the Armistice Agreements were Western-controlled. At the same time, a major and apparently unexpected complication had arisen, in the form of the Soviet Jewish response to the establishment of the Jewish state, a reaction which had actually been encouraged by the support given the Jewish state by the U.S.S.R. This response was particularly troublesome in that it came at a time when the U.S.S.R. was intensifying her tendency toward complete isolation from the capitalist world and was becoming notably averse to her Jewish population's connections with the West. The combination of the Soviet inability to exercise any physical presence in the Palestine area and the negative domestic results of Soviet support of Israel necessitated the ending of that support once it had achieved its principal objective.

The termination of the first stage, however, did not result in practice in any serious worsening in Soviet-Israel relations since the Soviets, although announcing their preparedness to substitute the Arabs for Israel as their allies in the Near East, found little response in the Arab world. The intensification of the Cold War, together with the identification by Soviet communications media of Israel with the U.S.A. and the new anti-Jewish drive of late 1952 and early 1953, brought about a deterioration which culminated in the severance of diplomatic relations in February 1953. In the period from May 1949 until this time, Soviet-Israel relations were, then, governed by the East-West conflict and developments on the Soviet domestic scene.

The final phase, which opened after Stalin's death, was, in contrast to the preceding one, dominated by regional considerations. The new leadership's slogan of normalization not only implied the resumption of relations with Israel, but led to a modification of the East-West confrontation on all the main fronts. At the same time, the Soviet Union found in the Near East a convenient arena for a careful offensive at a time when all initiative was being frozen elsewhere. The relatively improved relations with Israel were thus not a factor, let alone an end, in themselves, but a function of Soviet relations with the Arab states, and especially Egypt, as these became a major focus of the anti-imperialist struggle.

NOTES

[1] The diplomats—Secretary of the Soviet Embassy in Ankara, Sergei Mikhailov, and its press attaché, Nikolai Petrenko—spent about 10 days in Palestine. The founding meeting of the League for Friendly Relations with the U.S.S.R. took place on 25 August, 1942.

[2] Ivan Maiskii, who had various contacts with Zionist leaders while ambassador in London, was appointed Vice-Commissar for Foreign Affairs in August 1943. He visited Palestine from 2 to 4 October, 1943, and met with David Ben-Gurion and Eliezer Kaplan who took him to visit the kibbutzim of Ma'ale Haḥamisha and Qiryat 'Anavim.

[3] From an interview between Dr. Moshe Sneh and the *JTA* correspondent in Tel Aviv a year later—*Jewish Telegraphic Agency Daily News Bulletin*, 4 September, 1945.

[4] According to a Soviet representative who met with a delegation of the League for Friendly Relations with the U.S.S.R., which brought ambulances to Teheran toward the end of 1944.

[5] This information was given by President Roosevelt to Dr. Stephen Wise in March 1945. (Dr. Wise was at the time President of the World Jewish Congress and of the American Jewish Congress, and Chairman of the American Emergency Zionist Council.)

[6] *Jewish Chronicle*, 23 February, 1945.

[7] Eliyahu Elath, *Yoman San Francisco* (Tel Aviv 1971).

[8] For Soviet diplomacy in the Arab world, see, e.g., *Foreign Relations of the United States, Diplomatic Papers, 1945*, Vol. VIII, U.S. Government Printing Office, Washington 1967–8. For pro-Arab leanings in Soviet publications at the time, see: Lutskii and Vladimir, *Palestinskaia problema* (Moscow 1946).

[9] For the full text of the correspondence, see: *Foreign Relations of the United States, Diplomatic Papers, 1945*, Vol. VIII, *op. cit.*, pp. 734–740.

[10] For the Commission of Inquiry, see: Richard Crossman, *Palestine Mission* (London 1946); and Bartley Crum, *Behind the Silken Curtain* (London 1946). For the Soviet reaction to the setting up of the Committee, see: V. Milogradov, *Arabskii Vostok v mezhdunarodnykh otnosheniiakh* (Moscow 1946).

[11] *New Times*, 8 October, 1947.

[12] These Soviet contacts received a certain amount of publicity in the Arab press and in reports by Westerners from Arab countries.

[13] *Security Council, Official Records, 1st Year, 1st Series,* No. 1, pp. 301–309.

[14] *Security Council, Official Records, 2nd Year,* No. 80, pp. 2109–2211.

[15] *Cf.* Liudmila Vatolina, "Liga arabskikh stran," *Mirovoe Khoziaistvo i mirovaia politika,* 1945, No. 7.

[16] Articles to this effect began appearing in *Filastin* in December 1944.

[17] *Generally Assembly, Official Records, 1st Special Session,* Vol. 1, pp. 127–135.

[18] The enthusiastic Jewish reaction was shared by Jews in the West, in Palestine, and in Eastern Europe.

[19] Elizabeth Monroe, *Britain's Moment in the Middle East, 1914–1956* (London 1965), p. 157.

[20] David Horowitz, *State in the Making* (New York 1953), pp. 131 and 143.

[21] *General Assembly, Official Records, 2nd Session Supplement No. 11, UNSCOP Report to the General Assembly,* Vol. 1, pp. 47–49.

[22] *Security Council, Official Records, 2nd Year,* Nos. 87 and 88, 29 August and 10 September, 1947.

[23] E. Monroe, *op. cit.,* p. 165.

[24] *General Assembly, Official Records, 2nd Session, Ad Hoc Committee on the Palestine Question,* 13 October, 1947, pp. 69–71.

[25] *Ibid.,* 19 November, 1947.

[26] *Documents on American Relations, 1947,* pp. 613–618, reprinted *Documents on International Affairs 1947–8,* Royal Institute of International Affairs (Oxford 1952), p. 116.

[27] *Security Council, Official Records, 3rd Year,* 271st Meeting, 19 March, 1948.

[28] For the Soviet role in the deal, see: Meir Mardor, *Shelihut Aluma* (Ma'arakhot, Israel 1958), p. 158; Isaac Ramba, (ed.), *Shimshon Yunicman* (Hahanhala ha'olamit shel Brit Herut Hazohar, Tel Aviv 1962), pp. 238–239.

[29] David Ben-Gurion, *Medinat Yisrael Hamithadeshet* (Tel Aviv 1969), Vol. 1, p. 189.

[30] In accordance with the military treaties which bound Great Britain with Egypt, Iraq, and Transjordan.

[31] *Security Council, Official Records, 3rd Year,* No. 77, 29 May, 1948.

[32] *Ibid., 3rd Year,* No. 93, 15 June, 1948. There are numerous references by both sides in the U.N. official records to the problem of the international force, the role of the Security Council, etc.

[33] D. Ben-Gurion, *op. cit.,* p. 302.

[34] *New Times,* 8 September, 1948; see below.

[35] The decision to adopt this policy apparently preceded the murder of Solomon Mikhoels on 13 January, 1948.

[36] The institutions that were closed down included the Jewish Anti-Fascist Committee, its organ *Aynikayt,* and the "Der Emes" publishing house. The last Jewish cultural institutions, the Yiddish Theater in Moscow and a Jewish library in the same city, were closed a year later, in November 1949.

[37] *General Assembly, Official Records, 1st Special Session, 1st Committee,* 51st Meeting, 8 May, 1947.

[38] *Radio Moscow,* 22 May, 1948—*British Broadcasting Corporation, Summary of World Broadcasts, Part I,* 28 May, 1948.

[39] For the reaction of Soviet Jewry to the establishment of the State of Israel, the reception given Mrs. Meyerson in the Moscow main synagogue, and the connections which Soviet Jews sought to establish with the Israeli legation, see: Mordekhai Namir, *Sheliḥut Bemoskva* (Tel Aviv 1971).

[40] *Ibid.,* pp. 109–110.

[41] For the Slansky Trial and the role played in it by the U.S.S.R., see especially: Jan Pelikan, (ed.), *The Czechoslovak Political Trials, 1950–1954. The Suppressed Report of the Dubcek Government's Committee of Inquiry, 1968* (London 1971), and Karel Kaplan, "Thoughts about the Political Trials," *Radio Free Europe, Czechoslovak Press Survey,* Nos. 2147, 2148, 2149, 9, 10, 11 December, 1968.

[42] It is not unlikely that the anti-Jewish campaign of 1948–9 was also somehow connected with domestic Soviet developments and personnel changes in the Soviet leadership, the political apparatus, and intellectual circles. Yet, while Soviet sources confirmed the connection in the case of the events of late 1952-early 1953, there is only circumstantial evidence for the events of 1948–9. It should, however, be borne in mind that Malenkov succeeded Zhdanov early in 1948 as second-in-command after Stalin in the Soviet hierarchy (although Zhdanov died only on 31 August), and that the anti-cosmopolitan campaign reached its peak in the months which saw the purge of Zhdanov's followers (the Leningrad Case, etc.).

[43] Those tendencies were given pungent expression in the attack on George Kennan, U.S. ambassador to the Soviet Union, beginning in late September 1952 and culminating in his expulsion from the U.S.S.R.

[44] I[zrail'] A[dol'fovich] Genin, *Palestinskaia problema* (Moscow 1948). For the article in *New Times,* see n. 34 above.

[45] M. Namir, *op. cit.,* pp. 118–119 and 152. That the loan did not materialize was due first and foremost to the fact that the Soviets in the late 1940s had neither the material wherewithal nor the conceptual framework for giving aid or credits to countries outside the Soviet orbit.

[46] *Wochenzeitung,* Vienna, 12 November, 1955, quoted by *Current Events in Jewish Life,* October-December 1955, Institute of Jewish Affairs; *cf.* also: *Khrushchev Remembers,* Andre Deutsch, London 1971, pp. 259–261.

[47] See, e.g., *Ma'ariv,* 9 July, 1971.

[48] E.g., *General Assembly, Official Records, 2nd Session,* 125th Plenary Session, 26 November, 1947, p. 1360.

[49] "Doklady i diskussii: narodno-osvoboditel'naia bor'ba v kolonial'nykh i polukolonial'nykh stranakh posle vtoroi mirovoi voiny," *Voprosy Ekonomiki,* 1949, No. 10, pp. 84–87.

[50] *Al-Miṣrī*, 9 April, 1950.

[51] *Arab News Agency*, 30 April, 1950, and *Radio Israel* in Turkish, 2 May, 1950—*British Broadcasting Corporation, Summary of World Broadcasts, Part IV*, 9 May, 1950.

[52] *Radio Damascus*, 26 April, 1950—*ibid.*, 2 May, 1950.

[53] For the formation of the Neutralist Bloc at the United Nations, on Indian initiative, see: G. M. Jansen, *Afro-Asia and Non-Alignment* (London 1966), pp. 102–113.

[54] This appreciation was given expression in a note handed by Deputy Foreign Minister Andrei Gromyko to the Egyptian envoy to the U.S.S.R. on 21 November, 1951, which was published in *Izvestiia* on 23 November.

[55] The Soviet vote seems to have been intended first and foremost to undermine 'Abdallah's position in Jerusalem and the West Bank, and thereby to weaken that of Great Britain.

[56] In a note given by Iakob Malik to Trygve Lie on 17 April, 1950; the Soviet note stated that the U.S.S.R. no longer considered it possible to support the resolution favoring the internationalization of Jerusalem—*General Assembly, Official Records, 5th Session, Supplement No. 1 (Annual Report of the Secretary General on the Work of the Organization)*, p. 6.

[57] For these abstentions, see: *Security Council, Official Records, 4th Year, No. 38, 11 August, 1949*, and *6th Year, 545th, 547th, and 558th Meetings, 8, 18 May, 1 September, 1951.*

[58] The announcement of the release of the doctors was published in the name of the Ministry of the Interior in *Pravda*, 4 April, 1953.

[59] For the story of the resumption of relations, see: Ben Zion Rezin, "I conducted negotiations for the renewal of diplomatic relations with the Soviet Union," *Ma'ariv*, 10 March, 1972.

[60] *Izvestiia*, 21 July, 1953.

[61] *Pravda*, 28 November and 15 December, 1953.

[62] *New York Times*, 1 June, 1953.

[63] *Cf.* the entry on Egypt in the Soviet Encyclopedia which was sent to print early in September 1952: *Bol'shaia Sovetskaia Entsiklopediia*, 2nd ed., Vol. 15, p. 460.

[64] The delegation was in the Soviet Union from 16 January to 6 March, 1954, and visited a number of the East European People's Democracies on the way to and from the U.S.S.R.

[65] *Al-Ahrām*, 10 February, 1954.

[66] *Security Council, Official Records, 9th Year, No. 656, 22 January, 1954.*

[67] *Ibid.*, No. 664, 29 March, 1954.

[68] *Cf.*, e.g., the announcement of the Soviet Foreign Ministry on the situation in the Middle East of 17 April, 1956, which appeared in the central Soviet press on the same day.

[69] *Pravda,* 22 March, 1954.
[70] See, e.g., *Izvestiia,* 21 July, 1953, and the aforementioned article by B. Rezin.
[71] The agreement with Egypt was signed in Cairo on 27 March, 1954—*al-Ahrām,* 28 March, 1954.
[72] The identification of those particular leaders who were responsible for the change is not essential to this paper.

Yigal Allon

THE SOVIET INVOLVEMENT IN THE ARAB-ISRAEL CONFLICT*

The Soviet Union was until World War II the Great Power least involved in the Arab world. Since then she has reached a measure of involvement which at present is not inferior to that of the United States.

When the Soviet Union adopted a friendly attitude toward Israel, when her attitude became more reserved, or when she transferred her support to the Arab states—especially Egypt and Syria—her policy was not determined by any emotional or ideological considerations. The decisive factor was always how best she could maneuver for a better position in her global struggle for power. When the Soviet Union gave the *yishuv* (the Jewish Community in Palestine) her moral support in the struggle against the British Mandatory power, when she lent the Jewish Agency significant political support culminating in Gromyko's famous speech at the United Nations, in 1947, in which he took a firm stand in favor of the Jewish state (and this was, let us recall, in the days of Stalin), when she encouraged Czechoslovakia to supply Israel with arms, when she permitted the *'aliyah* (immigration) of Jews from the countries of Eastern Europe—it was not because she had been won over to Zionism or because the Israelis had turned Communist. This was simply political pragmatism on her part.

The Soviet objective in supporting the *yishuv* was to help edge out an imperialist power from an important part of the Middle East. This was meant to have a double effect: to serve as a precedent and as an example encouraging other peoples in the region to emulate the *yishuv*; and to create a vacuum which would cry out to be filled.

Against the background of the Nazi Holocaust, the Soviet position won general approval. At the same time, by supporting the U.N. Partition Plan which called for the establishment of an Arab state as well as a Jewish state, the Soviet Union did not endanger her ties with the Arab world which politically, in fact, were almost non-existent.

* This paper is in no way a statement of official government policy or position, but a personal opinion only.

147

Most of the Arab states had not yet achieved any real independence and no diplomatic relations existed between them and the U.S.S.R.

I shall not enlarge upon this point other than to recall that, in spite of all the vicissitudes in the Soviet Union's relations with Israel, in 1954 diplomatic representation was raised to ambassadorial level. Again, when the Soviets decided to cool off relations with Israel and to gamble on the Arabs, it was not because they had become pro-Arab, but because this was what, in their view, Soviet self-interest demanded.

It is interesting to note that after the Cairo military *coup* in 1952, *Pravda* claimed that the Americans were behind it. The Soviets did not regard the *coup*, at least in its preliminary stages, as revolutionary in character. Even after the Bandung Conference, when President Nasser embraced the policy of Positive Neutralism, the Soviet Union did not regard the Egyptian military regime as anything other than a transitional stage on the road from feudalism to Communist revolution. In the view of the Soviet Union, a country like Egypt belonged to the "strategic reserve of the revolution," as Leninist terminology described the subjugated colonial peoples (apparently not without justification). They believed that the Nasserite regime would undermine and even destroy the old social order, create a revolutionary situation, and advance the takeover of power by pro-Communist elements or at least strengthen Soviet influence in Egypt and Arab society in general.

Soviet policy, in its broad lines, is dictated—as it has already been noted—by ideology, by a "grand design," but its application is marked by pragmatism. Thus the Russians continued to support Nasser's military regime while Communists were being tortured in Egyptian prisons. There was a temporary diversion from this pro-Egypt policy when, at Khrushchev's instigation, the Soviet Union turned her attention toward Iraq—Egypt's traditional competitor for hegemony in the Arab world. However, it was not long before the Soviets returned to their first client. They did not falter when Egypt spread her wings over Syria by establishing the United Arab Republic, despite their distaste for this union. It can be assumed that the Soviet Union saw and continues to see in Egypt, Syria and Iraq bridgeheads for deeper penetration into the Middle East, Africa, the Persian Gulf and the Indian Ocean—on ideological and political as well as strategic levels.

While the Soviet interest in the Arab world is understandable, it is more difficult to explain why Arab states allowed themselves to be hugged by the Soviet bear while having no taste for Communism per se. To say that the Arab-Israel conflict is the prime motivation is true to some extent, but it oversimplifies matters. For while all the Arab states are hostile to Israel and regard themselves as being in a state of conflict with her, some of them have managed to keep at a safe distance from the Soviet Union even while praising her policy on this issue.

The creation of the Baghdad Pact in 1954 despite Egyptian opposition; the rise in the importance of the Third World with the Bandung Conference in 1955; the refusal of the United States to finance the Aswan Dam and later the Soviet Union's agreement to do so in 1956; the nationalization of the Suez Canal—all these created conditions which paved the way for Egypt's declaration of neutralism, a serious crime in the eyes of Washington in those days. Nasser attempted to have the best of several worlds, to be all things to all men: an Arab to the Arabs, a Muslim to the Muslims, an African to the Africans, an Asian to the Asians (thanks to the Sinai Peninsula, he was the only Afro-Asian in the Afro-Asian bloc), an anti-Communist to the Americans, an anti-colonialist to the Soviets, a land reformer to the Socialists, and, of course, a neutralist to the countries of the Third World.

True, military developments between Egypt and Israel were not without influence. When Fidayeen attacks became insupportable, Israel carried out a number of retaliatory raids. There are those who maintain that it was the Gaza raid, which took place four days after the signature of the Baghdad Pact, on February 28, 1955, that led Nasser to sign, in September of that year, the Czech arms deal and thus bypass the Tripartite Declaration which had imposed an arms balance preventing both Israel and Egypt from obtaining arms in substantial quantities. Chronologically, the Czech-Egyptian arms deal—which was presumably achieved through the mediation of Chou En-lai in Bandung with the blessing of Moscow—came after the Gaza operation (but, at any rate, before the Sabḥa operation in November). However, there are also solid grounds for believing that a commercial agreement, including an arms deal, between Egypt and Czechoslovakia had been concluded in February 1955, *before* the Gaza raid which took place on the last day of that month.[1] The obvious reply to Israel's retaliation would have been for Egypt to put an end to the terrorist incursions and not to opt for an arms race, for it should have been clear to her that Israel could not afford to remain inferior in arms. It was this arms race that made the 1956 Sinai Campaign inevitable.

In attempting to define more specifically the stages of the escalation of Soviet aid to the Arab cause, it may be said that the first stage was *support*, both moral and political. The second was *assistance*, including arms supplies, military instructors, and advisers. The third was *involvement*, which included the participation of Russian personnel in special defensive missions; this stage was reached in the latter part of the War of Attrition. The culmination would be *intervention*, which it is to be hoped will never be reached—on this point I am optimistic—for this would mean actual offensive military action on the part of the Soviet Union.

There is no knowing how the Soviet Union would have reacted to the five-day Sinai Campaign of 1956—in which Egypt's armed forces were destroyed—had the intervention of Britain and France not taken place and had there not been an American ultimative demand for a cease-fire and complete withdrawal. Without underestimating Bulganin's ultimatum, it was actually Eisenhower's demand which brought about the triple withdrawal. It is reasonable to suppose that the Soviet ultimatum was served only when it became clear to the Russians that they would be acting in accord with the Americans and not in opposition to them.

It is interesting to compare Ben-Gurion's reply to Bulganin on November 7, 1956, with his reply to Eisenhower on the following day. To Bulganin Ben-Gurion wrote, among other things: "Our foreign policy is determined by our vital needs. No foreign factor determines it or will determine it." To Eisenhower Ben-Gurion wrote: "We have willingly accepted your proposal."

It is clear from this that it was not the Soviet Union but the United States that restored Sinai to Egypt. The credit, of course, went to the Soviet Union. At this point the Russians saw no way of strengthening their position in Egypt other than by rebuilding and re-arming the Egyptian forces. The arms race began anew. The Soviet supply of arms to Egypt grew in scale and caliber and with it Egyptian dependence on the Soviet Union.

It may be interesting to compare the two cases in which Soviet action served as a catalyzing agent in the Arab-Israel conflict. In February 1960, and again in May 1967, the Soviet Union deliberately supplied Egypt with false information to the effect that Israel was about to attack Syria. The aim was to prevent Israeli retaliatory action against

Syria and the consequent threat to the Syrian regime. This was a Soviet diversionary move, the objective of which was to bring about the concentration of Egyptian forces on the Egyptian-Israeli border, to increase tension on that border and thus bring relief to the Syrian border.

In 1960, for various reasons, this did not result in war. In 1967, however, after the Egyptian blockade of the Tiran Straits, the Soviet Union lost control of the situation and the ball passed into the hands of Egypt and Israel.

When, after the first day of the Six-Day War, the extent of the Egyptian defeat became evident to Moscow, the Soviets were faced with a dilemma much greater than that which had confronted them after the 1956 Sinai Campaign. If they allowed the Egyptian army to collapse completely, they would be accused of desertion by the Egyptians and the Arabs in general. If they intervened with limited forces against Israel, there was the risk of being countered by Israel. If they sent an ultimatum, a meaningful ultimatum, it might involve them in a global confrontation. (President Johnson made it quite clear to Premier Kosygin that both powers must refrain from intervention, and in support of his words he sent the Sixth Fleet to the Eastern Mediterranean.) The speed of the Israeli action, however, denied the Russians sufficient time to maneuver or to redeem the situation.

This was repeated on the Syrian front a few days later. Once again, in order to save her position in Egypt and Syria, the Soviet Union took it upon herself to rebuild the armed forces of these two countries. The rapid supply of war matériel was unprecedented both in quantity and quality. This, in turn, necessitated an increasing number of Soviet advisers assigned to various formations down to battalion level. The recompense received by the Soviets was bases for their naval and air forces, as well as shore services for the former. These bases are part of the Soviet Union's global deployment and serve as a possible alternative to aircraft carriers.

Soviet aid to the Arab countries also took the form of support in the United Nations. At first, the Soviet condition for a cease-fire was a total Israel withdrawal. When the Americans rejected this and the Israelis continued to advance rapidly, the Russians agreed to a cease-fire without preconditions and without immediate withdrawal.

Again, when Security Council Resolution 242, of November 1967, was in the process of formulation, the Soviets attempted to pressurize the Council into passing a clear-cut resolution demanding

Israel's complete withdrawal from all occupied territories. This was rejected by the United States and Britain, and eventually the now-famous British proposal was adopted.

I shall not dwell on the War of Attrition, except for a few points. There is no doubt that the decision to start this was Egyptian, but it nevertheless had Soviet blessing. When it became clear that the network of S–2 missiles could not stand up to Israel's flying artillery—if I may so call the Israel Air Force—the Soviet Union supplied Egypt with more modern missiles, the Sam–3 and even more sophisticated models. As Israel remained superior in the air, the Soviet Union passed from assistance to involvement, with Soviet crews taking an active part in the defense of the Egyptian skies.

There are different views on the reasons for the Soviet decision to shift to involvement. Some maintain that it was taken when it became clear to them that their antiaircraft defenses had failed in the first phase of the War of Attrition. This is backed up by information gathered by Israel's intelligence services. Also, President Sadat, in an interview with James Reston,[2] actually gave support to this view. Others claim that the escalation of Soviet involvement came as a direct result of the Israeli air raids deep into Egyptian territory. Well, as the late President Ben-Zvi used to say, you do not argue with information: you either accept it or reject it. For my part, I think we can rely on Israel's intelligence services.

Nasser's appeal to the Soviet Union for direct involvement came as a result of Israel's devastating attacks along the Suez Canal zone, and this was *before* the beginning of the air raids in depth. At that time I was among those who supported the policy of air raids on military targets deep inside Egyptian territory. Bringing home to the Egyptian people, who were being fed false information, a true recognition of the war situation was not less important than causing damage to military targets. I hoped that these raids would achieve a cease-fire, for obviously it is easier to proceed from a cease-fire to a peace treaty than from active hostilities.

The American peace initiative which led to the cease-fire in August 1970—with all my appreciation for it, and I was among those who welcomed it—would not have been feasible had it not been made abundantly clear to Nasser that the War of Attrition against Israel, even if it caused Israel casualties, was wearing Egypt down to a much greater extent. I maintain that, despite the loss of several Phantoms,

Israel could have held out indefinitely in this type of war. It may be recalled, in this connection, that shortly before the cease-fire came into force several Soviet-manned planes were shot down. It was Israel's success in this limited war that paved the way for the American initiative designed by President Nixon.

The question is sometimes asked: Does the Soviet Union desire the destruction of Israel? My answer would be: No, but she might not do anything to prevent it. At any rate, Professor Kolkovicz is probably correct when he says that the Soviets find a continuing situation of no peace-no war quite to their liking. Israel, for her part, would prefer, for obvious reasons, a peace treaty to this uneasy situation of neither peace nor war.

Another question might be asked. Do Soviet and Egyptian interests in this conflict converge? My answer would be: Not always. While the Egyptians favor pan-Arabism under their hegemony, the Russians are cool toward this idea, although they do not always oppose it publicly. While the Egyptians desire an early resumption of hostilities and are interested in Soviet intervention, the Soviets exert a restraining influence upon them. Although the Soviets would, in my opinion, like to see the Suez reopened, the Egyptians are less enthusiastic about this for they are afraid of losing a bargaining position. However, were the Egyptians able to secure total Israeli withdrawal, they evidently would agree to the opening of the Canal.

Yet what interest could Israel have in a partial settlement that entailed complete withdrawal? Tito, after his recent visit to Cairo, declared that if Israel agreed to the Egyptian conditions, the Soviets would evacuate Egypt. President Sadat, on the other hand, has stated that even after peace with Israel is achieved, the Egyptian army would continue to rely on Soviet advisers and the Soviet navy would continue to receive services in Egyptian ports. By such contradictory declarations the Egyptians hope to appease both the Soviets and the Americans. I doubt if the Soviets would indeed agree to leave the Mediterranean for less than an American response in kind.

To sum up, so far Egypt has been on the losing side in three wars and has exchanged Western imperialism for a Soviet one—not particularly felicitous achievements. If Egypt does not wish to become totally subservient to the Soviet Union, if she really desires peace before the Brezhnev doctrine is imposed upon her,[3] she has little to lose and everything to gain from direct contact with Israel, exploring with her the way to a brighter future for the whole of this region.

NOTES

[1] See Uri Ra'anan, *The U.S.S.R. Arms the Third World* (M.I.T. Press, Boston 1969), p. 76 ff.

[2] *New York Times*, 28 December, 1970.

[3] For the development of this theme see Jigal Allon, . . . *und David ergriff die Schleuder* (Colloquium Verlag, Berlin 1971), pp. 127–136.

J. C. HUREWITZ

SUPERPOWER RIVALRY AND THE ARAB-ISRAEL DISPUTE: INVOLVEMENT OR COMMITMENT?

Ever since the start of the Cold War in the mid-1940s, the Soviet Union and the United States have been on a collision course. As the sharpening rivalry assumed a nuclear shape, the superpowers began to take precautions to avoid a nuclear war. By agreeing to such measures as the hot line, the Test Ban Treaty, the Nonproliferation Treaty, and the current Strategic Arms Limitation Talks (SALT), the Soviet Union has sought to negotiate with the United States from a position of parity. In the Middle East, the superpower rivalry has not yet risen above the stage of the Cold War.

Mutually infectious, the lingering Cold War in the Middle East and the unresolved Arab-Israel dispute have interlocked. Unlike the Suez-Sinai war of a decade earlier, the Six-Day War did not directly involve the extraregional powers, thus letting the regional belligerents reach their own temporary level of accommodation. The emphatically one-sided outcome deeply humiliated the Arab states. Egypt in particular has insisted on redressing the balance. It has been prepared to pay for increased military aid even in political coin, by the offer of bases to the Soviet Union. To appreciate the depth of Egyptian frustration that the consent to the continuous Soviet military presence on Egyptian soil must entail, one need only recall that it was little more than a decade and a half ago, after a bitter struggle, that Egypt finally rid itself of foreign bases under the hated preferential alliance with Britain.

Profoundly embarrassed by the massive defeat of its protégés (Egypt and Syria) in 1967, the Soviet Union also wanted to redress the balance and, in the process, to continue expanding its influence. It accordingly stepped up the arms resupply to Egypt, adding new types of weapons in the bargain. The Soviet Union also underwrote Egypt's attritional war of 1969–70, and when Egypt lost that war, took the quantum jump of sending missiles and planes from its current inventory for an air-defense system managed by Soviet combat personnel. The United States, which at first dragged its feet, resumed shipment of new weapons to Israel early in 1968 by delivering A-4 Skyhawks

155

which had been on order before the war. The F-4 Phantoms, the contract for which had been approved in December 1968, began reaching Israel in September 1969. Within four months, the Israel Air Force put the new planes into active service.

Did the Sovietization of the air defense of Egypt in 1970 mean that the U.S.S.R. was committing itself to defend Egypt in any fresh encounter with Israel? Did the United States balancing support to Israel imply a balancing commitment? If so, the superpower rivalry in the Arab-Israel zone might be recreating conditions comparable to those of July-August 1914 and capable of producing World War III. Are the superpowers actually on such a collision course in the Middle East? To answer that question, we must first examine the deepening superpower entanglement in the Arab-Israel dispute.

Traditionally, the Middle East has been an area of Western predominance and exclusive presence. It has also traditionally been an area of primary Russian strategic interest. This is the stuff of contention. The record of the past century and a half amply confirms that recurrent crises have divided tsarist and Soviet Russia from the Western maritime powers in the Middle East—in the 1830s, 1850s, and 1870s, in the two world wars and the years that immediately followed each, and then almost steadily since the mid-1950s. From the start of the interrupted rivalry in the 19th century, the concerned extraregional powers have used the offer of modern weapons and of training in modern methods of military organization as a form of bribery or coercion in efforts to bend to their will the regional governments.

The international environment in which Middle East regional politics has unfolded is now in transition. In the years between the two world wars, the Middle East was subordinated to a system of Anglo-French hegemony. That hegemony survived the first postwar decade behind the facade of the growing military-political engagement of the United States, only to be replaced after the Suez crisis of 1956 by a Pax Americana, which in turn began to disintegrate after the Six-Day War because of the reluctance of the United States to continue carrying such burdens alone. The self-contracting American influence induced an expanding Soviet influence in the Middle East, producing a lively competition whose outcome remains uncertain. One such outcome, a *Pax Sovietica*, seems almost certain, unless the two superpowers stabilize the international system in the Middle East under their joint sponsorship or find some multilateral alternative.

Actually, in the Middle East Cold War, which began before the end of World War II, the Soviet Union and the Western powers have been using a wide assortment of tactics—propaganda, economic and technical assistance, cultural export, mutual deterrence, and preeminently the attempted manipulation for political influence of arms transfers to their respective protégés. The Soviet-American arms-transfer rivalry, after 1967, has been unprecedented in scale, in sophistication of weaponry, and in risks taken by patrons and protégés alike. In propaganda rhetoric as in actual policy, the U.S.S.R. has deliberately tried to forestall the American attempt to preserve the "military balance" in the Arab-Israel zone by steadily enlarging its own presence in Egypt and by trying to force the United States to suspend its balancing support, and preferably to abandon it altogether. The Phantom or F-4 has become the symbol of such support, as has also in the past year the American endorsement of Israel's position for a limited agreement on reopening the Suez Canal.

In propaganda rhetoric and in actual policy, the United States has tried to keep the cease-fire alive and to help the parties move toward a limited canal settlement. In its search for such an accord, the United States has been seeking to hold Israel's loyalty while appealing for Egypt's confidence. American diplomatic tactics have rested on the assumption that goodwill toward Israel has been amply demonstrated by military, economic, and diplomatic assistance. The United States has solicited Egypt's cooperation by interrupting in June 1971 the flow of F-4s to Israel and by accepting for negotiating purposes the Egyptian terms that such a limited arrangement must be viewed as only the first step toward a full withdrawal with a fixed period for the next phase, and the right to deploy Egyptian soldiers in Sinai as the Israeli troops retire. In 1971, each of these concessions by the United States, acting as mediator, aroused distrust in Israel of its major benefactor.

Early in 1972, the United States reversed itself by resuming the delivery of F-4s and A-4s under a long-term contract and the support of Israel's negotiating position on Suez. As might have been expected, Egypt immediately backed away from the American initiatives. Israel sees no advantage in Egyptian terms, particularly in the six-month limit on the cease-fire before the next stage of withdrawal from Sinai, since Israel would be abandoning a position of military strength and therefore of diplomatic advantage without any concrete return. By the same token, Egypt sees no advantage in a limited withdrawal without a deadline, since it would be conceding to Israel the right to retain permanent possession of Sharm al-Sheikh and the Aqabah coast between there and Eilat. Little wonder that by February 1972 Egypt showed less enthusiasm for the renewed American proposal for proximity talks than for a renewal of Ambassador Gunnar V. Jarring's efforts at good offices. In brief, the diplomatic tactics of the United States, designed to pry Israel and Egypt loose, seemed instead to have fastened them all the harder to their fixed moorings.

Let us pause for a moment to get our analytical bearings. The present paper examines the military-political dimension of superpower rivalry as it focuses on the Arab-Israel dispute. The identity of the superpowers is clear. There are still only two, the United States and the Soviet Union. Whether the People's Republic of China (P.R.C.) will ever develop into a third superpower remains to be seen. In the present analysis, the P.R.C. receives no more than marginal consideration. Now that it is a member of the United Nations, with a permanent seat in the Security Council, its views on the Middle East will be heard more frequently than at any time in the past; and its actions, particularly if it should exercise the veto in the Security Council, as it may be expected to do, will occasionally command attention.

The P.R.C. has already signaled, for example, that it will uphold the Palestine Arab cause, which both superpowers have been trying to sweep under the rug. Security Council Resolution 242 of 22 November 1967, which sets forth the Council's unanimous guidelines for an Arab-Israel settlement, does not even mention the Palestine Arabs by name. It takes little imagination to foresee the likelihood that consistent Chinese opposition will neutralize even that slender instrument for the promotion of a settlement. Like the U.S.S.R. in the first postwar decade, the P.R.C. in the 1970s may be counted on to play the spoiler role in the Middle East, trading on Soviet-American rivalry and on the Arab-Israel dispute. Such a role may best be defined as the exercise of influence without responsibility, as a means of diminishing the influence of both superpowers.

To simplify the analysis, I shall consider on the Arab side Egypt alone, introducing other Arab states and the Palestine Arabs only when making a special point. What the analysis may thereby lose in precision, it should more than make up in simplicity and clarity. In the Arab-Israel dispute, when all is said and done, only Egypt can take the first step toward a settlement. Other Arab states may or may not follow. But if they do not follow, neither can they lead.

Even using such distortive shorthand, the analysis is bewildering enough. We are considering two pairs of actors, one regional and the other extraregional. Each actor, in order to uphold its own interests, pursues its own policies, either alone or in partnership with one or more of the other actors. For the superpowers, the Middle East is just one aspect of a rivalry that is global; in that global competition, the Middle East as such is important but not vital. Each superpower, moreover, is paired off with a regional protégé. Policy differences between the Soviet Union and Egypt over how to deal with the American-Israel coalition rarely come into the open. By contrast, American-Israel differences over how to deal with the Soviet-Egyptian coalition often form the subject of public debate, at times acrimonious. Egypt has not yet restored full diplomatic relations with the United States, but the *ad hoc* arrangements are sometimes as intimate as any formal relations in the past. The Soviet Union, which similarly has not resumed normal relations with Israel, has nonetheless signaled more than once in the past year a desire for reopening a diplomatic dialogue short of re-exchanging embassies. In a word, the superpowers have been trading on the regional dispute, and the regional disputants, on the super-power rivalry.

The four actors employ their own terminology. Their most favorite concept these days is "the military balance." There are of course two balances that come into account, the superpower and the regional. The two interplay. But we need not rehearse, let alone evaluate, the details of the evolving strategic balance between the superpowers. That is the concern of the peppery exchanges of SALT, which by all present testimony are moving ahead only a trifle less slowly than the multiple talks in varying spheres through many media on a limited or full, interim or final, bilateral or multilateral Arab-Israel settlement.

Even the regional military balance is not a concept that lends itself to exactitude. For Israel and the United States, a regional military balance means the preservation of Israel's military superiority. That doctrine's corollary is immutable inferiority for the other side. Such a corollary, no self-esteeming Egyptian government can accept. For Egypt and the Soviet Union, regional military balance means equality for Egypt now and superiority later. Almost all Israelis are convinced that Egyptian military superiority will lead ultimately to the destruction of their state. In such a doctrine, the Israelis can hardly be expected to acquiesce.

Superiority is achieved and kept through effectiveness in military organization, size of available and trained manpower, quantity and quality of weapons and their assimilation into the military organization, quality of military and political leadership, military doctrine and planning, economic mobilization, and morale of the population—to mention only the more significant elements that enter into the reckoning. When Melvin Laird or Moshe Dayan, Andrei Grechko, or Muhammad Ahmad Sadiq or any of his predecessors have mentioned the Arab-Israel military balance in the past year or two, they did not invariably have in mind all these considerations.

Commonly, they have thought of weapons, showing preference for quality, but not ignoring quantity altogether. Still, when Laird says that the balance has not been tipped in Israel's disfavor, he is using the concept in its more comprehensive sense and is thinking about present conditions. When Dayan expresses anxiety about the interruption of F-4 deliveries or the American refusal to sell more F-4s to Israel, he is thinking about a weapons balance and about the future conditions in the Arab-Israel zone.

One note of caution: this paper attempts to determine whether or not the accelerating superpower rivalry for influence through arms exports to Egypt and Israel carries with it a commitment by each superpower to insure that its protégé will not lose the next war. I am not writing policy, I am analyzing it. Nor is my analysis to be construed as advocacy.

Up to the decision by the Soviet and Egyptian governments early in 1970 to Sovietize the air defense of Egypt, the American intervention in Lebanon in 1958 excepted, the superpowers had refrained from deploying their own fighting personnel in the theater of dispute and intermittent combat. The appearance in Egypt of Soviet-manned SA-3s broke the ice. Moscow did not even share that untested missile system with North Vietnam. The United States received advance assurance that the introduction of Soviet fighting personnel into Egypt to operate such a sophisticated weapon system was essential for the defense of a hard-pressed protégé. The SA-3, the United States was told, would be emplaced only around Cairo, Alexandria, and the Aswan Dam. In March and April 1970, even before the concrete had been poured for the SA-3 launching pads in the enumerated localities and without prior notice to Washington, Soviet pilots and ground crews reached Egypt together with MiG-21Js, the latest version of the fighter interceptor, ostensibly to protect the launching pads. With the Sovietization of Egypt's air defense, the entangling superpower and regional military rivalry in the Arab-Israel zone changed character.

There was no longer need to inquire whether the Soviet Union would intervene in the Arab-Israel dispute. It had already done so. But did intervention mean commitment? That was the new question. The American pledge that the regional military balance would not be changed in Israel's disfavor, renewed on the eve of the cease-fire and confirmed soon after it went into effect, related to the balancing of equipment, not to the balancing of forces. Israel's military-political strategy nevertheless has been based on the assumption that American military power would remain in the eastern Mediterranean to deter the Soviet Union from open participation in a full-scale regional war.

Such a war would not necessarily be one that arrayed Israel against all the Arab states, or even against all its nextdoor neighbors. It might mean a war between Israel and Egypt alone. In the event of a fifth round—the fourth having been Egypt's attritional war—how would the superpowers react? Would they be compelled to take part openly and actively? Or would the Soviet Union, as it did in 1970, fight cautiously and anonymously, and on a severely circumscribed scale? Would the United States, as it has invariably done in the past in the Arab-Israel dispute, deter the Soviet Union from taking part in hostilities on a "grand scale"—viewed regionally—but otherwise remain on the sidelines as a generous weapons-supplier?

The central question of superpower commitment is not necessarily a legal one. Neither superpower, I suspect, has given its protégé an unequivocal security guarantee in the event of a military showdown. Whether or not this is a question of legality, the existence or nonexistence of a formal security guarantee does have a bearing on the superpower military balance in the Mediterranean and the Middle East, which is unavoidably affected by what the United States and Soviet Union do, or do not do, in the Arab-Israel zone. That balance is also conditioned by domestic considerations at each superpower's home, chiefly the resolve or lack of resolve to play the role of a global power.

As regards the superpower military balance in the Mediterranean and the Middle East, it could be said at the start of the cease-fire in August 1970 that the United States still clung to its superiority. It continued occupying the No. 1 position for technical rather than practical reasons, because of the unmatched firepower of the Sixth Fleet. What was uncertain then, and is even more uncertain today, is not the fire power but the will power of the United States to use that force.

The continuing domestic dissensus over Vietnam, and the consequent pressure for curtailing American military commitments, reflected in the Nixon Doctrine for winding them down, have progressively weakened American credibility in the use of military power to uphold a political principle. As No. 2, the Soviet Union has been trying harder to put an end to American paramountcy in the Middle East. It has done what any state that is expanding its power position across the globe would do in similar circumstances: it has taken advantage of its rival's disarray to expand its own influence.

From the outset in the mid-1950s, the Soviet Union has built its military-political position in the Arab-Israel zone by engaging in the diplomacy of polarization. It has created the image among Arabs that the U.S.S.R. alone among all interested extraregional powers has consistently supported the Arab case against Israel, and that the United States has no less consistently supported Israel. Before June 1967, the Kremlin distinguished between what it labeled "progressive" Arab governments (all of which were military republics, and all of them military clients of the Soviet Union) and the "reactionary" Arab governments (the nonmilitary regimes that still inclined toward the West). In those days, Moscow scarcely concealed its encouragement of the "progressives" to overthrow the "reactionary" regimes.

The United States pursued the reactive diplomacy of antipolarization. The United States backed Israel without formal guarantee, but with implied assurance that it would not allow the destruction of the state. At the same time, the United States continued its policy of keeping friendly Arab states friendly, although such activity has slowed down steadily, as one Arab state after another suffered military takeover, putting an end to civilian political systems and bringing to power military juntas that procured their arms from the Soviet Union. Even when they did not, as in the case of Libya after September 1969, the military republics nevertheless remained suspicious of the United States and the West. The diplomacy of antipolarization is commonly called a policy of evenhandedness, a cliché that has come to be associated with Governor Scranton's report to President-elect Nixon in December 1968, but was already in occasional use much earlier. The arms-transfer rivalry between the superpowers acquired a momentum of its own. The major changes over time can be briefly summarized. The Soviet Union did not take long to become a direct salesman to Egypt, after initially using Czechoslovakia as a facade. Moscow lifted most limits on quantity and progressively on quality, thus requiring the Western suppliers to do the same, although exceptionally the qualitative lead might be taken by the West as in the American sale of F-4s to Israel.

Meanwhile, the United States had preferred to let its European allies, chiefly France but also Britain and Germany, become the main suppliers of Israel. The United States served as the grand coordinator of allied arms exports to Israel and to friendly Arab states, but did not participate in the traffic of major equipment until 1963, when Washington started selling Hawk missiles to Israel. By 1965, the United States had become a principal dispenser to Israel and to neighboring Arab states, primarily Jordan and Saudi Arabia. These efforts formed part of the diplomacy of antipolarization, and the United States tried to balance sales—not quantities but systems—to Israel and to these Arab states, and to announce the sales in such a way as to make clear that its policy was evenhanded. The announcement itself on each occasion seemed more important to the Department of State than the sales themselves.

The massive defeat of Egypt and Syria in June 1967 proved a near disaster for Soviet policy in the Middle East. With its two major protégés so prostrated by the war, the U.S.S.R. had little choice but to airlift fresh supplies, particularly to Egypt, if it was to salvage any influence in the Arab East. Because of the distractions in Vietnam, however, the United States proved unable to derive any durable benefits. In the circumstances, the Soviet Union had sufficiently recovered by the spring of 1969 that it could go along with, if it did not actually take part in the planning of, the limited war that Egypt unleashed against Israel. The Soviet Union furnished the ammunition and replacements, presumably on its own account.

Not unrelated to the arms transfers to Egypt and Israel was the naval rivalry between the superpowers. The ease with which the United States was able by naval action to force the Soviet Union to withdraw its missiles from Cuba in October 1962 seems to have driven home the point to the security planners in Moscow that being a superpower is not the same as being a global power. In any event, whether by coincidence or design, only after that time did the U.S.S.R. begin to build a continuous naval presence in the Mediterranean. Slow before the Six-Day War, the buildup of the Soviet Mediterranean Squadron, after it, became impressive, commanding the attention of the United States and of the riverine members of N.A.T.O. In fact, by the fall of 1967 the squadron had acquired limited naval-base rights in Alexandria and Port Said for repair and replenishment, and by May 1968 even more limited air-base rights for Tu-16s on Soviet reconnaissance missions over the Sixth Fleet in the mid-Mediterranean.

The Red Navy does not now have aircraft carriers and therefore must depend on a land-based air arm. With the takeover of Egypt's air defense in 1970, the U.S.S.R. was able simultaneously to provide the Egyptian armed forces with air support and the Mediterranean Squadron with air cover. There is evidence that the Red Navy is building an experimental small carrier. Since the construction of large carriers in appropriate numbers and their assimilation into the navy would take more than a decade and cost billions of rubles, the procurement of air bases in Egypt in 1970—even at the price of paying for all the military equipment sent to Egypt since the Six-Day War—is a bargain.

The superpower naval rivalry in the Mediterranean is sometimes assumed to be leading toward World War III. The primary mission of the two navies in the Mediterranean is of course not strategic but conventional, in support of regional diplomacy. The Sixth Fleet, it is true, occasionally includes Polaris submarines with nuclear missiles, thus enabling it marginally to contribute to the strategic deterrence of the Soviet Union. But the Soviet Union cannot respond in kind in the Mediterranean because of the limited range of submarine-borne nuclear missiles. On strategic assignment, Soviet submarines must operate in the Atlantic or the Pacific.

The superpowers, it may safely be assumed, are more interested in each other than in their respective Middle East protégés. Despite the growing Soviet entanglement in Egypt, the decision-makers in the Kremlin seem to have taken every measure to elude formal commitment. Wholly understandable was the U.S.S.R.'s failure to intervene in the Suez crisis of 1956, except verbally, since it could not have taken any belligerent steps in the face of overwhelming American power. By agreement with the United States on Soviet initiative, the U.S.S.R. again stayed out of the war in June 1967. In the Egyptian attritional war of 1969, Russian soldiers did not fight, though many of the technicians and advisers in the military units, down to the battalion level, were doubtless caught in the exchange of fire from time to time. Even after the destruction of the four MiG-21Js on 30 July 1970, the Soviet Government insistently refused to acknowledge its combat presence in Egypt. Manifestly, the Kremlin was prepared to sacrifice manpower rather than escalate the fighting and invite possible confrontation with the United States.

We are now able to assess the significance of the cease-fire of August 1970. It is not generally recognized that the United States brought off its *coup* from a position of diplomatic weakness. Egypt, with Soviet approval, seems to have consented to the cease-fire precisely because of that. The Egyptians must have calculated in advance that going along with the United States would give them an opportunity to move their missile launching pads much closer to the canal without major loss of life and with only minimal risk of escalating the war. This was amply confirmed by the swiftness with which it was accomplished after the agreement. Whether or not the installations would have been withdrawn, had the United States taken a firm position immediately on detection of the violation, must remain a hypothetical question. Israel, too, benefited from the American diplomatic weakness, for once the United States belatedly acknowledged the Egyptian violations with Soviet connivance, it honored its pledge to restore Israel's military advantage. The United States replaced Israel aircraft lost in combat and agreed to sell additional Phantoms and Skyhawks. To these were now added Shrike missiles and Walleye winged bombs as countersystems to the Soviet antiaircraft missiles and radar, as well as a variety of highly sophisticated electronic equipment for jamming enemy radar and guidance signals.

The unexpected death of Nasser at the end of September 1970 changed the diplomatic game overnight. Ever since the Six-Day War the U.S.S.R. had come to rely increasingly on Egypt as the instrument and the center for erecting a solid military-political position in the eastern Mediterranean. That linchpin was suddenly removed. Nasser had created a one-man political system in Egypt and had used it to fill the role of Arab unity leader throughout the Arab world. His removal thus created a dual problem of succession, in Egypt and in the Arab unity movement. No other Arab state could claim a pervasive presence in the Arab world, and therefore none could take Egypt's place as unity leader.

This was amply demonstrated when Colonel Muammar al-Qadhafi tried but failed to use Libya's massive economic resources to buy such leadership. Moreover, the very acceptance of the cease-fire by Egypt (and Jordan) had already shattered Arab ranks. Deliberately ignored were the protests of the Palestine Arabs, who vociferously opposed the cease-fire, as did also the so-called radical Arab governments—Syria, Iraq, and Algeria. Even before Nasser's death, King Hussein had badly crippled the Palestine resistance movement in Jordan and destroyed its headquarters there. He later compelled Iraq to pull its troops out of his kingdom. Nasser's death before he could mediate the quarrels precipitated by Hussein's forcible action left the Arab world in even greater disarray.

The Kremlin had to take careful stock of the new but uncertain alignment of forces in Egypt and the Arab world. There could be no advance assurance that Anwar al-Sadat would develop staying powers. Even if he did, there was still less assurance that he would win wide popularity either at home or beyond Egypt's borders. Egypt's planned renewal of the cease-fire in November revealed the lack of diplomatic maneuverability. Even Israel's failure to respond imaginatively to Ambassador Jarring's diplomatic initiative in January-February 1971, supported by the two superpowers, although it weakened Israel's diplomatic position, did not measurably strengthen Egypt's.

Meanwhile, the de facto continuance of the cease-fire after March 1971 gave the United States, for the first time in many years, a practical opportunity to mediate between the contestants. The Department of State adopted and reshaped Dayan's vague suggestion for a limited agreement on the reopening of the Suez Canal. Whether or not Secretary William P. Rogers' personal negotiations in Egypt and Israel in May 1971 were beginning to produce results, the Soviet Union seemed to feel that they were. Moscow presumably discouraged Sadat from further cooperation with the United States on a canal agreement at that time. In doing so, the Kremlin was disclosing its displeasure at seeing any agreement under the sole sponsorship of the United States. From such an agreement the Soviet Union could neither gain any prestige nor be assured any voice in supervising the execution of the terms.

In brief, the diplomacy of polarization seemed to have run its course. Following the disappearance of Nasser, the U.S.S.R. had gained influence in Egypt but had lost flexibility in the Arab world. The Soviet Union was becoming committed to protecting Egypt against its Arab adversaries, while trying to avoid military commitments in Egypt's struggle with Israel. All the major political developments since May 1971 in Egypt, in the Arab states, and in the Arab dispute with Israel confirm the Soviet need to develop a fresh diplomatic strategy for dealing with this part of the world. The internal political crisis in Egypt in mid-May removed from the scene many of the ablest political opponents of Sadat, thus narrowing the Soviet choice. Sadat's support of Jafar al-Numeiri in Sudan in July underlined for the Kremlin that it had been dealing in Egypt with a nationalist movement that could not be taken for granted. This helps explain why President Nikolai V. Podgorny went to Cairo at the end of May to sign the treaty with Egypt in person as reinsurance against abrupt political changes in the future. The odds are against the Soviet Union's being able to hold on to its bases in Egypt indefinitely under such a treaty. It is saddled, meantime, with the rising cost of keeping an unreliable Egyptian friendship alive.

This of course does not mean that the United States is getting off scot free. Furthermore, the arms-transfer rivalry has brought to the Egyptian-Israel cease-fire line sophisticated military equipment that is not even available on the line dividing N.A.T.O. from the Warsaw Pact. Egypt and Israel have been overinvesting in their armed forces and have come to solicit more and more economic aid from their patrons. Egypt has never recovered from the severe economic depression into which it was plunged by the 1967 war. Similarly, Israel's crash investment in military industry in the same period has begun to overheat the economy and retard the expansion. Yet even these economic levers do not give the superpowers a commanding voice in the domestic policies of either country and give only a limited influence over the formulation of foreign policies. The United States clearly cannot induce Israel to take any step that its leaders regard as undermining the state's security. Nor can Egypt be expected invariably to resist the pressures that come from neighboring Arab states on policies affecting Arab unity. In short, the two regional protégés have been expressing less than unqualified confidence in their superpower patrons.

The Israel strategy before the Six-Day War of avoiding total or near-total reliance on a single outside power helps explain the high investment in military industry after that war. Israel's occasional defiance of the United States was most recently expressed on the proposed interim canal agreement. Comparably, in the attempted production of missiles and jet planes in the early 1960s, Egypt was barely concealing its basic suspicion of the political reliability of Soviet weapons. And, as we have seen, Egypt's stand on Sudan in the summer of 1971 openly courted Soviet wrath.

Nevertheless, despite these underlying differences, the superpower rivalry has reinforced the ties between the United States and Israel as well as between the U.S.S.R. and Egypt. Each superpower has tried in its own way to decouple its adversary's patron-protégé linkages. This the United States has sought to accomplish by trying to persuade Egypt to reach an interim agreement with Israel and also by playing on Egypt's manifest anxiety over its growing dependence on the Soviet Union. The U.S.S.R. in turn has promoted the separation of the United States from Israel, while simultaneously proclaiming their inseparability, by trying to pressure the United States into stopping arms aid to Israel and into forcing Israel to agree to the unconditional evacuation of Sinai.

While it is obvious that the superpowers are profoundly involved in the politics of their protégés, their inability to control protégé policies created the dilemma of how to deal with any war that might be started by either Egypt or Israel against its patron's wishes. Those who contend that the superpowers might slide unwillingly, and perhaps unwittingly, into an Arab-Israel war favor a scenario that looks like this: War breaks out because the Arab states feel they cannot allow the situation to harden the accomplished fact into an accepted fact. They therefore start a war that they know they will lose. The fighting escalates because Israel cannot allow the Arab states to nibble away at its limited manpower. The Arab states in turn escalate further to remain in the fighting. Then Israel escalates still further, finally bringing the Soviet Union in, first with antiaircraft and then with aircraft, with Israel responding in kind. But Israel cannot long sustain the fighting with the Soviet Union, and ultimately the United States too goes belligerent.

This is a grossly simplified scenario, but one that is not entirely implausible. In brief, unless the superpowers are able to restrain themselves in situations that begin to get out of hand, they may discover that they too are losing control. The Soviet Union, for example, could easily feel that its entire investment in the Arab area is at stake, and if it does not go to the aid of the Arabs it might lose everything. The

United States on its side cannot see Israel on the verge of destruction without going to its aid.

There is, however, an overriding restraint for the superpowers—the determination to avoid a nuclear confrontation. For neither super-power is the Middle East an area of supreme importance. It is therefore not a region in which such a confrontation is likely to take place. One may therefore assume that any war started by the protégés, without the concurrence of their patrons, would be fought by the regional powers alone. All of this rests on the further assumption that the Soviet Union is convinced that its own active participation would be likely to force the United States to come in as well. The high American domestic interest in Israel, which runs contrary to the prevailing mood of con-traction of foreign military commitments, must keep the Kremlin guessing.

Thus, we are left with the following assessment: Involvement without commitment is irresponsible. On the other hand, if the super-powers are to avoid confrontation which might lead to nuclear war, they must avoid such commitments. That is the responsible position to take. Responsibility in superpower politics thus becomes irresponsibility in regional politics. This is the superpower dilemma in the Middle East.[1]

[1] This paper was completed in January 1972 and has not been revised.

4. ECONOMIC CONSIDERATIONS

ABRAHAM S. BECKER

OIL AND THE PERSIAN GULF
IN SOVIET POLICY IN THE 1970s*

From the inception of the cold war at the end of World War II, the West has been concerned about the Soviet threat to the security of its Middle East oil investments and supply lines. Stalin's bid to set up a Soviet republic in Persian Azerbaidzhan and Kurdistan in 1946 was accompanied by an attempt to impose a joint Soviet-Iranian oil company on a reluctant Tehran. Just a few years later, an Iranian nationalist with chief support in the Tudeh Communists nationalized the oil industry, although only for a brief interval. As Western Europe increasingly turned from coal to oil for its chief energy source, the Soviet Union emerged as a major factor on the Middle East scene in alliance with vocally anti-Western Arab regimes. The closure of the Suez Canal in 1956 and the oil crisis it engendered spurred exploration and development of North African fields, located west of the vulnerable Canal and then still in friendly hands. The Arab-Israel War in June 1967, in the outbreak of which the U.S.S.R. played a conspicuous role, brought with it a second closure of the Canal and an attempt at an Arab embargo on oil sales to the U.S.A. and Britain.

With respect to oil, the events of 1967 were only a prelude to probably more significant developments. Over the last few years the host countries have forced the international oil companies to swallow stiff increases in posted prices and taxes. During the negotiations, the producers threatened nationalization of foreign-held assets and embargoes on shipments if the oil companies did not meet their demands. Partial or selective nationalization actually took place in four countries. In February 1971 Algeria took over majority control in all French oil interests in the country and nationalized French gas pipelines. At the end of that year, Libya, which had helped precipitate a world fuel crisis in 1970 by forcing the oil companies to curtail output, nationalized British Petroleum Co. assets in

* Any views expressed in this paper are those of the author. They should not be interpreted as reflecting the views of The Rand Corporation or the official opinion or policy of any of its governmental or private research sponsors. The author is grateful to William Quandt for his comments and criticisms. He has also benefited from reading an unpublished paper by Edward Luttwak.

173

reaction to the Iranian seizure of three islands in the Persian Gulf. On June 1, 1972, Iraq nationalized the Kirkuk fields and related assets of the Western-owned Iraq Petroleum Company, while Syria, in sympathy, seized the I.P.C. pipeline section running through her territory.

The growing militancy of the oil producers heightens Western anxieties already aroused by the deepening involvement of the Soviet Union in Middle East affairs. In one degree or another, the U.S.S.R. seems to be active all over the region's map, from the Atlantic to the Indian Ocean. Moscow is, or was, the largest arms supplier to Algeria, Egypt, Syria, Iraq, Sudan, Yemen, and South Yemen. The Soviet navy makes its presence known not just in the Mediterranean but in the Persian Gulf and Indian Ocean as well, and, no doubt, would do so more often if not for the continued closure of the Suez Canal. Moscow extends clear verbal support to the main guerrilla movement in Oman and may be supplying arms as well. At the same time, friendly relations are sought with Turkey and Iran, with whom trade and aid relations are by now surprisingly extensive.

But is the U.S.S.R. interested in Middle East oil? For what purposes and under what circumstances? Given the significance of oil in the Middle East, and especially in the Persian Gulf, there is a fine line that must distinguish Soviet interests in the region's oil from those related to other geopolitical considerations. Moscow is undoubtedly pressing to root out Anglo-American influence and presence. Especially in the Persian Gulf, these are intertwined with relations between the foreign oil companies and the producing states. The Soviet Union could not be indifferent to Persian Gulf oil affairs if she was at all concerned with the politics of the region.

Of course, proximity to the Soviet Union bears its own imperative. This was an area of interest to Russia's rulers long before its petroleum wealth was dreamed of. Up to the Bolshevik Revolution and beyond, Turkey and Persia (in an earlier period Afghanistan, too) were the focus of imperial interest, not the Arab provinces of the Ottoman Empire, and not even Egypt. When in the secret Nazi-Soviet negotiations in 1940 Stalin expressed longer-term territorial ambitions, it was in "the area south of Batum and Baku, in the general direction of the Persian Gulf." At the conclusion of the war, Moscow demanded parts of Eastern Turkey and restated its long-standing desire to control the Turkish straits. Even the first successful foothold the Soviet Union gained in the Arab world in the 1950s resulted from Moscow's efforts to frustrate Big Three attempts to organize an anti-Soviet alliance on the U.S.S.R.'s southern doorstep.

Since the breakthrough of the Egyptian arms agreement in 1955, Soviet Middle East policy has focused on the radical Arab states. However, in the middle 1960s increasing attention was paid to "non-progressive" states in the region—particularly Turkey and Iran. A revised policy line stressed rapprochement in contrast to the belligerence of an earlier period. The new line found receptive audiences in Ankara and Tehran, where for varying reasons dissatisfaction with American policy was rife. Moscow extended large credits to both countries, concluded an agreement with Tehran to purchase natural gas in exchange for the construction of a steel mill at Isfahan, and even sold Iran over $100 million worth of Soviet military equipment.

It is not intended here to survey the history of Soviet relations with the states of the Persian Gulf. The point is simply that contiguity of the region would have sufficed to keep Moscow on guard to secure as favorable a political environment in the area as she could. At the same time, however, growing Soviet naval power in the Mediterranean and in the Indian Ocean, the threat of radical upheaval in many countries of the region, and the increasing militancy of the oil producers, combine to pose the question of long-run Soviet objectives in the Gulf. Does Moscow seek to derive economic or political benefits from extension of her presence into the Gulf? Do the Soviets seek to import oil themselves or to deny the West the right to import? Or is the actual motivation some combination of the two? Such far-reaching questions cannot be definitively answered now. On the economic side, Soviet sources are reticent on important aspects of their long-term energy planning; on the political-military side, the scope of Soviet ambitions may not be entirely clear to the leadership itself.

This paper attempts only to develop some of the relevant considerations affecting Soviet policy in the Gulf. A first and major one is Soviet economic interest in Middle Eastern oil, an issue that is explored with the aid of an outline Soviet oil balance in 1975 and 1980. It is important to emphasize that the estimates to be presented are not the result of an exhaustive survey of the source materials, that they take into account only major components of the oil balance, and that they generally neglect tradeoffs with natural gas. The second section of the paper examines the implications of a probable change in the U.S.S.R.'s oil trade position in the context of the evolving oil politics of the Middle East. The paper concludes with a brief consideration of the regional environment of interstate conflict in which Soviet policy will have to operate.

THE PROSPECTIVE SOVIET OIL BALANCE

Western views of Soviet petroleum prospects tend to fluctuate violently. In the late 1950s fears of a Soviet export offensive were high and the production outlook seemed rosy. A decade later the U.S.S.R. appeared to some observers to be potentially in need of Middle Eastern supplies on a large scale.[1] Ambiguous Soviet signals have contributed to the uncertainties. At the end of 1967, Valentin D. Shashin, the Minister of the Oil Industry, indicated that the 1975 production goal for crude oil had been reduced from earlier plans of 470 million metric tons to 450–470 million tons.[2] Over a year later, in January 1969, the prospects apparently looked no brighter, and Shashin cited the 1975 production target as 460 MT (million tons).[3] The industry journal at the same time disclosed that so-called "A + B reserves"—a somewhat looser concept than "proved and probable"[4]—increased by 51 percent between 1960 and 1968, whereas production over the same interval had doubled. "As a result," the editor noted pessimistically, "the provision of explored reserves declines from year to year and arouses concern in connection with the necessity to maintain high rates of growth of oil extraction."[5] On this basis, the prestigious Petroleum Press Service estimated Soviet reserves as 4.5 billion tons in 1968, compared to 3 billions in 1960, and thus sufficient for perhaps 15 years at the current rate of output.[6]

Suddenly, Soviet claims took a decidedly more optimistic turn, emphasizing the richness of the West Siberian fields being brought into production. In his January 1969 press statement, Shashin had referred to a 1975 output goal for West Siberia of 75 MT. In June 1969, the Vice-President of the Siberian branch of the Academy of Sciences forecast an annual production rate of 500 MT, date unspecified.[7] Assuming the customary 10 percent output-reserves ratio, this claim implied reserves of 5 billion tons in West Siberia alone. Presumably, this particular output goal was still far off in the distance, but the 1975 target for West Siberia announced in January 1970 was 100–120 MT, 1/3–3/5 higher than the figure Shashin named a year earlier. The new fields were expected to yield 230–260 MT in 1980—that is, about 40 percent of a national goal of 600–620 MT released by Shashin in late 1967.[8] Recently, a Soviet source has claimed that production in West Siberia can be brought to the level of a billion tons annually. Again, no target date was specified.[9]

The latest authoritative word is that provided in the Ninth Five Year Plan (F.Y.P.): nationally, 1975 sights have been raised to 496 MT,[10] compared to the 450–470 MT announced at the end of 1967. The target for crude oil production represents an increase of 41 percent over the base year level of 353 MT, despite the expected leveling off or possibly even decline in production in the currently most important oil-producing area, the Ural-Volga region—the so-called "Second Baku."[11] Depletion of the Ural-Volga reserves is undoubtedly the chief factor making for a monotonic decline in the rate of growth of crude production, from 16 percent per year in 1956–60 to 7 percent in 1971–5 (Table A, see pp. 204–205).

Production and consumption of oil in the U.S.S.R. in the two decades since 1950 increased at the following compounded annual rates (percent; Tables A and C, see pp. 204–205, 208):

	1951–5	1955–60	1961–5	1966–70
Production	13.3	15.9	10.4	7.7
Consumption	10.9	11.5	8.5	7.6

In each time period, the rate of growth of production outstrips that of consumption, reflecting more rapid positive growth rates of net exports than of production. Therefore, in order to construct a first approximation to an estimate of the Soviet oil balance in 1975, we might assume that consumption in the Ninth F.Y.P. period is intended to grow slightly less rapidly than production, whose planned average annual rate of increase is 7.0 percent per year[12]—say, by 6.8 percent annually.

At the 24th Party Congress in 1971, Kosygin supplied another piece of the puzzle when he declared that shipments of oil to members of C.E.M.A., the Council of Economic Mutual Assistance, are to rise from 138 MT in 1966–70 to 243 MT in 1971–5.[13] The coverage of these figures is unclear, since the official trade statistics report 165 MT of crude and product exports in 1966–70 to the seven members of C.E.M.A.— Bulgaria, Czechoslovakia, G.D.R., Hungary, Mongolia, Poland, and Rumania; conversion of the refined products to a crude oil equivalent basis would raise the total further. Kosygin was probably referring to shipments of crude alone: these amounted to 44 MT in 1966–7, the last years for which the trade statistics distinguished between crude and refined products. The remainder of 94 MT for 1968–70 would represent 85 percent of the conglomerate crude and refined product exports in those years, an only slightly higher share than in 1966–7 (82 percent).[14]

Therefore, it is assumed that crude oil exports to C.E.M.A. members in 1970 were 85 percent of total crude plus refined exports to these countries (40.5 MT), or 34 MT; and that trade and consumption flows are to take place at constant average annual rates over the Ninth F.Y.P. period. On the basis of these assumptions and the indications on plan targets already supplied, a rough approximation to the 1975 petroleum balance may be worked out as in Table 1.

Table 1

SOVIET PETROLEUM OUTPUT, CONSUMPTION AND TRADE, 1970–75

(Million Tons of Crude or Equivalent)

	1970	1975
1. Crude production	353	496
2. Inland consumption	250	347
3. Exports of crude to C.E.M.A. area	34	60
4. The same at field equivalent	36	63
5. Net exports of products to C.E.M.A. and of crude and products to all others, field equivalent	67	86
6. The same in crude oil equivalent	64	82
Of which:		
6a. Net exports of products to C.E.M.A.	7	9–12
6b. Net exports to non-C.E.M.A. area	57	70–73

Sources:
1. Production. 1970 from Table A. 1975 from *Pravda*, 25 November, 1971.
2. Consumption. 1970 from Table C. 1975 computed on the assumption of growth at 6.8 percent per year.
3. Exports of crude to C.E.M.A. 1970: see text. 1975 level computed from 1970 and 1971–5 figures, the latter given in *Materialy XXIV s"ezda KPSS*, Moscow: Politizdat, 1971, p. 182.
4. Row 3 at field equivalent. Converted on the assumption of 5 percent loss rate.
5. Exports of products to C.E.M.A., etc. The difference between row 1 and the sum of rows 2 and 4.
6. Row 5 multiplied by .95.
6a. and 6b. See text.

In Table 1, consumption is projected at an annual rate of almost 7 percent. Kosygin's 1971–5 target for crude oil exports to C.E.M.A. member countries implies an annual rate of growth of 12 percent, on the assumption that he was referring to crude alone and that growth would take place at a constant yearly rate. In contrast, the net of other exports and imports—refined products to the C.E.M.A. area, crude and refined products to and from all other countries—would appear to be slated for growth only one-third as rapid, 4 percent per year. C.E.M.A. countries are assumed to have absorbed 7 MT in crude oil equivalent (C.O.E.) of refined products by 1970 (15 percent of 40.5 MT of crude and refined products, divided by refinery yield coefficient of .85—see Table C); they supplied the U.S.S.R. with less than 1 MT in return (Table B). Hence, the absence of the targeted rate of increase of product exports to the C.E.M.A. area is not critical for the present exercise. The difference between a 4-percent and a 12-percent rate of expansion of these exports is the difference between 9 and 12 MT C.O.E. in 1975. Thus, the ultimate residual, net exports to non-C.E.M.A. countries, may be slated for an increase of only 23–8 percent, from 57 to 70–3 MT C.O.E., or 4–5 percent per year. As roughly three-quarters of Soviet oil exports outside of the C.E.M.A. area was directed to Japan and Western Europe, this might be the anticipated rate of growth of the component of Soviet oil exports directed to the "West."

The cornerstone of this rough cut at a 1975 Soviet oil balance is projection of inland consumption at 6.8 percent per year, a rate just below the rate of increase of crude output. Is the projection a reasonable one? If it is too low—say, by one percentage point—then the volume of net exports to non-C.E.M.A. countries in 1975 would be less than or no more than in 1970. In view of the significant utility of such exports (on which more below), it seems unlikely that Moscow intends to cut them substantially in the next few years. Therefore, an upper limit on the projected rate of consumption may reasonably be set at about 8 percent. Can we establish a lower limit as well? Every one percent per year of growth in consumption foregone in 1971–5 would make available an additional 15 MT C.O.E., a fifth of the level shown in Table 1, for export outside the C.E.M.A. area in 1975. It is doubtful, however, that the planned rate of consumption growth can be held much below 5 percent per year, given the targets for increase in power output.[15]

Nothing has been said so far about natural gas. Soviet gas output seemed to be slowing down until 1971, although prospects were still described glowingly. The Eighth F.Y.P. target for 1970, 225–240 billion cubic meters (bm^3),[16] was underfulfilled by 13 percent, but the rate of growth was still a respectable 9.3 percent. The Ninth F.Y.P. goal implies a slightly higher rate of growth, about 10 percent (Table A). In the meantime, exports of gas have expanded rapidly; while production in 1970 was 55 percent greater than in 1965, exports increased eight times in the same period. The volume of gas exported by the U.S.S.R in 1970 was only two percent of her output, but the ratio can be expected to rise sharply as the Soviet Union expands her pipeline network into Eastern and Western Europe.[17] On the other hand, the U.S.S.R. has begun to import gas at a scale only slightly below her exports. Owing to imports of 2.6 bm^3 from Afghanistan, net exports in 1970 were but 0.7 bm^3. Imports from Iran alone are to reach 6 and then 10 bm^3 in the next few years.[18]

In brief, although there continues to be a marked deceleration in the growth rate of Soviet crude oil extraction, the 1975 target is probably adequate to provide not only a large boost in crude exports to C.E.M.A. countries but also to at least maintain the current level of hard-currency-earning exports to the West. Imports of oil and gas are still comparatively small and even with substantial expansion are not likely to assume large proportions by 1975.

Looking further ahead to 1980, it appears that the production outlook now is for more than the 600–620 MT announced in 1967[19] but also for continuation of the retardation in the rate of growth of output. Early in 1971, the deputy head of the oil ministry, Rafkhat Mingareev, indicated 625–645 MT as the 1980 mark toward which Soviet planners were reaching,[20] whereas simple extrapolation of the 7 percent rate of increase implied by 1970 realized extraction and the 1975 target would yield 697 MT. Thus, Mingareev's range implies deceleration to an annual growth rate of about 5 percent. If inland consumption continues to rise at the rate assumed earlier for 1971–5, 6.8 percent, the 1980 level would be somewhat over 480 MT. Several years ago, an O.E.C.D. forecast implied minimum Soviet internal needs in 1980 of 613 MT, virtually identical with the 1980 output target, as then known.[21] The lower consumption figure would leave roughly 145–165 MT for net exports to all countries, Communist and non-Communist; the higher O.E.C.D. figure would leave only the slimmest margin over internal needs, about 10–30 MT.

In February 1971, Mingareev concurred with a Western estimate of 680 MT as the combined requirements of the Soviet Union and the East European socialist countries in 1980. Since he simultaneously indicated that production in the European socialist area would approximate 650–670 MT at that date, there was an implied deficit of 10–30 MT net of exports to Cuba, North Korea, and North Vietnam, or to other Soviet clients. The C.O.E. deficit was larger, inasmuch as the demand projection of 680 MT referred to liquid products.[22] Allowance for exports to Western Europe and Japan would raise the deficit to a level of 100 MT or more.

The U.S.S.R. has, of course, been the chief supplier of oil to her major Communist allies. As indicated, exports to C.E.M.A. member countries reached 40 MT of crude and refined products in 1970, whereas these countries produced on their own less than 20 MT of crude in the same year.[23] Dependence on Soviet supplies encompasses not just the C.E.M.A. members but, in varying degree, Yugoslavia in Eastern Europe, North Vietnam and North Korea in East Asia, and Cuba on the other side of the globe. These four countries absorbed close to 10 MT of crude and products in 1970, 57 percent more than in 1965 and 244 percent more than in 1960. Thus, between 1965 and 1970, Soviet exports of crude and liquid products to the group of "socialist countries" jumped by almost three-quarters, from 29 to 50 MT. Eastern European requirements in 1980 are variously estimated, but they could reach 125–200 million tons.[24] Barring significant offshore discoveries in the Baltic Sea, which do not now seem likely, Eastern Europe will continue to depend almost completely on imported supplies.[25]

It is clear, however, that the Soviet Union is not planning to remain indefinitely as East Europe's virtually sole supplier. The large volume of crude supplies promised during the Ninth F.Y.P. is the last substantial slice of the Soviet pie that the East Europeans expect to see. They have been warned to begin searching out their own supply sources[26] so that the burden on the Soviet Union can begin to be eased after 1975. The warnings appear to have been heeded. The Poles, for example, have contracted with British Petroleum to buy 3 MT of crude annually for ten years beginning in 1975 (in 1970 the Soviet Union supplied Poland with 7 MT of crude and 1.5 MT of products), and Czechoslovakia and Hungary will evidently obtain 5 MT of crude each from Iraq in the same time period.[27] Presumably, other such contracts will be drawn up in the next few years, undoubtedly with Middle East producers. Thus, the apparent European Soviet bloc deficit in 1980 should be viewed as the reflection of a restructuring of trade flows, which will probably see East European requirements increasingly met from Middle East importation.

However, the redirection of Soviet-East European oil-trade flows will most likely insure a continuing and important role for Soviet exports to Western Europe and Japan. Such exports have been a favored means since the 1950s of earning convertible exchange. Between 1960 and 1965, exports of crude alone to Europe and Japan doubled and shipments of products rose by almost half; in the succeeding five years exports of crude and refined grew by half again. At the beginning of 1969, Minister

Shashin announced that the growth of exports to non-"socialist" countries would be curtailed.[28] The process seemed already to have been inaugurated in 1969: exports of petroleum and products to non-Communist Europe and Japan declined relative to the previous year's level by almost 4 percent, while Eastern Europe and Cuba continued to increase their imports of petroleum and products, by 5.7 MT, or 14 percent.[29] In 1970 shipments to Europe and Japan recovered to roughly the 1968 level and in 1971 they grew by an additional 4 MT.

The inclination in 1969–70 to constrain exports to the West may have been at least partly motivated by the recognition that the opportunity cost of a ton of exported crude, in terms of the required solid fuel replacement, was six times as high as the production cost of the crude.[30] Except to the extent that she wished to retain an instrument of political control over them, this also argued for a Soviet decision not to remain the sole supplier of oil to Communist Europe and Cuba. On the other hand, Soviet planners were not overendowed with commodities salable on the world market. Their machinery, for example, had yet to prove its worth in free competition among buyers with convertible exchange. In the early 1960s it required only 16 kopecks of expenditure in the U.S.S.R. to lift a dollar's worth of oil, if comparison is with mainland U.S. prices, or about 33 kopecks if Middle East prices are used instead.[31] On the other hand, the average price ratio for producers' durables has been estimated as about 50 kopecks per dollar.[32] Considering petroleum's more general marketability, there seemed to be a strong case for the argument that the Soviet Union had a comparative advantage in exporting oil.[33]

Yet the Soviet literature in the middle 1960s contained numerous complaints of the high investment and transportation costs involved in a fuel geography moving ever further eastward.[34] Until 1967, moreover, internal Soviet prices of petroleum failed to reflect the relationship to a protected high-cost coal industry which necessarily provided the basic substitutes in use for oil. The price reform in that year saw prices of petroleum tied to those of coal and therefore raised by four-fifths.[35] An editorial in the journal of the State Planning Commission observed that raising oil prices had the additional advantage of enabling "more correct determination of the effectiveness of exporting oil."[36] West Siberian oil, the hope of the next decade, is actually relatively cheap to extract and transport: by Soviet calculations and allowing for investment outlays, average production costs in the Tiumen come to 6.2 rubles per ton of standard fuel (equivalent to 8.9 rubles per actual ton, assuming the usual conversion coefficient of 1.43 standard tons per actual ton), compared with 11.5 rubles for Kuznetsk (mine) coal, 15.3 rubles for Donets coal, and 230 rubles for Moscow Basin coal. It costs only 44 kopecks per ton of standard fuel and for each 1,000 km of distance to move oil by 102-cm (40-inch) pipeline.[37]

The question is, what replaces the exported oil? Transporting Kuznetsk coal 1,000 kilometers by electric main-line rail adds 3.23 rubles per standard ton to an already swollen production cost. Moving coal of lower unit calorific value involves even larger expenditures per standard ton. One would think natural gas would be much cheaper. It is, in terms of production cost—Tiumen gas is only a third as costly to produce as the companion crude—but pipeline transport of gas is six times as expensive as oil for the same diameter pipe. It requires doubling the pipe diameter to reduce the cost of shipping gas 1,000 km by 40 percent. [38] The coal of Kansk-Achinsk, a thousand miles east of Tiumen, is by far the cheapest of all major Soviet fuel sources—cheaper even than Tiumen natural gas—but railroad transport would seem to be prohibitively high. [39] Academician Kantorovich, of linear-programming and shadow-pricing fame, asserts, however, that the rail freight rates are set irrationally. Rates are virtually uniform for short and long hauls; they reflect average costs while incremental fixed and operating costs are 2–3 times lower than average expenditures per ton-km. For the entire rail network the tariff for shipping coal per 1,000 ton-km is 3 rubles; average cost is 1.75 rubles, but incremental cost is only 0.70 rubles. [40] If Kantorovich is right, Kansk-Achinsk coal might compete favorably with Tiumen gas or oil on a delivered basis to the central industrial regions of European Russia if not its western borders.

Thus, apart from expansion of the scale of output, the ultimate availability of oil (or gas) for export depends, at least on economic grounds, on transformation of the patterns of output and transportation of Soviet fuel. The structure of fuel output has already undergone radical change since the middle 1950s. Coal accounted for 65 percent of total fuel output in 1955 while oil and gas accounted for only 24 percent; by 1970, the share of coal was down to 36 percent, whereas that of oil and gas had reached 40 percent (Table A). But there are large reserves of relatively cheap fuel in Siberia—coal as well as gas and oil—whose exploitation is linked to the development of the transport network and changes in the perception of rational pricing. If the development of Siberia proceeds rapidly enough, the more costly seams of European Russian coal can be abandoned—and the gradually exhausted oil fields of the Caucasus and the Ural-Volga region too—and the opportunity cost of Soviet oil and gas exports will, at least on this account, decline.

Price movements on the world oil market will obviously affect the outcome of these developments. To judge from the last year or two, delivered prices of Middle East oil are likely to move up sharply by the end of the decade, while real internal opportunity costs in the U.S.S.R. can be expected to remain relatively stable. Manifestly, the incentive to export oil and gas will be strengthened under these circumstances.

Will there be a comparable economic rationale for substantial imports of liquid fuel, especially from the Middle East? Production costs are undoubtedly lower in the Persian Gulf than in the U.S.S.R.[41] However, the price Moscow would have to pay for Persian Gulf oil depends on the circumstances under which the oil is obtained. That is, the opportunity cost of Soviet resources expended on Middle Eastern oil would vary depending on whether the Soviet Union herself removed the oil she withdrew, under some form of development contract, or whether she purchased it: in the latter case, the terms of purchase—barter or hard currency—could make a crucial difference; in the former case, much depends on the volume of royalties and taxes that would have to be paid, and on the accounting-ruble valuation of hard currency proceeds.[42]

The development of the Siberian reserves will take decades, not years, and in the meantime the U.S.S.R. will continue to face a fundamental problem of energy economics, the substantial expense of lifting and moving fuel from relatively inaccessible eastern deposits to western points of consumption. Tiumen oil and gas will be needed in Siberia (and for export to Japan?[43]) as well as in European Russia. Under appropriate conditions, Middle East oil and gas could profitably be imported for consumption in the southern regions of the U.S.S.R.[44] This rationale was strongly implied by Mingareev in the interview early in 1971, cited above. A prototype arrangement is now in operation: On 28 October, 1970, Podgorny and the Shah of Iran met at the Astura border bridge on the Caspian Sea to open the world's largest gas trunkline, built jointly by the Russians and the Iranians, to supply the U.S.S.R. with 6 bm^3 of gas annually. After 1973 the capacity of the pipeline is to be raised to allow annual import of 10 bm^3.[45] As is the case with imports of oil from the Gulf, imports of gas to the southern regions of the U.S.S.R. would free supplies further north for local use or for export.

At the same time, it may turn out that the relatively optimistic picture presented in Soviet sources of the economics of future hydrocarbon production is overdrawn. Rising costs in older regions of production may be matched by unexpectedly higher costs of production and transportation in the newer fields. Such a development could significantly affect the government's trade policy.

To sum up: Presently observable schedules of production and internal consumption in the European Communist area indicate that the net export position of the group will be under no threat in the next few years, but by 1980 an overall C.E.M.A. deficit is likely.[46] At the same time, the Soviet Union may have an economic interest in importing oil and gas on a tangible scale that reflects the vast sprawl of the Soviet economy and would depend on the terms on which foreign supplies could be obtained. Moreover, on the assumption that Soviet payments imbalances with the industrialized countries will not have evaporated by the end of the decade, oil and gas will continue to offer an attractive vehicle for augmenting Soviet hard currency earnings, particularly in view of the apparent trend to rising world market prices. It seems a reasonable bet that by the end of the decade the C.E.M.A. countries as a group will be shopping for something of the order of 100 million tons of crude oil equivalent. To a yet limited extent, the Soviet Union is already importing Middle Eastern oil and gas—from Algeria in the west to Iran (and Afghanistan) in the east. Conceivably, the scale of Soviet imports will grow much larger.

SOVIET POLICY IN THE GULF: TOWARD STABILITY OR UPHEAVAL?

If there is indeed to be such a change in the bloc's and in the U.S.S.R.'s oil trade role, what are the political implications for Soviet policy in the Persian Gulf? Here one observes polarization of views. It has been argued, on one hand, that if the U.S.S.R. is prepared to become a substantial importer of Middle Eastern oil, she will perceive her self-interest in stabilizing rather than agitating the region. In this view, Moscow would wish to prevent serious disruptions in production and should therefore be loath to encourage political radicalization of the region. On the other hand, there are fears that the Soviet Union would attempt to deny oil supplies to the West or permit access only under restrictive conditions. If this were her goal, the U.S.S.R. might be expected to promote radical nationalist militancy within the producing countries.

Presented in these terms, the dichotomy seems outdated. In the last few years, the producers have already displayed a new and strident militancy that has alarmed the West, and the Soviet Union has not displayed any reluctance to extend her full moral support to the host countries. But how far is Moscow prepared to go? Will she be content to applaud as the show unfolds, or will she in fact attempt to guide the performance? And in which direction? Toward complete nationalization, for example?

Boris Rachkov, a Soviet writer on Arab oil affairs, argued the necessity of nationalization on the grounds that the monopolists would never grant producer country demands for a share in equity. He acknowledged the danger of Western boycott that could be triggered by nationalization in one country alone, but declared: "If, on the other hand, all, or at least several large oil-producing countries nationalize their oil concessions simultaneously, this would make an oil boycott by the cartel impossible." In this connection, Rachkov noted the significance of the "victory of democratic forces in Libya" in the fall of 1969, which narrowed the room for maneuver of the oil cartel in countering nationalization moves in Iraq and Algeria. "The victory of the democratic forces in Libya has brought the oil-producing countries closer to the stage in their development where they can take a firmer stand in defense of their economic interests." Rachkov concluded with the prediction that the growing unity of the Arab oil producers and "deepening democratization of their socio-political system will undoubtedly lead to the development of conditions in which the imperialist oil cartel, with all its insiduous means of blackmail and oppression, will be powerless to prevent the transfer of control over Arab oil into the hands of its real owners."[47]

Although Rachkov's article appeared in 1970, it has the flavor of another era. Events have moved beyond him. Two decades ago nationalization in Iran was a radical alteration of the environment that drew forth the equally drastic response of boycott from the international oil companies. The Mossadegh government felt powerless otherwise to effect control over the disposition of its resources; the cartel felt free to punish Iran because the Middle East producers were unorganized. Both conditions have changed drastically. In 1960 the Organization of Petroleum Exporting Countries (O.P.E.C.) was formed; a decade later it succeeded in extracting from the international companies the largest monetary concessions in the history of the industry. On top of the $750 million annual incremental payment obtained by the Middle Eastern members of

O.P.E.C. in 1970, the companies agreed in Tehran on 14 February, 1971, to increased levies of more than $10 billion over five years to the six Persian Gulf producer-members.[48] This was followed on April 2, by a grant of $1.00 per barrel additional to Libya and in June by a sharp jump in prices of Iraqi oil.[49] Finally, on 20 January, 1972, the companies agreed to compensate the Gulf producers for the devaluation of the dollar through an increase in the posted prices of 8.49 percent, raising annual payments by an anticipated $700 million.[50]

Over the last two decades, moreover, there has been increasing impetus within the Middle East oil-producing countries to alter the ownership and control patterns under which their petroleum is produced and sold. The 18th Conference of O.P.E.C. in July 1969 sought to dispel "any lingering doubts that there may have been about the determination of the oil-producing countries to press ahead with their demand for participation in the ownership of their concession-holding companies."[51] The Persian Gulf producers have begun by demanding a 20 percent share in the equity interests of the oil companies, but the former are clearly bent on achieving majority control.[52] The ultimate scope of this effort will remain unclear until the producing countries indicate "how greater country influence on domestic producing operations and investment can be accommodated to the worldwide supply logistics and financial operations of the international parent companies."[53] Few will doubt, however, that the era of concessionary arrangements for oil production in the Middle East is coming to an end. Early in 1971 Algeria took over majority control of the French oil company and completely nationalized natural gas operations. Iran seems little disposed now to allow the concessionaire to exercise his option of renewing in 1979. The years 1983–4 will see the reversion of oil company assets to the government of Venezuela without compensation. Other Middle East producer governments are expected to terminate the concessions, even though their agreements with the majors are not scheduled to expire until the end of the century or later. Everywhere the minimum objective seems to be "a state of affairs in which, as fully as possible, the role of government is progressively enlarged, in the pursuit of the economic and political interests of the countries."[54]

The objective is complicated by a major dilemma of relations between foreign oil companies and the Middle East producers. On one hand, in pursuit of more rapid economic growth and in response to domestic nationalist pressures, the governments are intent on raising their oil revenues as rapidly as possible. On the other hand, there are limits to the amount of economic rent (considered from a worldwide viewpoint) that can be siphoned off locally before the monopoly position of the Middle East is seriously undermined. The line beyond which the concessionaire is squeezed out of production is increasingly short of production cost by the growing margin of taxes and royalties that are in effect costs to the concessionaire. For this reason, Adelman asserts that the critical issue is not so much expropriation or nationalization as "continued *appropriation* of all the surplus between the bare minimum profit necessary to keep the company operating, and the real price of crude oil."[55] Only part of the 1970–2 revolutionary upsurge in producer revenues constitutes "appropriation" in Adelman's sense, for the companies will have passed on almost all of the increase in higher prices to consuming countries. To the latter, the choice is only between reducing the "take" of governments in the form of taxes or raising prices to ultimate consumers. Both constitute redistribution in favor of the producing countries (although the profits of the cartel may also grow) and thus may be termed another form of "appropriation."

The consequences of accelerated "appropriation"—in the narrower sense of reduced oil company profit margins or in the broader one of creeping inflation of world oil prices—are surely predictable; utilization of fields previously considered unprofitable, intensification of exploratory drilling in new fields, enhanced incentives for the development of substitute energy sources—ultimately, therefore, the redirection of oil trade. This is not likely to be a significant factor in the near term, perhaps not before the next decade, for the world is too heavily dependent on Middle Eastern oil to be able to redirect its supply lines quickly and easily. Four-fifths of Western Europe's oil imports originate in the Middle East, and Japan's dependence is even greater. The Middle East still contains better than 70 percent of the non-Communist world's proved reserves, a fact of life that is only marginally affected by the rosiest of forecasts for Alaskan or North Sea fields.

For a while at least, we are not likely to see a break in the upward trend of oil prices. It is true that the current situation is a relatively recent phenomenon which reversed a protracted decline in oil prices. But a return to the pre-existing environment seems improbable. The trauma of the first Suez closure in 1956 intensified the search for West-of-Suez supplies, and these were found in abundance in the North African and Nigerian oil fields. Paradoxically, an added factor helping to keep prices down was the flow of surplus oil from the Soviet Union's new Volga-Ural fields. At the same time, economies of scale were being realized in transportation with the progressively increasing size of oil tankers. The reversal of the price decline of the 1960s was brought about by supply interruption in the wake of the Six-Day War and by unexpected increases in the industrial countries' demand. Though temporary stringencies on the demand side may be alleviated, the world demand for energy seems bound to continue to grow at a rapid rate. The transition from the oil age to that of nuclear energy—if only in power production—seems some distance away.[56] On the supply side, adjustments in the form of construction of additional tankers and pipelines are in full swing, but the exploitation of economies of scale in transport may be in the region of diminishing returns. The transport bottleneck is beginning to be opened, but this does not seem sufficient in itself to trigger the turnaround.

A major factor in keeping oil prices firm is the developing solidarity of the Middle Eastern producers, whose perception of the utility of not breaking ranks has been sharpened by the experiences of the last few years. If that solidarity can be maintained or strengthened, the upward pressure on prices is likely to continue, whatever the future direction of oil company-producer country relations, whether to increasing "appropriation" or growing "participation." For this reason, the threat of old-fashioned nationalization seems less relevant. True, nationalization has taken place in Algeria, Libya, and Iraq. Additional nationalization may occur during the coming years as a reaction of frustration during the tensions of negotiations. But in the Persian Gulf at least, sights seem to be fixed on rapid transition to full producer-country involvement in "upstream" and "downstream" operations.

If the Soviet Union emerges as a significant oil importer, how will she fit into this scheme of oil market development? Rising prices (if Moscow comes forward as a simple buyer from state-owned companies) and escalating tax royalty rates (if the import is the end result of a development contract) could adversely affect short-run Soviet economic interests. As a buyer of oil extracted by others, the U.S.S.R. is unlikely to offer a straight hard currency deal. Her trade in oil as in other goods will continue to depend heavily on bilateral agreements in which technical assistance and producers' goods—or arms—are offered in exchange for the desired imports. It could be expected that Moscow would have to offer favorable terms in order to offset the disadvantages of barter and the often doubtful quality of her goods in trade. If the producer-countries' oil revenues are rising faster than the world market prices for the manufactured goods they seek in exchange, the Soviet barter position would be undermined.

On the other hand, the Soviet foreign-trade planner might foresee the eventual reversal of the seller's market and the development of alternative sources of supply in response to continued rise in the delivered price of Middle East oil. He might look forward to the time of reversal as one in which Gulf producers would be likely to turn a more attentive ear to Soviet barter offers, if the nominal terms of trade appeared favorable. Even if the Middle East continued to hold its dominant position in world supply, the Soviet Union might still find it cheaper to deal with national companies than with the affiliates of the international cartel. National companies, compelled to accept quotas on sales to the cartel-controlled markets or faced by price-elastic demand there, might be eager to sell to the Soviet Union on relatively favorable terms. The desired volume of Soviet imports might also be obtained in exchange for aid to the national companies in developing "downstream" operations. Therefore, Moscow's purely economic interest in the processes of Middle East "participation" and "appropriation" perhaps should have a time identification: in the short run it may be negative; in the longer term there may be a distinct gain that can be anticipated.

But the economic argument should not be overdrawn. If it is valid, it is yet relatively new and concerns a future that is distant to harried policymakers. Soviet concern with and involvement in Gulf affairs are of much longer standing, and the classic motivations have been political. The reasons why Moscow has long made the international oil companies her favorite whipping boy in the Middle East are a function of the real or imagined connections between the companies and their home governments. The Kremlin is no less intent now than before on expelling the West—that is, essentially the United States and Britain—from the Middle East, and in the struggle between developing-country producers and the oil cartel, she sees a ready-made instrument to hand. The struggle has the potential for radicalizing the region, pulling it to closer identification with the Soviet Union and alienation from the West. Possibly, Moscow even thinks that displacement of the Western concessionaires will diminish the security interests the West still perceives in the area and therefore will make the Soviet task of penetration less costly.

In her effort to eject the West from the Middle East, Moscow can be expected to support to the hilt producer demands for "participation" and perhaps, as Rachkov, the Soviet writer cited earlier, suggests, to try to shift that effort into a drive for nationalization. Rachkov was careful to include the assurance that after nationalization "the present concessionaires would become simply purchasers of oil, to whom the Arab countries would give firm guarantees of steady and reliable deliveries."[57] However, can it be safely presumed that Moscow will in fact back an orderly transition to new but stable supply relationships with the West? Or are Soviet leaders likely to see opportunities for dealing the West a crippling economic blow by attempting to turn off the oil tap? Those who are inclined to discount that possibility point to the Soviet Union's approval of the decision by the Khartoum Summit Conference in August 1967 to lift the Arab oil embargo that followed the Six-Day War.[58] However, it is equally true that Moscow publicly endorsed the embargo idea while it was still under discussion. Because it is the most recent and relevant case in point, the abortive 1967 embargo merits brief examination here.

Commenting on the Baghdad Conference of Arab economics ministers that preceded Khartoum, Evgenii Primakov, Deputy Director of the Academy of Sciences' Institute of World Economics and International Relations, observed: "Powerful economic controls are in the hands of the Arabs. If the controls are used skillfully under the conditions of unanimity of the Arab States, they will undoubtedly prove exceedingly effective. Because of the closure of the Suez Canal alone, Western Europe and the United States have to spend an additional $250 million per month."[59] A Radio Moscow broadcast in Arabic on 15 August reported that the Iraqis planned to ask for a complete embargo of oil exports to the United States, Britain, and West Germany, as well as withdrawal of Arab bank deposits and a boycott of all imports from these countries.[60] The Soviet commentator implied that these were "necessary measures to mobilize all Arab resources to remove the traces of Israeli aggression" and declared: "We can see that the decisive provision for realizing these proposals is the firmness of Arab solidarity and unity."[61]

As the Khartoum Summit Conference approached, Radio Moscow's domestic service affirmed (25 August): " . . . the Arabs assume rightly that a blow against the oil interests of the West will accelerate the elimination of the consequences of aggression." Implicit approval was given to the reputed agreement at the prior Baghdad Conference on gradual nationalization of the Anglo-American oil companies. Igor Beliaev, *Pravda's* editor for Afro-Asian affairs, noted with satisfaction the difficulties caused in the West by the oil boycott and asserted that "if the Arab countries will now manage to strengthen the position they agreed upon in Baghdad, there is no doubt that the imperialist powers who support Israel, the aggressor in the Near and Middle East, will find themselves in a very tight position."[62] On 28 August, as the Arab heads of state prepared to gather at Khartoum, Radio Moscow counseled them that

> ... the implementation of [the Baghdad Conference] resolutions and recommendations, particularly those connected with Arab oil, would be the most potent weapon against the aggression and the powers supporting it. The closure of the Suez Canal, particularly to westbound tankers, as well as total economic boycott—the withdrawal of funds deposited in Western banks and so forth—are all, in conjunction with the above, measures the implementation of which, collectively and *in toto,* would, it is hoped, be thoroughly considered by the Summit Conference so that all Arab leaders would be committed effectively and soundly to enforce these measures.

Similar statements were made in comments on the proceedings during the meeting.[63]

The Khartoum Conference, of course, decided to terminate the oil embargo and this met with Soviet approval. Perhaps the approval was more readily granted because the decision was accompanied by a promise of an indefinite annual subsidy to Egypt from Saudi Arabia, Libya, and Kuwait, of £ 95 million, thus lifting part of the economic burden of support for Nasser from the Soviet back. However, Moscow's major concern was undoubtedly to secure as close a measure of Arab unity in support of the Soviet line of "political solution" as possible, and it was probably recognized that general agreement on embargo, boycott, or nationalization could not be achieved at that time. Failing general agreement, such measures could prove self-defeating. Radio Moscow therefore felt obliged to acknowledge the existence of serious inter-Arab conflicts (2 September): "It would be naive, of course, to expect the first summit to resolve all the controversial issues between the Arab countries ... it must be borne in mind that for a long time the imperialists have been heating up discord between them and setting one Arab state against the other." Soviet commentary stressed the agreement "for joint political and diplomatic moves by the Arab countries on the international level toward liquidating the consequences of the aggression."

Moscow revealed distinct sensitivity to the charge that the Summit

Conference had been a failure, and much of the post-conference radio and press material was devoted to defense against the charge.[64] From the Soviet point of view, the repudiation of the extremist Algerian-Syrian line of resumption of the war and the agreement instead on pursuit of the "political solution" was of fundamental importance for the security of the Soviet position in the Middle East. On this account, Moscow was entitled to see some success in the Khartoum outcome, although the apparent expectation that the West would yield on the Arab-Israel question in the face of interruption in the oil supply was frustrated.

There are two aspects of this remarkable episode that are worth stressing here. First, the Soviet campaign, however intensively pursued, seemed to be aimed at distinctly limited objectives. The series of anti-Western acts the Soviet Union endorsed on the eve of Khartoum were defended as measures aimed to secure Israel's military withdrawal. In contrast, the theme of "national liberation" and obtaining control of national resources for national development was conspicuous by its absence in the Soviet media. We cannot know whether the Kremlin privately hoped to achieve as a byproduct a permanent alteration in the control and ownership arrangements of Middle East oil production. It seems doubtful that such illusions were harbored, but in any case the public discussion focused on boycotts and embargoes, rather than on nationalization.[65]

Boycotts and embargoes are measures of economic warfare, and this is the second important feature of the episode. Moscow did vocally support economic warfare against the West, not in the distant Stalinist past but just a few years ago. The Soviet Union had suffered a humiliating defeat in June 1967 and saw her painfully won position in the Middle East seriously endangered. A reversal of even greater proportions than the Six-Day War itself had to be averted, and in pursuit of that major goal the U.S.S.R. was prepared to endorse extraordinary measures.

With the failure of the Arab oil embargo in the summer of 1967, Soviet propaganda stress on the significance of the vast Arab oil reserves as a weapon against the West was retired to the back burner.[66] The reasons for the failure were clear enough. The impact of closing the Suez Canal in 1967 (along with the temporary embargo) was not as severe as in 1956, largely because of intervening increases in the size of Europe's emergency stocks[67] and in the average carrying capacity of the world tanker fleet. Thus, between 1957 and 1967, the average size of the tanker in the world fleet increased by 76 percent and the total tonnage by 123 percent.[68]

The closure of the Canal also provided strong incentives for producers with Mediterranean outlets to increase production substantially. This concerned Libya primarily, then still under conservative monarchist rule. At the same time, Iran was delighted to pay its Arab neighbors back in kind for their eagerness during the Mossadegh period in the early 1950s to support the cartel boycott of Iranian oil by stepping up production in the rest of the Gulf. In this respect the situation has changed in the last few years. Libya under the Revolutionary Command Council is the most militant of the major oil producers. The solidarity of the O.P.E.C. coalition, with Iran at the fore, has held through the tempestuous negotiations of 1970–2. Since the virtual monopoly enjoyed by Middle Eastern oil on the world market is not likely to be seriously threatened in the near future, the short-term prospects of an aggressive O.P.E.C. policy vis-à-vis the concessionaires and through them the major industrial consumers would seem bright.

This does not, however, mean that Moscow stands a good chance of controlling the West's access to Middle East oil. O.P.E.C. is not now and is not likely to become a Soviet instrument. The experience of the last two years has brought sharply increased revenues to state coffers in the Persian Gulf and perhaps an equal leap of self confidence. But the producers recognize their dependence on the oil companies for the transportation, refining, and distribution of Middle East crude. Iran, Kuwait, and Saudi Arabia are anxious to keep the miraculous goose in steady production. They are aware that adventurist tactics could boomerang, spurring an intensive search for alternative sources of supply. This could mean not only accelerated development of areas already in operation, like the Arctic or the North Sea, but also emergency measures to augment the fuel supply from unconvential sources—e.g., shale, tar sands—for which the technology is evidently on the doorstep of profitability.[69] It would mean that if the immediate dislocations caused by the supply interruption could be successfully overcome, the world would adjust to a new pattern of trade flows that could be disastrous to the Middle East.

Would Moscow be inclined to try to induce the Arab producers to a more radical course of action? In the summer of 1967 the Soviet Union did not lead the pack; she supported an initiative that had been taken by the Arabs. A Soviet attempt to push one or two radical Arab states to shut off the flow of oil to the West in the future would probably cause general alarm among the other Middle East producers who recognize their dependence on Western markets even while manipulating and exploiting

Western dependence on Middle East supply. The same may also be said of any Soviet attempt to establish a monopoly position in a major Middle East producer state. Moreover, such ploys would risk undermining objectives that must be more valuable to the U.S.S.R.—for example, detente in Europe—than either the particular Soviet clients in the Middle East or any possible gains from blocking oil supply lines to the West.

However, should the militancy of O.P.E.C. result in the stalemating of a future set of oil negotiations and the Middle East producers undertake to make good their ultimatums, it would be imprudent to count on the U.S.S.R. playing a moderating or even neutral role. Soviet reactions to more recent crises suggest that the 1967 episode was not an aberration. After the seizure of British Petroleum's assets in Libya, Radio Moscow declared in an Arabic-language broadcast on 13 December, 1971, that "all sincere friends of the Arabs . . . regard Libya's action as part of the struggle of all Arabs against imperialism." Indications of the resumption of U.S. aircraft sales to Israel brought Radio Moscow on 3 and 18 January, 1972 (again to the Arab world) to link the U.S. Government and the "U.S. oil monopolies, who seek to plunder and rob the Arab countries" and to declare that there was only one way to stop the flow of Arab oil wealth "financing" Israeli "aggression": "strike at the positions of the imperialist monopolies in the Arab countries."

The Soviet commentator reminded the Arab countries that they "possess all the necessary potential to take such decisive measures." Recalling the oil boycott of 1956 (but, tactfully, not the abortive try of 1967), he warned: "It looks as if history will repeat itself." Finally, the Iraqi and Syrian seizure of I.P.C. assets was hailed in *Pravda* on 4 June, 1972, as "undoubtedly one of the heaviest blows dealt at the positions of the oil monopolies and a resolute step toward liquidation of the positions of monopoly capital on Arab soil."

The lesson of 1967 and of more recent history as well is that the Soviet Union is not averse to economic warfare in principle. A future oil crisis might see Moscow enthusiastically backing radical measures undertaken by the producer states, depending on the breadth of the producer coalition and the objectives at stake. If that support resulted in hastening the development of alternative sources of energy supply, the Soviet Union might count that as an additional benefit, for reasons set out earlier. Following in the wake of the producer states rather than playing the leading role might also diminish the probability that the Soviet stance would be costly to her major global objectives. In any case, Moscow might feel that her future prospects in the Middle East would be more badly endangered by allowing herself to be outflanked on the left in Arab oil politics.[70]

PROSPECTS FOR SOVIET POWER AND DIPLOMACY

"One cannot safely look more than a year or two ahead in the Gulf," the chief foreign correspondent of the (London) *Sunday Times* has warned us. " . . . The Gulf has already entered a new period of flux in which neither existing boundaries nor traditional regimes can be expected to prevail."[71] An arena made to order for Soviet maneuvering? Perhaps, but it may also be one in which Moscow will find it considerably more difficult to acquire and maintain a foothold than in the maelstrom of Arab-Israel conflict. It would be misleading to conclude a discussion of the U.S.S.R. and Middle East oil without at least a brief consideration of the political environment in which Soviet policy will have to function.

Leonard Binder has pointed out that the situation in the Gulf bears the significant imprint of the Six-Day War.[72] Before, the major threat to the stability of the region had come from Egypt. Nasser battled royalists in Yemen, involved himself in the revolution in South Yemen, incited to revolt against Faisal in Saudi Arabia, and proclaimed the right to national liberation of Arab Khuzistan in Iran. His massive defeat in June 1967 meant the disappearance, at least temporarily, of a powerful Egyptian voice from Arabian and Persian Gulf affairs. The death of Nasser may mean that even a settlement of the Arab-Israel conflict is unlikely to be followed by renewal of the former Egyptian role in this region.

As Egypt is the Soviet Union's major client in the Middle East, she may be viewed as having acted in proxy for the patron. But if this is so, Moscow could hardly have drawn unqualified encouragement from the record of her surrogate's activities even before June 1967. The war in Yemen went badly, and in South Yemen, now the People's Democratic Republic of Yemen (P.D.R.Y.), Nasser had backed the wrong horse in the struggle between rival revolutionary groups. Iran's "White Revolution" was going from strength to strength, while the protracted Kurdish revolt effectively kept Iraq, presumably a Soviet client too, internally busy and externally harmless.

The post-June War scene finds the Soviet Union without Egypt's corrosive aid and with still limited naval access, due to the continued closure of the Suez Canal, but more active in the region than before. Britain's decision to withdraw from east of Suez must have quickened Soviet anticipation. Iraq and the P.D.R.Y. are already counted Moscow clients—although the former especially is prone to ignore its patron's wishes[73] and the latter has significant ties to Peking. Iraq, however, settled its long and bitter conflict with the Kurds in March 1970 and should, therefore, be more readily inclined to external involvement.[74] The Republic of Yemen is attempting to tread warily between East and West, after an era of civil war in which the Soviets were directly engaged for a brief period, but it may not be able to play the balancing game too long. Two attempted *coups* were reported in Saudi Arabia in 1969, and the problem of succession to King Faisal may generate more visible turmoil. The first fruits of a "national liberation" struggle in Muscat and Oman came in the overthrow of the Sultan by his son in July 1970. The Federation of Arab Amirates, which was to help stabilize the region following British departure, has been brought into existence (in truncated form), but disunity and internal subversion may pose a significant threat to its future. Few of these developments can be traced back to Moscow, but radicalization of the region might be seen as improving the prospects for extending Soviet influence.

Since 1965 a guerrilla force has been operating in the Dhofar province of what used to be called the Sultanate of Muscat and Oman. In the fall of 1968 the Dhofar Liberation Front was renamed the Popular Front for the Liberation of the Occupied Arab Gulf and its program broadened and radicalized. The Front embraced Marxism-Leninism and vowed to supplant Western oil monopolies generally, and British protectorate forces in particular, by socialist regimes. As the insistence on the "Arabism" of the Gulf in the title implies, the scope of the Front's concern reaches also to Iranian difficulties with her Arab neighbors.[75] The Front's immediate target, Sultan Sa'id bin Taymur, was obviously inviting—a caricature of a medieval tyrant, whose efforts to shut out the external world were doomed even before his oil revenues began to mount to $50–100 million a year. On 23 July, 1970, the Sultan was overthrown by his son with the acquiescence if not actual assistance of the small British protector forces. The new Sultan, Sayyed Qabus, has succeeded in winning over some of the disgruntled elements in the country, now renamed the Sultanate of Oman, by his promises of significant reform, but clearly the P.F.L.O.A.G. will not be satisfied with reform.

Radical sentiment is not new to other parts of the Gulf. Kuwait and Bahrein are perhaps the more likely breeding grounds. The Trucial States are surely not immune but seem to have escaped major infection for the time being. Their fears on this score were partly responsible for the opposition to the inclusion of Bahrein in the Federation of Arab Amirates. With British protection now withdrawn, and troubled by internal rivalries, the Gulf sheikhdoms may find it more difficult to cope with radical nationalist movements, particularly if these groups parade under the flag of anti-Iranian imperialism.

Growing Soviet blue-water power east of Suez would dramatize the increasing interest of the U.S.S.R. in the Gulf region. Assuming the reopening of the Suez Canal, Moscow would be able to deploy quickly and in strength a Red Sea-Arabian Sea force from elements of her Black Sea and Mediterranean units. The distance from the nearest Soviet home ports in the Black Sea would be radically shortened and a valuable base would be available in Aden. By air, the Soviet frontier is minutes to only a few hours away. Thus, the U.S.S.R., and perhaps only the U.S.S.R. among the Great Powers, would be capable of effective intervention in the affairs of the Arabian Peninsula. When the Labour Government announced its intention to withdraw from east of Suez, the British had 4,700 troops in the region (approximately two battalions plus service troops), 2,400–2,500 R.A.F. personnel, with three frigates and a half dozen coastal minesweepers cruising the Gulf waters.[76] This force has now departed the region. The current U.S. military presence is far smaller: there are no American ground forces, only a flagship on the Gulf, usually augmented by two destroyers from the Atlantic Fleet. Reopening of the Suez Canal should make movement of American naval forces from the Mediterranean to the Indian Ocean no more difficult than for the Soviet forces, but in the present atmosphere of U.S. politics would the opportunities be utilized to the same extent by Washington as by Moscow?

But there is another side to the ledger. On the Arabian Peninsula, as in the Near East before the Six-Day War, the U.S.S.R. could find herself plunged headlong into the swirling waters of interstate rivalries, should she choose to exercise a more direct role. In the southwest, the triangular relations of Yemen, P.D.R.Y., and Saudi Arabia are far from an equilibrium point. A gradual rapprochement seems to be in the making between Riyadh and Sana but, despite the talk of unity, Sana and Aden came to violent blows in mid-1972. At the same time, there is continuing border conflict between the Saudis and the southern Yemenis, with the former supporting a dissident conservative movement operating in the P.D.R.Y. hinterland. The P.D.R.Y. is the base of the P.F.L.O.A.G., not the least reason being the former's envy of the oil wealth of the Gulf states, which contrasts so sharply with the depression-ridden economy of the P.D.R.Y.

After its brief fling of direct participation in the Yemeni civil war, Moscow seems to have decided on a more circumspect approach in south-west Arabia. For example, the communiqué issued at the conclusion of the October 1971 visit to the U.S.S.R. by the P.D.R.Y.'s Prime and Defense Minister, Ali Nasser Muhammed, declared that the two sides

> . . . confirmed their solidarity with the peoples of the Persian Gulf who are struggling for the complete elimination of the presence and domination of colonialism and neocolonialism, for the dismantling of all foreign military bases, and for national liberation and social programs in the area.

The communiqué made no mention of Dhofar, Oman, the P.F.L.O.A.G., or the "threat to the Arabism of the Gulf" (Iranian claims to the islands of Tumbs and Abu Musa at the neck of the Gulf).[77]

The most difficult problem for Soviet policy is presented by the region's most significant rivalry, that between Iraq and Iran. The Iraqis in 1970 awoke "with a jolt to the imminence of the British withdrawal and the prospect that the Iranians and the Saudis will exclude them from the area."[78] Attempting to ward off that event, Baghdad has been vehement in denunciation of the Iranian takeover of Abu Musa and the Tumbs on 30 November, 1971, declared her support for the Federation of Arab Amirates, increased her offers of economic aid to the Arab states, and expanded her trade network in the region. At the same time, her acquisitive interest in Kuwait seems to have been reawakened, and Iraq is spreading her own revolutionary gospel along the shores of the Gulf. Baghdad and Tehran are directly at loggerheads over a number of other issues, including navigation on the Shatt al-Arab and offshore oil rights, but these are only the accompaniment to the major theme of who controls the Gulf.

Moscow is in the delicate position of cultivating both sides to the dispute. Thus, the cumulative amount of Soviet and East European economic aid offered to Iran is exceeded in the underdeveloped world only by extensions to India and Egypt. Among non-Communist developing nations, Iran is the second biggest customer of Soviet exports (after Egypt but before India). The Soviet Union is now Iran's biggest customer for exports other than oil. As for Iraq, until 1972 she had been tendered a cumulative total of over $500 million in Communist economic aid and an equivalent volume of Soviet military assistance.[79] The June 1972 nationalization has brought Moscow and Baghdad even closer together.

Financial or military assistance to both sides will not, however, obviate the necessity of deciding how to support rival claims. Will the U.S.S.R., in support of her client Iraq, be prepared to challenge the pretensions of Iran, seeking acknowledgment as protector and stabilizer of the Gulf? How would Moscow respond to a restaging of the Iraq-Kuwait crisis of 1961, but this time with Saudi Arabia and Iran, or the latter alone, playing the lifeguard role of Britain? The Kremlin is surely interested in preserving a militant radical Iraq as counterweight to the Western-oriented states, but it is doubtful that much profit would be seen in backing the Iraqi land grab. Such a policy might appear to the Gulf states as the preliminary to moving on other oil-rich principalities, and some of the possible adverse (to the U.S.S.R.) consequences of that have already been indicated.

Moscow's attitude to the growth and deployment of Iranian power must be at best ambivalent. If during the 1960s the U.S.S.R. believed that she too would "benefit from a strong and independent Iran,"[80] the motives were likely to have included interest in separating Iran from the United States. Even then, the Kremlin may have had another string to its bow. Mustafa Barzani, leader of the Iraqi Kurds, told a Western correspondent that in August 1962 "Communists" had tried to persuade him to incite fellow Kurds across the border in Iran, for which he was promised arms, supplies, and money. According to Barzani, pressure to turn the Iranian flank in this manner continued to be exerted on him at the time of the negotiations with the Iraqi government at the beginning of 1970.[81] If and when Soviet involvement in Gulf affairs increases, there may be greater temptation to take a harder line toward Iran. On the other hand, the rapid development of the Shah's military power, particularly if it operates in concert with the Arab states of the Gulf, may force the Soviet Union to weigh more carefully the risks and rewards of intervention in the region.

The key to future political stability in the Gulf seems to be the tripartite relation between Iran, Saudi Arabia, and the principalities. Iran is eager to fill singlehandedly the power vacuum left by British withdrawal, but the Shah must reckon with Faisal's (or his successor's) notions of the proper Saudi role in Gulf affairs. In contrast to the balance-of-power policy followed with respect to neighbors in the northwest and southwest, Riyadh "pursues instead something akin to an imperial policy" in the

Gulf region, where the future of the vital national resource, oil, is at stake.[82] Weakness and disorganization among the principalities could engender conflict between Riyadh and Tehran, as well as between the latter and Baghdad. Conversely, an internally cohesive Federation of Arab Amirates, even without Bahrain and Qatar, might enable Shah and King to cooperate in containing Soviet or Iraqi ambitions.

Soviet policy in the Middle East has often perceived a constraint on the left in Chinese Communist rivalry for leadership in the "Third World." But it may be a mistake to assume that the Chinese will play a purely radicalizing role in Persian Gulf affairs. Admittedly, Peking has already obtained a foothold in the P.D.R.Y. and the P.F.L.O.A.G., but it is also on good terms with Tehran. The Shah's attempt to develop an "Indian Ocean strategy" is surely directed at containment of the Soviet Union. It is unlikely that the Chinese would be unsympathetic with this objective.[83]

As an arena for Soviet penetration, the Persian Gulf "suffers" by comparison with the Near East. Iraq is not Egypt and no dispute in the Gulf region offers the U.S.S.R. as comfortable a perch as the Arab-Israel conflict. Moscow forged a position for herself in the Eastern Mediterranean by alliance with the largest and most stable Arab power, led by a figure of commanding presence, on an issue in which general (if usually only minimal) Arab support was guaranteed. The Soviet client in the Gulf region is chronically *coup*-ridden and universally distrusted; its fundamental conflict is with a state that enjoys the patron's largesse to an almost equal degree. With the development of militant Arab nationalism in Egypt and Syria, Moscow felt no hesitation in choosing between Israel and the Arabs. On the other hand, the rivalry of Iraq and Egypt posed difficult problems for Soviet policy after the overthrow of the Baghdad monarchy in July 1958.

The dilemma inherent in backing regional rivals is undoubtedly one of the major weak points of a possible activist Soviet stance in the Persian Gulf region. Another is the danger of alarming Middle East and West alike about the scope of Soviet ambitions with respect to control of a major share of the Eastern Hemisphere's oil production. In attempting to achieve a delicate balance among inconsistent and potentially dangerous alternatives, Moscow may unwittingly leave the door open to a regional equilibrium of forces.

Table A

FUEL OUTPUT IN THE USSR, 1940–70 (Million Tons, Except as Otherwise Indicated)

	1940	1950	1955	1960	1965	1970	1975
In natural units							
Oil	31.1	37.9	70.8	147.9	242.9	352.6	496
Natural gas[1] (billion cubic meters)	3.2	5.8	9.0	45.3	127.7	197.9	320
Coal	165.9	261.1	389.9	509.6	577.7	624.1	695
Peat	33.2	36.0	50.8	53.6	45.7	57.5	n.a.
Shale	1.7	4.7	10.8	14.1	21.3	24.3	n.a.
In standard fuel units[2] (million tons)							
Oil	44.5	54.2	101.2	211.4	346.4	504.2	709
Natural gas[1]	4.4	7.3	11.4	54.4	149.8	235.6	381
Coal	140.5	205.7	310.8	373.1	412.5	451.2	500
Peat	13.6	14.8	20.8	20.4	17.0	21.4	44–58
Shale	0.6	1.3	3.3	4.8	7.4	8.5	
Firewood[3]	34.1	27.9	32.4	28.7	33.5	27.7	
Total	237.7	311.2	479.9	692.8	966.6	1,248.6	1,634–1,648
Percent of total							
Oil	18.7	17.4	21.1	30.5	35.8	40.4	43
Natural gas[1]	1.9	2.3	2.4	7.9	15.5	18.9	23
Coal	59.1	66.1	64.8	53.9	42.7	36.1	30–31
Peat	5.7	4.8	4.3	2.9	1.7	1.7	3–4
Shale	0.3	0.4	0.7	0.7	0.8	0.7	
Firewood	14.3	9.0	6.7	4.1	3.5	2.2	

Notes:

n.a. means not available.

[1] Including by-product gas. Output of by-product gas alone came to 1.8 billion cubic meters in 1950, 7.7 in 1960, 16.5 in 1965, and 21.6 in 1969.

[2] 7,000 kilocalories calorific value per ton.

[3] Centralized output only; excludes output by households for own use. See Robert W. Campbell, *The Economics of Soviet Oil and Gas*, Johns Hopkins University Press, 1968, pp. 4–5.

Sources:

1940–70. TsSU SSSR: *Promyshlennost' SSSR*, Statistika, 1964, p. 228; *Narodnoe khoziaistvo SSSR v 1970 g.*, Statistika, 1971, pp. 142–3, 183–5, 187, 189.

1975. Targets in natural units from *Pravda*, 25 November, 1971. Natural units were converted to standard fuel units at rates implied for 1970.

The 9th F.Y.P. directives (*Materialy XXIV s"ezda KPSS*, Politizdat, 1971, p. 248) had called for a minimum two-thirds share for oil and gas in total fuel output. In conjunction with the revised coal, oil, and gas targets, this implies a total output goal of 1,634 MT and a residual figure of 44 MT for peat, shale, and firewood. The latter figure seems low, requiring perhaps a considerable decline in firewood use. Arbitrarily, the 1970 level of output of the three minor fuel sources is included as a maximum 1975 goal.

Table B

U.S.S.R. FOREIGN TRADE IN OIL AND GAS, 1955–70

I. Oil Exports by Country Group (Million tons)		Non-"Socialist" Europe[1] and Japan	"Socialist" Countries				Rest of the World	Total
			C.E.M.A. Member States[2]	China	Other[3]	Arab Clients[4]		
1955	crude	0.3	1.7	[5]	0.2	0.2	0.5	2.9
	refined	2.0	0.6	1.2	0.1	0.2	1.0	5.1
	C & R	2.3	2.3	1.2	0.3	0.4	1.5	8.0
1960	crude	8.2	6.3	0.6	2.0	0.7	—	17.8
	refined	7.7	3.1	2.4	0.9	0.9	0.4	15.4
	C & R	15.9	9.3	3.0	2.9	1.6	0.5	33.2
1965	crude	16.4	18.3	[5]	4.1	0.7	3.9	43.4
	refined	11.3	4.3	—	2.1	0.2	3.1	21.0
	C & R	27.7	22.6	—	6.3	0.9	6.9	64.4
1970	crude	} 41.2	} 40.5	[6]	} 9.9	1.8	} 2.4	66.8
	refined			data not available				29.0
	C & R							95.8

II. Oil Imports (Million tons)

	1955	1960	1965	1970
Crude	0.6	1.2	—	2.5[7]
of which: from				
Austria	0.5	1.0	—	—
Algeria	—	—	—	0.5
Egypt	—	—	—	2.0
Refined	3.8	3.2	1.9	1.1
of which: from				
Rumania	3.4	2.8	1.6	0.5
G.D.R.	0.2	0.2	0.3	—

III. Gas Exports and Imports (Billion cubic meters)

	1955	1960	1965	1970
Imports	—	—	—	2.6[8]
Exports	0.1	0.2	0.4	3.3

Notes:

Totals may differ from sums of components because of rounding.   [1]Excluding Turkey and Cyprus.
[2]Bulgaria, Hungary, G.D.R, Poland, Rumania, Czechoslovakia, Mongolia.
[3]Yugoslavia, N. Vietnam, N. Korea, Cuba (after 1959).   [4]Egypt, Syria, Yemen, S. Yemen, Somalia.
[5]No entry.   [6]Less than 50 thousand tons.   [7]The sum of identified imports from Algeria and Egypt.
[8]Identified imports from Afghanistan.

Sources:

Ministerstvo vneshnei torgovli SSR: *Vneshniaia torgovlia SSSR, Statisticheskii sbornik, 1918–1966*, I.M.O., 1967; *Vneshniaia torgovlia SSSR za 1961 god*, Vneshtorgizdat, 1962; *Vneshniaia torgovlia SSSR za 1966 god*, I.M.O., 1967; *Vneshniaia torgovlia SSSR za 1970 god*, I.M.O., 1971.

Table C
SOVIET OIL CONSUMPTION, 1940–70
(Million Tons)

	1940	1950	1955	1960	1965	1970
1. Ouput of crude	31.1	37.9	70.8	147.9	242.9	352.6
2. Exports of crude	—	0.3	2.9	17.8	43.4	66.8
3. Imports of crude	—	0.3	0.6	1.2	—	2.5
4. Net exports of crude at field equivalent	—	—	2.4	17.5	45.7	67.7
5. Exports of refined products	0.9	0.8	5.1	15.4	21.0	29.0
6. Imports of refined products	0.1	2.3	3.8	3.2	1.9	1.1
7. Net exports of products at C.O.E.	0.9	-1.8	1.5	14.4	22.5	32.8
8. Net exports of products at field equivalent	0.9	-1.9	1.6	15.2	23.7	34.5
9. Consumption, row 1 minus rows 4 and 8	30.2	39.8	66.8	115.2	173.5	250.4
Index, 1960 = 100	26.2	34.5	58.0	100.0	150.6	217.4

Sources :
Output from Table A, trade from Table B. Refinery losses and fuel expenditure are assumed to be 15 percent, following Campbell, *Economics of Soviet Oil and Gas*, p. 226 (Jaroslav G. Polach, "The Energy Gap in the Communist World," *East Europe*, April 1969, **18**:4, p. 21 uses 13 percent). Losses in storage and transportation of crude or crude equivalents are assumed at 5 percent, again following Campbell, pp. 160 and 226.

Table D

U.S.S.R. AGGREGATE ENERGY BALANCE, 1960–75

(Million Tons of Standard Fuel)

	1960	1965	1970	1975
Resources (net)				
Fuel output	692.8	966.6	1,248.6	1,634–1,648
Hydroelectricity output	6.3	10.0	15.3	⎰ 60
Other	32.7	35.5	35.4	⎱
Total	731.8	1,012.1	1,299.3	1,694–1,708
Utilization (net)				
Consumption for:				
production of electricity				
and heat	221.2	335.0	452.0	n.a.
production-technical				
and other needs (including				
storage and				
transportation losses)	456.8	562.8	678.2	n.a.
Total	678.0	897.8	1,130.3	1,478–1,492[1]
Net exports	49.1	107.6	149.5	216
Net change in stocks	4.7	6.7	19.6	[2]
Total	731.8	1,012.1	1,299.3	1,694–1,708

Notes:

n.a. means not available.

[1] Including net change in stocks.

[2] Included with consumption.

Sources:

1960–70: TsSU, *Narodnoe khoziaistvo SSSR v 1970 g.,* p. 63. 1975: Output from Table A. Remaining components of resources extrapolated from prior years. Net exports: 1975 net exports of oil in Table 1 (rows 3 and 6) are 142 MT C.O.E., equivalent to 203 MT of standard fuel (see Table A for conversion ratio). The foreign trade yearbook for 1970 reports 17.4 MT of net exports of coal in that year, equivalent to 12.5 MT of standard fuel. It is assumed that coal net exports are the same in 1975. (Note that 1970 net exports of crude and products in C.O.E. were 97.1 MT (Table C), equivalent to 138.9 MT of standard fuel. The sum of this and the figure for coal exports, 12.5 MT, is 151.4 MT, or only 1.3 percent different from the official figure shown above.) Total consumption, including net change in stocks, in 1975 is obtained as a residual— total utilization less net exports.

NOTES

[1] For example, see "When Oil Flows East," *Economist,* 10 January, 1970, pp. 51–2.

[2] V. D. Shashin, "Neftedobyvaiushchaia promyshlennost' SSSR za 50 let Sovetskoi vlasti," *Neftianoe khoziaistvo,* 1967, No. 10, p. 7; Tass dispatch, 27 October, 1967. Khrushchev's ambitious 20-year plan had called for 690–710 million tons by 1980 (*Pravda,* 19 October, 1961); Shashin disclosed a 1980 target of 600–620 MT.

[3] "Soviet Bars Increase in Exports of Oil," *New York Times,* 11 January, 1969.

[4] For discussion of the Soviet reserve concepts, see Robert W. Campbell, *The Economics of Soviet Oil and Gas,* Baltimore, Md.: Johns Hopkins University Press, 1968, pp. 60–2.

[5] "Za novye rubezhi v razvitii neftedobyvaiushchei promyshlennosti," *Neftianoe khoziaistvo,* 1969, No. 1, p. 2. The increase in $A + B + C_1$ reserves came to 70 percent, yet only a year earlier, Shashin had claimed a 120 percent increase in the same category of reserves over the previous ten years. Shashin, "Neftedobyvaiushchaia promyshlennost' SSSR za 50 let . . .," p. 7.

[6] "Russian Reserves Are Inadequate," *Petroleum Press Service,* **36**:4, April 1969, p. 122.

[7] Radio Moscow in English, 2 June, 1969.

[8] *Pravda,* 15 January, 1970, and Shashin (as cited in n. 2 above). Output from the Siberian fields was to exceed 30 MT in 1970, whereas the Directives approved by the 23rd Party Congress in 1966 had called for 20–25 MT.

[9] Iu Sokolov and N. Feitel'man, "'Neft' i gaz Tiumeni'—novyi nauchno-tekhnicheskii sbornik," *Izvestiia Akademiia nauk SSSR, Seriia ekonomicheskaia,* 1971, No. 3, p. 131. In early 1972, the Tiumen fields were said to have "recoverable" reserves of about 7 billion tons ("Soviet Seeks Japan Loan," *New York Times,* 25 February, 1972).

[10] Kosygin's speech to the Supreme Soviet, 24 November, 1971, printed in *Pravda* the following day. At the 24th Party Congress in April, Kosygin stated a range, 480–500 MT. *Materialy XXIV s"ezda KPSS,* Moscow: Politizdat, 1971, p. 248.

[11] *Ekonomicheskaia gazeta,* No. 4, January 1970, p. 6 (interview with Shashin).

[12] This is the growth rate implied by comparison of the initial and terminal years only. For the first time since the prewar era, annual goals as well as the

ultimate year's target have been supplied for industrial output (in Kosygin's speech, n. 10 above). The rate of increase is not constant over the period.

[13] *Materialy XXIV s"ezda*, p. 182.

[14] The source of all Soviet foreign trade data in this paper is the series of official yearbooks, Ministerstvo vneshnei torgovli, *Vneshniaia torgovlia SSSR za—god*, annually for the years 1960–70 and the special volumes for 1959–63 (published in 1965) and 1918–66 (published in 1967). See Table B.

[15] The 9th F.Y.P. calls for 44 percent growth in electricity output. Between 1960 and 1965 the increase in fuel consumed for power and heat production was two-thirds as large as the growth of electric power output (net of hydropower). Between 1965 and 1970, the ratio was raised to 78 percent (Table D and TsSU, *Narodnoe khozaistvo SSSR v 1970 g.*, Moscow: Statistika, 1971—abbreviated to *NK 1970*—p. 179). The Directives promise "significant fuel economies" from the construction of very large power units of 500, 800 and 1,200 thousand kilowatts, reflected in 1975 fuel expenditure per kilowatt-hour of 340–342 grams, compared with a 1970 level of about 367 grams (*Materialy XXIV s"ezda*, pp. 147, 247, and *NK 1970*, p. 181). The anticipated saving is about 7 percent per unit of electricity output. Therefore, aggregate fuel inputs for a 44 percent increase in power output would have to grow by a third or slightly more.

In Table D, an energy balance for 1975 is calculated from the known fuel output targets and the estimate of oil exports in Table 1. If fuel utilization for production of electricity and heat is scheduled to grow by a third, the second component of consumption (production-technical needs, etc.) could increase by about 30 percent. Suppose, however, that Table 1 is constructed on the assumption of a 4.8 percent per year growth in inland consumption, rather than 6.8 percent. Then total net exports of oil in C.O.E. would be 171 MT, equivalent to 245 MT of standard fuel. On the assumption that non-petroleum (chiefly coal) exports remain at the level of 13 MT indicated in the sources to Table D, total fuel net exports would rise to 258 M.T. This forces the total consumption (including stock increments) figure in Table D down from 1,478–1,492 to 1,446–1,460 MT. If consumption for electricity and heat is still to increase by one-third, the implied allowance for the residual component of utilization is 835–849 MT, or roughly one-quarter more than in 1970.

[16] *Pravda*, 20 February, 1966.

[17] By 1972, for example, the Soviet Union was to begin delivering natural gas to Italy at the rate of 6 billion cubic meters annually ("Italy to Import Natural Gas From Soviet," *The New York Times*, 11 December, 1969). *Total* Soviet exports in 1970 were only half as large—3.3 billion cubic meters. Latest figures (*Vneshniaia torgovlia SSSR za 1971 god,* IMO, 1972, and TsSU, *SSSR v tsifrakh v 1971 godu*, Statistika, 1972) show that Soviet gas exports rose

by almost two-fifths in the single year 1971 but gas production increased in proportion.

18 See below, p. 186. *Vneshniaia torgovlia SSSR za 1971* reports a 122 percent jump in gas imports during 1971, as the flow of Iranian gas rose to 5.6 bm^3 from 1.0 bm^3 in 1970.

19 However, according to the *Petroleum Press Service* ("Soviet Bloc Trade Marks Time," **36**:5, May 1969, p. 164), "the country's crude oil production target for 1980 was stated [in April 1969] to be 550–600 million tons."

20 *Ibid*: **38**:2, February 1971, p. 64.

21 O.E.C.D., *Energy Policy, Problems and Objectives,* Paris 1966, cited in Stanislaw Wasowski, "The Fuel Situation in Eastern Europe," *Soviet Studies,* **21**:1, July 1969, p. 44. A recent American forecast for 1980 is 100 MT higher but seems of doubtful reliability. *International Petroleum Encyclopedia 1970,* Tulsa, Oklahoma: Petroleum Publishing Co., 1970, p. 7. According to the *Petroleum Press Service* ("Soviet Oil in the Seventies," **37**:1, January 1970, pp. 3–5), the U.N.'s Economic Commission for Europe projected Soviet inland consumption in 1980 as 595 MT.

22 See n. 20.

23 *Petroleum Press Service,* **38**:8, August 1971, p. 286.

24 *International Petroleum Encyclopedia 1970,* p. 7; Wasowski, "The Fuel Situation in Eastern Europe," pp. 40–1.

25 One might also add into account the imports of Soviet oil by the U.S.S.R.'s Arab clients—Egypt, Somalia, Syria and Yemen. The imports of these four countries came to 1.8 MT in 1970, almost 90 percent of which was destined for Egypt. However, Egyptian production is rising steadily.

26 See, for example, "Soviet Tells Bloc to Buy Crude Oil in Middle East," *New York Times,* 24 November, 1969.

27 "Poland Signs Pact to Buy Oil from British Concern," *New York Times,* 3 July, 1971; "Poland Turns West," *Economist,* 10 July, 1971; *Financial Times* (London), 22 October, 1971. In the aftermath of the Iraqi nationalization, East European imports are being stepped up. See *Reuters East-West Trade News,* 3 August, 1972, and *Middle East Economic Digest,* 8 September, 1972.

28 See n. 3 above.

29 It is not clear whether the changes occurred in exports of crude oil or refined products or both. In 1967 crude accounted for 60 percent of the imports by non-Communist Europe and Japan but almost 80 percent of imports by Eastern Europe and Cuba.

30 Campbell, *op. cit.,* p. 237. See also E. Kuprinov, "Raschetnye tseny i rentabel'-nost' predpriiatii," *Voprosy ekonomiki,* 1968, No. 3, p. 49.

31 Campbell, *op. cit.,* pp. 136–7.

32 A. S. Becker, *Prices of Producers' Durables in the U.S. and the USSR,* RM-

2432, Santa Monica, California: The RAND Corp., August 1959, pp. 47–9; and unpublished estimates by the author.

[33] This brief summary hardly does justice to a complex question. For additional discussion that takes into account transportation cost as well, see Campbell, *op. cit.*, pp. 236–41.

[34] The complaints are still being voiced. E.g., Iu. Savenko, "Problemy toplivno-energeticheskogo balansa v stranakh-chlenakh SEV," *Voprosy ekonomiki,* 1969, No. 7, p. 123.

[35] A. I. Komin, *Problemy planovogo tsenoobrazovaniia,* Moscow: Ekonomika, 1971, p. 121.

[36] "Novye tseny—etap khoziaistvennoi reformy," *Planovoe khoziaistvo,* 1967, No. 7, p. 15.

[37] A. Probst, "Puti razvitiia toplivnogo khoziaistva SSSR," *Voprosy ekonomiki,* 1971, No. 6, pp. 52–3. An earlier Soviet source claimed average production cost of Tiumen oil was no more than 4 rubles per (natural) ton (*Sotsialisticheskaia industriia,* 13 September, 1970), equivalent to 2.8 rubles per standard ton, but this figure probably excludes investment costs.

[38] Probst, *op. cit.,* p. 53.

[39] *Ibid.,* pp. 52, 57.

[40] L. Kantorovich, "O tsenakh, tarifakh i effektivnosti ekonomiki," *Ekonomika i organizatsiia promyshlennogo proizvodstva,* 1971, No. 1, p. 27.

[41] Middle Eastern costs are of the order of 12–20 cents per barrel (estimate by M. A. Adelman, cited in Sam H. Schurr and Paul T. Homan, *Middle Eastern Oil and The Western World: Prospects and Problems,* New York: American Elsevier, 1971, p. 123), equivalent to 88–146 cents per ton.

[42] It would pay the U.S.S.R. to barter for oil so long as the real foreign trade earnings foregone by selling the exported commodity for oil rather than something else are no higher than the value of the imported oil. If the oil is destined for internal consumption, its value is sales proceeds foregone on the foreign market.

[43] The Soviet Union has apparently offered to supply Japan with 25–40 MT of Tiumen oil annually for 20 years as part of a package deal that includes a $1.5 billion Japanese loan to the U.S.S.R. and Soviet purchase of steel tube in Japan. The tube would be used to extend a pipeline from the Tiumen oil fields to the Sea of Japan. "Soviet Seeks Japan Loan," *New York Times,* 25 February, 1972.

[44] "Approximate comparison of outlays on oil and gas extraction in the Soviet Union and on her imports from several developing countries shows that under specified conditions, importing can be advantageous even for the U.S.S.R." L. Zevin, "Voprosy povysheniia ustoichivosti i effektivnosti ekonomicheskikh sviazei SSSR s razvivaiushchimsia stranami," *Planovoe khoziaistvo,* 1971, No. 7, p. 23. Zevin adds that the scale of imports would

depend in large degree on "the readiness and capability of the relevant developing countries to open wider access for goods from the socialist states on their markets on mutually advantageous conditions" (*ibid.*, p. 24).

45 *Jerusalem Post*, 29 October, 1970.

46 See, however, Zevin (cited in n. 44 above) who believes that a significant scale of C.E.M.A. oil imports (60–90 MT) from the developing countries would not come before the late 1980s (p. 24).

47 B. Rachkov, "The Future of Arab Oil," *International Affairs* (Moscow), 1970, No. 8, pp. 32–7. Rachkov touched briefly on this theme in an earlier article, "Neftianye monopolii i agressiia Izrailia," *Kommunist*, No. 12, August 1967, pp. 113–4.

48 "Five Year Oil Accord Is Reached in Iran by 23 Companies," *New York Times*, 15 February, 1971.

49 For convenient summaries see *International Financial News Survey*, Vol. XXIII, p. 141 (No. 18) and pp. 196–7 (No. 25, 30 June, 1971). See also J. E. Hartshorn, "From Tripoli to Teheran and Back: The Size and Meaning of the Oil Game," *The World Today*, July 1971, pp. 293–7.

50 T. J. Hamilton, "Six Persian Gulf Oil Nations Win Price Increase at Geneva Talks," *New York Times*, 21 January, 1972.

51 *Middle East Economic Survey, Supplement*, 11 July, 1969, cited in Schurr and Homan, *op. cit.*, p. 137.

52 "Oil Nations Seeking Role in Companies," *New York Times*, 3 November, 1971; "Oil Under the Gun," *Forbes*, 15 March 1972.

53 Schurr and Homan, *op. cit.*, p. 139.

54 *Ibid.*

55 M. A. Adelman, *The World Petroleum Market*, cited in Schurr and Homan, *op. cit.*, p. 144. Emphasis in the original.

56 Most informed projections indicate non-Communist world consumption of oil growing at rates approximating 5–6 percent annually to the end of the decade and perhaps beyond. See, for example, Shurr and Homan, *op. cit.*, pp. 23–9.

57 Rachkov, "The Future of Arab Oil," p. 36.

58 D.L.M., "Soviet Interest in Middle East Oil," *Mizan*, 10:3, May–June 1968, p. 81.

59 *Pravda*, 16 August, 1967.

60 The proposal was actually for a full boycott for three months, with selective penalties thereafter.

61 Earlier, on 14 August, Radio Moscow had declared that "the actions of the oil-producing countries are fully legitimate and are totally consistent with the provisions of the concession agreements, which entitle the governments of the oil-producing countries to withhold sales from the countries whose policy is deemed hostile to them."

[62] Radio Moscow, Domestic Service, 27 August, 1967.

[63] For example, Radio Moscow, International Service in English, 29 August; *Trud*, 31 August, 1967.

[64] See, for example, V. Kudriavtsev in *Izvestiia*, 5 September, 1967.

[65] Compare Rachkov's 1967 and 1970 articles (see n. 47).

[66] The theme has begun to be sounded more often recently. See R. Petrov, "Antiarabskaia politika SShA," *Novoe vremia*, No. 24, 11 June, 1971, p. 14, but especially, below, p. 27.

[67] Before the Six-Day War, Britain's stockpile was sufficient for four months normal consumption. In addition, there are routine stocks that are said to equal 45 days consumption. Schurr and Homan, *op. cit.*, pp. 80, 82.

[68] T.T. Connors, *An Examination of the International Flow of Crude Oil, With Special Reference to the Middle East*, P-4209, Santa Monica, California: The RAND Corp., October 1969, p. 29. The trend was still sharply upward. Whereas the existing fleet at the end of 1967 averaged 31,000 DWT, the average size of tankers on order in November 1968 was 92,000 tons, and that figure would be substantially higher if the 90 small carriers ordered by the U.S.S.R. were excluded. It should be noted, in this connection, that at its pre-closure depth of 38 feet, the Suez Canal could accept fully loaded vessels only up to 50,000 tons. Thus, the trend to even larger tankers threatened the future utility of the Canal, if it stayed closed too long. *Ibid.*, pp. 30, 32,39.

[69] Schurr and Homan, *op. cit.*, Chapter 4.

[70] It will be apparent that the approach set out in this section departs somewhat from Robert E. Hunter's, *The Soviet Dilemma in the Middle East. Part II: Oil and the Persian Gulf*, London Institute of Strategic Studies, October 1969. Hunter judges that the U.S.S.R. is unlikely to pursue a "colonial" policy with respect to Persian Gulf oil; Soviet policy instead "is likely to be exclusively commercial" (p. 9). Hunter's dichotomy seems to be too neatly drawn for the rapidly changing arena of Gulf politics and economics. In this respect I have modified the view expressed in A. S. Becker and A. L. Horelick, *Soviet Policy in the Middle East*, R-504-FF, Santa Monica, California: The RAND Corporation, September 1970, p. 103 (published in S. S. Alexander and P.Y. Hammond, eds., *Political Dynamics in the Middle East*, New York: American Elsevier, 1972). Hunter's approach is shared by John A. Berry, "Oil and Soviet Policy in the Middle East," *Middle East Journal*, **26**:2, Spring 1972, pp. 149–160.

[71] David Holden, "The Persian Gulf After the British Raj," *Foreign Affairs*, **49**:4, July 1971, p. 734.

[72] Leonard Binder, *Factors Influencing Iran's International Role*, RM-5968-FF, Santa Monica, California: The RAND Corporation, October 1969, pp. 37–8 (published as "Iran's Potential as a Regional Power," in Alexander and Hammond, eds., *Political Dynamics in the Middle East*).

[73] E.g., on acceptance of the Suez Canal cease-fire agreement in the summer of 1970. The Iraqi Ba'th has also engaged in bloody repression of Communist Party activities. *An-Nida* (Beirut), 5 April, 30 May, 1970, and 21 January, 1971; *al-Akhbar* (Beirut), 13 December, 1970, and 23 May, 1971; *Pravda,* 26 September, 1970.

[74] The embers of Kurdish dissatisfaction are, nonetheless, still smoldering. See, for example, *Jeune Afrique*, No. 507, 22 September, 1970, p. 49; *L'Orient-Le Jour* (Beirut), 18 November, 1971.

[75] Through the promotion of "people's war," the Front aims to create a single socialist Arab state, already named the Arab People's Republic of the Gulf, which is to include Oman, the Trucial States, Qatar, Bahrein and Kuwait. See Sevinc Carlson, "The Chinese Intrusion," *New Middle East*, No. 27, December 1970, p. 39.

[76] *The Gulf: Implications of British Withdrawal*, The Center for Strategic and International Studies, Georgetown University, Washington, D.C. Special Report Series: No. 8, February 1969, p. 79.

[77] *Pravda*, 11 October, 1971. However, the Soviet press has treated the Dhofar rebels with great sympathy. See the articles by A. Vasilev in *Pravda*, 29 September and 4 October, 1969; 3 August, 1971.

[78] *The Economist*, 20 June, 1970, p. 32.

[79] Department of State, Bureau of Intelligence and Research, *Communist States and Developing Countries: Aid and Trade in 1970*, RECS-15, 22 September, 1971, pp. 2–4, 18–19; *Vneshniaia torgovlia SSSR za 1970 god*, 1971, pp. 11–15; "Growing Soviet Economic Stake in Middle East," *Middle East Economic Digest*, 28 August, 1970, p. 1010.

[80] Binder, *op. cit.*, p. 36.

[81] Barzani maintained that he refused to lend himself to such purposes at any time. His response to a question posed by the Iraq News Agency on Baghdad Radio, 15 March, 1970, is consistent with his claim.

[82] Robert R. Sullivan, "Saudi Arabia in International Politics," *The Review of Politics*, 32:4, October 1970, p. 451.

[83] Hossein Amirsadeghi, "Iran's New Outward Look," *New Middle East*, No. 35, August 1971, pp. 9–10.

Gur Ofer

THE ECONOMIC BURDEN OF SOVIET INVOLVEMENT IN THE MIDDLE EAST*

I. INTRODUCTION

From 1954, when its aid program to (non-Communist) developing countries started, until the end of 1970, the Soviet Union has extended over $7 billion of economic-aid credits and almost the same amount of military aid. By the end of 1971 at least another billion dollars will have been made available. The Soviet Union's East European satellites were also induced to join in this effort with close to $3 billion of economic aid as well as considerable amounts of military aid (see Table 1).[1] While most military credits have already been taken up, less than half of the economic aid had been drawn by the end of 1970. All in all, the aid effort is by now close to $20 billion.

What stands out is the large share of aid going to the region extending from North Africa to the Indian subcontinent, and within this region the concentration on the Middle East. Of the total, 80 percent was extended to the wider region, and more than half the military aid and a quarter of the economic aid, to the Middle East (Egypt, Iraq, and Syria). Egypt alone received a full 40 percent of all military supplies and more than 16 percent of all economic support, and has thus become the largest single recipient of aid from the Soviet Union and Eastern Europe. The new economic agreement concluded in March 1971 provides for about half a billion dollars of economic aid, and military supplies poured in throughout

* This paper is part of a project on Soviet Middle-East involvement at present under way at the Russian and East European Research Centre, The Hebrew University of Jerusalem. An earlier version was read at the Tel Aviv Conference on the Soviet Union and the Middle East (December 26–30, 1971). I would like to thank Edward Lutwak for his advice on military matters (especially on Section III) and for his many valuable comments on an earlier draft. Thanks are due also to Abraham Becker for his important comments. The paper presented here is, with only minor alterations, the one that was read at the conference; thus no changes were introduced following the ouster of Soviet personnel from Egypt.

Table 1.

ECONOMIC AND MILITARY AID BY THE SOVIET UNION AND EASTERN EUROPE, BY REGION AND COUNTRY OF DESTINATION: 1954–70[1]

		Millions of U.S. dollars			Percent			
	Total	Soviet Union		Eastern Europe Economic	Total	Soviet Union		Eastern Europe Economic
		Military	Economic			Military	Economic	
1. Total	**16,705**	**6,785**	**7,039**	**2,881**	**100.0**	**100.0**	**100.0**	**100.0**
2. North Africa, Middle East, Central Asia	13,506	5,520	5,887	2,099	80.8	81.4	83.6	72.8
3. North Africa[2]	826	270[3]	354	202	4.9	4.0	5.0	7.0
4. Iran and Turkey	1,502	135[4]	1,022[4]	345	9.0	2.0	14.5	12.0
5. Red Sea[5]	607	195[6]	324	88	3.6	2.9	4.6	3.0
6. Middle East[7]	6,159	3,650	1,571	938	36.9	53.8	22.3	32.6
7. Egypt	(4,273)	(2,700)	(1,011)	(562)	(25.6)	(39.8)	(14.4)	(19.5)
8. Iraq	(1,009)	(500)	(327)	(182)	(6.0)	(7.4)	(4.6)	(6.3)
9. Syria	(877)	(450)	(233)	(194)	(5.3)	(6.6)	(3.3)	(6.8)
10. Central Asia[8]	4,411	1,270	2,616	525	26.4	18.7	37.2	18.2
11. of which: India	(2,980)	(1,000)	(1,593)	(387)	(17.8)	(14.7)	(22.6)	(13.4)
12. Black Africa[9]	678	50	458	170	4.1	0.7	6.5	5.9
13. Latin America	590	—	283	307	3.5	—	4.0	10.7
14. South East Asia	1,932	1,215	411	306	11.6	17.9	5.9	10.6

[1] i. The figures in the source were apparently converted from rubles at the official exchange rate of 0.9 rubles/$1.
ii. No figures are available on military aid extended by Eastern European countries.
iii. Military aid figures refer to actual deliveries. Economic aid and figures refer to credits extended; the proportion of deliveries to credits is about 45 percent for the Soviet Union and much less for Eastern Europe

[2] Algeria, Libya, Morocco, and Tunisia.   [3] Does not include military aid to Libya since the figure is not available.
[4] Includes small sums for Cyprus and Greece.   [5] Ethiopia, Somalia, Southern Yemen, Sudan, and Yemen.
[6] Does not include military aid to Southern Yemen since the figure is not available.   [7] Egypt, Iraq, and Syria.
[8] Afghanistan, Ceylon, India, Nepal, and Pakistan.   [9] Other than countries included in line 5.

Source:
U.S. Department of State, Bureau of Intelligence and Research, Communist States and Developing Countries: Aid and Trade in 1970 (Research Study: RECS-15: September 1971), Table 1, pp. 2–4 and Table 8, pp. 18–19.

the year. The flow of aid was accompanied by increased trade with the recipient countries, more or less matching the aid distribution.[2]

On the one hand, these totals are impressive; and their distribution clearly indicates the direction and intensity of Soviet interests in the non-Communist world in general and in the Middle East in particular. On the other, the entire aid effort can be shown to be only a fraction of one percent of Soviet resources during the period, a fact that alone could support the argument that economic factors are of minor or even negligible importance in Soviet decisions on involvement in the Middle East (or elsewhere for that matter).

This paper concentrates on only one facet of the economic side of the Soviet involvement in the area, namely, on the economic burden that military aid imposes on the Soviet Union. Its main purpose is to evaluate this burden against various yardsticks and thus to locate it more precisely between the two extreme and contradictory impressions given above. Such an evaluation of the military aid (M.A.) burden is only one aspect, admittedly not a major one, of a general evaluation of Soviet involvement. Clearly any complete assessment would involve a full-scale cost-benefit analysis, weighing the expected strategic and political benefits and risks as well as the entire economic cost and possible advantages. I believe that the Soviet Union's strategic-political goals in the region are the decisive factors in this calculation and that economic considerations—on both the benefit and cost sides—are secondary. However, I am also of the belief that economic considerations enter into the decision-making process, on the cost side, at least. Stopping short of attempting the full cost-benefit calculation—not least because of the lack of comparability of economic costs and political and other benefits—precludes any definite conclusions about Soviet involvement. Nevertheless, I hope that this very partial analysis, dealing only with M.A., will enable us to get some idea of the factors which influence the Soviet Union and of the importance it attaches to penetrating the area.

The investigation will be pursued along three distinct, though interdependent lines. First, there is the perennial problem of evaluating Soviet ruble figures which are generally known not to represent real economic costs. Soviet aid prices should be evaluated in terms of their real alternative costs to the Soviet economy. These in turn may be different in the short and the long run. Second, once the right prices have been established the burden of the aid program is estimated. This burden may be defined as the ratio between the amount of aid and the amount of relevant alternative uses. The problem is to find the appropriate denominators of such ratios. There is an inverse relationship between the relative weight of a cost within a given alternative use and the scope of the relevant alternatives to be considered. For example, if the planners have full control over all Soviet resources and can shift them at will from one use to another, then the aid program should be compared with the whole Soviet G.N.P. and it will then be relatively unimportant. If, on the other hand, it is assumed that the realistic alternative is within the government budget or a special part of it, then the share and importance of the same aid program becomes much larger. Finally, it might be appropriate to compare the cost of the Soviet Union's international activity with that of its opposite number, the United States.

Problems of valuation are discussed in Section II. In Section III an attempt is made to estimate the share of M.A. programs in total Soviet military production. Section IV evaluates the M.A. burden of the Middle East conflict on the Soviet economy, and compares it with the corresponding burden on the United States. The connection between M.A. and other Soviet military and strategic interests in the region is briefly outlined in the concluding section.

II. PROBLEMS OF VALUATION OF MILITARY AID

What we refer to as military aid also includes deployment of Soviet military units in foreign (non-Communist) countries, which in essence means Egypt. It does not include Soviet deployment on the high seas even if its purpose is military support to an aid recipient.

The two main problems in estimating military aid are to obtain information on the actual flows of military equipment, ammunition, advisers, and so on, and how to evaluate these physical flows. The first problem must be left to the various intelligence agencies, private and governmental. No attempt is made here to double-check or improve on the information which they choose to supply to the general public.

The problem of valuation, although it has its informational aspects, also involves some economic considerations. Even when known or inferred, the very low ruble prices of military hardware are often rejected as not being the 'right' standard of valuation, and much higher Western prices are substituted. This is done on two grounds: (a) That Soviet prices for military equipment are scaled down artificially and that the right alternative or 'shadow' prices are much higher. To estimate the burden of military production on the Soviet economy, it is necessary to assign some set of higher prices.[3] (b) That even if Soviet ruble prices are 'correct,' where the military capabilities of the Soviet Union and the United States or of Egypt and Israel are to be compared, it is necessary to use prices that reflect those capabilities; thus, if the MIG-21 is comparable in its military characteristics with, say, the French Mirage, then for this type of comparison the same price tag should be put on both[4]—whether in dollars or in rubles.

These valuation problems are encountered whenever Soviet military production is involved and are widely discussed in the literature. As against the official exchange rate of 0.9 rubles/U.S. $1 and a rate based on relative G.N.P. prices[5] which is not much different, the value of the 'defense-equipment ruble' based on official Soviet prices comes within the range of 0.32–0.50 rubles per dollar. [6] This means that *relative* Soviet prices for military and space equipment are somewhere between two to three times lower than the comparative U.S. prices. The discussion in the literature on the source of this apparent price advantage may be summarized as follows. First, military equipment prices are kept down, at least to some extent, by means of the Soviet turnover tax system and by several open and many hidden subsidies to producers of military equipment.[7] Second, the heavy and military industries are more efficient than light industry and other branches thanks to the preferential treatment they have been given over the years—as regards investment, resources, skilled manpower, quality of materials and their prompt supply, and technological development inputs.[8] Third, as long as the production advantages of the heavy industry or military establishment stem only from these policy factors and not from any 'natural' or intrinsic advantages, the cost to the Soviet society and economy of having to live with backward consumer industries and agriculture should be charged against this sector. Consequently, the 'shadow' prices of every piece of equipment would have to carry this very great cost. This is the basic argument behind what is referred to as the "qualitative aspects" of the defense burden[9] or what Hanson calls "long-run military opportunity costs."[10] Fourth, Becker has advanced the argument that in centrally planned economies military-type industries have a natural advantage deriving directly from the nature of the system. In such a system only the military can impose the production and delivery discipline and quality control whose absence is the main source of inefficiency in the civilian, consumer-oriented industries.[11] While this may be so, there still remains the preferential treatment of military-type industries in supplies, materials, R & D, skilled manpower, etc., some of which are of major importance in a centrally planned economy. Finally, there is the argument that in the comparisons with the United States the Soviet products are of inferior quality; the inferiority is in part unintentional, but in part it represents a "deliberate emphasis on simplicity, commonality, and specialized function." Becker, from whose comment I have just quoted, thinks the second point is more apparent in military production while the first applies to civilian production.[12] Be that as it may, all differences between products should be allowed for before prices are compared.[13]

To sum up, it seems that even for the purpose of estimating the Soviet defense burden it is justified to set the prices of the equipment produced considerably higher than the official, though not necessarily as high as Western, prices.

The evaluation of Soviet military aid, by itself and in relation to Soviet military production, involves additional problems. First, the financial terms of the aid programs (prices, grants or loans, interest, etc.) must be ascertained. Second, the value depends on whether supplies consist of first-line weapons currently produced for the Soviet armed forces, of older vintages of equipment in use, or of surplus stocks. Third, it is necessary to know whether there are any biases in the Soviet pricing of conventional as distinct from nuclear, long-range delivery, and space equipment. No specific information is available on this point. Finally, it is doubtful whether any R & D costs should be charged to military aid. Here no such allowance is attempted beyond what is included in the price.

Under ordinary circumstances, Soviet military aid is extended in the form of medium-term to long-term low-interest credits. While not as productive as domestic investment, the returns on the loan, in the form of cotton, foodstuffs, natural gas, or oil, cover at least part of the original costs. The drawback of military aid loans is that they do not generate the economic potential from which they can be repaid, as economic aid funds sometimes do. In case of war, moreover, the equipment not only has to be replaced but the economic capability of the recipient to pay for this rearmament may be drastically reduced, as was the case with Egypt. Up to the early 1960s Egypt duly paid for Czech and Soviet arms with the best of its cotton and rice. In 1965, however, payments were suspended and an arms debt of $460 million was written off by the Soviet Union.[14] Since then, Egypt has paid little if anything, for military aid. In this case, as in a number of others, what started out as credit ended up as a grant-in-aid.

The vintage of the military equipment supplied can make a great deal of difference to the value of any specific Soviet M.A. program. There seem to be three economically relevant phases for an item of military equipment. In the first, the equipment is being introduced. At this stage, which takes a number of years, production lines are working full steam and the generals are impatient to get supplies. Any demand to supply the weapons to other countries is bound to create strong economic and other pressures, and such supplies should be charged at the full cost, if not more. The second phase comes when the item has been fully introduced; there is excess production capacity, with replacements being supplied on a small scale and part of the capacity diverted to civilian production.[15] Here it is the civilian production, whose supply has probably already been delayed by prior military needs, that is the main competitor of the foreign recipients. Nevertheless, the price of the equipment may be lower at this stage. In the third phase, the equipment has gone out of use in the Soviet Union and its alternative economic price is of course very low. A considerable share of Soviet military supplies to many countries has consisted of this third, surplus type.[16] As will be seen below, however, this hardly applies to the Middle East, certainly not to recent supplies to Egypt.

Finally, as the short history of Soviet M.A. has demonstrated more than once, it contains a large unplanned element. A substantial proportion of Soviet M.A. has had to be supplied under emergency conditions, and at very short notice. This stands in sharp contrast to the preplanned build-up and development programs of the Soviet forces. Short-notice orders are more costly and disrupt production and deployment schedules.

With these observations in mind, we can now turn to the figures.

III. THE SHARE OF MILITARY AID IN SOVIET MILITARY PRODUCTION

In this section, two calculations are juxtaposed, a monetary ruble-valued calculation of Soviet M.A. as a percentage of Soviet military production; and a similar calculation for M.A. to Egypt only, based mainly on a comparison of military equipment stocks.

Cost Comparisons

Table 2 presents Soviet military assistance to Egypt and the Middle East and to North Africa, the Middle East, and Central Asia combined,

Table 2.

THE MILITARY AID BURDEN OF THE SOVIET UNION: 1955–70[1]

	1955–70	1955–62	1963–67	1968–70
A. *Soviet military aid* (million rubles)				
1. To Egypt	2,430	900	495	1,035
2. To Middle East	3,285	1,510	743	1,035
3. To North Africa, Middle East, and Central Asia	4,968	1,746	1,769	1,454
B. *Soviet expenditures* (billion rubles)				
4. Defense equipment	74.8	20.7	28.9	25.2
5. Defense other than personnel and R & D	131.9	47.6	46.2	38.1
6. Total defense	257.9	98.1	88.7	71.1
7. Production of machinery & equipment	380.8	116.4	133.6	130.8
C. *The military aid burden* (percent)				
Aid to Egypt: panel A, line 1 divided by panel B				
Line 4	3.2	4.3	1.7	4.1
5	1.8	1.9	1.1	2.7
6	0.9	0.9	0.6	1.5
7	0.6	0.8	0.4	0.8
Aid to Middle East: panel A, line 2 divided by panel B				
Line 4	4.4	7.2	2.6	4.1
5	2.5	3.2	1.6	2.7
6	1.3	1.5	0.8	1.5
7	0.9	1.3	0.6	0.8
Aid to North Africa, Middle East, and Central Asia: panel A, line 3 divided by panel B				
Line 4	6.6	8.2	6.1	5.8
5	3.7	3.6	3.8	3.8
6	1.9	1.7	2.0	2.0
7	1.3	1.5	1.3	1.1

and compares it with Soviet expenditures on defense, defense equipment, and total production of machinery.

The U.S. State Department's Soviet M.A. figures used in our tables are somewhat on the conservative side compared with the figures given by other sources. M.A. to Egypt during 1963–70 is set at $1.7 billion, whereas the I.I.S.S. *Strategic Survey* estimates it at $4.5 billion, at free market prices, for the shorter 1967–70 period.[17] The I.I.S.S. figure goes down to about 2.5 billion at the official exchange rate, which is still above the State Department's figure,[18] and above the figure for total Soviet M.A. ($1.8 billion) given by the State Department for 1967–70.[19] Though differences are only to be expected, the discrepancy here is such that it may be due to the omission from the State Department figures of the deployment of Soviet units in Egypt in 1970. If so, and taking the Soviet deployment (which includes some 15,000 men, 150 MIG-2IJ and other planes in six air bases, about 80 SA-3 SAM sites, and a modern

---

[1]The regions are as in Table 1.

Source:

Panel A—the dollar figures of Table 1 converted to rubles by the official exchange rate of 0.9 rubles/$1; for the subperiods, U.S. Department of State, Director of Intelligence and Research, *Communist Governments and Developing Nations: Aid and Trade in 1967* (Research Memorandum: RSE–120), August 1968, p. 6, Table 2.

Panel B—Line 6 is the sum of the 'Defense' and 'Science' entries in the Soviet government budget. Line 5 is based on Stanley H. Cohn, "The Economic Burden of Soviet Defense Outlays," in U.S. Congress, Joint Economic Committee, *Economic Performance and the Military Burden in the Soviet Union* (91st Cong., 2nd Sess.: 1970), p. 183, Table A–2; figures for the missing years (1956–7, 1959, and 1968–70) were estimated on the basis of the proportion of the total in adjacent years (Cohn's total is also the sum of the official 'Defense' and 'Science' entries).

Lines 4 and 7 are based on Michael Boretsky, "The Technological Base of Soviet Military Power," in the Joint Economic Committee's report cited above, p. 227, Table A–3, and p. 214 (for 1970). Boretsky's figures are for 'machine-building products net of intra-industry sales' and he gives the amount out of this item going to defense. Figures for the missing years were interpolated on the basis of adjacent years. Boretsky's figures (in 1955 rubles) were converted to current rubles using the wholesale enterprise price index for machinery derivable from Cohn, *loc. cit.*

radar system)[20] to be about $500 million at Soviet prices, the two sources are much closer to each other. In view of this, the M.A. figures in Table 2 should be regarded as minimum estimates, at least for the last few years.

All the figures in Table 2 are shown in current rubles. However, discounts are given on some military aid, either when old or surplus equipment is supplied or for political reasons. The first type of discount represents real economic considerations; the second may lead to some understatement of the figures.[21] The most relevant comparison is between M.A. and Soviet production of military equipment as a whole. Of the two series that relate to total purchases, Beretsky's (line 6) is conceptually more appropriate than Cohn's (line 5), which in addition to equipment also includes construction, maintenance, and operations. Before using the results based on Boretsky's and Cohn's series it must be said that both are open to quite serious objections. Cohn's series contain a large element of guesswork, in his assumption that science allocations that are not devoted to defense are roughly equal to defense items hidden elsewhere in the budget. There is no way of knowing whether the procedure overstates or understates the figures. Boretsky's figures have been attacked as exaggerating both the level and the growth rate of Soviet military production.[22] If this is so, then both the level and growth rate of the figures in lines 7 of panel C are underestimated; as will become clear below, this is preferable to an overestimate.

As can be seen in the table (panel C, lines 4 and lines 5), the military equipment supplied to Egypt over the whole period came to 1.8–3.2 percent of the Soviet Union's defense production; when Syria and Iraq are added the figures go up to 2.5–4.4, and for North Africa, Middle East, and Central Asia combined, to 3.7–6.6.

The available data allow only a very rough breakdown into subperiods. The trend that emerges is of a relatively heavy burden in the initial build-up period followed by a decline in the early 1960s and an increase since 1967 or 1968. The series do not agree on whether the burden is greater or smaller at the beginning or the end of the period. The most important of the factors that have been pushing the burden down is the very marked increase in Soviet military production over the period. The real trend, however, may be steeper than some of the figures in the table suggest, considering the possible exaggeration in the growth rate of Boretsky's military production series (this affects lines 4 in panel C), the marked increase in the porportion of first-line equipment supplied, and the decline in the proportion of surplus-type weapons—presumably not all of this shift is reflected in the reported prices.[23] This last point applies especially to Egypt. Military aid to Egypt alone may well have reached 5 percent of Soviet military production in the last few years.[24]

One other point should be made. Since M.A. consists of only the conventional types of equipment, while a considerable share of Soviet production is devoted to strategic-nuclear and space systems, the aid burden is much heavier on the 'conventional' production.[25] Assuming that strategic weapons (as here defined) constitute one-quarter to one-third of military production, the burden on the non-strategic part is between one-third and one-half higher than that on the total. For Egypt alone it may come to 7.5 percent and for the entire Mediterranean-Central Asia region to 10 percent or more.

Comparison of Military Stocks

The following exercise is an attempt to compare Egyptian with Soviet non-strategic military stocks in mid-1971 and to arrive at the Soviet burden in Egypt, taking into account differences in the speed of build-up or turnover, losses, amortization, maintenance, and current operating costs, as well as differences in the type of equipment.

Units and Stocks[26]

Table 3 gives the relevant information on the army.

Although the comparison is necessarily selective, it does suggest that the present equipment stock of the Egyptian army is about 5 percent of the Soviet Union's. However, unlike the Soviet army, Egyptian divisional units are not equipped with tactical atomic weapons and battlefield surface-to-air missiles. Moreover, the Soviet army has been introducing the new T-62 tanks while the bulk of the Egyptian tank force is made up of the T-54/55 types which are being phased out although they will still be used in large numbers for several years.[27] Surplus T-54/55 tanks may have an alternative use in the formation of the new divisions for the Soviet Far East (prepositioning of equipment). These two factors bring the figure down to below 5 percent.

Air power is compared in Table 4. If only the tactical and non-strategic air defense segments of the Soviet air power are considered, then the Soviet effort in Egypt appears to be in excess of 5 percent. What is more, although the Soviet Air Force's equipment is on the whole somewhat

Table 3.
SOVIET AND EGYPTIAN ARMY STRENGTH: MID-1971[a]

	Egypt	Soviet Union	Egypt as per cent of Soviet Union	Remarks
Men (thousands)	275	1,750	16	
Divisions				
Tank	3	51	6	The Soviet division has about 30 percent fewer men than the Egyptian.
Mechanized	4	102	4	The Soviet division has about 10 percent fewer men than the Egyptian.
Infantry	5	—	..	
Parachute, commando, and airborne	3	7	[b]	
Equipment				
Medium tanks (thousands)	1.5–2.0	30–37	4–6	The higher Soviet figure is based on full strength of Soviet tank and mechanized divisions. The lower figure assumes that some units are below full strength. The number of Soviet guns is estimated at a 1:1 ratio with tanks.
Guns and howitzers (thousands)	1.5	30–37	4.5	
Frog and other surface-to-surface missiles	25	500	5	
Personnel carriers (thousands)	1.2	43	3	The Egyptian figure is probably an underestimate.

[a]Excluding Air Defense Command.
[b]No percentage is entered here since the figures are probably not comparable owing to classification differences.

Table 4.
SOVIET AND EGYPTIAN AIR STRENGTH: MID-1971

	Egypt	Soviet Union	Egypt as percent of Soviet Union	Remarks
Tactical air force	523	5,000–7,500	7½–10	For Egypt, 'combat aircraft' as in *The Military Balance*. For the Soviet Union, 5,000 is the figure for 'tactical aircraft' not including strategic, air defense, naval, and transport aircraft. The 7,500 includes the last two.
Helicopters	140	1,750–2,000	7–8	Egyptian helicopters are on the average smaller than Soviet ones.
Air defense				
Aircraft	150–200	3,200	5–6	Of about the same types: in Egypt, 150 MIG-21J and up to 50 SU-11 and MIG-23 operated by Soviet pilots.
SA-2 SAM				
(Guidelines)	420	8,000	5	
SA-3 SAM	320	2,000–3,000	14–16	
Radar-based integrated				
air defense unit	1	··	5 or more	The radar system in Egypt was taken to be equivalent to a Soviet Air Defense District (P.V.O.), of which there are 20. Software investment in Egypt is assumed to be higher than in a Soviet district.

more modern than the Egyptian, the difference is not so great as in the army, especially if the Soviet-operated squadrons of MIG-21J, SU-11, and MIG-23 interceptors are taken into account. Also of first-line quality are the radar system and the SA-3 missiles, likewise operated by Soviet crews.

As for naval power, most of the Soviet vessels are larger and more modern than either the submarines or the surface ships supplied to the Egyptian navy. The main exceptions are the *Osa* and *Komar* missile boats of which, according to *The Military Balance 1971–1972*, the Egyptians received 20, or about 15 percent, of a total Soviet stock of 140. The Egyptians have 12 diesel submarines, compared with 210, mostly bigger, Soviet submarines (not, of course, counting nuclear or cruise-missile submarines); 5 older destroyers, as against over 120 bigger and more modern Soviet destroyers, and so on. The Middle East conflict has not yet acquired a significant naval dimension and the Soviet aid burden in this region has consequently remained relatively light. Even so it appears that here, too, the Egyptian stock is upward of 5 percent when only the smaller vessels are included in the comparison.

Setting the Egyptian military stock at about 5 percent of the Soviet non-strategic stock seems to be a reasonable estimate. The percentage may be somewhat lower, considering that quite a number of M.A. items, while still used in large numbers in the Soviet and Warsaw-Pact armies, are no longer being produced in large numbers for first-line deployment. On the other hand, the large build-up of land and air power in the Far East, along the Chinese border, has increased the Soviet Union's own demand for most of these still operational items.

Build-up Rates, Replacements, Operations

The annual *flow* of Soviet military equipment, at least in the last five years, has evidently constituted a much higher percentage of the corresponding Soviet production than the 5 percent estimated for the stock. First, the present Egyptian stock has been built up mainly during the last five years, while the average full replacement period of Soviet stock is much longer. Second, the replacement rate in Egypt is higher even in peacetime owing to the high rate of wear and tear and to damage caused by poor maintenance and unqualified manpower. Third, actual fighting during much of 1968 through 1970 upped the rate of equipment amortization and increased the consumption of parts and ammunition. The fighting and its outcome were also responsible for at least two large unplanned spurts of arms shipments to Egypt: immediately after the 1967 war, and during 1970.[28] Finally, the cost of deploying up to 20,000 Soviet cadres and outfitting and operating at least six airfields should also be added to the cost of the equipment. Taking all these factors into account, post-1967 military aid to Egypt alone may well come up to 10 percent of the parallel non-strategic Soviet effort, a figure of the same order of magnitude as was arrived at by the value calculations in Table 2.

IV. THE MILITARY AID BURDEN

On the face of it, the share of M.A. in conventional or total Soviet military production seems to be rather large—large enough to indicate major commitment. For a more precise evaluation, however, we must ask ourselves whether the allocation used as a denominator for estimating the M.A. share is the relevant one, and if it is, or if the relevant denominator is found, how a given share can be shown and not just sensed to be large. Admittedly, it is not easy to decide whether a 2 percent or a 5 percent share of some kind of allocation is large or small. One possible solution is offered by the comparative method: considering the movement of the share of M.A. over time or comparing similar shares in some other countries. An attempt to compare the M.A. burdens of the Soviet Union and the United States is made later on, but first the question of the relevant denominator is taken up.

In evaluating burdens of relatively small shares of a given allocation, there seems to be a sort of 'small-share illusion' at work, a fallacious tendency to disregard as unimportant any share below a certain figure. It arises from the assumption that the yearly, or periodical, allocation process can each time be started from scratch, the suballocation to competing claimants being made without regard to past allocations. In fact, however, most of the total available for allocation is already tied up in advance of the formal budgetary process by the cumulative effect of earlier decisions, so that only a relatively small part of the total is disposable. All additional claims should be compared with the small share of the total that is available of reallocation. M.A. as such is nondomestic and this suggests that it may not be backed up by a strong pressure group within the military establishment and that it is generally not among the most vital security priorities. Clearly, therefore, the difficulties involved in securing the 2 or 5 or more percent of Soviet military production may be much greater that the actual percentages would imply. Many of the difficulties may be political; but there may be economic ones too, such as short-run pressure on production capacity and the resultant delays in deliveries to high-priority domestic military sectors.

The actual burden becomes heavier the tighter the military production schedules and the more rigid the total allocation. As has been pointed out, an increase in non-strategic military production probably comes at the expense of consumer durables and other civilian products. Using Boretsky's figures it may be seen that a 2-percent share of total military production, for instance, amounts to over 5 percent of the production of consumer durables.[29] And in the Soviet case, as we have seen, this substitution is very tangible and immediate.[30]

In Table 2 the amount of M.A. is compared to two other, much more comprehensive figures: the total Soviet defense allocation, as estimated by Cohn, and the total volume of machine-building and metal-work production; these two allocations come next to military production in scope, one from the budgetary and the other from the productive-capacity point of view. Naturally, the M.A. shares are much lower (see lines 6 and lines 7 in panel C of Table 2); still lower is the M.A. share in the government budget or in G.N.P. Measured against G.N.P., total M.A. is of the order of magnitude of about two-tenths of 1 percent and M.A. to Egypt is less than half that; when measured against the government budget the ratios are about double (these shares are estimated at official Soviet prices). Assuming that the Soviet defense-production prices have to be doubled and adding economic-aid deliveries, total aid does not come to more than half of 1 percent of G.N.P. and aid to Egypt comes to no more than one-tenth of 1 percent.[31] The possibility of actually shifting resources to M.A. increases much less than indicated by the widening of the base, especially in the short run. The substitution of M.A. for any other use becomes economically and politically more expensive as the dissimilarity between production characteristics increases and as the interested parties belong to more divergent administrative or economic sectors. Nevertheless, the broad-based figures of fractions of 1 percent should be kept in mind in considering the Soviet Union's ability to engage in military or economic aid programs, if it finds them essential. The burden they impose may be much higher than these fractions indicate, but the resources are clearly there.

Another way of evaluating the burden is to compare it with the corresponding burden on the countervailing world power, in this case the

United States. Let us assume a fully symmetrical power contest for influence in a given region, each superpower supporting its allies in a local conflict. Leaving aside any additional goals, the advantage goes to the superpower which manages to achieve a desired 'balance' at less cost than— while imposing heavy burdens on—the other side. One power may, however, be willing to invest more than the other if it considers a particular region to be more than just an arena for superpower rivalry. This seems to be so in the case of the Soviet Union vis-à-vis the United States in the Middle East: in the context of the naive symmetric model the Soviet Union is certainly the loser here, since its Middle East burden is much greater than that of the United States. The extra burden carried by the Soviet Union is the product of three disadvantages, which I shall only mention briefly. First, the Soviet economic base (G.N.P.) is only about one-half that of the United States, so that any confrontation that demands the same military effort bears down twice as heavily on the Soviet Union. This is only partly, if at all, compensated for by the higher efficiency of Soviet military production.[32] Second, to achieve some sort of balance Egypt alone has to deploy more forces and weapons than Israel, not to mention the military power of other Arab countries confronting Israel, most of which also receive Soviet M.A. Third, Egypt's ability to finance its own defense requirements is less than Israel's, so that the Soviet Union has to contribute a higher proportion.

The first disadvantage is discussed extensively in the literature and although there is no general agreement on the exact difference between the Soviet and American burdens, it is agreed that the Soviet Union's is the greater. The most frequently used index of burden is the share of defense spending in total G.N.P., and the main disagreement is on the value of the 'defense ruble.' A secondary issue is the size of the undisclosed portion of Soviet defense spending. The share of defense in G.N.P., based on rather conservative estimates of the undisclosed items and on Soviet factor-cost prices (thus correcting market-price biases introduced by the turnover taxes), has ranged from 10 to 13 percent over the last 15 years.[33] In the United States, during the same period, defense expenditure amounted to 8–10 percent of G.N.P., the upper limit being reached in the 1950s and in 1967–8, at the height of the Vietnam war.[34] This comparison, at current prices, shows that the Soviet burden is on the average about 3 percentage points—or 30 percent—above the American. The Soviet excess burden is much higher when the figures are corrected for the artificially low ruble defense prices, as shown in Section II.[35]

Naturally, the machine-building industry and the R & D establishments bear the brunt of the Soviet excess defense burden. Boretsky has shown that the production level of the Soviet machine-building industry has risen from 70 percent of the American level in the early 1960s to almost 90 percent around 1970.[36] Even allowing for some exaggeration, the ratio is certainly well over 50 percent which is the U.S.S.R./U.S. G.N.P. ratio. The Soviet effort to promote the machine-building industry is designed to support a high level of investment and a large military production, and at least one-quarter of its production goes to military uses compared with about one-fifth in the United States. Consequently, the Soviet Union may in the last few years have been coming close to the United States in its military production.[37] Also, the relative Soviet military and space R & D effort is much higher than that of the United States.[38]

This resource-base disadvantage is a factor that the Soviet Union has to live with in its role as a superpower, in the Middle East no less than elsewhere.

The other two disadvantages are peculiar to the Middle East. The first is that in order to maintain some kind of balance, Egypt has to deploy a much larger army and far more equipment than Israel. The disparity is still greater when other Arab states are taken into account as well. From the annual defense expenditures for 1951–64 as calculated by Nadav Safran, it is apparent that in most years Egypt spent at least one-third more than Israel and in some years as much as or more than 60–70 percent more. Further, the combined military budget of Egypt, Iraq, Syria, and Jordan was between two-and-a-half and five times that of Israel.[39] These are the figures presented in Table 5 for Egypt and Israel, with additional data for the period since 1964. As may be seen, it is only since 1967 that Israel's expenditures have come up to the reported Egyptian level; they are, of course, still far below the combined budget of the surrounding Arab states.

These money-value comparisons require some qualifications. There is some doubt whether the Egyptian figures include Soviet M.A., at least the hardware part of it. It is almost certain that they do not include replacements of the 1967 war losses and the Soviet Union's own large air defense and air base build-up in Egypt since 1970. If M.A. is included, it is likely to be shown at the artificially low Soviet prices, resulting in an underestimate of the Egyptian defense budget. Both factors thus cause an upward bias in the Israeli-Egyptian expenditure ratio. It should also be

Table 5.
DEFENSE EXPENDITURES, G.N.P. AND MILITARY AID, ISRAEL AND EGYPT: 1955-70

	1955	1970	1955-70	1955-62	1963-70	1963-6	1967-70
Defense expenditure (million U.S. dollars)							
1. Israel	89	1,370	6,347	1,355	4,992	1,198	3,794
2. Egypt	212	1,223	7,962	2,017	5,945	2,111	3,834
3. Israel/Egypt, percent	42.0	112.0	79.7	67.2	84.0	56.8	99.0
Gross National Product (million U.S. dollars)							
4. Israel	1,186	5,273	46,214	15,764	30,450	12,638	17,812
5. Egypt	2,996	6,425	72,974	29,336	43,638	19,341	24,297
6. Israel/Egypt, percent	39.6	82.1	63.3	53.7	69.8	65.3	73.3
Defense expenditure as percent of G.N.P.							
7. Israel	7.0	26.0	13.7	8.0	16.4	9.4	21.3
8. Egypt	7.0	19.0	10.9	6.8	13.6	10.9	15.7
Soviet military aid as percent of Egypt's defense expenditure	..	..	34.2	50.0	28.8	..	..
G.N.P. per capita (U.S. dollars)							
9. Israel	678	1,783					
10. Egypt	131	193					

Source:
Defense expenditure and G.N.P.
1955-65: based on Nadav Safran, *From War to War* (New York: Pegasus 1969), p. 148, Table I (Egypt); p. 158, Table II (Israel); and Appendixes.
1966-70: Israel, Don Patinkin, "The Economic Development of Israel" (unpublished draft; Jerusalem 1970); Appendix Table (1966-9) and Bank of Israel, *Annual Report 1970*, pp. 12 and 147 (1970); Egypt, I.I.S.S., *The Military Balance*, various issues.
Soviet aid: Table 2.
Per capita G.N.P.: figures in lines 4 and 5 divided by the following population figures (thousands) Israel, 1,750 in 1955 and 2,958 in 1970 (*Statistical Abstract of Israel 1971*, No. 22, p. 21, Table B/1); Egypt, 22,900 in 1955 (U.N., *Demographic Yearbook 1956*) and 33,300 in 1970 (*The Military Balance 1970-1971*, p. 45).

noted that there may be biases in the prices of both countries, the official rates of exchange may not be suitable for comparative purposes, and different procedures are probably used in recording the defense expenditures. None of these considerations alter the basic fact that Israel is spending less than Egypt and of course much less than all the Arab countries together. This conclusion is also borne out by the respective army strengths and arsenals of the two sides.[49]

The parties' actual expenditure should now be compared with the kind of military balance that was in fact achieved. So far, it has been clearly demonstrated by past events that considering the expenditure levels and in the absence of direct superpower participation Israel has throughout had and still has a wide margin of superiority. The 1967 war has made this previously not fully recognized and not publicly admitted superiority common knowledge and helped to enhance it. The fact that this superiority became obvious forced the Soviet Union to become directly involved in order to establish some kind of balance.[41] The Soviet Union correctly estimated that, at least within a reasonably short period, the balance could not be righted by M.A. in the form of equipment alone. The U.S.S.R. is therefore incurring the high political-strategic risks of direct military involvement on top of the economic costs.

Finally, the Soviet Union finds itself in a position where its contribution to the military supplies and expenditures of its allies is higher, both absolutely and relatively, than the corresponding contribution of the United States. Israel has enjoyed several advantages over Egypt in its ability to divert resources to defense and procure the necessary arms supplies. Consequently, its claims for American support in the Middle East were until very recently rather limited. They are still much less onerous than the demands made by Egypt on the Soviet Union. First among Israel's advantages are its fast-growing G.N.P. and its quite high per capita G.N.P. Other things being fairly equal, the ability to support a large defense budget is a direct function of national economic growth and per capita production. As may be seen from Table 5, over the last 15 years Israel has almost managed to close the G.N.P. gap with Egypt, thus further widening the gap in G.N.P. per capita. By now an equal defense budget in Egypt and Israel also means that the percentage burden on G.N.P. is almost the same. Second, Israel enjoys a stream of economic support from world Jewry as well as from German restitutions and reparations. Though the second is gradually diminishing, both flows are to a very large extent independent of the local conflict and the superpower struggle. Largely thanks to these two advantages, Israel has been in a position to buy weapons in quite a number of countries other than the United States, and is not exclusively dependent on American supplies, which until recently have for the most part been paid for. The political circumstances which made France willing to *sell* military equipment up to 1967 also contributed to Israel's superior procurement position. Finally, Israel has a much higher technical capacity to produce its own military equipment and this also relieves its superpower supporter of the responsibility of being the sole supplier as well as of part of the cost. As can be seen from line 9 of Table 5, the Soviet Union contributed at least one-quarter of the Egyptian military effort over the entire 1955–70 period if Soviet M.A. is not included in the Egyptian budgets, and up to one-third if it is.[42] Again, these figures should be adjusted upwards to take account of the low Soviet M.A. prices and of the cost of Soviet-run facilities in Egypt, assuming that they are not included in the M.A. figures. As has been pointed out, only a small part of this aid has so far been paid back on schedule.

On the Western side of the conflict, there has been nothing remotely matching such massive participation. There was the $160 million German arms grant in 1959–64,[43] and during the last two years there has been a fairly large American M.A. program on a credit basis. Until 1967, U.S. government grants and loans to the government of Israel amounted to $30–50 million a year, mostly for economic projects. In 1969 Israel received $86 million and in 1970 $367 million in U.S. government long-term credits, mostly to finance military purchases.[44] If the current request for $300 million a year in M.A. is granted, this will constitute about twenty percent of Israel's total military spending in 1971, but unless there is a sustained, rapid escalation of the armament race, Israel will not continue to depend on the United States to such an extent.

Altogether, the Soviet Union has poured several times as much military aid into the region as the United States.[45]

V.   CONCLUSIONS

All these rather tedious calculations seem to lead to the same conclusion, namely that the economic burden of Soviet M.A. to the Middle East and especially to Egypt is rather high, though not exorbitant, and that the situation cannot be explained simply as a superpower struggle for influence. This implies the conclusion, which has already been reached by others on different grounds, that the Soviet M.A. program only makes sense if it serves goals much higher on the priority list than is assumed by the naive symmetric model.

Even this general conclusion is valid only insofar as the M.A. costs incurred by the Russians were preplanned or at least expected. Naturally, only preplanned costs allowing for a wide risk margin can be attributed to goals and intentions. Although I have no documentary evidence on this question, it is clear that Soviet M.A. costs exceeded any *ex ante* estimate— even with a large risk element included—by a considerable margin. This is so mainly because of the unanticipated developments of 1967. Without the 1967 war the balance of power between Israel and the Arab states could have been maintained with a much lower level of armaments and slower escalation, and possibly without creating the threat of a direct Israeli-Soviet confrontation. The war smashed the laboriously manufactured Arab-Israel military balance sustained by a large measure of bluff and by the uncertainties created by a long period without direct confrontation. After the war the Soviet Union not only had to replace the equipment lost but also to restore the credibility of its allies. They must have then realized that in order to rehabilitate the Egyptian armed forces they would not only have to be equipped at a much higher level than before, but that sooner or later they would have to be provided with a dependable air defense system which would have to include Soviet personnel.

Accordingly, Israel's deep air-raids into Egypt at the end of 1969 appear to have done no more than speed up—probably quite considerably— a deployment that would have become necessary in any case. Whatever margin of error they may have included in their calculations, the Russians were in 1967 undoubtedly confident of achieving their major aims with less tension than actually developed, and consequently they expected the cost to be lower. Any attempt to estimate the unforeseen element in the Soviet M.A. expenditure is bound to be speculative. One suggestion I venture to offer is that it is small enough to sustain the conclusion that the Soviet commitment in the Middle East, especially to Egypt, remains impressive in economic terms. As was pointed out in the introduction, no conclusions as to Soviet goals and policies can be drawn from a partial cost-benefit account. The following observations should, therefore, be considered merely as supporting evidence for hypotheses advanced in the literature and backed up by many other considerations. The partial nature of our calculations precludes any assessment of the 'profitability' of the Soviet effort in the region. Nor can we, on the basis of the present analysis, identify specific Soviet goals that would explain a commitment of the order estimated. What can be done is to list some of the usually cited goals which may account for it singly or in combination. One such high-priority goal which may explain Soviet M.A. to the region has recently been described by MccGwire in his article on soviet naval developments.[46] According to him, the strategic threat to the Soviet Union of American aircraft carriers (in the late 1950s and the 1960s) and the deployment (since 1963) of Polaris submarines in the Eastern Mediterranean found the Soviet Union unprepared. Faced with a serious threat to its national security, the Soviet Union, although aware of the limited prospects of success, reacted by a premature long-distance naval deployment.[47] In addition to the lag in nuclear submarine design and production, MccGwire lists several major deficiencies: inferior submarine detection systems; lack of control over territory adjacent to essential sea areas needed, in the absence of carriers, for both naval installations and air bases, particularly after the Albanian ouster in 1961; and finally, the lack of floating mid-ocean support as a partial substitute for shore bases. Until the 1967 war, Russian entry into the Eastern Mediterranean was, owing to these deficiencies, mainly bluff: "it was not until after the June 1967 war that the availability of sheltered berths for Soviet support ships in Egyptian harbours enabled a substantial jump in the average number of ships deployed . . . . The Arab-Israeli war also led to the use of Egyptian airfields in support of naval operations . . . ."[48] It appears that the Russians badly needed naval and air bases in Egypt (and Syria) for strategic defense. The alternatives to the choice made—going on with the bluff or putting still greater pressure on the already hard-pressed naval design bureaus and shipyards—were apparently considered either impractical or too costly. Compared with these alternatives, the economic M.A. costs as originally stated must certainly have appeared more than reasonable.[49]

Other global-strategic Soviet interests usually cited as reasons for the direct Soviet involvement in Egypt are the containment of the U.S. Sixth Fleet, in order to deny it the freedom it had enjoyed, if not for immediate defense purposes; to threaten the southern flank of Europe; or, on the eastern flank, the containment of China, the support of India, and a strategic naval deployment in the Indian Ocean as a counterforce to the possible American deployment of Poseidon missile submarines. The Mediterranean-based goals would require, though less urgently, shore facilities and air bases along the Mediterranean coast of the kind envisaged by MccGwire. Bases in Egypt are of great importance to Soviet goals in

Asia. None of these possibilities excludes MccGwire's, while each of them alone and certainly several together would justify the cost of the M.A. extended. Finally there is James Cable's contention that the role of the Soviet navy in the Mediterranean is to support peacetime diplomacy, and to use superpower capabilities in local disputes.[50] It stands to reason, however, that, as Cable says, "governments build navies . . . for war. The peacetime existence and presence of warships is a mere by-product . . . ."[51]

Undoubtedly many interests are intended to be served by the Soviet Union's military and economic aid to the Middle East, but if it is to serve the purpose of providing a, possibly temporary, substitute for carriers and open anchorage equipment, it becomes a much more reasonable and attractive proposition from the point of view of the economically hard-pressed Soviet leadership. Two more conclusions or inferences may be drawn from the findings of this inquiry. One is that while the Soviet Union is interested in keeping the Israel-Arab conflict going, it is also interested in keeping the arms race in the Middle East from moving or escalating too fast to a higher level and more expensive weapons. This is so provided, of course, that the Soviet Union can achieve its basic goals. This last qualification to my mind explains the Soviet initiative in increasing tension in 1967 (even though they ultimately got more than they bargained for). The escalation of 1970 was altogether too fast for their taste. Second, it is doubtful whether the Soviet Union can afford, emergencies apart, to engage in massive M.A. programs in two regions at the same time. This may be relevant to the Middle East in view of the possibility, widely discussed these days, that the Soviet Union is moving toward strategic deployment in the Indian Ocean and massive support for the Indian military forces.

NOTES

[1] The dollar figures apparently reflect the values of the various aid agreements as signed, i.e., at Soviet prices, and thus represent the ruble values at the official exchange rate of 0.9 rubles /$1. On the economic meaning of these values see Section II. After some hesitation I decided to use *current* dollars (and current rubles) as the value units throughout this paper. As will be seen below, this is quite appropriate for most of the issues raised; in any case conversion to constant dollars (and rubles) involves a good deal of arbitrariness. The reader should, however, be aware that the internal value of the U.S. dollar declined by about 50 percent over the period under discussion (1955–70): the implicit price deflator for G.N.P. (1951 = 100) stood at 90.9 in 1955, 110.9 in 1965, 122.3 in 1968, and 135 in 1970 (see U.S. Department of Commerce, *Survey of Current Business,* various issues).

[2] Of the $2.6 billion total trade with developing countries in 1970, about $2.1 billion were with North Africa, the Middle East, and Central Asia. Trade with Egypt, Iraq, and Syria came close to $1 billion, and with Egypt alone to $0.7 billion [U.S. Department of State, Bureau of Intelligence and Research, *Communist States and Developing Countries: Aid and Trade in 1970* (Research Study: RECS-15), September 1971 (henceforth State Department 1971), pp. 23–27]. See also Hertha W. Heiss, "The Soviet Union in the World Market," in U.S. Congress, Joint Economic Committee, *New Directions in the Soviet Economy.* Part IV: *The World Outside* (89th Cong., 2nd Sess. 1966; henceforth *New Directions*), pp. 917–33; and Lev L. Klochkovsky, "U.S.S.R. Trade Partner," *International Trade Forum* (December 1970), pp. 17–29.

[3] Western prices are applied for this purpose(among others)by Abram Bergson, "The Comparative National Income of the USSR and USA" (1969 draft of paper read at the Toronto Conference on Research in Income and Wealth), pp. 5–6, Table 1 and pp. A-18 to A-21; and by Michael Boretsky, "The Technological Base of Soviet Military Power," in U.S. Congress, Joint Economic Committee, *Economic Performance and the Military Burden in the Soviet Union* (91st Cong., 2nd Sess. 1970; henceforth *Economic Performance*), pp. 203–204, 220–21.

[4] Institute of Strategic Studies, *The Military Balance 1970–1971* (London 1970), p. 11.

[5] The geometric average of exchange rates calculated with United States and Soviet quantity weights (on the basis of Cohn's G.N.P. calculations and the

239

sources cited in Stanley H. Cohn, "General Growth Performance of the Soviet Economy," in *Economic Performance, op. cit.,* pp. 13–14).

6   The lowest figure for the ruble (indicating the largest difference between Soviet and American prices) is given by Boretsky (*op. cit.,* p. 204); higher rates are estimated by Bergson for 1955 (0.41 ruble/$1) and Bornstein, as calculated by Benoit and Lubell (0.50 ruble/$1) [Bergson, *op. cit.,* Emile Benoit and Harold Lubell, "The World Burden of National Defense," in *Disarmament and World Economic Interdependence,* ed. Emile Benoit (International Peace Research Institute, Oslo: Monograph No. 1; Oslo, New York, and London 1967), p. 40]. All estimates are based on comparative prices of mainly civilian machinery and equipment, assumed to be similar to those of their military counterparts.

7   Turnover tax is relevant here only to the extent that it should be added to the normal price of the goods. Hidden subsidies are in the form of low capital charges, no charges for R & D, etc. When the same plant carries on mixed military and civilian production (a usual procedure in the Soviet Union), a disproportionate share of the costs is charged to the latter, a point made by Michael Henchinsky in a forthcoming paper.

8   In the paper mentioned in n.7, Henchinsky attributes the efficiency of civilian production in East Germany to the absence of a big defense industry in that country and at least part of the decline in the quality of the Czech civilian industry to the growth of military production. He also states that people who are in the know prefer consumer goods from plants mainly producing military equipment, because they know that they get better quality for the same price.

9   Stanley H. Cohn, "The Economic Burden of Soviet Defense Outlays," in *Economic Performance, op. cit.,* pp. 166–88, especially pp. 176–78.

10   Philip Hanson, "The Economic Background to Soviet Defence Capabilities," in Royal United Service Institution (R.U.S.I.), *The Soviet Union in Europe and the Near East: Her Capabilities and Intentions* (London 1970), p. 66; and Morris Bornstein, "Economic Factors in Soviet Attitudes Towards Arms Control," in Benoit (ed.), *op. cit.,* pp. 70–73.

11   Abraham S. Becker in a talk in Brussels in Spring 1971.

12   In a private communication to the author.

13   See Michael Boretsky, *op. cit.,* pp. 221–23. Alec Nove, criticizing Boretsky's article, seems inclined to explain most of the price difference by quality differences (see his "Soviet Defence Spending," *Survival,* XIII, October 1971, p. 330). See also F.E.C. Gregory, "Soviet Army Procurement," in R.U.S.I., *op. cit.,* p. 95. Extra gadgets, most of which may not confer any major combat advantage, are considered to be one of the factors that make American weapons much more expensive than their Soviet counterparts.

14   Marshall I. Goldman, *Soviet Foreign Aid* (New York 1967), p. 240. Examples of the terms of early Soviet M.A. agreements are given in Joseph S. Berliner,

Soviet Economic Aid (New York 1958), p. 48. See also Goldman, *op. cit., pp.* 61–62 and 195–96, and Leo Tansky, "Soviet Foreign Aid to the Less Developed Countries," in *New Directions, op. cit., Part IV, pp.* 966–67, who also describe the repayment difficulties.

[15] Thus the Ministry of Defense produces tractors as well as tanks, artillery, and armored vehicles; the Ministry of Radio Industry is responsible for the supply of radio and TV sets to the public but is controlled by the military; and the Ministry of Aviation Industry also produces consumer durables. See Andrew Sheren, "Structure and Organization of Defense-Related Industries," in *Economic Performance, op. cit., pp.* 128–32.

[16] See also Tansky, *op. cit.,* p. 966.

[17] International Institute of Strategic Studies (I.I.S.S.) *Strategic Survey 1970* (London 1971), pp. 46–50.

[18] Institute of Strategic Studies, *The Military Balance 1970–1971, op. cit.,* p. 11.

[19] State Department 1971, *op. cit.,* p. 17, Table 7.

[20] I.I.S.S., *Strategic Survey 1970, op. cit.,* p. 47, whose figure is based on a rate of 9.45 ruble/$1.

[21] See U.S. Department of State, Bureau of Intelligence and Research, *The Communist Economic Offensive Through 1963* (Research Memorandum: RSB-43), June 1964, p. 10.

[22] See Nove, *op. cit.,* especially p. 330. Becker has made similar comments, especially as regards the level.

[23] The *level* of the burden is also overstated to the extent that reported prices of various old and surplus-type weapons are higher than the alternative value to the Soviet Union.

[24] This is certainly so if the quoted M.A. figures do not include the Soviet deployment in Egypt during 1970.

[25] By 'strategic military equipment' in this paper we mean weapon systems which are used exclusively by world powers. In addition to nuclear delivery, detection and defense systems, and space equipment, it also includes most large vessels and heavy (transport) aircraft. Other types of military equipment fall under the 'conventional' or non-strategic heading.

[26] The main sources for this section are: I.I.S.S., *The Military Balance 1971–1972* (and other issues); John Erickson, *Soviet Military Power* (London 1971), pp. 52–82 and especially p. 75. Also consulted were: Gregory, *op. cit.;* Michael MccGwire, "Soviet Naval Procurement," R.U.S.I., *op. cit.,* pp. 74–87, and John Simpson, "The Military Aircraft Procurement Process in the the USSR," *ibid.,* pp. 88–94. In writing this section I benefited from the help and expertise of Edward Lutwak. I tried to stay on the conservative side as regards the Egyptian/Soviet stock ratio, and despite much evidence that the Egyptian military stock as presented in I.I.S.S. *The Military Balance 1971–1972* is underestimated, these were the stock figures I usually adopted.

[27] Egypt is also using several hundred T-34/85 medium tanks which are definitely obsolete for the Russians.

[28] This shipment, which included modern SAMs, MIG 21-Js, and about 15,000 Soviet men, may have been planned, but events certainly dictated considerable prescheduling.

[29] Boretsky, *op. cit.*, p. 218, Table 9.

[30] See n.15 above.

[31] Data on Soviet G.N.P. up to 1965 are from Abraham S. Becker, *Soviet National Income, 1958–1964* (Berkeley and Los Angeles 1969), pp. 24–25, Table 6, and from Bergson, *op. cit.*, pp. 5–6, Table 1. Estimates for later years were projected on the basis of the above, using growth rates from Cohn, "General Growth Performance of the Soviet Economy," *op. cit.*, p. 9. Government budget figures are from Soviet Union, Tsentralnoe Statisticheskoe Upravlenia, *Narodnoe Khoziaistvo SSSR* (various years). Data on economic-aid deliveries are from Department of State 1971, *op. cit.*, p. 9, Table 2.

[32] See the discussion of valuation problems in Section II.

[33] See Cohn, "The Economic Burden of Soviet Defense Outlays," *op. cit.*, p. 185. Using a different method, Becker (*op. cit.*, p. 96, Table 15, and pp. 163–64) estimates the defense/G.N.P. ratio for 1959–64 at up to 10 percent at unadjusted prices; at factor cost, the ratio should go up by 1 to 2 points.

[34] I.I.S.S., *The Military Balance 1971–1972, op. cit.*, p. 62; Bergson, *op. cit.*, p. 5, Table 1 and pp. B-5, B-6; see also U.S. Department of Commerce, Office of Business Economics, *The National Income and Product Accounts of the United States, 1929–1965. Statistical Tables* (supplement to *Survey of Current Business;* Washington, D.C. 1966), various tables. The range of 8–10 percent is sufficiently broad to accommodate somewhat different definitions of "defense."

[35] Calculations for 1955 made by Bergson at the same prices (dollars or rubles) for both the United States and the Soviet Union show that the Soviet defense burden is 180 percent of the American (Bergson, *op. cit.*, pp. 4–5, Table 1). A somewhat different calculation for 1968 by Boretsky shows a Soviet excess burden of 150–170 percent (Boretsky, *op. cit.*, pp. 199 ff.).

[36] This figure refers to "machine and machine-like products" only, a somewhat narrower category than "machine-building and metal-working"; see Boretsky, *op. cit.*, p. 206, Table 5, and p. 216, Table 7.

[37] As calculated in *ibid.*, p. 206, Table 5, and pp. 215–19. See also Bornstein, *op. cit.*, pp. 68–69.

[38] Boretsky, *op. cit.*, pp. 223–25; see also Cohn, "The Economic Burden of Soviet Defense Outlays," *op. cit.*, pp. 176–78.

[39] Nadav Safran, *From War to War: The Arab-Israeli Confrontation, 1948–1967* (New York 1969), p. 148, Table I (Egypt), and p. 158, Table II (Israel).

[40] See units, figures, and equipment lists of both countries in I.I.S.S., *The Mili-*

tary Balance. The latest (*1971–1972*) issue (pp. 29 and 32-33) shows that Israel has about two-thirds as many combat planes and tanks as Egypt.

[41] Direct Soviet involvement and the high level of uncertainty that goes with it explain the relative increase in Israel's defense budget since 1967, compared with Egypt's.

[42] The figures assuming that Soviet M.A. is not included in the Egyptian defense expenditures are arrived at by dividing Soviet M.A. by the sum of Soviet M.A. and Egyptian defense expenditure.

[43] Safran, *op. cit.,* pp. 157–58.

[44] Based on balance-of-payments accounts in Israel, Central Bureau of Statistics, *Statistical Abstract of Israel* (Jerusalem: various years).

[45] This remains true even if United States aid to Arab states is included in the calculation.

[46] Michael MccGwire, "The Background to Soviet Naval Developments," *The World Today,* XXVII (March 1971), pp. 93–103.

[47] *Ibid.,* p. 100.

[48] *Ibid.,* pp. 100–101.

[49] The price of a modern carrier is of the order of hundreds of millions of dollars (American prices).

[50] James Cable, "Political Applications of Limited Naval Force," in R.U.S.I., *op. cit.,* pp. 52–58.

[51] *Ibid.,* p. 57.

REFERENCES

Bank of Israel, *Annual Report 1970*. Jerusalem 1971.

Becker, Abraham S. *Soviet National Income, 1958–1964*. Berkeley and Los Angeles: University of California Press 1969.

Benoit, Emile and Lubell, Harold. "The World Burden of National Defense," in *Disarmament and World Economic Interdependence*. Edited by Emile Benoit. (International Peace Research Institute, Oslo: Monograph No. 1.) Oslo: Universitetsforlaget; New York and London: Columbia University Press 1967, pp. 29–59.

Bergson, Abram. "The Comparative National Income of the USSR and USA." Draft (1969) of paper read at the Toronto Conference on Research in Income and Wealth, May 1970.

Berliner, Joseph S. *Soviet Economic Aid*. New York: Praeger for Council on Foreign Relations, 1958.

Boretsky, Michael. "The Technological Base of Soviet Military Power," in *Economic Performance and the Military Burden in the Soviet Union*. (U.S. Congress. Joint Economic Committee.) 91st Cong., 2nd Sess., 1970, pp. 189–231.

Bornstein, Morris. "Economic Factors in Soviet Attitudes Towards Arms Control," in *Disarmament and World Economic Interdependence*. Edited by Emile Benoit. (International Peace Research Institute, Oslo: Monograph No. 1.) Oslo: Universitetsforlaget; New York and London: Columbia University Press 1967, pp. 60–85.

Cable, James. "Political Applications of Limited Naval Force," in Royal United Service Institution (R.U.S.I.), *The Soviet Union in Europe and the Near East: Her Capabilities and Intentions*. London 1970, pp. 52–58.

Cohn, Stanley H. "General Growth Performance of the Soviet Economy," in *Economic Performance and the Military Burden in the Soviet Union*. (U.S. Congress. Joint Economic Committee.) 91st Cong., 2nd Sess., 1970, pp. 9–17.

――――. "The Economic Burden of Soviet Defense Outlays," in *Economic Performance and the Military Burden in the Soviet Union*. (U.S. Congress. Joint Economic Committee.) 91st Cong., 2nd Sess., 1970, pp. 166–88.

Erickson, John. *Soviet Military Power*. London: Royal United Service Institute for Defence Studies, 1971.

Goldman, Marshall, I. *Soviet Foreign Aid*. New York: Praeger 1967.

Gregory, F.E.C. "Soviet Army Procurement," in Royal United Service Institution (R.U.S.I.), *The Soviet Union in Europe and the Near East: Her Capabilities and Intentions.* London 1970, pp. 95–99.

Hanson, Philip. "The Economic Background to Soviet Defence Capabilities," in Royal United Service Institution (R.U.S.I.), *The Soviet Union in Europe and the Near East: Her Capabilities and Intentions.* London 1970, pp. 64–67.

Heiss, Hertha W. "The Soviet Union in the World Market," in *New Directions in the Soviet Economy.* Part IV: *The World Outside.* (U.S. Congress. Joint Economic Committee.) 89th Cong., 2nd Sess., 1966, pp. 917–33.

Institute for Strategic Studies, see International Institute for Strategic Studies.

International Institute for Strategic Studies (I.I.S.S.). *The Military Balance 1971–1972.* London 1971 (and other annual issues).

———. *Strategic Survey 1970.* London 1971 (and other annual issues).

Israel. Central Bureau of Statistics. *Statistical Abstract of Israel.* Jerusalem: annual issue.

Klochkovsky, Lev L. "U.S.S.R. Trade Partner," *International Trade Forum* (December 1970), pp. 17–29.

MccGwire, Michael. "Soviet Naval Procurement," in Royal United Service Institution (R.U.S.I.), *The Soviet Union in Europe and the Near East: Her Capabilities and Intentions*, London 1970, pp. 74–80.

———. "The Background to Soviet Naval Developments." *The World Today,* XXVII (March 1971), pp. 93–103.

Nove, Alec. "Soviet Defence Spending," *Survival*, XIII (October 1971), pp. 328–32.

Patinkin, Don. "The Economic Development of Israel." (Unpublished draft.) Jerusalem 1970.

Royal United Service Institution (R.U.S.I.). *The Soviet Union in Europe and the Near East: Her Capabilities and Intentions.* London 1970.

Safran, Nadav. *From War to War: The Arab-Israeli Confrontation, 1948–1967.* New York: Pegasus 1969.

Sheren, Andrew. "Structure and Organization of Defense-Related Industries," in *Economic Performance and the Military Burden in the Soviet Union.* (U.S. Congress. Joint Economic Committee.) 91st Cong., 2nd Sess., 1970, pp. 123–32.

Simpson, John. "The Military Aircraft Procurement Process in the USSR," in Royal United Service Institution (R.U.S.I.), *The Soviet Union in Europe and the Near East: Her Capabilities and Intentions.* London 1970, pp. 88–94.

Soviet Union. Tsentralnoe Statisticheskoe Upravlenia. *Narodnoe Khoziaistvo SSSR.* Moscow: annual issue.

Tansky, Leo. "Soviet Foreign Aid to the Less Developed Countries," in *New Directions in the Soviet Economy.* Part IV: *The World Outside.* (U.S. Congress. Joint Economic Committee.) 89th Cong., 2nd Sess., 1966, pp. 947–74.

United Nations, *Demographic Yearbook 1956*. New York 1957.

U.S. Department of Commerce. Office of Business Economics. *Survey of Current Business*.

———. *The National Income and Product Accounts of the United States, 1929–1965. Statistical Tables*. (Supplement to *Survey of Current Business*.) Washington, D.C. 1966.

U.S. Department of State. Bureau of Intelligence and Research. *The Communist Economic Offensive Through 1963*. (Research Memorandum: RSB-43.) June 1964.

———. *Communist States and Developing Countries: Aid and Trade in 1970*. (Research Study: RECS-15.) September 1971.

———. Director of Intelligence and Research, *Communist Governments and Developing Nations: Aid and Trade in 1967*. (Research Memorandum: RSE-120.) August 1968.

PART TWO

MIDDLE EASTERN
REPERCUSSIONS

5. TRENDS IN MIDDLE EASTERN POLITICS

LEONARD BINDER
TRANSFORMATION IN THE MIDDLE EASTERN SUBORDINATE SYSTEM AFTER 1967

From 1956 to 1967, at least, the structure of the Middle Eastern system of international relations was more or less stable. Indeed, it is difficult to understand the origins and the course of the 1967 conflict without the perspective of the surprises and disappointments of the earlier confrontation. But the issues of navigation, of the disposition of U.N. forces, and even the demilitarization of evacuated territories were not the essential questions they are now thought to be. The essential characteristic of the Middle Eastern subordinate system in 1956 was its relative autonomy of the dominant global system. The Great Powers had a good deal of leverage, but Britain and France felt that they could not intrude without the pretext of containing a local, regional, conflict. Their intervention was decisively opposed by both the United States and the Soviet Union, and both these powers combined to press Israel to withdraw. The subsequent autonomy of the regional process was in large part due to the new Egyptian domination of Arab political affairs—a domination which persisted from 1957 to 1961, before it commenced a long and continuous decline. During the first phase of Egyptian dominance there was not a single Arab country that was not influenced in greater or lesser measure by Egyptian pressure. American pressures were exerted on Lebanon, Jordan and Syria, but these efforts were more than counterbalanced by Egyptian diplomacy. The Soviet Union tried to establish a position in revolutionary Iraq, but it did not succeed.

During the second phase of the period under discussion even Egyptian influence diminished in effectiveness as Syria broke with the U.A.R., the Yemen adventure turned into a disaster, Iraq went its own stumbling way, Lebanon became more independent, Tunisia criticized Egyptian dominance of the Arab League, and both the Sudan and Libya eluded Egyptian domination. Thus even within the bloc of Arab states, effective autonomy was much stronger than the questionable legitimacy afforded each state by prevailing doctrines of Arab nationalism and Arab unity. But whether Egypt pressed the other

251

Arab states, or the other Arab states resisted Egyptian demands, the intensity of this inter-Arab process precluded extra-area powers from predominant influence.

The pattern thus established had significant impact on the relations of non-Arab powers with the Great Powers as well. The more intractable the general situation in the Middle East, the less was it worth making major political investments in the area. Above all, it was not worth antagonizing Middle Eastern governments in order to advance regional projects which had less and less chance of overall success. Hence, the failure of Turkey to successfully mediate the Palestine dispute and its failure to intimidate Syria in 1957 and Iraq in 1958, coupled with inadequate American support for Turkey during the crisis of the Menderes regime, in the organizational framework of the Baghdad pact, in the aftermath of the Cuban missile crisis, and especially in the Cyprus dispute, have led the United States, and Turkey, too, to the conclusion that a looser arrangement between the two is preferable. A similar pattern of limited American responsibility along with a diminution of concern for regional collective security has characterized recent United States relations with Iran. A parallel relationship of substantial but limited concern has always been the American orientation toward Israel. In the case of American-Israeli relations more so than in other cases, it is clear that a fuller control over the policies of regional states would entail a fuller guarantee of the existing situation of those states. At various times Lebanon, Israel, Jordan, and Tunisia have each hinted that such an arrangement with the U.S. was possible. But the United States was, understandably, reluctant to base its regional policy on the trust reposed in it by these small states—and instead wished to keep its options open with regard to the other states in the region, and especially Egypt.

The Soviet Union, in contrast to the United States, starting from the outsider's position wished to gain some sort of foothold. Its strategy was as simple as it has been effective. The Soviet Union offered assistance in competition with the weaker powers, but it did not seek to influence policy other than to decrease the dependence of Middle Eastern states (other than Israel) upon the Western powers. The U.S.S.R. did criticize those Middle Eastern governments which harrassed or oppressed their local Communists but these were generally mild protests.

Regional autonomy, or more accurately, the autonomy of the regional political process may thus be attributed to the rise of Egypt, to the advent of the Soviet Union, and to the gradual alteration of American goals. This autonomy was principally manifested by the increased availability of political alternatives for the major states of the region, for Egypt, for Turkey, for Iran, and later for Algeria. The smaller states have been affected by the flexibility of the larger states, so that Tunisia, Libya, Sudan, Lebanon, Jordan, Kuwait, Saudi-Arabia, Bahrain, and Qatar have been less pro-West but also regionally more independent than would otherwise have been the case. Israel has not inherited a similar flexibility of policy because of Soviet and Arab hostility, but it has acquired some policy resiliency as a result of the influence of Turkey and Iran. These elements of autonomy are the most important structural elements in the pattern of Middle Eastern international relations. The rest, such as the distribution of military power, the ability to command economic resources, and the pattern of diplomatic communication, are all secondary and dependent upon the central feature of autonomy. But after 11 years and an illusion-shattering war, the question is not so much how the system worked in the past, but whether it still works that way now and how might it work in the future?

In order to examine the proposition that the Middle Eastern subordinate international system has been transformed as a consequence of the Six-Day War, there are two kinds of changes that have to be examined. The first and most obvious changes are those that have occurred in the Middle East itself. The second set of changes are those affecting the dominant global system. If the Middle Eastern system has become more closely integrated with the global system—if it is less meaningfully a subordinate system in itself—then its greater dependence will be manifested in its reflection of the influences of the dominant system as it is now and not as it was thought to be in 1956.

Starting with the major regional changes, the most important to consider is the decline of Egypt. The diminution of Egypt's influence began in 1961 with the successful separation of Syria, and it continued through the Yemen campaign, the deposition of Ben Bella, the election of Helou in Lebanon, the emergence of the Palestinian al-Fatah movement with Syrian assistance, and above all, in the series of Arab Summit Conferences in 1964 and 1965. Despite this decline, Egypt still maintained the key position in Arab and Middle Eastern affairs, and was still capable of applying pressure on almost every Arab country and even on Iran. After the Six-Day War, these tendencies, which portended an Egyptian decline, were effectively realized. Egypt could no longer wield influence in the Maghreb, Egyptian armed forces were withdrawn from Yemen, Egypt ceased maneuvering against the Ba'th regime and against King Hussein, and Egypt put the best face on its relations with Lebanon and with the Palestinians. Iran is no longer concerned about Egyptian encroachment. The closure of the Suez Canal has also severely limited any possible Egyptian leverage in the sphere of petroleum politics.

This decline began immediately after the Egyptian defeat and continued up to and after Nasser's death. Still, while Nasser was alive Egypt was still felt to be potentially able to return to its previous role. Nasser skillfully weakened the Palestinian movement, he won an ally in King Hussein, he kept up the pressure on King Feisal, he mastered the political forces within his own country, and he was thought to be able to manage the newly enlarged Soviet presence in Egypt. Perhaps this assessment of Nasser was more wishful thinking than truth; nevertheless, in his final mediatory action between Hussein and the Fidayeen, he played the role of elder statesman and of the exponent of the interests of the whole Arab nation rather than merely one component thereof. Had Nasser been able to gain some decisive advantage over Israel, an advantage that might have undone some of the stigma of the 1967 defeat, then the way might possibly have been opened for a restoration, at least in part, of the earlier Egyptian position, and with it, of the earlier structure of the Middle Eastern system.

Nasser's death brought out in sharper relief those vulnerabilities of the Egyptian position that had not been so clearly seen in the shadow of his imposing personality. The potential of domestic political instability, the disunity of the armed forces, the divided loyalties of the left wing, the depth and permanence of the Soviet position in Egypt, the Soviet potential for influencing domestic politics and foreign policy, and the loss of Egyptian initiative in inter-Arab affairs all became more apparent. The government of Sadat, having weathered its first domestic storm in the preemption of the Ṣabrī-Jum'a plot, and its first international storm in the aftermath of the Rogers visit, has now gone to substantial lengths in repudiating some of the policies identified with Nasser. It is evident that these new trends are not unpopular with some segments of Egyptian society, but these new policies enhance the fear of some that Egypt is once again turning to its own problems and concerning itself less with those of all the Arabs.

This new Egyptian trend does not dismay their Soviet allies, because even though the Soviets wish to expand their influence in the region, they prefer to do so by developing parallel strong pro-Soviet apparati in each country rather than strengthening the regional role of their major ally. It is for this reason, that the initiative for the confederation of Arab republics seems to have emanated from Libya and Syria more than from Egypt or the Sudan. Nasser had begun the search for a new Arab alignment at the time he broke up the Rabat Summit Conference. He talked of a special alliance of Libya, Egypt, and the Sudan, an alliance which Egypt might be able to dominate, but more importantly one which signaled Egypt's withdrawal from Fertile Crescent politics. The prominence of Syria in the current plan is the work of Qadhafi of Libya, and it represents his favorable estimate of the more moderate Ba'thi government of Syria as well as his fear that an unattached Egypt might fall totally under the influence of the Soviet Union.

The major consequence of the changed Egyptian circumstances is that Egypt is no longer the hub of an essentially centripetal Arab and Middle Eastern political process. The multilateral pattern of Fertile Crescent interaction has been altered to the point that even bilateral relationships are relatively unimportant. Egypt used to play an essential role in the affairs of the Fertile Crescent, but both Egypt's role and the framework within which that role was significant have changed. Egypt does not challenge Syria, cannot help Jordan or Iraq, and does not threaten Lebanon. Multilateralism has increased in the Maghreb, but Egypt is not a part of that development. In Egypt's immediate vicinity, it used to dominate the foreign affairs of Libya and the Sudan in parallel bilateral relationships. Now Libya was shown to have played a more vital role in Sudanese affairs during the attempted pro-Communist *coup*. The confederation will, if it ever becomes effective, become a framework for a new multilateral pattern in which Egypt will not necessarily have the initiative. In the Persian Gulf region, another pattern of multilateralism, potentially dominated by Iran, is emerging. This new and vitally important arena was formerly a target of Egyptian ambitions, but now it is likely that Egypt will be largely excluded from significant influence in the Persian Gulf. Prior to the outbreak of the War of 1967, Egyptian-Saudi relations had chilled over the Yemen conflict to a point approaching absolute zero. Since the Egyptian defeat, Saudi-Arabia has been compensating Egypt for part of its losses due to the closure of the Canal. As a consequence of these payments and the end of the Yemen conflict, Egyptian-Saudi relations improved somewhat, but not a great deal, as Nasser tried to keep the Saudis from supporting his enemies. Since Nasser's death, however, Sadat's "liberal" policies have laid the groundwork for improved relations and for increased private Saudi investment in Egypt, if the Saudis can overcome their apprehensions regarding the influential presence of the Russians.

The thorough realignment of the structure of the Middle Eastern political process has been indicated in this discussion of Egypt's position, and it will be further illustrated when we now look at the new situation in the Fertile Crescent. The Arab states of the Fertile Crescent—Lebanon, Syria, Iraq, and Jordan—experienced a higher degree of political and diplomatic multilateralism than any other segment of the Arab world. In part this characteristic was due to the proximity of these countries, but it was also due to the fact that they were all administered in similar fashion under a single regime in Ottoman times. The political projects aimed at unifying the Fertile Crescent were also more realistic than the grander projects of "comprehensive" unity which were devised, in part, to prevent unification in the Crescent. The territories of "Greater Syria" stand in the closest relationship, but for years the really burning issue was the unification, by force or otherwise, of Syria and Iraq. Iraq, more than the other states of the Crescent, has had closer if not always more congenial relations with Turkey, Iran, and Kuwait.

During the mandatory period, the successor states of the Fertile Crescent were isolated from each other by Britain and France, so that even territories under the same imperial power became more estranged from one another. The period from the end of World War II until 1957 was one of intense rivalry and political involvement which took primacy over relations with Arab states outside of the Fertile Crescent— although at times both Egypt and Saudi Arabia played important subordinate roles in support of Syria and in opposition to the Hashemites of Iraq and Jordan. From 1957 to 1967, Egypt dominated the Fertile Crescent and all but succeeded in isolating each of the four states from one another and in substituting four parallel bilateral patterns relating each of the countries to Egypt, for a single multilateral subsystem.

After the War of 1967 a number of notable changes took place, the most important of which was, doubtlessly, the reduction of Egyptian influence. Sudden and important changes of this type often go un- recognized at first, and this was particularly the case with regard to Syria and Jordan, both of which had suffered serious military defeats. The heavy Egyptian pressure on both these countries was reduced and, despite their poor military showing, each regime was immediately strengthened and more stable. Syria tried to force issues of regime significance in both Jordan and Lebanon, but Iraq and Egypt came to Jordan's assistance, and Egypt and the Western powers supported Lebanon. With Nasser's death Egypt is less likely to intervene in the Fertile Crescent, but Jordan seems to be able to withstand Syrian pressures with American and Israeli support, and Lebanon is in a similar situation except that it has reached a more equivocal compromise with the Palestinian Fidayeen.

It is evident that the last four years have been a transitional period, rendered ambiguous in part by misleading expectations regarding Egyptian influence and the rising power of the Palestinian movement; the latter movement has experienced a meteoric rise and a nearly identical decline. It is, of course, important in itself, but first let us consider its significance for the Fertile Crescent subsystem. The Palestinian movement, while emphasizing a relatively parochial problem within the general problem of pan-Arabism, has taken the whole of Arab territory as the field for their operations, thus detracting from the integrity of both boundaries and sovereign authority. Had it been otherwise, and had they been willing to respect the sovereignty of the territories from which they operated (as they have come to do in Syria), the Fidayeen might now be a significant factor. Perhaps it would have been sufficient had the Fidayeen merely insisted on control of certain areas along the border with Israel, as they did later in Lebanon. But in Jordan the Fidayeen went much further, calling into doubt any distinction between Palestine and Jordan as Arab political entities.

The Palestinian movement is an anomaly in the context of the wider Arab movement, for although all of the Arab states are at war with Israel the goal of an Arab victory has never been explicitly tied to the creation of a Palestinian political entity. The rights of Palestinians rather than Palestine have been the object of Arab mottos. Emphasis on Palestine as a potential political entity necessarily, if dialectically, calls to mind the sovereignty of other Arab states and, consequently, raises the question: In what way can derogations from their sovereignty be justified in the course of the Palestinian struggle? Two ideologically relevant answers may be given. The first is that the other Arab states, having been derelict in their duty or simply having failed in their historic responsibility to their fellow Arabs of Palestine, must suffer some diminution of their rights in the course of allowing the Palestinians to fend for themselves. The second answer is that Arab states cannot or ought not claim full sovereign rights against Arab individuals or groups who lack formal citizenship. The latter is more acceptable, but it has far-reaching implications for Arab politics as well as for the future of any Palestinian entity.

Despite the exaggerated challenge extended to the government of Jordan by the Fidayeen, the guerrilla groups do not appear to have been prepared to overthrow Hussein's regime and to take over routine government. Nevertheless, the position of the Jordanian government was growing progressively weaker until it appeared that it might collapse. This possibility kept all of the neighboring countries on edge, and while the Syria of Atāsī and Zuaʻyyin appeared content to witness the rise of anarchy in Jordan, Israel, Iraq, Lebanon, and Egypt, not to mention the Great Powers, were all apprehensive of what each of the others and Syria might do in Jordan.

Thus, with Egyptian influence in the Fertile Crescent reduced to moral suasion, and with the Palestinian guerrilla movement operating across boundary lines throughout the area, there began to develop a renewed multilateralism in the Fertile Crescent. The growth of this multilateralist pattern continued from 1968 through 1970 before it was countermanded by two contradictory developments. The most important event was, of course, the so-called Eleven-Day Civil War in Jordan in September 1970. The military defeat of the Fidayeen drew only mild rebukes for Jordan from all the Arab states except Syria, and even Syria under the more moderate leadership of Ḥāfiẓ al-Asad has done no more than close its border. This act symbolizes the isolation of Jordan, but it is an incomplete isolation at most. Nevertheless, the defeat of the Fidayeen has reversed the multilateralist trend. The second event has been the increased dependence of Egypt on Soviet political and military beneficence. Egypt's military dependence is generally acknowledged to be immense, but its political dependence is somewhat less clear. Sadat's agility in avoiding a *coup* by ʻAli Ṣabrī, Shaʻrawī Jumʻa and their cliques was less an indication of his ability to control Soviet political influence within Egypt than it was due to the contemptuous and hence impolitic attitude of the central bureaucracy of the Arab Socialist Union. The seriousness of Soviet pressures against any renewal of Egyptian-American relations, against the background of Soviet activities in Ceylon and the Sudan, conjure up the possibility of Soviet intervention in Egypt as well. These possibilities are of concern not only to Egypt itself but to many other regional states, and especially Libya, the Sudan, and Syria. Syrian concern has been enhanced, perhaps by the solicitousness of Qadhafi, but it is nevertheless real. Hence, Syria has for the time being subordinated its interest in Jordanian affairs to the Federation of Arab Republics, by which it was hoped to strengthen Egypt politically. The founding of the Federation, as ineffective as it might be, reestablishes the political link between Egypt and Syria although it is now Syria that lends support to Egypt. This renewed link has also mitigated the multilateralist pattern of the Fertile Crescent.

It remains a constant of mechanistic thinking regarding Arab affairs that any linking of two Fertile Crescent countries will bring imbalance to the international relations of the Arab states. Presumably, if a predominant power emerged in the Fertile Crescent, it would soon come to control all the territories of the Crescent and would constitute a potential if not an actual rival to Egyptian influence. It has been fears of this sort shared by Egypt, Israel, the Great Powers, and the Arab states of the Arabian Peninsula, which led them first to oppose Iraqi acquisitiveness and then to resist Syrian ambitions. Early after World War II, the Iraqi elite, motivated by old-fashioned Arab nationalism, sought an opportunity to annex Syria. Their aspirations and their failure were revealed in the sensational trials which followed the military *coup* of July 1958. Thereafter, there has been only one real promise or threat of unification in the Fertile Crescent and that has come from the Ba'th Party. Ba'thi political potential appeared to be high on two occasions. The first was in 1963 at the time of the so-called "unity talks" among Nasser and the delegations of the Ba'thi regimes of Syria and Iraq. The second was just after Nasser's death when it appeared that somewhat similarly moderate Ba'this were in or near power in Damascus and in Baghdad. In 1963 the Ba'th had to contend with the severe hostility of Nasser, a hostility which ultimately drove the Ba'th of Syria toward extremism and which pushed the Ba'th of Iraq toward moderation. No joint action was possible at the time. The emergence of "moderate" regimes in Iraq and Syria in 1970, after Nasser's death and after the most significant defeats of the Palestinians, seemed to set the stage for a renascence of Ba'thi influence. The "heroic" role played by Nasser was going begging and the Fidayeen were no longer in a position to play that part. Apparently, however, the Ba'this were still far too tied up in their own domestic squabbles to be able to undertake such important international responsibilities. The Baʻth remains a potential vehicle for more effective multilateralization of Fertile Crescent politics, but the potential has not yet been realized. In fact, Baʻthi international performance is now far lower than it was in 1963, and not only east of Suez. Both the Libyan and the Tunisian authorities have been very apprehensive about the consequences of possible Baʻthi influence on their younger intellectuals. Despite the availability of significant opportunities, it appears that the Baʻth has made no outstanding effort to gain influence outside of Syria and Iraq.

Perhaps the most important change in the international arrangements of the Fertile Crescent has been the outcome of the Israeli occupation of the West Bank and the partial lowering of international barriers between Jordan and the occupied zone on the one hand and between the occupied zone and Israel on the other. The impact of this peculiar arrangement has been limited by Jordan's bad relations with the other Arab states. The uniqueness of the arrangement is manifested in the fact that the "open doors" policy of Israel has allowed for substantial interaction, including important economic transactions, at the personal level, while there is almost no official contact at the governmental level. The movement of persons and goods back and forth across the truce lines produces only a minimal level of international social interaction, but at times the Jordan River is the easiest border to cross in the Fertile Crescent. It is conceivable that this trickle could expand the bureaucratic loopholes even without the attainment of a formal settlement, or a comprehensive settlement, but in order for it to become really significant as a cause of international political structural change, Jordan will have to improve its relations with Syria and Iraq.

Such Israel-Arab unofficial interaction as is the consequence of the "open doors" policy occurs only to the east of Suez. Paradoxically, most government-level contacts, albeit indirect, are between Israel and Egypt. The reason for this asymmetry is easy enough to find. Government-level activity between Israel and Egypt is the outcome of occasional pressures applied by the United States and the Soviet Union. The earlier prevalence of hostilities and the precarious appearance of the cease-fire on the Canal, militate against any extension of the "open doors" policy to Suez. Moreover, the political ambivalence of the West Bank Palestinians, who are not at all certain that they wish to renew an effective allegiance to King Hussein, is not matched by the unambigous political attachments of the former residents of the Canal Zone to Egypt.

A year after Nasser's death the characteristic tendency of the governments and elites of the Fertile Crescent countries is isolative, and this tendency has been strengthened by the political and military decline of the Palestinian movement. Even Lebanon, which has responded to Syrian and Palestinian pressures, allowing a number of Fidayeen to use parts of the south Lebanon region as a staging area for attacks on northern Israel, has attempted to seal off the area of hostilities. Lebanon has further indicated by word and deed that it will resist the efforts of Palestinians to turn Beirut into an arena of of Palestinian politics. Lebanon has also shown that she will oppose Syrian or Iraqi attempts to use the Palestine issue or events in Jordan as a pretext for intervention in its affairs. This vigorous, if slightly ambiguous, Lebanese policy has not been entirely successful in precluding Israeli retaliatory incursions into Lebanese territory, but it has resulted in the prompt return of Israeli troops after each punitive raid.

It is premature to draw conclusions regarding the future of the Palestinian movement on the basis of recent Jordanian successes in repressing it. Palestinian guerrilla and terrorist elements remain active in Syria and Lebanon, and of course, many have gone underground in Jordan. A daring act of terror may signal a new rise of enthusiasm, or an agreement on a temporary or partial settlement in the Sinai area may bring a Palestinian reaction. It is far more likely that the Palestinian movement will go through an extensive and much needed rethinking phase. The ideological pretenses and inept leadership of the past will have to be changed. Above all, the lessons of their unacknowledged dependence on host Arab states must be learned by the Palestinians. It is difficult to know how soon such lessons will be fully studied and whence will come more responsible and pragmatic thinking. For the transitional moment, however, it seems that the Palestinians of the West Bank are in the best position to determine the Palestinian future. Not only are they resident in Palestine, but their communities are more or less intact, they have an immediate grasp of both Israeli and Jordanian political realities, they enjoy a high degree of autonomy, they are still uncommitted for the most part, and their cooperation is being sought by Israel, by Jordan, by expatriated Palestinian groups, and by international agencies. The population of the West Bank has also been allowed to enjoy some economic benefits of their key position, in that both Israel and Jordan subsidize the West Bank region, and it has not been called upon or forced to expend resources on warlike or guerrilla activities. For all of these reasons, it is not likely that the leaders of the West Bank will soon commit themselves, but at this time it is no longer true that the Palestinian die could be cast by other Palestinians without taking account of West Bank attitudes. At present it is more likely that the West Bank leadership could, if it could or would achieve a consensus, determine the fate of the Palestinian movement.

As the Fertile Crescent pattern becomes more isolative, and the Egyptian region strives for greater integration, the more remote sectors of the Middle East system have become more autonomous, more politically significant, and more politically active. The Maghreb and the Persian Gulf, both remote from the scene of the 1967 war but both indirectly affected by that conflict, have emerged to prominence. Algeria in the Maghreb and Iran in the Gulf have each gained considerable influence—primarily due to their petroleum resources but also to their relatively substantial populations and extensive territories. Each resisted Egyptian predominance, even though Algeria claimed to be more radical and Iran more conservative. Each has also been wooed by the Great Powers, believing that friendly relations with Algeria or Iran might facilitate their policies in the Mediterranean or the Persian Gulf.

Iran's role in the Persian Gulf looms as the larger of the two because more changes are taking place in the Gulf, there are more states in the vicinity of the Gulf, and more states in and out of the Gulf are at present willing to see Iran play a leadership role. Iran will be able to act as a politically stabilizing force during the withdrawal of direct British influence from the Gulf. But Iran is also likely to avoid threatening Western petroleum interests in the area. It will also probably continue to improve relations with Saudi-Arabia, Kuwait, Bahrain, Qatar, and the Trucial Shaikhdoms, thus drawing them a little further out of the frequently uncomfortable orbit of Egyptian and Arab League politics. If Iran is successful in doing this, then some more substance will be lent to the idea of an Islamic political bloc. Iran will act as a restraint on Iraq, and as a regulator of Kurdish political activity. Iran can also have a regulatory influence on Afghanistan if such a need should arise. This new, active, Iranian role has been welcomed not only by Tehran, but also in Washington and Moscow. The longer such a pattern continues, the less likely will it be that the earlier centripetal domination of the subordinate system will be reestablished.

Algeria has begun to emerge as a stable and independent power in the Maghreb. Its influence with its two neighbors is limited because Algeria became embroiled in minor border disputes with both and because of the ideological tension among these regimes. Algeria has been suspect since its attainment of independence as an adventurous state given to overenthusiastic support of Egypt, China, the Soviet Union, and the Palestinians. Boumedienne has run a much tighter ship than Ben Bella, and despite Algeria's retention of the ideological and tactical initiative, Boumedienne has improved relations with Morocco and Tunisia, and if relations with France have become strained over petroleum matters, relations with the United States have improved somewhat. Relations with the Soviet Union are good even though it seems that Algeria has stopped short of granting the U.S.S.R. bases on the Mediterranean. Algeria's role in the western Mediterranean is still more potential than actual, but it appears that all of the prerequisites are present. Algeria has the wealth, population, international prestige, political cadres, geographical location, and size to play an extremely important role in the Maghreb not only as the predominant Arab power but also as the primary mediator or broker of Great-Power influence.

Egypt might have been able to play a role in the central part of the Middle East similar to that of Algeria and Iran. While it lacks petroleum resources of the same order, Egypt has an even more important strategic position and plays an influential ideological role. Certainly both the United States and the Soviet Union sought to implement their Middle East policies through cooperation with Egypt. For its part Egypt could not seem to bring itself into a sufficiently neutral position to benefit from this immensely strengthening attitude of both superpowers. Initially, the United States was far more willing to strengthen Egypt as an area power than was the Soviet Union, which preferred to strengthen domestic Communists. The United States was willing to go a long way, although not all the way, toward establishing a regime in the Yemen which would be responsive to Egypt. The Soviet Union, on the other hand, offered aid in building the dam at Aswan. The Soviets also sought to develop attractive situations of influence in Syria, Iraq, and the Sudan. The United States already had relatively reliable friends in Israel,

Jordan, Lebanon, Turkey, Iran, Arabia, Tunisia, and Morocco. But the United States was still willing to weaken those friendships by courting Cairo, except perhaps during the worst period of U.S.– Egyptian relations in 1964 and 1965. Moscow was unwilling to support Egypt all the way, however, except perhaps for a brief period in 1964 when Egypt was declared to be on the non-capitalist road to development. Egypt's calculations were probably most based on its policy of maintaining influence over the policies of the Arab states—the real basis of Egypt's appeal to the Great Powers. The United States wished to exploit Egypt's influence over the other Arab states. The Soviet Union wished to diminish that influence. Egypt feared that cooperation with the United States, unless the U.S. first sold out Israel, would cause the loss of Egyptian influence in the Fertile Crescent. The Soviet alliance sustained the Egyptian image abroad but it also resulted in domestic policies which increased internal political tension and strengthened the opposition to Nasser's regime. In the aftermath of the 1967 war, Egypt lost on both counts; its influence in the Fertile Crescent diminished, and internal dissension over economic and social issues increased.

Egypt's political weakness, within and without, was more than matched by its military vulnerability immediately after the Six-Day War. The combination of vulnerabilities and the loss of confidence rendered Egypt a virtually open field for Soviet influence. The major outward aspect of the ensuing process of the building of that influence was, of course, the rebuilding of Egyptian armament. This did not replace the armies shattered in the June war, nor did it restore morale, but it was, at least, a promise of Soviet commitment. That commitment was ultimately expressed in the deployment of Soviet manpower along with advanced missiles and aircraft as a response to the impatient Israeli bombing-in-depth policy. The stationing of large numbers of Soviet troops in Egypt doubtlessly had its counterpart in the growth of Soviet influence over Egyptian policy and may have contributed to the emergence of a group of pro-Soviets among the political elite. How close such a group ever got, or is at present, to taking over the regime is a matter about which we can only conjecture.

The myth of Egyptian autonomy, given the expanded Soviet presence, could be maintained as long as Nasser lived, but it was soon thereafter dispelled. Sadat's conflict with 'Alī Ṣabrī and various members of the Arab Socialist Union executive did not reveal the presence of direct Soviet influence. On the other hand, the ousted group was clearly identified as a pro-Soviet faction. Soviet influence was more in evidence immediately after Rogers' trip to Cairo. It would seem that Sadat's success in forestalling a *coup* by the pro-Soviet faction was deemed both by Sadat and by the United States to have produced a situation conducive to renewed U.S.–Egyptian relations, preceded perhaps by an interim Israeli-Egyptian agreement on the Suez Canal. So obvious was Sadat's welcome to Rogers, and so obvious was Rogers' optimism, that the Soviet Union became alarmed. Some pressures were immediately and decisively applied. Egypt was offered, and accepted, a long-term Treaty of Friendship and Cooperation with the Soviet Union. Sadat then crudely rejected any idea of a more friendly approach to the United States or a compromise position on an interim agreement with Israel.

The United States has not offered Israel a parallel alliance, nor have American soldiers been committed to Israel's defense. The United States has not even given Israel a guarantee of a continued arms supply. Despite many superficial appearances, there is no real symmetry of the Soviet and American positions, although there is great potential for a Great-Power confrontation. Israel is free to renew diplomatic relations with the Soviet Union, but the Soviet Union is unlikely to desire to do so at the cost of allowing Egypt to renew its diplomatic relations with the United States. Israel may well be able to resist American pressures to agree to a partial withdrawal from the Suez Canal, but such pressures will not become decisive unless the result will include renewed diplomatic relations with Egypt. The Soviet Union, once thought to be anxiously desirous of opening the Canal, is no longer so anxious, and certainly will not allow Egypt to compromise if the consequence of an interim Suez agreement will be the normalization of U.S.–Egyptian relations.

If a military confrontation, on land, in the Middle East, is less likely now than it was in the past, the possibility of a confrontation at sea has increased. The important strengthening of the Soviet fleet in the Mediterranean has more than a single aim, the least of which may be to protect the landed Soviet position in the Middle East. The Soviet Mediterranean fleet is meant to strengthen the Soviet Union over against Western Europe, to allow a more flexible response to demands for autonomy in Eastern Europe, to expand Soviet influence in Africa and in the Persian Gulf, and, in the longer run, to better the Soviet position vis-à-vis Chinese political and military efforts. The

Soviet presence in Egypt is thus similar to that of the former imperial British occupation.

Soviet bases in Egypt were primarily geared to the support of the Soviet fleet. But insofar as those bases might be threatened by Israel, they had to be defended by keeping the Israelis from attacking them and by preserving the regime which offered this military hospitality. During the Six-Day War, when it may have occurred to the Soviet Union to intervene militarily on behalf of Egypt by means of Soviet air power, it was doubtlessly revealed that the Soviets were in no position to do so. The lack of bases, ground crews, equipment, and antiaircraft defenses made it impossible for the Soviets to intervene had they wished to. That problem has now been remedied even though the defense of Egypt itself may be subordinated to support of the Soviet fleet. The Soviet Union can if it wishes, and will if it chooses, use Soviet men and equipment against Israeli forces. Furthermore, the general utility of these bases may be of such broad importance from the perspective of the Soviet military that their protection may outweigh the benefit to be won by peaceful accommodation with the United States. Again, if an interim or comprehensive Middle East settlement might weaken the Soviet control of these bases, it is unlikely that the Soviet military will agree to such an accommodation.

Thus the Soviet Union has gradually but consistently moved toward imposing a dual bilateralism in American and Soviet relations with Egypt and Israel. The United States has resisted this pattern, but has been forced by circumstances to accommodate itself to it. Early after the fighting, in the summer of 1967, there was a good deal of talk about the possibility of a Soviet-American agreement to regulate the situation in the Middle East. Now it seems more probable that any joint Great-Power regulation of the conflict is more likely to be manifested in a prolongation of the present cease-fire rather than in any peaceful settlement. The Soviet Union does not appear to want to withdraw to a position of joint supervisor of a peace treaty, a position which appears very attractive to the United States at this time.

The Great-Power position in the Egyptian-Israeli conflict remains fluid, but it has already moved far from what it was in May 1967. As the eastern and western extremities of the Middle East have enhanced the autonomy of their regions, the central core of the Middle East appears to have declined decisively in its autonomy. On the banks of the Suez Canal the distinction between the dominant global system and the subordinate Middle Eastern system appears no longer to exist. Now, more than ever, it seems that the small states of the Middle East will be compelled to serve as expendable pawns in a global conflict in which the superpowers will seek to gain advantages while minimizing the risk of nuclear war. For the peoples of the Middle East, and for the Egyptians and the Israelis, the dilemma is as simple as it is insoluble: peace does not seem to be attainable without the aid and encouragement of the Great Powers; but the Great Powers cannot agree either to withdraw from the region or to regulate it jointly and collectively; hence cooperation with the Great Powers has tended and still tends to perpetuate a dual bilateral balance of Egypt and the U.S.S.R. against Israel and the U.S. The problem for which no solution is obvious is how to achieve peace while restoring the autonomy of the Middle Eastern subordinate system.

The breakdown of the Middle Eastern system culminated in the war of June 1967, it did not start then. As we have seen, the change began at least two years earlier with the decline in the Egyptian position. Egypt's centralizing role was the determinative factor in the pre-1967 system, but that role could not be sustained. The power differential of Middle Eastern states, taken by themselves and without foreign military assistance, was so small as to render them nearly equal. In any case, Egypt's advantage was not great enough to sustain its aspiration to leadership and regional predominance without the support of the Great Powers. For Egypt to have been completely successful, Nasser would have required the support of both Great Powers and not merely one. As it was he had neither the complete support of the one nor the other.

The particular form which the transformation of the Middle Eastern system is now taking is also not so much the consequence of the war of 1967 as it is due to certain changes which have affected the relations of the United States and the Soviet Union. A decade and a half ago, the assumptions of bipolarity still prevailed as adequate guides to understanding global politics. At the same time neutralism or non-alignment was developed as a doctrine accounting for the significance of international political roles in opposition to the universalization of bipolarity. Today neither bipolarity nor neutralism have meaningful applications. The bloc structure of bipolarity has broken down. New and powerful international actors have emerged. The smaller states are less apprehensive of aggression by the major bloc leaders and less willing to serve as trip-wires or early warning systems. Accomodative agreements between the Great Powers are viewed with mixed feelings, as smaller powers welcome hopeful agreements on such topics as disarmament, but also fear the consequences of agreements which resolve regional tensions by imposing restrictions or territorial hindrances on smaller powers. The protected security spheres of the Great Powers have been penetrated and they grow progressively more porous. Even economic prosperity is no longer tied to bloc loyalties, but is often the result of fiscal and commercial flexibility in a world which is becoming more and more pluralistic. Neutrality means far less, too, in a situation where some NATO bloc members, and some Communist states have more political maneuverability than many so-called neutrals. In any case no really strong (morally or militarily) bloc of neutral states has emerged. Neither Egypt, nor Indonesia, nor India, nor Ghana, nor even Yugoslavia or Algeria has been able to sustain the political initiative of the neutralist movement. No significant political force has emerged in the Third World. No moral force has been exerted on Great-Power politics. No alternative way of ordering world politics has developed out of the policies of non-alignment. It cannot even be argued that the various U.N. organs have been strengthened as a result of the efforts of the neutralist powers.

The Great Powers are still concerned with regional defense, but their approach is more flexible, and they are willing to accept the fact of one another's presence as an assurance as well as an annoyance. Both sides are far more willing to rely on seapower than they were before. The greatly enhanced capacity of both the United States and the Soviet Union to destroy one another from whatever place on earth is the key to the decline of bipolarity as an explanation of international politics and to the lowering of the stakes in local, land-based conflicts from Viet Nam to Cuba. At one time the West considered the Middle East to be the flank of NATO, and a conflict in the Middle East to be a mere prelude to a conflict in Europe. The Soviet Union thought of the Middle East as a staging area for a Western attack on southern Russia and, in the absence of a protective belt of satellite states, stationed many armies along its southern borders. Had a sizeable conflict broken out in the Middle East both sides would have become locked in mortal combat there and elsewhere in the world. Now no one expects such a result from fighting in the Middle East unles the U.S. and the U.S.S.R. come under the leadership of greater fools than ever before.

But the decline of bipolarity and of the threat of war has had a differential impact on the policies of the United States and the Soviet Union. As the fear of immediate, all-out war recedes, Middle East policy is less dominated by considerations of military strategy and less geared to the limitations of a given military technology. Political and economic considerations of a more ordinary kind may come to prevail. It is not surprising, then, that while still desirous of preserving its contractually privileged petroleum position, the United States is willing to adopt more of a laisser faire attitude toward the Soviet Union. The Soviets, on the other hand, have been reconsidering the positive attitude that Khrushchev took toward neutralism. Khrushchev's policy was effective in weakening the Western hold on many countries in the Third World, but it was feared that this concession might have far-reaching ideological consequences. Perhaps most of all, it was feared that it would result in the ruin of the Communist Party and its best cadres in the countries most praised by Khrushchev and the countries which were most influential in their own regions. Khrushchev's removal from power did not result in an immediate reversal of his policy toward those who were on the non-capitalist path, but gradually a strong alternative tendency has appeared. This alternative tendency has been manifest in Ceylon, the Sudan, Turkey, Syria, and possibly even Egypt. Soviet policy in the Third World is not univocal, and bourgeois nationalist allies are not yet being abandoned. Yet it does seem that the alternative of establishing Castro-type regimes based on pro-Communist intellectuals has been seriously considered, has been strongly advocated, and has been applied tentatively in a number of cases. The lack of conspicuous success thus far achieved is no warrant for the imminent abandonment of such a secondary policy. Russia's rivalry with China is too serious to allow the Soviets to contemplate the relaxing joys of peaceful coexistence, competition, and political accommodation with the United States. If the stakes in a possible U.S.–U.S.S.R. conflict have become less, well that circumstance allows a firmer ideological and Communist organizational line to be followed with less attendant risk. In Egypt, where the Soviet Union's position is so strong, both alternatives are available. So long as cooperation with the bourgeois-nationalist regime is possible, the pro-Soviet members of the intellectual and military elite will not be called upon to act—even though Egypt condemned the opponents of Sudan's Numeiri.

Consequently, it is not easy to foresee the basis of either an interim settlement dealing only with the Suez Canal or a more comprehensive settlement. For an agreement to be reached, the United States would have to agree to the continuation of Soviet dominance in Cairo. If not, the Soviet Union will induce Cairo to raise its conditions beyond what might be considered reasonable by Israel, and it will compensate Egypt with additional arms. An additional difficulty, even if the United States wished to acquiesce in such an arrangement, is that there is no proper way to specify the exclusion of American influence in Cairo as a precondition of an agreement, and it may be embarrassing to insist on an explicit Egyptian commitment not to renew diplomatic relations with the U.S. without Soviet approval. It may be safer, from the Soviet point of view, to avoid an agreement.

As the United States seeks to defuse the dangerous situation along the Canal, it turns consistently to the difficult conditions which Israel puts forward. Israeli conditions for a partial withdrawal are demanding because Israel fears that the United States will shift to a more neutral stance as soon as an interim agreement is signed. But American pressure can probably succeed in wearing down Israeli resistance. If and when it does, the United States is bound to elicit some assurances that Egypt, too, will pursue a more "evenhanded" policy. In this, it is unlikely that the United States will succeed, because an interim agreement for a partial withdrawal will not eliminate Egypt's dependence on the Soviet Union and it will not alleviate Israeli fears of a renewal of hostilities. Insofar as any line across the Sinai Peninsula will be more difficult to maintain than the present line along the Canal, such an interim arrangement may require the immediate implementive presence of both powers. It is evident that peace between Egypt and Israel is unattainable without the withdrawal of the Great Powers from immediate involvement in the subsystem, and that withdrawal of the Great Powers is impossible without peace. The unexpected expulsion from Egypt of Soviet troops and specialists seems to offer a way out of this vicious circle.

Two important events occurred since the end of 1971 when this paper was completed. These were the expulsion of Soviet troops and advisors from Egypt in July of 1972 and the dismissal of General Muḥammad Ṣādiq from his post as commander-in-chief of the Egyptian army and minister of war. Both actions of President Sadat surprised observers. The first seemed to be a decisive break in the recent history of close Soviet-Egyptian cooperation, and foreshadowed an attempted rapprochement with the U.S. The second was a partial reversal of the first and was widely interpreted as a concession to the Soviet Union. Both events sustain the view that domestic political considerations still outweigh "cold-war" issues in determining Egyptian policy. Sadat, and the general public, were believed to be opposed to continuing so vast a Soviet presence in Egypt. The Soviets were too friendly to Sadat's enemies and the Communist ideology is uncongenial to the ideological predilections of Sadat's propertied and religious supporters. While the dismissal of General Ṣādiq was generally acknowledged to be desired by the Soviets, there is also some suggestion that his ouster and the return of a limited number of Russian specialists was the demand of a group of Egyptian army officers.

These two events taken together indicate how difficult it will be for Sadat to alter his relations with the U.S.S.R. and the U.S. The U.S. is widely expected to seek to improve its relations with Egypt after the elections of November 1972, but it is also apparent that Egypt's political importance to the United States has declined in the measure that Egypt's influence over the other Arab states has declined. On the other hand, American and Soviet interest will increasingly shift to the oil-producing countries because of the impending energy shortages in both countries and because of the recent bargaining successes of these countries. It is premature to speculate on the nature of these newly emerging patterns, but it is possible to argue on the basis of these events that the dual bilateral arrangement which has thus far prevailed among the U.S., U.S.S.R., Egypt, and Israel will be altered only by agreement between the U.S. and the U.S.S.R.

P. J. Vatikiotis

NOTES FOR AN ASSESSMENT OF THE SOVIET IMPACT ON EGYPT

I

It is difficult amidst the different interpretations given and glosses which have been put on the Soviet-Egyptian and Soviet-Arab relationships to isolate with any precision the impact of the Soviet Union on these societies. One prominent Syrian academic, for instance, asserted in the summer of 1958: "Egypt and we are now united, the Soviet Union is behind us, our Arab adversaries are cowed and in disarray, the Israelis are nervous, and the world better watch out". If an academic's perception of the situation was that euphoric 13 years ago—even though the euphoria may have concealed a more typical cynicism—one can only imagine what the propaganda-fed perception of the masses must have been.

There is also the temptation for one to try and depict say, the Egyptian-Soviet relationship on the basis of what the Egyptian press says about it, with an assiduous reference to its content. The danger here would be that the discussion of that relationship by the Egyptian press is primarily motivated by considerations of domestic policy, often by those of inter-Arab and regional politics, and significantly by the requirements of the Egyptian belief that an unequal relationship with the Soviet Union, with themselves as the junior partner, or client, can only be mitigated by some relationship with the Western powers, particularly the United States.

Leading students of the Soviet Union have written extensively about the U.S.S.R. in the Middle East, and have particularly covered the story of the coming of the Soviet Union to the Middle East from 1955 to the present time. They have, I think, dealt at some length with the question of why and how the Soviet Union came to be in the position it is today in the Middle East generally, and in Egypt particularly. Moreover, they have discussed an important aspect of Soviet-Arab and Soviet-Egyptian relations, namely, the relevance of Communist ideology to Soviet foreign policy, and its implications for local Communists and socialists in the Arab states.

273

One could, for example, seek to formulate the reaction and response of Egyptians to their relationship with the Soviet Union from a tedious recitation of, or reference to, the commentaries penned by state-appointed editors and feature writers of newspapers and magazines. But that, in my view, would be a useless exercise for I am certain our colleagues follow closely such publications as *al-Ṭalīʿa, al-Kātib, al-Muṣawwar, Rūz al-Yūsuf, Ṣabāḥ al-Khayr* and *al-Hilāl,* not to mention the daily newspapers. Moreover, the readership of these publications is still limited to a relatively small proportion of the Egyptian population, indeed, of the Arabic-speaking peoples generally.

One is inclined to argue that, not unlike the British Empire before them, the Soviets are in the Middle East primarily because of their vital interests in Europe and the subcontinent of Asia. Currently, the overriding preoccupation of Soviet policy on a global scale is the containment of the United States. Egypt and the Arab states in the Middle East constitute only one area in Russia's consideration of the problems and requirements of its foreign policy. The role of these states therefore is, in the Soviet view, instrumental to the containment of the United States and the defence of the Russian empire. The relationship, or alliance, with Egypt can therefore fluctuate up or down the order of priorities of Soviet foreign policy. To this overall consideration one should append the added Soviet concern and preoccupation with the challenge (real or potential) of China—in Asia certainly, the Middle East and Africa probably—as well as that of a larger European community. To this extent, Soviet bilateral relations with the Arab states are not prompted, so far, by any specific, tangible Soviet interest in the Middle East itself.

Until five years ago, Middle Eastern oil was mentioned only in connection with Western economic and strategic interests. The newcomer in this field has been Japan from the Far East. The assumption was that the Soviet Union and its East European satellites were self-sufficient in this primary commodity. Since that time, some economists and strategists have argued a direct Soviet interest in Middle Eastern oil on the basis of the rate of consumption in Russia and Eastern Europe, which now exceeds production. To this extent, they argue that Middle Eastern oil must become a major factor in Soviet strategy and therefore a direct Soviet interest in the Middle East. But Egypt is not a major oil producer, although it could conceivably become one. One would think nevertheless that Soviet interest should, in the next decade, shift to the

Persian Gulf in the east and also to Algeria (and Morocco) in the west.

A strong case cannot be made at this time for a Soviet interest in the establishment of Communist regimes in the Middle East, even though this could be considered an ultimate objective for two reasons. First, there is the official attachment of the U.S.S.R. to Communist ideology. Second, the Soviet Union claims to lead the world revolution of Communist states or regimes. But in Egypt—or in other Arab states—local Communist parties have hardly exhibited marks of strength, or even potential strength. In fact, the establishment of closer relations between Arab regimes, particularly the one in Egypt, and the U.S.S.R. has resulted in their further weakening, decimation, and suppression. For it is clear that so long as the Soviet Union can help the installation of regimes in Egypt, or elsewhere, on which it can rely for close collaboration on the local, inter-Arab, or regional, and international level, it is not particularly concerned whether these regions are controlled by local Communists or others.

In the last fifteen years, Egypt presented to the U.S.S.R. a convenient, in parts, ideal centre in which to plant the Middle Eastern adjunct, or flank, of their more active and aggressive global policy. The Russians had no prior educational, cultural, or other contacts in Egypt. Until World War I, Russia's policy in the Middle East was constrained by and limited to its relations with the Ottoman State over the Balkans and the Levant. In fact, excluding one or another group of the eternally fragmented Egyptian Communist Party since 1920, there were hardly any Russophones or Russophiles in the country. The miniscule Russian community in Egypt had consisted of a few White Russian emigrés and refugees from the Revolution and its aftermath (1917–20). Even the few Egyptian Marxists and Communists in Egypt were intellectually of purely British and French provenance. A great number of them were foreigners resident in Egypt. The Russians could not match—and they did not try to—the overwhelming English and French educational, cultural, and political influence of a century. Furthermore, by 1920 Russia retreated from any involvement in world affairs and, in effect, became isolationist. There was a temporary break in the pursuit of its traditional policy, since Catherine the Great, of seeking an outlet to southern warm waters towards the Mediterranean. Yet the break was of short duration, from 1917 to 1945, when the traditional policy was revived, in fact resumed, in connection with Turkey and Iran, not to mention the civil war in Greece from 1944 to 1949.

Before the establishment of diplomatic relations between Egypt and the U.S.S.R. in 1943, most Egyptians could hardly recall their previous, peripheral contacts in the 19th century, when Egypt sent an expeditionary force to fight alongside the Turkish armies in the Crimean War (1854–6), and again in the Russo-Turkish War of 1877.

Shifting Great Power interests and Arab state policy reorientations occurred after World War II, which contributed to the development of a Soviet-Arab, and especially a Soviet-Egyptian, relationship. A corollary of America's containment policy against the Soviet Union after 1947 was the search for regional security pacts in the Middle East and other zones of contention and conflict in the Cold War. In view of the weakened position and retreating influence of Britain in the Middle East, the United States sought to incorporate the region into its global "system" of security arrangements. The Arab states, however, were not interested in the Cold War. The overthrow of *ancien régimes* by military *coups d'état* brought to power rulers who were more interested in the further erosion of the Western position in the Middle East, in short, the evacuation of bases in Egypt, Arabia, and the Persian Gulf. In the meantime, after the death of Stalin in 1953, a reorientation of Soviet policy marked the abandonment of the Zhdanovite world dichotomy, and a willingness to support local nationalist and revolutionary trends in the Middle East and Africa. The Soviets were now ready to work actively in thwarting the West's attempts to incorporate the Middle East into its global defence system. At that point Soviet interests coincided with those of the new rulers of Egypt.

In Egypt, as in Syria and other Arab states, the myth was quickly fostered of a new friendly superpower which was fundamentally opposed to their erstwhile Western "masters". A relationship with the Soviet Union came to be seen as a counterweight to what they believed was certain American hostility; so that as Western bases were evacuated, one after the other, Egyptians—and other Arabs—believed that much of this welcome development was due to Soviet assistance.

Greater dependence on massive Soviet economic, technical, and military aid, together with a continued inability to deal successfully with the Israeli adversary, as well as the need to maintain a leading position in inter-Arab state conflicts and rivalries, inevitably led Egypt to the acceptance of a Soviet alliance. The belief was nurtured that such an alliance would help Egypt attain its objectives at home, in the region, and especially against Israel. Initially, Nasser and his colleagues may have felt that a closer relationship with the Soviet Union would spare them a total dependence on the West and, after 1955–6, the consequences of Israel's military superiority.

More generally, the Egyptians and other Arab states came to consider the relationship with the Soviet superpower as a way of buttressing internationally their rejection of Western domination. Since many of them view Israel as a Western "intruder" into what they consider an Arab land, the relationship with the U.S.S.R. was also adjudged as regionally, locally efficacious. Since 1966, at least, the Soviet Union has been, in Egyptian eyes, the only power willing to support them in their conflict with Israel.

This, in broad terms, has been the Egyptian perception of the relationship with the U.S.S.R.—at least until the death of President Nasser in September 1970. Since that time, however, it has become clear to some Egyptians that their superpower ally may desire the benefits of the relationship with Egypt in the wider context of their global policy, but without the measure of involvement that could be most favourable to Egypt.

It is odd, but nonetheless uncanny, in its parallelism that both Russia and the United States, roughly at about the same time (1953–6), saw in the rise of Nasser the possibility of extending their influence throughout the Arab Middle East. Both were attracted and tantalized by the emergence of that apparently powerful man, whose personality came to mesmerize, if not in fact dominate, the Arab states for nearly a decade (1957–67). They saw Nasser as the anchor with which to moor their policies in the Arab states. Both superpowers had tried their luck before with the ostensibly more Arab centre of the region, Syria in the Fertile Crescent, "the pulsating heart of Arab Nationalism": the United States in the period 1947–57; the Soviet Union after that. In the years 1961 to 1965, however, both superpowers had shifted their attention to the least Arab of these states, Egypt.

The Americans soon parted company with their presumed Bismarck over the Yemen and other issues which were intricately connected with their vast commercial interests, their relations with the so-called conservative Arab rulers in the Peninsula and elsewhere, and their support of Israel. The Soviets, on the other hand, had no such irreconcilable interests, and hoped to utilize their Mazzini more effectively throughout the Arab Middle East. Yet even they, in the last two years, have tried to diversify their "investment", by proliferating hopefully similar if not better relations with Algeria, for instance (and Morocco), in the Maghreb, and now Iraq in the Fertile Crescent.

II

Leaving the matters of military assistance and the Arab-Israel conflict aside for the moment, clearly the greatest impact of the Soviet Union on Egypt has been on its economy generally, and the pattern of trade particularly. Ideologically and socially the Soviet impact on economic practice has been minimal—almost none. Under Nasser, the government deliberately planned its economic schemes with an orientation towards the middle, state-employed technical, educated urban groups. To this extent these consumers who could have been squeezed, or sacrificed, in favour of a production-oriented economy in the cause of rapid industrialization, were consciously, deliberately, that is, as a matter of politics, catered for—in fact, pampered. Even when defence expenditure rose in the 1971–2 fiscal year to nearly £700 million in a state budget of £2,500 million, taxes had hardly risen in the preceding three years. There also persisted a marked continuity in the economic system from the *ancien* to the Nasser regime. By any set of criteria, the socialist revolution of the Free Officers hardly qualified as socialist according to the economic definitions of that condition.

The fact that the major transformation in the Egyptian economy from private to public enterprise occurred after 1956 and more rapidly after 1961 cannot be gainsaid. The regime argued that an underdeveloped country can achieve both a more equitable distribution of income and a higher rate of growth when the means of production are publicly owned. The state under this system would realize a higher rate of savings and investment, both of which could be channelled into activities that are far more productive for society as a whole. This argument, I think, constituted the extent of socialist economic doctrine; but one which is not confined to the U.S.S.R. Without suggesting that the Egyptian economy has been successful under this doctrine, one must assert that it was not led by convinced socialists or Marxists. Moreover, at no time did the regime accept any of the other essential ingredients or features of political socialism, viz., the role of the party, the class struggle, etc.

Ironically, the pattern of trade was quickly reoriented away from its traditional Western direction to the East mainly for political reasons.

While this entailed some imports from the Eastern bloc but not neces-sarily the U.S.S.R. to Egypt, it consisted largely of massive exports of Egyptian cotton, and some petrochemicals. The single largest import item has been military and economic aid.

In view of the construction of the Aswan High Dam over a period of ten years and the massive supply of arms, Soviet technology has conceivably had some impact on Egypt. With it has gone the training of Egyptian personnel. Some of these have had to make the effort to learn Russian. There is no clear evidence, however, to date that Egyptians have been eagerly flocking to learn Russian or any other East European language for that matter. Even though Russian has been in the school curriculum for some years now, it is still not as widely taught a language as English or French. It is moreover an optional language. English, for a long time now, has been a compulsory foreign language in most schools.

Whereas over trade, technology, and military training the Russians have achieved a virtual hegemony in Egypt, in the essential infrastruc-ture areas of education and culture their impact, so far, has been negli-gible. Even in trade, technology, and the broader field of economic development the Russians have not completely rendered Egypt inac-cessible to Western diplomacy and trade. Their monopoly of military aid is a fact; so is their military and technological presence in the country, in whatever guise, a fact.

It can be argued that within a generation, Russian or some other politically less ominous East European language may well displace English or French as the first foreign language of educated Egyptians— of the élite. Almost simultaneously with the signing of the Soviet-Egyptian Treaty of Friendship and Cooperation in May 1971, a new cultural agreement was signed between the two countries. It provides for more Russian teachers in Egypt in 1971 and 1972. On the face of it, this may seem insignificant. Considering the clause in the Treaty regard-ing cultural cooperation between the two countries and the undertaking of the Soviet Union to help build socialism in Egypt, the Russians could be quite serious about teaching in Egypt. Their educational and cultural efforts in the past—after 1955 and especially in 1958–60—failed for several reasons. They were in fact rendered useless by the wooden re-sponse of young Egyptians who continued to flock mainly to the West for higher education. Moreover, the Russian attempt to promote Muslim-oriented cultural activities in Egypt could have back-fired at home, in the face of their cultural and political treatment of their own Muslims in the U.S.S.R.

It would be dangerous, however, to assume that given their military and political investment in Cairo at the present time, a new Russian effort to implement such an agreement must automatically fail. Since say, 1966, the difficult economic situation in the country, the strained relations with the West, the overcrowding in schools and universities, the lack of research funds and access to European sources of educational and cultural materials could force more and more Egyptians, seeking technical and higher education, to settle for what the Russians can provide on the spot, or in Russia, cheaply or gratis—whatever the quality.

This possibility lay perhaps behind the recent apprehension of several Egyptian leaders in education, science, literature, and the arts, that in ten to fifteen years time a whole new generation of Egyptians could grow up with Russian as their only second language. In the meantime, they complain about their own isolation from the major sources of their inspiration in Europe, which provided the basis of their literary endeavour and modern cultural formation over the last 150 years. This, despite the fact that these same men of letters did, in the last twenty-five years, manage to produce an original native, or local, literature of high quality in the short story, novel, poetry, and the theatre.

Yet the novel experience of these Egyptians with the Russians in Egypt, and more significantly, as a result of their visits to Russia and Communist Eastern Europe, has undermined their earlier romantic vision of the Communist revolution and eroded their paradisical image of Russian government and society. They have come to wonder why it is so necessary for a successful, long-established revolutionary state and doctrine in Moscow to continue to regiment, persecute, and punish its more curious and courageous intellectuals. There is, in other words, a disenchantment among the Egyptian Left of the period 1945–65 with the object of their past adulation.

At home, Egyptians of all classes and backgrounds find it difficult to become acquainted with the Russians in their country. They hardly have a chance to mix with them socially. Moreover, the Russians working in Egypt tend to live in their own physical and cultural ghetto. Many of them consider Egypt a "hardship post", preferring postings abroad to the few countries left in the world with a royal court. They are suspicious of the average Egyptian and detest his levitous insouciance, as well as his native cynical sense of humour. In many respects, the Russian's chauvinism, which makes him see for his country an even greater, hopefully dominant, global role, tends to manifest itself in near-racist attitudes towards the Arabs and the Egyptians. This is further complicated by the instinctive apprehension of his own authorities were he inclined to establish a closer personal, social relationship with Egyptians.

Another obstacle to the Russian impact on Egyptian society derives from the supple, subtle resilience of the Egyptian to outside influences. This characteristic has manifested itself historically often enough. Only the Arab conquest in the seventh century, for singularly compelling reasons, produced an epochal religious, linguistic, and partly societal change. It is thus difficult to brainwash an Egyptian ideologically. Ideological commitment is not his forte for several reasons one need not enumerate here in detail.

Any meaningful impact the Russians could hope to have in Egypt, which could facilitate and accelerate their control over the country—if that is their objective, and I see no good reason why they should eschew it—would have to come from their relations with the state, that is, the ruler, and its major agencies or structures of power: the army, the bureaucracy, the state security and intelligence agencies (e.g., the Ministry of Interior and the several "special vanguard organizations", *al-tanẓīm al-ṭalī'ī al-khāṣṣ*).

It is not at all clear, so far, that the Russians have acquired any political control over the one institution of the state, the army, in which they are best entrenched and with which they are most concerned. Both its political core and penumbra are still very much under the control of whatever the established Egyptian power élite of the day may be. Similarly, the trials of those implicated in the alleged conspiracy of Field Marshal Amer in the summer of 1967 and those in that of 'Alī Ṣabrī in the summer and autumn of 1971 indicate that the Russians were politically only peripherally placed in such institutions as the army, the Arab Socialist Union (A.S.U.), the security services, and the administrative agencies of presidential affairs. The same seems to be true of the disturbances among workers in Helwan in 1968 and 1971, as well as among the students in February and November 1968, and January 1972.

The apparatchiks in the troika of state power seemed so far to consider the relationship with Russia mainly in terms of their domestic conspiracies for power. The episode of 14 May, 1971, suggests that there was no clearly formed "Moscow party" in the A.S.U., the presidential office, the security services, or the army. A careful reading of the testimony in the trial proceedings of the alleged conspirators gives added strength to this impression. It is plausible that so long as the relationship with Russia is not drastically modified, shaken, or undermined, the Soviets are not particular about who governs in Cairo. On the other hand, and significantly because under the circumstances whoever governs in Cairo must still depend on the U.S.S.R., the spectacle of unsolicited explanations of domestic upheavals to the patron power and the sharp, swift response of the latter with the demand of a formal treaty become logical consequences of these arrangements.

Nor is there a Moscow-oriented Egyptian Communist Party of any consequence. Any members of such grouping, when not out in the political wilderness but, on the contrary, actively serving on some committee of the A.S.U., the boards of public companies, or the editorial boards of the press media, are circumscribed and inhibited by the nature and ethos of these state organizations. Their behaviour is very much affected and determined by the state-decreed functions of these organizations, as well as by their internal conspiratorial cabals. Whatever the degree of its authenticity, the crucial testimony of Aḥmad Kāmil, Chief of Egyptian Intelligence until 13 May, 1971, before the State Prosecutor, as published in al-Nahār of Beirut, leaves little doubt about this condition. The forms, foundations, and patterns of political behaviour appear to remain of local—almost in-bred—provenance.

It is also problematic for the Russians that, unlike Hungary or Czechoslovakia, Egypt is not contiguous to the Soviet Union. To this extent, military action on their part for political ends remained a remote, and impractical, option. Alternatively, a Soviet-sponsored coup by an Egyptian army cabal, which has often been considered as a venue open to the Russians, has not materialized. The restraining factor here may be that so long as whoever emerges as the ruler in Cairo must, within the present Egyptian political context, be a despot, and so long as he continues to depend on the U.S.S.R. for military and economic assistance, it is irrelevant who he is: I would go as far as saying even if he was a Muslim Brother. This, in my view, would be the case, provided that the despot perpetuates the political convention and practice of not allowing the formation and development of alternative political groups in the country.

It is clear, so far, that the nature of the local political and economic regime is not of the essence to Soviet policy, so long as that regime guarantees an orientation in regional and international affairs which is complementary and acceptable to that of the U.S.S.R. This view, in itself, constitutes a self-imposed Russian limitation on their influence over, or involvement in, Egypt's domestic politics.

Nevertheless, the Treaty of May 1971, while for the time being possibly not affording clear instruments of Russian control over domestic Egyptian politics, offers the Soviets a regional and international advantage in the pursuit of their wider policies. Sadat's visits to Moscow in October 1971 and February 1972, for example, support this hypothesis. The Treaty also allows the Soviets to entertain longer-term hopes.

Until recently, everyone assumed that the U.S.S.R. was only interested in a relationship with friendly countries where their fleet could call, possibly be serviced on a limited scale, or have its stores replenished: the U.S.S.R. was not anxious to secure shore facilities or land bases over which they would have exclusive control. The assumption was reasonable insofar as over a period of fifteen years (1955–70) the U.S.S.R. could coordinate its policy of supporting Arab nationalist agitation for the evacuation of all military bases from the Middle East with that of its Arab friends. Except for Cyprus, Turkey, and Greece there are hardly any Western bases left in the Near East. The question now is whether given the Treaty of May 1971 with Egypt [and of April 1972 with Iraq] —and the possibility of similar treaties being concluded with other Arab states—the Soviet Union might reorient its negative anti-Western Middle Eastern policy into a positive one of demanding land bases or at least facilities in the area beyond what she already has in Egypt. If the crucial consideration—the constant—in Soviet foreign policy remains the containment of the United States, say in the Mediterranean and Europe, the reorientation cannot be ruled out. On the other hand, a case can be made against this happening if one accepts the recently better-entrenched Soviet position in the Asian subcontinent—although this could conceivably have the opposite effect.

The disadvantages of the Treaty are in its psychological impact on the Egyptians. Whatever its military and political advantages and disadvantages for the Soviet Union and Egypt, the Treaty could, like the Anglo-Egyptian Treaty of 1936, become once more an arena of bitter domestic political conflict. The *al-mu'āhada* (the Treaty) versus *al-istiqlāl al-tāmm* (complete independence) antithesis could once more plague the Egyptians, adding to their resentment of a new "Cromerism". As one Egyptian put it, *majī' al-tatar,* "the coming of the Tatars", was an inevitable consequence of *al-tamantāshar sana,* the "18 years" of Nasser's rule and policies.

III

It is widely accepted that so long as the Arab-Israel conflict persists and a territorial settlement between Egypt and Israel is not forthcoming, Egypt will remain a client state of the U.S.S.R. The implied antithesis of this proposition is that once the Egyptian-Israeli dispute is settled, the Egyptians can proceed to free themselves of this dependent relationship with Russia, and even rid themselves of the Soviet presence in their country. I am not too sanguine about this eventuality, especially when the Soviet-Egyptian relationship is not exclusively predicated upon the Arab-Israel or Egyptian-Israeli conflicts. As I tried to suggest earlier on in this essay, the patron-client relationship was perhaps facilitated and further developed by these conflicts; it did not, however, originate with them. In fact, from the Soviet point of view, it was also very much related to their European, Asian, and African, in short, their global, policies. Moreover, to any Egyptian ruler who finds it necessary to indulge in an Arab, or regional Middle Eastern policy, the dependence on the Soviet Union may become a less transitory consideration or phenomenon. It could even become essential for domestic purposes.

One now often hears the suggestion that the emergence of China on the international political stage will affect relationships like the one between Egypt and the Soviet Union. It may very well do so. But this remains, for the time being, in the realm of speculation and I prefer not to speculate about it. It may circumscribe and cramp the patron power; it may even afford the client state greater room for manoeuvre in dealing with its patron.

The question to be posed perhaps is, if the Arab-Israel conflict were to be settled to the satisfaction of Egypt, would the relationship with the Soviet Union be undermined, or rendered anachronistic and therefore undesirable for both parties? Would it change? Given this, the generation of new conflict in the Persian Gulf, East and North Africa, the Asian subcontinent, and assuming the greater involvement of China in these areas, would the massive Russian commitment in Egypt become expensively counter-productive or superfluous? As Egypt becomes less and less inclined to involve itself in wider Arab problems, would its regional utility to the Soviet Union diminish? As Egyptian resentment of their relationship to the Russians mounts and as the disappointment of the Russians with their Egyptian protégés becomes deeper, can one assume a drastic, dramatic change in that relationship?

The fact remains that despite Egyptian resentment and Russian disappointment, the Soviet Union continues to support the regime in Egypt. On their part, the Egyptians continue to publicly recognize its necessity, emphasize their gratitude for Soviet support, and swear their eternal friendship to the U.S.S.R., while privately deploring and resenting it for a variety of reasons. The question is, can they do anything about it, one way or the other? The nationalists' assumption is, for instance, that if they were able in the past to will the severance of their relationship with Britain, they could well do so again regarding their relationship with the Soviet Union. But a nationalist's perspective is rarely precise or balanced. No one can underestimate the conditions extraneous to Egypt which militated against the continuation of the particular relationship between Britain and Egypt. I am therefore inclined to suggest that the Egyptian-Soviet relationship will be equally fundamentally affected more by the shifting and changing regional and international conditions outside Egypt and less by what the Egyptians themselves do about it.

One area of direct Egyptian action, for example, which one can allude to only as an unpalatable gloss on Egyptian-Russian relations, is the option of direct talks with their enemy, Israel. To what degree their Russian patrons would try to prevent them from exercising such, in these days unorthodox, initiative (assuming the Egyptians themselves may ever wish to do so) I cannot say. For the time being, Egyptian resentment of the relationship with Russia also derives from the fact that their patron has been unable to remove their enemy from the Sinai without themselves having to do anything directly about it. This approach in itself betrays a fundamental Egyptian disability in this relationship, as well as the general Egyptian perception of inter-Arab and international politics. Central to this preception is their belief that their adversary has a similar relationship with the United States. This, in part, also explains their common assumption that in any armed conflict with Israel, whether in the past or in the future, they face American military might. It is finally this curious perception which, at least by the end of 1970, made Egyptians question their relationship with the Soviet Union. They wondered what they had gained from it in terms of war and peace.

And that, in turn, led them to question what they had gained from the Nasser regime.

One had the impression in Cairo in 1971 that the Egyptian regime was willing to live, even if temporarily, under an arrangement devised and sanctioned by the superpowers. They were not averse, that is, to a more classically imperialist drawing of the political map of the Middle East. They could not, or were not prepared to, understand why their adversary, because of his situation, seemed to prefer an accommodation arrived at by the local parties to the dispute. And in this attitude, which partly derives from their relationship with the Soviet Union and their own image of the Israeli-American relationship, lurk greater long-term dangers. It ignores the difficulty with superpower arrangements, namely, the fact that their respective clients can refuse to be bound by them, and, therefore, to use a slang expression, can muck them up. One is reminded that the Peloponnesian War, some 2,400 years ago, abounded with such arrangements, from which the two great powers of the time, Athens and Sparta, suffered greatly. One is also reminded of the classical admonition that indirect arrangements, where "great hatreds exist", can achieve no lasting settlement under overwhelming external pressures. The pressures may be relaxed, lifted, or they may simply change. Moreover, recurrent warfare at sporting intervals involves the incalculable risk that the "course of war is governed by the total chances in operation and can never be restricted to the conditions that one or the other of the two sides would like to see permanently fixed".

Most, if not all, of the Arab states as presently constituted will continue to require arms and economic, financial, and technical assistance for so-called rapid development; but also, perhaps more importantly, in order to change occasionally the *status quo* both within their own boundaries and in those of their neighbours. Domestically, they need arms absolutely (perhaps not in great quantities) for the coercion so essential to their retention of power. Some Arab states, chief among them Egypt, for purposes of their own quite unrelated to those of the Soviet Union (except for a fortuitous convergence of the common interest to undermine and remove Western influence in the area) accepted first massive military, then economic aid from the U.S.S.R. Such assistance has been eminently profitable for Egypt so long as it was used to buttress its policy within an inter-Arab, inter-African context (Syria, Yemen, South Arabia, Afro-Asian Solidarity Conferences, etc.). But how useful or profitable has it been since June 1967?

It would be inaccurate to explain or justify Egypt's relationship to the U.S.S.R. in the last decade by its relevance to the 1952 revolution or its ideology. Rightly or wrongly, this relationship evolved from a policy based on the national-state interest of Egypt as understood by Nasser and his regime. It was deemed essential in three areas of state endeavour: internal development, Arab policy, and in order to meet the problems engendered by any relationship—confrontation or otherwise—with the West and Israel.

The Egyptians consider their relationship with the Russians a necessary one. Both they and the Russians feel it has been an unhappy one. The relationship was further strained by regional developments in August–September 1971—the *coup* and counter*coup* in the Sudan, and the support of General Numeiri by President Sadat of Egypt and Colonel Qadhafi of Libya. The new closer relations between Sadat and King Faisal of Saudi Arabia represent yet another departure from President Nasser's so-called radical Arab policy. The pressing demand by Egypt for more offensive weapons in order to pursue a more aggressive policy towards Israel, put forward by President Sadat during his visit to Moscow in February 1972, may have soured the alliance even more. The suspicion that the Russians may still be interested in a situation of controlled tension in the Middle East pending their pursuit of a wider *détente* with the United States tends to push Egyptians to the heights of desperation and depths of depression regarding Sinai and the Canal.

* * *

The crisis between Cairo and Moscow which began in February 1972 culminated in the expulsion from Egypt of Soviet technicians and advisers in July 1972. By last April, it was becoming clear that a gesture of Egyptian defiance, calculated both to reassert the regime's independence and mollify domestic discontent, was necessary, indeed inevitable. The abrasive relationship and daily friction between Egyptian officers and Soviet advisers led to demands for the latter's removal. Such peripheral developments as the underground "Egyptian National Front" with its violently anti-Russian leaflet tracts and communiqués, the petition signed and presented to President Sadat by erstwhile Free Officer colleagues (but not published until later in the summer), the notorious *al-Ahrām*-sponsored Seminar on the Soviet Union and the Arabs which led to the Russian demand for the censure and suspension of certain Egyptian Foreign Ministry officials were all indicative of the highly strained atmosphere surrounding Soviet-Egyptian relations. The parameters of anti-Soviet Arab feeling also were extended with further developments in the relations between Egypt and Libya, as well as in the restoration of more correct, if not friendly, relations with the West by the Sudan and the Yemen Republic. Further afield, Algeria diversified its options; Arab states in the East and West of the Islamic world gave clear indications of conducting policy on a practical bilateral basis.

When the Soviet advisers and technicians left, Egyptians assumed that at least Western Europe would step into the breach with relish and alacrity. Egypt's subsequent diplomatic, economic, and political démarche in Europe in the late summer of 1972, though reflecting a genuine need for new influential friends, foreign exchange, and new sources of arms, betrayed a misconception of Western Europe as a political unit or monolith, an anachronistic appreciation of the role smaller states can play in Great-Power politics, and a misreading of Western Europe's capabilities as a credible arbiter of the Middle East conflict.

What was, in my view, traumatic for the Egyptians in the 1972 crisis with the Russians was not the fact that their allies and patrons were unwilling to furnish them with the instruments of offensive war. Rather the trauma lay in two bitter realizations. One was their resentment of the Russians' patronizing attitude towards and near racist scorn for Egyptian officers. The other was the discovery that in certain areas of the facilities extended to the Soviet navy and air force in Egypt the Russians had acquired virtually sovereign rights. One of President Nasser's greatest gifts was his ability to convince Egyptians that whatever arrangements or agreements he concluded with foreign powers, they were always on his own terms. The apparent reality in the summer of 1972 was, for many Egyptians, I daresay quite shocking.

The Soviet technicians and advisers have left Egypt. As of this writing, the Soviet Mediterranean fleet at least continues to enjoy the use of shore facilities in Alexandria, Port Said, and Marsa Matruh. The Egyptian campaign to win friends in and assistance from the Western European countries has so far produced indifferent, in fact meagre, results. By the autumn of 1972, therefore, serious efforts to rehabilitate the alliance with the Soviet Union were being made. It is not easy or wise to predict what pressures and/or demands the Soviets may impose on that rehabilitation. Both parties to the treaty seem theoretically at least to dispose of certain bargaining strengths. The fact remains that, for the time being, the Russians have chosen to strengthen their presence in countries like Iraq and Syria to the east and the north; and this tends to weaken the Egyptian position in its continuing need of the Soviet connection. Yet it may have the salutory effect of urging Egyptians to consider the possibility that regional conflicts are best dealt with regionally or locally between the protagonists; that expecting the "perfect solution" in this imperfect world to be magically contrived and imposed by outside powers could be a chimera.

In these circumstances, the Soviet presence in Egypt and/or the Middle East is as stable or as guaranteed as that of Britain was earlier in this century. It would be foolish of anyone, however, to assess with any measure of accuracy the kinds of risks the Soviets are prepared to take in order to retain, strengthen, and defend their newly acquired position in the area which, to a great extent, derives from their relationship with Egypt. It would be equally foolish for anyone to assert that the Egyptians are particularly happy with it, or that there is much they themselves are willing or can do about it at the present time. Finally, it would be a mistake for Israel to view its conflict with Egypt from a narrow perspective, even from one which simply includes the other Arab states. Rather, an assessment of its dangers and possible future evolution should be based also on a consideration of the Soviet Union's interest in their so-called strategic *cordon sanitaire* encompassing the Asian subcontinent, East Africa, the Persian Gulf, and the Mediterranean.

6. COMMUNISM IN EGYPT
AND SUDAN

SHIMON SHAMIR

THE MARXISTS IN EGYPT: THE "LICENSED INFILTRATION" DOCTRINE IN PRACTICE

This paper deals with the voluntary dissolution of the Communist Party in Egypt and with the subsequent entrance, or "licensed infiltration," of the Communists into the political institutions of the Nasser regime. That extraordinary development in the history of Communism in Egypt may be regarded as a threefold solution to the particular problem faced by each of the principals: the Communists, the Nasserists, and the Soviets. Each of the three regarded the solution as promising but, in varying degrees, each has failed to see its expectations materialize.

For the Communists, the problem was survival—the preservation, in some form, of the struggle for a Marxist-Leninist revolution in Egyptian political life. However, as they were soon to learn, the path they chose led them not to a political foothold but rather to what one observer called *ghettos dorés*[1]—positions seemingly influential but which proved to be void of any effective power.

For the Nasserists, the problem was not merely one of removing an obstacle to the Egyptian-Soviet rapprochement, but also one of self-assertion. Having demonstrated their ability to monopolize power in the state, they now wished to prove that their own social formula, the indigenous Arab Socialism, was the unanimous and inevitable choice of a united nation. Absorbing the Marxist cadres and putting them to good use within the nationalist system seemed to be a profitable way to accomplish this. Yet, as it turned out, by allowing a confrontation, within their institutions, with a systematic doctrine like Marxism, they only stressed the eclectic, amorphous, and ambiguous nature of their own ideology.

The problem facing the Soviets was to reconcile their global strategy in this part of the world with their avowed ideological commitment to the Socialist revolution. The arrangement arrived at seemed to be well suited to the Soviets' immediate political needs and they had elaborated a theory to go with it. Their handiwork, however, proved to be incapable of removing much of the skepticism among Communists inside and outside the Soviet Union. For it was too obvious that the

293

theory, instead of interpreting realities in Egypt, sought to explain them away, and the arrangement, instead of serving as a basis for revolutionary action, was meant to justify expedient acceptance of the Nasserist system.

The paper, following a brief description of the negotiation of that arrangement, presents a preliminary account of the gains and losses experienced by the three parties.

THE SELF-DISSOLUTION OF THE COMMUNIST PARTY

At the beginning of the sixties, some 600 Communists, constituting most of the cadres of the Egyptian Communist Party (which had first become a unified organization in January 1958 but had existed as such for only a brief period), were kept in custody—most of them since 1959. By and large they were detained at the Abu-Za'bal concentration camp, which the Communists bitterly dubbed *maqbarat al-aḥyā'* ("the graveyard of the living"). The camp had become the highest synod of Egyptian Communism, where ideological and political questions were deliberated. The Nasser regime's adoption of Arab Socialism, as articulated in the nationalization laws of July 1961 and the National Charter of May 1962, strengthened among the Communists a trend to opt for close cooperation with the regime as the best course under the circumstances, even at the expense of the party's formal existence. This issue sparked heated debates, in which many Communists rejected the idea of collaboration and argued that the Nasser regime was "a form of capitalism that cannot serve the aims of the working class." Apparently, the first Communist faction to adopt the new line was the Mouvement Démocratique de Libération Nationale (*ḥaditu*). Its members had already expressed their moderate attitude vis-à-vis the regime during a somewhat similar debate in 1959. Soon members of another faction, the Egyptian Communist Party, followed suit.[2]

The main points of a settlement, according to which the Communists were to dissolve their organizations and join those of the regime, were worked out in negotiations with the authorities. It seems that prominent members of the Italian C.P., which had always maintained close ties with the Egyptian Communist movement, were instrumental in bringing about the agreement. The new line was discussed in Communist cells and in the central Communist forums. Those few who had opposed cooperation with the Nasser regime yielded to the majority (with the exception of a small Maoist group), and an official procla-mation to this effect was made public on 25 April, 1965.[3] By that time, the Communists had already been released from detention; some had been set free as early as 1962 or 1963, but most had remained in custody until the eve of Khrushchev's visit to Egypt in May 1964.

The operational clause in the proclamation announced:

> ... the termination of the existence of the Egyptian Com-munist Party as an independent body and the instruction of all its members to submit—as individuals—their applications for membership in the Arab Socialist Union, and to struggle for the formation of a single Socialist party which would comprise all the revolutionary forces in our country.

Reviewing the evolution of the situation which had made this decision possible, the proclamation indicated that the Nasser regime had in the past followed a path of trial and error but in 1961 had started down the road of "non-capitalist development toward Socialism." Nasser had inaugurated a transitional period and had sounded the need for a political organization able to direct the development toward Socialism. Therefore, said the proclamation, it was the duty of all socialist forces to lay aside their differences, to join ranks and form a single revolutionary vanguard party *(hizb thawri tali'i wāhid)*. This party would adopt "scientific socialism," bearing in mind that "there exists only one kind of scientific socialism"; it would be organized on a democratic basis; it would express the interests of the working class and eventually be based on it exclusively; within it the "new socialist forces" would gradually become a majority; and it was to operate under the leadership of Nasser.

THE MARXISTS

The decision of the Egyptian Communists—henceforth referred to as "the Marxists"—was not met with enthusiasm by Communists outside Egypt. At that time, Egyptian Communists were attending the Conference of Arab Communist Movements in Prague. Their reaction was to repudiate the legitimacy of this development, attrib-uting responsibility for it to "persons who do not represent the real Egyptian Communist movement."[4] They declared that the struggle against Nasser's "dictatorial and reactionary" regime would continue.

Some of the leaders of Arab Communist parties, notably Khaled Baqdash, questioned the wisdom and propriety of the self-dissolution and thereafter maintained their negative attitude.[5]

Indeed, the deliberate renunciation of independence was a most unusual step to be taken by a Communist Party. To understand its motives one must first consider the position in which the Communists found themselves at that stage. Comprising only some 800 to 1,000 active members and divided internally into several factions, they were conscious of the inherent weakness of their position in Egyptian society. The regime had practically neutralized them by cutting off their resources, destroying their organizational apparatus, and holding in custody their whole leadership. Their long detention in camps and prisons, where some prominent members had died, had not been without effect.[6] The failure of the Communist parties of Syria and Iraq after 1958 was another source of discouragement. Above all, the close collaboration between the Soviet Union and the Nasser regime proved to them that they could expect very little from their traditional patron.

A second set of motives for the Communists' decision to submerge themselves in the Nasserist system rested on positive considerations. A tendency to conditional cooperation had already appeared among Egyptian Communists in the years 1956–8, when some of them had pointed out that the anti-feudal and anti-imperialist nature of the regime justified such collaboration. (One faction, centered at *Dār al-Fikr*, went as far as to suggest absorption by the regime's National Union.) Nasser's National Charter, of course, did not win the approval of the Communists but they could not remain unimpressed by the Marxist concepts and slogans which were scattered throughout this and other Nasserist documents, such as "the liquidation of exploitation," "historical inevitability," "political regimes being a reflection of economic interests," "imperialism being the high stage of capitalism," "the concentration of the means of production in the hands of the people," and "the struggle against reaction." They wondered whether the Charter was not in fact a commitment by Nasser to go in the direction of a socialist revolution, or, in the event that Nasser had no intention of going all the way to Socialism—whether his actions would not, "objectively," lead him there. They calculated that after the proclamation of the *thawrat 'ummāl wa-fāllāḥīn* ("Workers and Peasants Revolution") Nasser might need them, for they considered themselves experts in the field of social revolution while he was merely a dilettante. They apparently wished to see themselves participating in the transformation of Egypt into a socialist country and even accelerating that process through officially sanctioned activity inside the system. The crucial factor in their decision must have been the promise of key positions in the propaganda machinery and the vanguard apparatus of the A.S.U. The considerations that had led to the shift in the Communist strategy were expounded by the leading Egyptian Marxist Lotfi al-Kholi as follows:

> Revolutionary leaders in a number of Arab countries have broken with anti-Communism and have overcome their mistrust of Arab Marxists. At the same time, one can observe a certain evolution among Arab Marxists in their assessment of the socio-economic changes in the U.A.R.[7]

It may be assumed that at least some of the Communists went further than that and actually contemplated subversive action under the cover of their legitimate positions. The April 1965 proclamation hinted at such a possibility. It certainly reflected the intention to bring about a revolution more radical than that desired by the regime. It made clear that the agreement was valid only during the transitional period that required unity, and even during that period Marxists within this alignment would uphold the principles that set them apart. The proclamation's wording was understandably cautious, so as not to compromise its authors, but it was also ambiguous enough for an alert party member to take the hint if he wished.

Finally, it should always be borne in mind that the Soviets, as will be shown below, had approved self-dissolution and integration into one-party regimes of the Nasserist type, and that Soviet opinion carried great weight with the overwhelmingly pro-Soviet Egyptian Communists.

The Egyptian Marxists themselves justified the drastic step they had taken by adducing the "special circumstances" existing in Egypt: on the one hand, the weakness of the leadership of the working people (i.e., the Communist Party), which did not leave them much choice other than to start afresh under new auspices, and on the other, the positive role being played by the leadership of the national revolution movement (i.e., Nasser) and the great influence of the socialist camp in Egypt (i.e., the Soviet Union), which limited the risks of extinction involved in dissolution and ensured eventual triumph.[8] Henceforth the operational principle of Marxists' activities within the Nasserist system would be to profess loyalty to the regime's policy, even when they opposed it, while at the same time attempting cautiously to radicalize it so as to bring it closer to the Marxist formulas.

Accordingly, the Marxists set out to establish themselves as firmly as possible within the system of the A.S.U. Quantitatively their entry had no great impact: initially, not more than 100 ex-Communists were admitted to the various levels of the A.S.U. hierarchy; three and-a-half years later, when elections were being held in the A.S.U., the number of ex-Communists running for office was put at 75, of whom 68 were elected. Nevertheless, in terms of quality, the list of positions they were allowed to occupy, for shorter or longer periods, was impressive. Marxists who had been associated with the disbanded Communist parties in varying degrees of affiliation were appointed to important offices at the Ministry of Education (under Tharwat 'Ukāsha) and in institutions of higher learning. Many of them were given conspicuously responsible positions in the mass media—the press, publishing houses, radio, and television (and some in the theater and cinema as well). The leading Marxist figures were appointed to the top jobs: Khaled Mohieddin became chairman of the board of Akhbār al-Yawm and secretary of the A.S.U. Press Committee; Lotfi al-Kholi became editor of al-Ṭali'a and was named a member of the editorial board of al-Ahrām; Maḥmūd Amīn al-'Ālim became director of al-Hilāl and supervisor of the Egyptian Establishment for Publications and Printing. Particularly significant was the fact that Marxists were given the management of the Institute for Socialist Studies which had been established to train cadres for the A.S.U. (notably Ibrahim Sa'd ad-Dīn). In addition, they occupied central positions in the Youth Bureau (Muḥammad al-Khafīf), the External Relations Committee (Kholi—chairman), and the A.S.U. Central Committee (Sa'd ad-Dīn, Kholi, 'Ālim, Mohieddin). Furthermore, some were elected or appointed to the National Council (Fu'ād Mursī, Mohieddin). In a few cases, they received appointments to economic bodies in the public sector (Mursī—chairman of the board of the "Nasr" Automobile Company, chairman of the council of the Industrial Bank). Eventually, they attained ministerial level (Ismā'il Ṣabrī 'Abdalla—Deputy Minister of Planning.)[9]

In addition to occupying important offices in the domestic institutions, Marxists played significant roles in maintaining the regime's extensive network of relations with foreign organizations, particularly with Socialist or Communist parties, international front-organizations, Afro-Asian and non-aligned forums, Soviet cultural and ideological institutes, and Palestinian Fidayeen organizations. Perhaps the most active in this field was Mohieddin who, among other things, served on the presidium of the World Peace Council.

The types of positions the Marxists occupied reflect, to some extent, the scope of their deployment among the various sections of Egyptian society. Undoubtedly their main foothold was among the intelligentsia—university graduates, professionals, writers, journalists, etc. The Marxists sought to increase their influence among the educated and to concentrate principally on gaining ground in institutions of higher learning. Evidently, they attempted to draw into their circles the students who had attended universities in Eastern Europe. Less conspicuously, they tried to strengthen their ties with trade unions. They voiced the demand to extend political activities to the army as well, but there are no indications that they have acquired influence among military officers. A development which may have altered this situation somewhat is the regime's policy, since the Six-Day War, to recruit and commission university graduates; it is possible that Marxist influence has permeated through this channel the lower levels of the officers' corps.

The ideological line followed by the Marxists, according to Kholi, was based on both the National Charter's program and the ideas of "scientific socialism."[10] This combination contains the same contradiction on the ideological level as that which the collaboration of the Marxists with the regime entailed on the operational level—for, just as the Marxists could not ignore the powerful "reactionary elements" in the Nasser regime, so could they not help noting the "utopian, petite-bourgeois, and subjective-idealistic" concepts in the doctrine of Arab Socialism. Accordingly, the same principle that guided their practical efforts within the regime was applied in formulating their ideological programs. Initially, the Marxists premised a broad common denominator with Nasserism for the purpose of giving their position a legitimate basis; secondly, they suggested a few of their own points gradually diverging from Nasserism toward Marxism-Leninism.

Their agreement with Nasserism was on those themes in the National Charter that had paved the way to cooperation; such as: the nationalization of industry and finances, and the allocation of seats to peasants and workers in the regime's various political and economic institutions. (However, Mohieddin obviously overstated the case when he declared in a press interview: "Three-quarters of the Egyptian National Charter is based on Marxist foundations."[11]) Agreement on principles of foreign policy was stressed in particular. These principles included the struggle against imperialism and colonialism, support for the policies of the Soviet Union (up to July 1972), polarization of Arab regimes into "progressives" and "reactionaries" (up to the Six-Day War), struggle with Israel as an imperialist base, support for the Palestinian Fidayeen (the Fath, rather than the radical organizations).[12] The Marxists expressed their approval also of concepts that were not in accord with their own ideology. These were tenets deeply rooted in the ideals of society or in the doctrines of the regime, but which either lacked any immediate practical consequences and therefore *could* be accepted, or reflected such a broad concensus that they *had* to be accepted. Thus, Marxists professed their allegiance to the "revolutionary values of religion and Islam,"[13] to the Nasserist concept of Nationalism, and to the vision of Arab Unity.

When it came to the divergences from Nasserism, the Marxists made their points with great care so as to avoid an open rift with the leadership of the regime. The Marxists sought to play down the differences by directing their polemics away from the Nasserist leadership and against the bourgeois elements in the national *taḥāluf* (alliance) on which the A.S.U. and the regime in general rested. Just as in the two previous generations the modernists of the Islamic Reform trend would cite the Quran and the *ḥadīth* to legitimize basically non-Islamic concepts, so the Marxists would draw upon Nasser's speeches and statements to demonstrate that the non-Nasserist ideas they preached were, in fact, those which Nasser had in mind. The more their views conflicted with Nasserism, the more intensively did they cite Nasser or, after his death, his successor Sadat.[14]

When they felt it necessary to challenge concepts which had been explicitly expounded by Nasser himself, the Marxists usually resorted to another tactic: they would choose a less prominent spokesman of the regime, who had happened to echo the same views, and then direct their attack against him. The Marxists employed this method in their treatment of the issue which touched them most closely: Nasser's definition of the basic differences between Arab Socialism and Marxism. Nasser, recapitulating the views of Heykal, had articulated the differences as follows: Arab Socialism rejects class struggle and the dictatorship of the proletariat, places national unity above everything else, allows private ownership, upholds individual liberty, and believes in Islam. When Fu'ād Mursī wished to debate these points, he chose a certain Ṭal'at 'Īsā as his interlocutor and then launched a frontal attack on "'Īsā's" views, arguing that adherence to these principles permeated socialism in Egypt with vestiges of capitalism.[15]

The Marxists sneered at their opponents who, they said, were ignorant of the "scientific laws" of social development and imagined that theirs was an original middle-road between historical materialism and idealistic relativism. However, deliberations of philosophical differences occurred quite infrequently in the polemics of the Egyptian Marxists. Their writing focused on the polarity which had immediate practical implications and was seen as the crux of the matter: "national unity" versus "class struggle."

The Marxists managed to avoid a confrontation on this issue by offering a new interpretation of the Nasserist slogan "the fusion (tadhwīb) of the differences between classes." For Nasserists this usually meant an alliance, more or less static, among the five "forces"—peasants, workers, intelligentsia, national capitalism, and the military—based on their common allegiance to the national goals. The Marxists, on the other hand, maintained that "fusion" implied a dynamic process by which the working class would gradually eliminate the forces whose interests clashed with its own. They rejected the notion that a nationalist regime could maintain a stable balance and harmony between conflicting social forces or that it could exist outside the context of class interests. The regime, they said, had necessarily to reflect the interests of either the bourgeoisie or the working class, and they hinted that in fact it was tending to the former rather than to the latter.[16] Feudal families, they charged, still maintained their influence in many villages while capitalists were still powerful in the cities. The state machinery was controlled by "bourgeois military and bureaucratic cadres" who constituted the "New Class" in Egyptian society. Those elements used their power to serve their own interests, and under their guidance nationalization had led to State Capitalism instead of Socialism.

The Marxists demanded a fundamental change in the structure of the regime. Instead of speaking of the five "forces" of the national alliance, they spoke of three classes: peasants, workers and national capitalists. They wished to alter the official definitions of the first two "forces" so as to exclude reactionary elements, such as exploiting landowners and bourgeois intellectuals and managers. They demanded that the workers be inculcated with class consciousness and encouraged to participate not only in the implementation of the regime's policies but also in their making.[17]

Acording to the Marxists, the chief instrument of action could be the A.S.U. They repeatedly pressed the regime to carry out its commitment to form within it a vanguard party to be established exclusively on cadres that would represent the interests of the working class and be faithful to the tenets of "scientific socialism."

These general guidelines were applied by the Marxists to a list of specific issues. They demanded organizational changes in the A.S.U., such as freedom of political action (i.e., for Communists), subjection of the constitutional system to the changing requirements of the revolution, protection of peasants from the bureaucracy, prevention of the development of a *kulak* class in the country, and extension of the powers of the trade unions. These demands naturally implied criticism of the regime's policies and actions, and sometimes it was made clear, without mentioning names, that their criticism was directed at the leadership itself. Thus, for example, when Michel Kamel wrote in *al-Ṭalīʿa* (February 1971)[18] that concentrating on "problems of cleanness, transportation, housing, and education" was important but did not cope with the roots of the problems of Egyptian society, his readers would not fail to grasp that this was a negative response to the Fawzī-Sadat program to build a "Modern Egypt," based on "science and faith."

Whenever the regime underwent a crisis, the Marxists amplified their criticism to the point of political pressure. This has happened several times in the last few years. Following the defeat of 1967, the Marxists demanded a realignment of forces, deepening of the revolution, liquidation of the regime's right wing, and the transfer of power to the revolutionary cadres. During the demonstrations of 1968 and the subsequent reorganizations, the Marxists again increased their pressure. After Nasser's death, the Marxists demanded more positions in the A.S.U. secretariat, the youth organization, the regional war committees, and the trade unions (at that point, reportedly, some Marxists threatened that, failing any official response to their requests, they would "act on their own"). After the arrest of the Ṣabrī and Jumʿa-Sharaf cliques in May 1971, and the exposure of the internal inspection system, "the secret apparatus" of the A.S.U., the Marxists pressed for the formation of a non-secret vanguard party based exclusively on cadres from the "progressive force" within the A.S.U.

Whether Marxists have actually engaged in oppositional or sub-versive activities, which go beyond verbal criticism and political pressure, is difficult to tell. The Marxists themselves, of course, firmly deny any activities of this sort,[19] and most observers tend to believe them. Marxists may have joined the workers' demonstrations of 1968 and 1971 but they could hardly have instigated them. Reports of illegal leaflets distributed by Marxists exist but they are rarely convincingly confirmed. It should be recalled that the identity of all the leading Marxists is known to the authorities. As will be shown, the security services have kept them under surveillance and made periodic arrests among their number, even at the senior level. It seems that the combi-nation of attractive appointments, on the one hand, and deterrent police action, on the other, has effectively neutralized all the leading Marxists. It may very well be that younger Marxists are more militant than those of the former generation and that their chances to evade surveillance are better, but whether they have already developed the capacity for independent action remains to be seen.

In retrospect, the Marxists cannot escape the conclusion that the deal they made with the regime in 1964-5 has not had the intended results. Some of the promises to which their proclamation referred have never been fulfilled. Instead of being allowed to function as an active partner forming a new revolutionary party, they were simply ab-sorbed by the A.S.U. which has remained a governmental organization differing in no essential way from its two predecessors—the National Union and the Liberation Rally. Marxists did not form vanguard cadres within the A.S.U. and were not given any real executive power. True, they enjoyed considerable latitude, perhaps much wider than they could have expected in the past, in the pursuance of their propaganda activities, but they soon discovered that disseminating ideas without any power to work for their materialization led nowhere—all the more so since the need to phrase these ideas circumspectly often robbed them of all force. Accordingly, their publications—characterized by a tortuous and repetitious style and verbal acrobatics—did not attain wide circulation. (It is not rare to meet educated Egyptians who have never held a copy of *al-Ṭali'a* in their hands.) Thus, their hopes for the rapid expansion of Marxism have not been realized and there are no indications that the number of their supporters has increased appreciably since 1965. (Nor are there signs of the emergence of a serious radical—Maoist or other—Marxist movement in that period.)

Confined to these *ghettos dorés*, their regulated and controlled activities struck a sharp contrast to their action in the past when, despite their weakness, they sometimes managed to organize workers' strikes, draw students to street demonstrations, and even conduct terrorist operations and violent resistance (notably in Port Said).

Although leftist trends have been noted among students and industrial workers, the lack of organized participation of Marxists in the protest demonstrations of these two groups in 1971–2 was conspicuous. The numerous decisions adopted by the striking students in January 1972 hardly included any with social content.[20] As for the workers' strike in Helwan in August 1971, not only did it fail to receive effective backing from the Marxists, but one of their prominent spokesmen, Lotfi al-Kholi, tried to belittle the whole affair.[21]

Above all stands the fact that the Marxists did not manage to bring about in Egypt a leftward trend of development. The regime, which had been expected to head in the direction of socialism, is not more socialistic today than it was in the mid-sixties; certainly, the A.S.U. has not become more of a Marxist party than it was seven years ago. In 1972, as will be shown below, the regime took a distinct turn to the right, which was manifested in a reshuffle of personnel and reformulation of ideas in the A.S.U. and in the wave of anti-Communism which accompanied the ouster of the Soviets. These developments have revealed how powerless and insecure the Marxists' position was and to what little extent they could put their trust in the two pillars of their political status: the patronage by the Soviets and the entente with the regime. All this has invalidated the rationale given by the Communist organization for its disbandment and exposed the Egyptian Marxists to charges of opportunism.

While the Marxists failed to gain the objective of their deal with the regime, they paid the price in full. The integration of the Marxists into the system and their compromise with Arab Socialism obliterated their particularity. Today, it is not at all clear what Marxists in Egypt indeed stand for. It should be noted that the term "Marxists," which is employed throughout this paper, no longer refers to a homogeneous group but to a spectrum which extends from the hard-core zealots, whose compromise with the regime remains tactical only, through ambivalent "National Marxists," to pragmatists whose present affiliation with Marxism is at best doubtful. Some of the Marxists, and especially those in high-ranking positions, would probably find it difficult to determine their precise position in this spectrum today. In some cases, former Communists rationalized their new position by referring to Arab Socialism as a "post-Marxist" phenomenon—the most progressive movement in terms of Third World realities.[22]

The disintegration of the Marxist movement was accelerated because the Marxists were not absorbed by an entirely monolithic regime but, in effect, by a web of competing factions at its top (see below). Thus, they often found themselves on opposing sides, serving as pawns in the hands of rival personalities at the higher echelons of the regime.

The Marxists do not hide their frustration. One Marxist told a visiting American political scientist: "We Communists no longer really exist. We compromised ourselves away years ago. We suffer from a national weakness whereby Egyptians lose their convictions by the age of 40. If there's to be any revival, it will have to come from among the students."[23] Another Marxist admitted to a correspondent of *Jeune Afrique*: "We have committed major errors. We have been 'drooling' so much during the years because Nasser had permitted us to participate in the national life and had given us posts in editorial offices and the university that we have become *embourgeoisés*. We have lost all contact with the masses. . . . The truth is that we are tired and not at all prepared to return to prison."[24]

Why did the Marxists fail to attain their objectives? Their inherent weaknesses have been too often described in the relevant literature to require more than brief recapitulation here. Their shortcomings were due to: persecution by the regime, the alien character of their ideology, dissociation from the lower classes, the limited size and rural character of the workers' class, mediocre leadership, internal conflicts, and low capacity for conspiratorial action. The paradoxical position of the Marxists vis-à-vis the Soviet Union should be particularly stressed: on the one hand, the deep involvement of the Soviet Union in the affairs of Egypt has been for them an asset that they wished to cherish, and on the other hand, they have become the victims of the same deep involvement, sacrificed by the Soviet Union for the sake of her political interests. Hence, the Egyptian Marxist movement, while being one of the Soviet Union's most consistent supporters in the Afro-Asian world, is at the same time one of her most expendable.

Marxists also faced difficulties with regard to what was supposed

to have been the source of their vitality and appeal for potential supporters—ideology. Although, compared to Nasserism, the exposition
of their ideas was markedly systematic and coherent, in the final analysis
these ideas, in their own Marxist terms, have not afforded much insight
into the problems of Egypt. As has been shown, the Marxists were
restricted in their attempts to make a clear distinction between Marxism
and Arab Socialism. The Marxists, who had pondered the feasibility
of applying the Cuban and Yugoslav models to the Egyptian case,
did not arrive at any conclusive ideas. Finally, the obvious gap between
theory and practice, which was already manifested in the terms of
their collaboration with the regime, has seriously damaged the credibility of their ideology.

It has been suggested that because Communism, like Islam, pro-
fesses a totalitarian doctrine with complete and final answers to questions
in all spheres of life, it might be spread more readily against the background of modernization and secularization, throughout the Muslim
lands.[25] However, apparent developments on the Egyptian scene do not
indicate that this similarity has contributed substantially to the appeal of
Communism. There are no indications that the Marxists' indoctrination
activities are geared to satisfy a genuine need for a totalitarian doctrine.
The fact is that the publications of the Marxists in Egypt cover only a
narrow range of subjects and very rarely treat such questions as philosophy, ethics, family life, aesthetics, or education. Moreover, the
Communist doctrine has lost much of its authoritarian character
because of the inevitable heterogeneity of a polycentric Communist
world.

Neither can the more conventional theory, regarding Islam as
the principal barrier to Marxism, be satisfactorily substantiated by
the Egyptian experience. True, the Islamic outlook of the masses and
the deliberate attacks on Communism by conservative Islamic intellectuals have not made the task of the Marxist easier.[26] However, the
major obstacles to the spread of Communism did not originate from
Islam but from Nasserist-type Nationalism (although it may be argued
that in the last count this Nationalism should be regarded as a manifestation of Islamic undercurrents). Nasser's messianic Nationalism
appropriated some of the Marxists' most popular strong points, such as
stands on anti-imperialism and social reform, affiliation with a powerful
bloc of nations and a vision of New Dawn. The Marxists could attempt
to outbid the Nasserists among intellectuals or the underpriviledged

classes but, in the political and social realities of Egypt, those groups could not easily be recruited for effective political action.

This may change with the accumulating setbacks and defeats of Nasserist Nationalism. But we are on no firmer ground today than we were twenty years ago—when the debate on this issue emerged—in our ability to gauge the potential capacity of Marxism to become a serious challenge in Islamic and nationalistic countries like Egypt.

The Marxists can claim at least one achievement: in one form or another they have managed to maintain a presence in Egyptian political life. Should Egyptian politics take an unexpected turn to the left—as a result of external or internal pressure—they would be there to offer their services.

THE NASSERISTS

Nasser's decision to release the Communists, to admit them into the A.S.U. and other institutions, and to appoint them to high positions in the propaganda network came as a surprise to the public and the functionaries of the regime. Yet it was not entirely an innovation, since Nasser had already countenanced cooperation with Communists in 1956–8. His split with the Communists in 1959, against the background of their activities in Syria and Iraq, had left this trend in abeyance, but in 1964–5 the conditions were again ripe for resumption of joint action.

By that time the crisis in Iraq and Syria had subsided. Khrushchev had demonstrated his deep interest in the Egyptian regime, his pragmatism, and his readiness to compromise. He insisted, however, that the imprisonment of the Communists hindered closer relations. It may very well be that the principles of the Nasserist-Communist arrangement had actually been worked out between the Egyptian regime and the Soviets; Sabri's trip to Moscow in September 1964 and Mohieddin's visit which followed in November may have been connected with such negotiations.[27]

For Nasser, the release of the Communists became expedient not only because of the Soviet pressure, but because their suppression was proving to be an ever greater embarrassment to the regime in its dealings with the Afro-Asian and non-aligned countries, whose ranks included a growing number of leftist regimes. It should also be recalled that in the Arab world, Egypt was trying to consolidate a bloc of "progressive" regimes opposed to those branded as "reactionary"—an action not in accord with the domestic suppression of the Communists.

Internal considerations also played a part in Nasser's decision. Although the adoption of Arab Socialism and the articulation of its basic tenets had taken place before the release of the Communists and without their participation, once he had opted for this policy, Nasser felt the need for an added infusion of socialist activism to uphold it. He needed a stronger left wing to counterbalance his right wing's opposition to the socialist decrees. The new policy had shifted Nasser's own position in the regime from the center to the left, and only by rallying more leftists could he restore his centricity. In addition, Nasser simply needed assistance in the sphere where, by his own admission, he was weakest— ideological articulation. Against the background of his previous failures with the Liberation Rally and the National Union, and the tensions which existed between the regime and the Egyptian intellectuals (referred to as "the crisis of intellectuals"), his readiness to come to terms with the Communists is comprehensible. Besides, he had few other alternatives: the Communists were probably the only available group with all the necessary qualifications to activate a Socialist in- doctrination system in the A.S.U. and effectively disseminate Socialist ideas through the mass media.

Apparently, Nasser judged that, at that point, the admittance of Communists did not involve a great risk. They had been sufficiently weakened by systematic persecution while Nasser's own leadership was well established inside Egypt. Furthermore, they could be con- trolled inside the regime's institutions no less, if not more, effectively than outside them.

The public pronouncements of Nasser and Heykal, on the eve of the self-dissolution of the Communist Party, sought to make the public clearly understand that the Communists were joining the regime on its own terms. In his meetings with the Parliamentary Committee of the A.S.U., on February 25, 1965, Nasser recapitulated the basic differences between Arab Socialism and Communism. He declared that no Communist could join the A.S.U. without his loyalty to the tenets of the National Charter having been checked, and therefore "there was no reason to be afraid of them."[28] Heykal's article on the Communists, in the 29 January, 1965 issue of *al-Ahrām,* had par- ticularly widespread repercussions. He pointed out the inherent weaknesses of Arab Communists, listed their "sins" against the National movement, and affirmed that they were "unable to discern the truth of the unity of Arab history, the unity of Arab struggle, and the unity of Arab destiny," and therefore "there is no future for Communism and Communists in Egypt and the Arab world."

Hence, what the Communists (and the Soviets) regarded as a fresh starting-point was seen by the leaders of the regime as the end of the road for Communism in Egypt. Retrospectively, Heykal speculated: "This may have been the greatest accomplishment of the Egyptian experience. Its Marxist left was honest with itself, from a historical and realistic point of view, when it decided to dissolve its organization and join the alliance of the working forces. There could not be more."[29]

Nasserist statements reflected more than the desire to dispose of a troublesome opposition party. In a way, Communism had challenged the Nasser regime's claim of embodying the common will of the entire nation and of offering the only authentic and effective solutions to the problems of society. It was therefore imperative to demonstrate that the Communist movement, as an alien and subversive force, was disintegrating and that its former members were one by one embracing the tenets of the National Charter. The regime wished to prove that its Nationalist movement would prevail because there was no alternative for Egyptian society.

Thus, while admitting the ex-Communists into the regime's institutions, the Nasserists continued the campaign to prove the superiority of their Nationalist ideology over Marxism. They argued that compared with Marxism, their concept was more humanistic, spiritual, liberal, humane, just, and genuine. No other ideology could be so well geared to the political, social, and emotional needs of a basically Arab-Muslim nation. Communism in this part of the world was doomed, not because it had been physically suppressed but because it was irrelevant.[30]

Confident as Nasser may have been of the popular aversion to Communism, he nevertheless took measures to ensure its neutralization. A fact which sometimes escapes attention is that in 1964–5, while the Communist cadres were being accepted into the A.S.U., Nasser simultaneously initiated the formation of a much more powerful cadre-system in that body.

In October 1965, 'Alī Ṣabrī was appointed Secretary-General of the A.S.U. and charged with converting it into an effective political instrument. Born into the Egyptian upper class, he had been known among the "Free Officers" as the most pro-American. He had no leftist background. Now he wished to use the opportunity afforded him in order to concentrate power in his own hands, through the development of a vigorous leftist force within the A.S.U. He outlined a leftist platform in his *al-Jumhūriyya* articles and gathered around him a group of leftist ideologues and functionaries. The line he presented was identical in many respects with that of the Marxists (i.e., liquidating the "feudal" elements, in the villages and the bourgeoisie and "New Class" in the towns, relying on a vanguard cadre-system in the A.S.U., etc.), but basically he did not overstep the boundaries of Nasserism. Ideology, at any rate, was of secondary importance for Ṣabrī, who pursued his objectives in an entirely pragmatic manner.[31]

His activities were closely linked with the efforts to set up the surreptitious cadre apparatus, known by names as *al-jihāz al-sirri* or *al-khāṣṣ* (the "secret," or "special," apparatus). It seems that Sha'rāwi Jum'a was in charge of this enterprise, with the assistance of Sāmī Sharaf. Both brought to this endeavor the experience they had gained in the internal security services. The apparatus was constructed as an undercover system of cells *(majmū'āt)*. This hierarchy served both as a channel for the directives of the center and as a network of surveillance. The apparatus penetrated universities, factories, clubs, etc., and was much feared and hated.[32]

Thus, two systems had emerged within the A.S.U. and the regime in general: one, that of the Marxist left, advocated the concept of an elite vanguard party but was not allowed to organize for its implementation; the other, that of the "official left," managed to set up a secret internal ring of cadres but without any real roots in a revolutionary vanguard concept. This dichotomy was sometimes described in Egypt as "a head without a body and a body without a head."

Since so little information has been made available on the position of the Marxists within the A.S.U., and nothing at all on the secret apparatus, the two have often been confused by observers. Some outsiders, principally the Soviets, may have had an interest in presenting this whole complex as a single homogeneous cadre-system which maintained a high level of both ideological and operational performance. Reference to the existence of such a monolithic structure made it easier to project an image of the A.S.U. which was dynamic and revolutionary.[33]

In fact, the two systems were not only separate but mutually hostile. This conflict partly overlapped that between Ṣabrī and Heykal—since Heykal, whose image was that of a Western-oriented person and did not wish to be identified with the regime's extreme right wing, had become the patron of a Marxist group centered round Kholi and *al-Ṭalī'a*. Ṣabrī, for his part, attracted to his side a few prominent Marxists, such as Maḥmūd Amīn al-'Ālim, and offered them the chance to participate in *al-Jumhūriyya* and *al-Kātib*, thus further splitting the Egyptian Marxist movement.

The arrests that were made from time to time among Marxists (see below) often reflected this conflict, with Ṣabrī attempting to imprison Heykal's protégés and the latter trying to set them free and smear Ṣabrī's name. Following the first deposition of Ṣabrī and the arrest of 'Ālim in September 1969, the contest became more equal and in May 1971, with the arrest of Ṣabrī and his clique, it was definitely decided in favor of the Heykal-Kholi clique.[34]

The regime's chief consideration was to keep the activities of the Marxists under control. Nasser often stressed that the opportunity they had been afforded was not meant for self-entrenchment in the regime's institutions. They had not been invited in order to change the regime but because they themselves had changed and no longer constituted a political entity. He made it clear that any attempt to form blocs *(takattulāt)* would be mercilessly crushed. He was reported to have told a group of Marxists who had complained about the restrictions imposed on their activities: "You should thank God that you are out of prison."[35]

The regime carefully kept them away from positions of power. According to Abdel-Malek, instructions from the top said: "Collaborate with them, absorb them, but at all costs keep all decision-making power in our hands."[36]

The Marxists were under constant surveillance and were occasionally hindered in the pursuit of their work or their quest for advancement. Occasionally, reports told of the removal or arrest of some Marxists. The following is a list of instances: In January 1965, a number of Marxists were arrested for distributing illegal leaflets; in October 1965, Mohieddin was dropped from the staff of *Akhbār al-Yawm* and other Marxists were dismissed from the communication media system; in April 1966, six Marxists (four from the former M.D.L.N. and two from the former E.C.P. factions) were arrested on the charge of having attempted to set up a Communist cell; in September 1966,

the verdicts in the case of 11 Communists who had rejected the collaboration agreement (and, therefore, should perhaps be separately
considered) were announced; in October 1966, 24 Marxists, Kholi
and other *Ṭalī'a* people among them, were arrested on a charge of
having established an underground organization; in January 1967, Kholi
was rearrested and held for 24 hours, followed by the arrest of Sa'd
ad-Dīn; in September 1969, 'Ālim was removed from *Akhbār al-Yawm*;
in May 1970, Kholi, Heykal's secretary, and her husband (also a Marxist) ·
were arrested on a charge of having made hostile statements—this time
Kholi remained in prison for five months; in August 1971, Mohieddin
and Sa'd ad-Dīn were arrested—the former was soon released but
the latter was tried together with the Ṣabrī-Jum'a-Sharaf group and
received a suspended sentence.

These ousters and arrests should not be regarded as identical
in background and source. As shown above, they sometimes reflected
the rivalries between competing cliques. Some of the earlier arrests
were thought to be the work of the security services which needed
time to readjust to a situation in which Marxists could operate overtly.
Other cases should be seen against the background of broader political
developments, such as tension with the Soviet Union or Communist
pressure in a neighboring country. But aside from all this, the basic
purpose of such measures was simply to regulate the activities of the
Marxists—by sanction or deterrent action. This differed fundamentally from the measures taken before 1964–5, which were meant
not to regulate but to suppress. Thereafter, detainees were usually held
for a very short time and it was not uncommon for some of them to be
sent abroad in an Egyptian delegation upon their release from detention.
Similarly, deposed Marxists were usually soon reinstalled in their former
positions or given similar posts.

Sadat's attitude toward the Marxists did not differ at the beginning
from that of Nasser. The striking feature of his policy, at that stage, was
that, in spite of his distinctly rightist outlook, the position of the Marxists
under his rule improved. This may be explained by a combination of
factors: the need to counterbalance his rightist image, the desire for
national unity, the wish to make a gesture toward the Soviet Union
and, perhaps, toward other leftist regimes. The decisive factor
may have been the need to broaden the basis of his regime, which
resulted in the admission of both rightists and leftists into his cabinet
and administration. Two ex-Communists were appointed to Sadat's

second cabinet: Fu'ād Mursī as Minister of Supply, and Ismā'īl Ṣabrī 'Abdalla as Minister of Planning. In January 1972 it was announced that a new Marxist publication, *Socialist Studies*, would begin appearing in Egypt with the aim of "strengthening, molding and defending the revolutionary line of the Egyptian leadership."

The Marxists—who had felt relief since the purge of their oppressors, the Ṣabrī and Sharaf cliques—were elated by this development. In several interviews Lotfi al-Kholi declared that, although basically the nature of the regime remained unaltered, "for the first time since 1952" there existed in Egypt a National Front in which Marxists participated as such and were recognized as a Marxist trend and not only as individual leftists. He and his colleagues expressed their confidence that soon the regime would allow the formation of Marxist cadres within the A.S.U. to replace the disbanded secret apparatus. The new organization would act openly and would devote its efforts to the concept of class-struggle.[37]

However, their elation proved to be premature. With the appointment of Sayyid Mar'ī—a landowner with no leftist inclination—as First Secretary of the A.S.U., developments seemed to have taken a reverse course. The A.S.U.'s General Secretariat was reorganized, resulting in the transfer of responsibility for the indoctrination system to conservatives and the ouster of the Marxist Fu'ād Mursī.

Mar'ī's principal assignment was to prepare proposals for reconstructing the A.S.U. and formulate for it a systematic political program. For this purpose he set up a Working Committee of 20, with nine subcommittees, which, in March 1972, began discussing the whole complex of A.S.U. problems.[38] Although prominent Marxists—such as Khaled Mohieddin, Lotfi al-Kholi, Jamāl al-'Uṭayfī, and Muḥammad al-Khafīf—played a central role in the deliberations of the committees, the draft that was produced in August[39] amounted to a serious defeat for the A.S.U.'s Marxist wing. This document, the "Guide for Political Action," defined the A.S.U. as an alliance in which all "forces," workers and national capitalists alike, had basically similar standing. It also rejected the Marxists' notion that these "forces" could be identified with social classes. The "Guide" denounced those "interpretations of Arab Socialism which are not rooted in Egyptian and Arab reality and do not respect the religious values but are based on beliefs and doctrines current in the world." Small wonder that *al-Ṭalī'a*, which published the document, described it as an unwarranted assault on Egyptian Marxists, a distortion of the principles of the National Charter, and a victory for Reaction.

The last stages of these developments coincided with the rift with the Soviets. This was accompanied by a wave of anti-Soviet, and therefore anti-Communist feelings. Sadat, in delivering his marathon 24 July speech, received the warmest ovations when he solemnly declared that he would never embrace Marxism. There were reports of harassment of Marxists in various places and the newspapers forecast a purge of "deviationists." Heykal told the al-Ṭalī'a staff that it was only through his intercession that Sadat gave up the idea of closing down that journal.[40] The new National Unity Law, which prescribed heavy punishment for any political activity outside the A.S.U., was interpreted to have been directed against the Marxists, among others. The Soviet accusation that the Egyptians were withdrawing from the "orientation to Socialism" and giving free hand to "reactionaries," drew a sharp reply from Premier 'Azīz Ṣidqī during his talks in Moscow in mid-October.[41] Heykal, apparently referring to the same accusation, wrote: "We are not obliged to grant any individual or any group the right to serve, in Arab-Soviet relations, as interpreters or intermediaries in a way that would affect our domestic policies."[42] The tide of anti-Communism, fed by growing frustration and Qadhafi-type fervor, was rapidly rising.

Sadat, however, was determined not to allow this attitude to go too far. When urged, in a meeting with press and information staff, to tighten surveillance measures against Marxists and curb Marxist propaganda, he said: "I cannot take extra measures against anyone. If somebody wants to be a Marxist, he is free to do so, as long as he does not endanger the security of the State . . . . I refuse to conduct a campaign [against them]."[43]

In the final analysis, the regime profited from the Marxists' collaboration. So far this collaboration has not threatened the safety of the regime but rather has served it in many ways: the regime had at its disposal the good offices of "professional" Socialists; it could regulate its attitude toward the Marxists in order to demonstrate its changing policies toward East and West; it dispatched Marxists to international forums where the projection of a Socialist image was desired; it employed them as spokesmen to express attitudes on sensitive questions upon which the regime did not want to commit itself (see, e.g., the criticism of the Fidayeen voiced by Mohieddin and Ḥamrūsh at the Kuwait Palestinian Seminar); and it used them to present moderate views on the Arab-Israeli conflict to foreign leftists and liberals.

However, this did not leave the Egyptian ruling circles with a sense of triumph. As the deliberations of Mar'ī's Working Committee have demonstrated once again, the confrontation with the Marxists only serves to expose the endless contradictions in the regime's ideology and its hopeless shallowness. Therefore, no matter how effective the regime's suppressive measures may be, the challenge of a radical leftist opposition is ever present.

THE SOVIETS

The dilemma of the Soviet Union in her relations with non-Communist regimes in the ex-colonial world—i.e., the need to choose between her big-power interests and ideological commitments—has been amply discussed in the literature on Communism and the Soviet Union. A brief summary, mostly based on that literature, will therefore suffice to cover the third aspect of our subject.

Within the period under discussion, the following stages are usually noted:

Between 1959 and 1962 (a period of high tension between the Soviets and the Nasser regime, evolving against the background of the suppression of the Communists in Iraq and Syria), the Soviets expounded the concept of the "national democratic state" in which Communists were supposed to act vigorously, in alliance with other national-revolutionary forces, in order to progress from what was basically a colonial regime directly to the "non-capitalist road of development."

In 1962 (when the Soviet-Nasserist crisis was subsiding), this idea was replaced by that of "revolutionary democracy," i.e., it was possible to advance along the "non-capitalist road of development" toward socialism, even under leaderships that were not socialist. Local Communists were required to assist in this process.[44]

Against this background there appeared, in the summer of 1963, an innovative concept which allowed for the self-dissolution of the Communist parties under one-party regimes of this kind and the integration of individual Communists into the ruling parties. This remarkable departure in the doctrine of the Soviet Union and the world Communist movement was discerned, dated, and analyzed by Richard Löwenthal in his essay "Russia, the one-party system, and the third world,"[45] and by Oded Eran in another article in this volume. It has been shown that behind the new doctrine lay the basic assumption that it was incorrect to regard a regime, such as that of Nasser, as representing the "national bourgeoisie," for it struggled against capitalism and had opted for progress toward socialism. Hence, it would be wrong for local Communists to hinder the actions of such a regime; on the contrary, by providing guidance and assistance from within, they could encourage the process of its transformation into a Socialist regime. This new strategy, dubbed by Western observers "licensed infiltration," was applied first to Algeria and next to Egypt.

In the case of Egypt, at least, it should be stressed that the term "infiltration" does not imply a hidden intention not to accept the agreements with the one-party regimes at their face value and secretly pursue a strategy of expansion and ultimate takeover. It is unlikely that the Soviet leadership, especially Khrushchev, wished the Communists to adopt such a subversive strategy. On the contrary, they seemed to convey the impression that they were relieved to see the Communists reach an entente with the Egyptian regime and thus remove from the Soviet Union the burden of an embarrassing problem. Surely, the last thing they could possibly have wished for was to see the local Communists start rocking the boat again. Henceforth the Soviet leadership spoke and acted as though this arrangement were functioning flawlessly and the Marxists' collaboration with the Nasser regime, nourished by the presence of strong Soviet influence in Egypt, was automatically leading to the attainment of the designed objective. Accordingly, they spoke of vanguard cadres within the A.S.U., which, in fact, were non-existent; depicted the A.S.U. to the Communist world as a sister-party with which they maintained relations on the party level; conducted joint seminars with Egyptian Marxists, and honored and decorated their leading members; and glorified the social and political achievements of the Nasser regime.[46]

The sharp contrast between this image and reality could not escape the notice of Communists in the Soviet Union and the world Communist movement, especially since Communists from other Arab countries were openly grumbling. The critics of this strategy, who were more party-oriented and rejected the big-power approach on which this strategy was based, expressed their criticism in Soviet and Marxist publications. They pointed out that in Egypt there existed a striking lack of correlation between the declared goals of the regime and the machinery that was supposed to achieve them, that the problem of the vanguard party in the A.S.U. had, in fact, not yet been satisfactorily solved, that the bourgeoisie was still deeply entrenched in local society, and that under such circumstances, no progress toward Socialism could be detected.[42]

There are indications that this criticism has been intensified since the rise of Sadat, whom it is extremely difficult, much more difficult than Nasser, to describe as one "treading the road toward socialism." His formal commitment to this road, in the Soviet-Egyptian Treaty of of Cooperation and Friendship of May 1971, does not seem to be very reassuring. Ibrahīm 'Āmir, the al-Muṣawwar correspondent, reported that while he was in the U.S.S.R. Soviet youth and others repeatedly asked him to explain:

> What is the nature of this Socialism? Could it be a new form of Capitalism disguised in the form of Socialism? Does the non-capitalist road, taken by states in the Third World, lead inevitably to Socialism, or perhaps it might—under certain circumstances and in the absence of specific elements guaranteeing the effectiveness of the forces leading toward Socialism [i.e., freedom of action for local Communists]— lead to Capitalism of a new kind?[48]

Such doubts and soul-searching have not produced any change in the official Soviet line, which is based on pragmatic considerations. Of primary importance are the Soviet interests in Egypt, the stability of the Nationalist regime, and the uncertainty that, even in the remote event of a Marxist-Leninist triumph, Soviet influence would predominate. Their 1971 experience in the Sudan demonstrated once more that they had nothing to win from Communist agitation and bids for power against basically pro-Soviet non-Communist regimes; on the contrary, under cross-fire from both friendly Nationalist regimes and world Communist movements, they have everything to lose. It remains to be seen whether the Soviets will maintain this policy in the face of the recent rift with the Egyptian regime.

NOTES

[1] Michel Salomon, *Méditerranée rouge* (Paris 1970), p. 201.

[2] Interview with Maḥmūd Amīn al-'Ālim, *al-Ḥawādith*, 21 October, 1966; Fu'ād Maṭar in *al-Nahār*, 15 October, 1966; *Rūz al-Yūsuf*, 22 March, 1965.

[3] Text in *al-Nahār*, 12–14 October, 1966.

[4] *Foreign Report*, May 1965, pp. 3–4. It should, however, be noted that an earlier, and much more important conference, that of the Representatives of the Arab Communists meeting in Vienna, December 1964, had adopted resolutions which were in line with the self-dissolution.

[5] *World Marxist Review*, December, 1965, p. 17.

[6] *Al-Jadīd*, 4 February, 1972.

[7] *World Marxist Review*, October, 1966, pp. 49–53.

[8] M.S. Agwani, *Communism in the Arab East* (Bombay 1969), p. 191.

[9] Appointments under Sadat—see below.

[10] *Op. cit.* For the views of the Marxists see the collection of essays *La voie egyptienne vers le socialisme* (Cairo n.d.). The views expressed in *al-Ṭalī'a* are described in a seminar paper by Yossi Amitay, included in a collection of articles on *Nasserism in Crisis* to be published by the Shiloah Center (Hebrew).

[11] Interview by Maṭar, *al-Nahār*, 30 May, 1971.

[12] Amitay, p. 27.

[13] See, for example, the text of the proclamation of self-dissolution.

[14] *Al-Ṭalī'a*, September, 1971, pp. 11–15.

[15] *Al-Ṭalī'a*, February, 1966, pp. 17–29.

[16] *Al-Ṭalī'a*, October, 1966, p. 23.

[17] *Al-Ṭalī'a*, July, 1971, pp. 11–19.

[18] P. 13.

[19] 'Ālim, *loc. cit.*

[20] See text of decisions in *al-Masīra*, February, 1972.

[21] *Al-Nahār*, 6 January, 1972.

[22] See Nājī 'Alūsh, "Yasār lā ya'rif al-yamīn min al-yasār," *al-Ādāb*, October, 1967.

[23] Malcolm H. Kerr in *Los Angeles Times*, 28 July, 1968.

[24] 1 October, 1967.

[25] See Bernard Lewis, "Communism and Islam," *Int. Aff.*, January, 1954, p. 320.

318

[26] See Muhammad Jallāl Kishk, *Mādhā yurīdu al-ṭalaba al-misriyyūn* (Beirut 1968).

[27] See also Mohieddin's interview with Khrushchev in *Rūz-al-Yūsuf,* 3 July, 1964.

[28] *Al-Ahrām,* 12–13 March, 1965.

[29] *Al-Ahrām,* 29 July, 1971.

[30] The differences between Nasserism and Marxism were best defined by Heykal (7 points) and Kamāl Rif'at (13 points), cited by Anouar Abdel-Malek, *Egypt—a Military Society* (English tr; New York 1968), pp. 292–7.

[31] *Middle East Record,* III (1967), pp. 529–547.

[32] Kishk, p. 47; Ḥalīq in *al-Ḥayāt,* 13 October, 1968; Protocols of the investigation of Aḥmad Kāmil, *al-Nahār,* September, 1971; *Rūz al-Yūsuf,* 27 March, 1972.

[33] Thus Mirsky in *New Times,* 1 December, 1965, spoke of Mohieddin and Ṣabrī as working together to reconstruct the A.S.U., with the purpose of "creating within the A.S.U. a vanguard Party, the political core of the Union." (According to Jean Pennar, "Moscow and Socialism in Egypt," *Problems of Communism,* September-October, 1966, p. 43.) It is interesting to note that after the purge of Ṣabrī, Kholi blamed the West for the false image of Ṣabrī as a leftist. *Elements,* Vols. 7–8, 1971, p. 12.

[34] *Al-Jarīda,* 28 April, 17 September, 1969; *al-Ḥayāt,* 28 September, 1969; *al-Jarīda,* 24 April, 1970; *al-Usbū' al-'Arabī,* 29 March, 1971.

[35] *Al-Ḥayāt,* 17, 24 October, 1965; *al-Jarida,* 9 November, 1965; *al-Ḥawādith,* 21 October, 1166.

[36] *Loc. cit.*

[37] Interviews with Kholi, *Jeune Afrique,* 20 November, 1971; *Elements,* Nos. 7–8, 1971; *al-Nahār,* 6 January, 1972; *al-Yawm,* 8 January, 1972; interview with Mursī, *al-Nahār,* 29 May, 1971; Muḥammad al-Khafīf in *al-Akhbār,* 12 December, 1971. Cf. *New Middle East,* January, 1972, pp. 12–13.

[38] Text in *al-Ṭalī'a,* May, June and July, 1972.

[39] Text in *al-Ṭalī'a,* October, 1972.

[40] *Al-Balāgh,* 11 September, 1972.

[41] See text of his report to the A.S.U. Central Committee, 25 October, 1972.

[42] *Al-Ahrām,* 13 October, 1972.

[43] *Al-Nahār,* 13 September, 1972.

[44] Walter Laqueur, *The Struggle for the Middle East* (London 1969), pp. 173–80; Aryeh Yodfat, *Arab Politics in the Soviet Mirror* (Jerusalem 1972), pp. 12–13.

[45] *Survey,* January, 1966, pp. 43–58.

[46] *Al-Ḥayāt,* 28 August 1966; *al-Ahrām,* 6 February, 1965; Mirsky, *op. cit.*

[47] Yodfat, pp. 215 ff., Belyaev and Primakov, *Za Rubezhom,* No. 39, 22–28 September, 1967; G. Mirsky, *Literaturnaia Gazeta,* No. 32, 1967.

[48] *Al-Muṣawwar,* 29 October, 1971.

ELIE KEDOURIE
ANTI-MARXISM IN EGYPT

Political thought in modern Egypt is, in its categories and arguments, derivative from European thought. It has been entirely produced by the small Westernized minority which, ever since Muḥammad 'Alī's time, has increasingly dominated the intellectual and official classes. Both before and after World War I, the trend of thought of these classes has revolved around two issues, namely: how to rid Egypt of the British occupation; and what ought to be the character and limits of government. Both issues were formulated in European terms and debated according to European assumptions and categories. They were thus of little import or significance for the mass of the Egyptians whose universe of discourse was quite different from that of their Westernized rulers.

It is true that the Wafd Party, both under Zaghlūl and Naḥḥās, attempted now and again to mobilize the masses, by appealing to them in the traditional Islamic terms,[1] but such attempts were intermittent, adventitious, opportunistic, non-systematic, and never buttressed with a theoretical foundation or justification. In fact, before 1952, only three groups in Egypt possessed a theory by which they justified an appeal to, and a mobilization of, the masses. The first was the Communist Party which, under the monarchy, was a small, clandestine group inspired and led to a very large extent by non-Muslim foreigners. What was even more incapacitating was that their notion of Egyptian politics, based as it was on a Marxist-Leninist analysis of class divisions and revolutionary action, was as irrelevant to Egyptian conditions as the political thought of the Westernized politicians who called themselves Wafdist or Sa'dist or Liberal Constitutionalist.

The second group was Aḥmad Ḥusayn's Young Egypt Party.[2] Its doctrine did recommend and require mobilization of the masses, in the European totalitarian style, and its ideology of Egyptianism, Islam, and xenophobia was more intelligible and acceptable to the masses. But the Young Egypt Party did not prove very successful. This was perhaps owing to the fact that it became involved in political intrigues with Fu'ād and Fārūq very soon after its foundation in 1933,

321

before having seriously recruited and organized a mass following. The powerful political opponents which it thus attracted were able therefore largely to limit and even at times to suppress its activities. The outbreak of war in 1939 added to its difficulties, since it was suspected of having Nazi connections, and was thus in bad odor with the British. But, what is perhaps equally important, the ideology of Young Egypt could not rival that of the third group which seriously and systematically attempted to mobilize and indoctrinate the masses.

This group was that of the Muslim Brothers which Ḥassan al-Bannā founded at Isma'iliyya in 1928. While the ideology of Young Egypt was an artificial hodge-podge made up of Islamic and European elements, that of the Muslim Brothers was purely Islamic, deliberately evoking and recalling beliefs, ways of thought and behavior, and exemplary deeds which the ordinary Egyptian Muslim held in familiar affection. Thus, where Young Egypt adopted for its slogan "God, Fatherland, and King," the Muslim Brothers proclaimed that Islam was their banner and the Qur'an their constitution. There can be no doubt that the latter was incomparably more powerful and attractive than the former. To say that the Muslim Brothers appealed to purely Islamic sentiments is, of course, by no means to deny that they were themselves profoundly touched by European ways of thought. For their very reaction to, and attack upon, what they considered as deeply harmful Western-Christian influences forced them to deal with and in European concepts and categories. In this respect, the thought of the Muslim Brothers is quite similar to modern Islamic apologetics, whether emanating from al-Azhar or from writers who have no official connections. All these writings, those of the Muslim Brothers included, consciously and militantly defending Islam against the West, are traditionalist rather than traditional in character. They are impregnated by European thought.[3] But the fact remains that, whatever its underlying tendency, the thought of the Muslim Brothers is expressed in traditional Islamic terms, and thus appeals to those Egyptians who have not been much touched by Europe, as well as to those who have become acquainted with, and been discomforted by it. Another reason for the superior appeal of the Muslim Brothers lay in the fact that, unlike the Young Egypt Party, Ḥasan al-Bannā and his lieutenants were at the outset, and for many years afterwards, not directly concerned with politics. Originally they looked upon their mission as one of social reconstruction. Their mission was directed toward the urban workers who were in acute danger of disorientation and alienation. The Muslim Brothers worked to recuperate these lost souls for the Islamic community, to make a place within the body politic for "the inhabitants of the caves who were outside the laws and the constitution," and give them a pride in their heritage.[4] It was really only after 1945 that the energies of Ḥasan al-Bannā and the other leaders began to be mainly directed to political intrigues and terrorism.

Of the success of the Brothers in creating a very large and tenaciously loyal following there can be no doubt. They were throughout a private organization. Unlike the Wafd and the other political machines under the monarchy or the military regime, the Brothers had no access to official patronage and could by no means reward their adherents or punish their opponents in the way these machines could. But in spite of this fact, they managed to attract a very large following indeed. Professor Mitchell has estimated that in 1946–8 the Society had some half-million members and another half-million sympathizers, and that in 1953, a year or so before its dissolution by the military regime, there were between 200,000 and 300,000 Brothers.[5] Such figures in a country like Egypt are remarkable on any reckoning, and it is difficult to believe that the loyalties and commitments which these figures represent should have disappeared so quickly. Such scant evidence as we have leads us rather to suspect that even now, persecution, repression, and proscription have succeeded in driving them underground rather than in absolutely destroying them. The vicissitudes of the Brothers may be laid at the door of their leaders who twice misjudged the political situation and their own power, and thus wrecked the organization which had been built up with such arduous labor and devotion. In 1948–9 they resorted to terrorism in order to gain power, and proved unequal to the contest with the authorities. The *coup d'état* of July 1952 gave them new hope of playing a large role on the political scene. But the scene was extraordinarily confused. Nasser and his fellow-officers were, it is true, very unpopular in the period 1952–4, and the leaders of the Brothers may have thought that in trying conclusions with these officers they could not possibly lose. But again they were proved wrong, and discovered to their cost that in an oriental despotism to him who controls the tanks obedience is due. So they suffered their second repression in the autumn of 1954. They were allowed to re-emerge briefly in 1965, but even in their enfeebled condition they must have represented a threat to the regime which subjected them to a new repression and condemned their most prominent surviving leaders to death. They have now been bludgeoned into passivity; but to judge by the nervousness of the authorities in 1965–6, their criticism of the military regime must enjoy a wide audience among a population still staunchly Islamic, more alienated from its Westernized rulers, and more sceptical of their purposes than ever.

Under the monarchy, the Brothers criticized the West and Westernization in Egypt for encouraging sexual immorality, unrestrained cupidity, the merciless exploitation by man of his fellow men, corruption, and atheism. That society in Egypt was a chaos and a shambles, that an increasingly large number of Egyptians were living in conditions of increasing misery was attributed to the abandonment of Islam by the rulers of this Muslim society, and to their infatuation with the West. The Muslim Brothers were not at that time particularly interested in Marxism or Communism, which seemed to them mere variants of European materialism and godlessness. After the *coup d'état* of July 1952 and the subsequent abolition of the monarchy, a great change came over the terms in which political debate was conducted in Egypt. The officers now in power—many of them greatly influenced by the outlook and doctrines of the Muslim Brothers—declared that, as the Brothers had argued, the miseries of Egypt stemmed from the corrupt political institutions of the Monarchy, whose parties pursued their own narrow and selfish interests at the expense of the people. All this was now to be changed: the welfare of the masses would become the object of government, the magnates would be divested of their extensive landholdings, and the administration would become clean, and be put at the service of the citizens. There was a moment when all this must have seemed very promising to the Brothers, to be indeed the vindication of their teaching and their struggle. But, as has been seen, these hopes were soon dashed and if Ibrahīm 'Abd al-Hādī in 1949 had chastised the Brothers with whips, Nasser in 1954 began chastising them with scorpions. Furthermore, from the arms deal of 1955 onwards, the military regime was becoming increasingly tied to the Soviet Union, increasingly inclined to adopt "socialist" policies—which to the Brothers were tainted with a European origin—and increasingly tolerant of literary and publicistic activity by Egyptian Marxists and Communists. The defeat of June 1967 seemed to the Brothers—and no doubt also to a large number of Egyptians—proof conclusive that the foreign policy which the regime had pursued for 12 years, with its dependence on the Soviets, and the internal economic and social policies which were believed to be the concomitant of this dependence, were an unmitigated catastrophe. If political debate had been free in Egypt, the Egyptians would surely have manifested their dislike of the military regime, in the same way in which they spontaneously manifested it in February 1954 before Nasser had been able fully to establish his hegemony.[6] As it was, this feeling of discontent had perforce to remain inchoate, expressed more in the gallows humor of which the Egyptians are such masters, than in reasoned criticism or in putting forward alternative policies.

To this there is an exception. A trenchant criticism of the regime, its tendencies, and the ideology it favors, of what is alleged to be its betrayal of Islam (and hence of Egypt) has been expressed by the Muslim Brothers and by those who seem sympathetic to their tenets. It is true that the Brothers were subject to great persecution in 1954–5 and 1965–6, but this does not seem to have led them to abandon their views, and we may suspect that these views find a large audience of passive sympathizers. Before the repression of 1965–6, in which he was executed, Sayyid Quṭb published, in 1964, a remarkable work *Ma'ālim fī'l-ṭarīq* ("Signposts on the Road") which was thought by the authorities important enough to warrant a refutation which the Arab Socialist Union published in 1966 under the title *Ma'ālim fī ṭarīq al-khiyāna wa'l-raj'iyya* ("Signposts on the Road of Treason and Reaction"). Significantly, the title of this pamphlet echoed that of Quṭb's book, and the layout and design of its cover were an exact copy of the work it was attempting to refute. One of the grave charges which this pamphlet levels against Quṭb is that he is a "reactionary inimical to socialism," and the charge is proved from his statement that the West is bankrupt because it has begun to adopt socialism from the Eastern camp. The writer of the pamphlet comments: "There are some who disagree with him, and who consider that the necessity for the capitalist system to adopt socialism is a confirmation of the triumph of socialism, which realizes the sublime principles which Islam has proclaimed."[7] The pamphlet's author is at any rate right in asserting that Quṭb is strongly opposed to socialism. For him it is one species of that *jāhiliyya* which now has the world in its grip. Communism, he declares, is class-rule "based on the union of the proletariat (*al-ṣa'ālīk*), and the sentiment which is dominant in it is a black hatred for all other classes! Such a petty and hateful union could not but bring out what is worst in the human being. For it is *ab initio* based on emphasizing the animal characteristics alone, on allowing them to strike root and to grow, in the belief that the basic needs of man are food, shelter, and sex—and these are the basic needs of the animal—and in the belief that the history of man is the history of the quest for food."[8] Communist society, Quṭb also says, is, like all the other societies existing in the world today, a *mujtama' jāhilī*, an idolatrous society which denies the sovereignty of God. Communist society is such because it denies the existence of God, making matter or nature the active principle in the universe, and economics and the means of production the active principle in human history. Communist society is also idolatrous because it establishes a regime in which complete submission is given not to God but to the Party.[9] Quṭb's criticism, however, reaches beyond Communism and the Soviet regime. His readers are left in no doubt that he rejects equally some of the most basic notions by which the military regime justifies itself, and the very foundations of its ideology. A regime, he asserts, cannot claim inspiration from God or Islam unless it proclaims that it is God, not the People or the Party, or any other human being, who is the source of authority. It is not only Communism and Capitalism which are idolatrous, we Muslims are also living in a *jāhiliyya*: "All that is around us is *jāhiliyya*. Peoples' imaginings, their beliefs, customs, and traditions, the sources of their culture, their art and literature, their laws and statutes, much even of what we take to be Islamic culture, Islamic authorities, Islamic philosophy, Islamic thought: all this too is of the making of this *jāhiliyya*." It follows, therefore, that the fatherland of the Muslim, his *waṭan*, is where Islam is supreme; as for the solidarity based on clan, tribe, nation (*qawm*), race (*jins*), color, and land, all these are petty and retarded types of solidarity which humanity adopts only when it is in a state of spiritual degradation. This kind of solidarity the Prophet had described as "rotten," an expression denoting repugnance and disgust.[10]

The repression of the Brothers in 1965–6 made it difficult if not impossible for such views to be publicly expressed. But the very fact of the repression showed perhaps that the authorities feared the popularity of views such as Quṭb's. After the defeat of 1967, and the shock which it administered to the military regime, the passive sympathizers with the Brothers and their ideas must have increased. Criticism of the regime, of its Soviet connections, of its emphasis on "socialism" and its tolerance of Marxist writings most likely gained an increasing audience. But such criticism, though certainly voiced in private conversation, could not possibly find public expression in Egypt. To gain an idea of their tenor we may refer to two pamphlets published in Beirut by the Egyptian publicist and journalist, Muḥammad Jallāl Kishk. Though the pamphlets were published outside Egypt, the author himself was apparently still living in Egypt at the time of their publication, and what he has to say in these pamphlets may therefore be taken as an exposition by a close and interested observer of the vicissitudes affecting Egypt, and of their causes and remedies. As will be seen, what he has to say makes it unlikely that his is an isolated and unrepresentative voice. His criticisms and proposals seem rather the continuation and the echo of what the Muslim Brothers, and all those Egyptians who have desired to transform Egypt into a true Islamic polity, have been saying for many decades now. The pamphlets therefore may be considered a sign of the obstinate continuity of certain currents of thought which, in spite of repression and persecution by different governments, have had the power to attract and hold for many decades now a very large proportion of the Egyptian intellectual classes.

The first pamphlet, *What the Egyptian Students Want* (*Mādhā yurīd al-ṭalaba al-miṣrūyyūn*), was published in November 1968, and dealt with the student demonstrations of the previous February. The second, *What the Egyptian People Want* (*Mādhā yurīd al-sha'b al-miṣrī*), taking the form of an open letter to President Sadat, was published in October 1970, and thus at the very moment when the latter was chosen to succeed Nasser.

Of the two pamphlets the second is the more cutting and outspoken; but many themes are common to the two publications, though since they are *oeuvres de circonstance* the emphasis changes from the one to the other. Writing in 1968 Kishk has no doubt that the Egyptian people is the absolute enemy of Communism: "The Egyptian people is a people which has faith, which clings to Islam. It has never known fanaticism in all its history, but it likewise will not allow itself to be uprooted." The Egyptian opposition to Communism has been on the increase since 1964 after Khrushchev's provocative visit, when he behaved as though he was a Cromer or an American Vice-President visiting South Vietnam. This enmity became clear when the Soviet Union adopted a defeatist attitude in May-June 1967, the crowd going so far as to throw stones and spit at the car of the Soviet Ambassador on 9 June, 1967. Kishk goes on to affirm that this dislike extends to the Egyptian Communists who have followed one of two policies: beginning by attacking the regime as fascist, they then changed their policy and gave it absolute support. They thus formed "the greatest reactionary force opposed to any criticism or change" and became the enemies of democracy and the supremacy of law. But who, anyway, are these Egyptian Communists? They are either Copts or Jews or Baha'is whose main interest is the struggle against Islam. Consider for instance their support of Emperor Haile Selasie in spite of his inimical position toward the Arabs, or how they have taken Makarios' side in the Cyprus dispute and prevented any publicity being given to the Turkish case. Many of them are opportunists who have taken up Marxism in order to teach in Government institutes, so that they may earn high salaries and "smoke American cigarettes imported in an illegal fashion."[11]

But it is clear that Kishk's attack is directed against a wider target than that of the Egyptian Communists. His quarrel is really with the military regime itself. This regime, he argues, is in effect composed of a congeries of organizations (*tashkīlāt*) whose members form a new ruling class. In order to perpetuate its rule, this new class has to repress the people, since if the people were in control of politics, these organizations would lose their *raison d'être*: they are "a natural phenomenon of class rule transforming the government into a secret group, and politics into a conspiracy." In order to describe the character of these organizations, Kishk has recourse to an analogy drawn from an earlier period of Egyptian history: it is mamlukes, he says, who run *al-Ahrām*, and this newspaper is in effect their fief (*sanjaqiyya*). The Egyptian Communists are but part of these organizations where they have succeeded in lodging themselves.[12]

What Kishk has been describing is in fact Nasserism, the bankruptcy of which appeared in 1967. Why, asks Kishk in his 1968 pamphlet, did the masses maintain Nasser in power on 9 June, 1967? Because the disastrous alternative was Nasserism without Nasser, and what they wanted was Nasser without Nasserism. It is this again which the Egyptian students wanted in their demonstrations of February 1968. The passage is eloquent enough to warrant extensive quotation:

When the regime sustained a military defeat, the justification for its existence disappeared, having previously lost any justification in internal affairs. If the President had not announced his retirement and the retirement of all the leadership of the regime, the masses would have marched on Cairo after the cease-fire, and it is impossible to foresee what would have happened.

But President Nasser was able, on the evening of 9 June, to prevent this march, rather to deflect it to another direction, when he faced the masses with the only possibility contingent on his resignation, namely the continuation of the Nasserite regime without Nasser; he was careful to emphasize this by appointing a successor.

Since this was the worst possible solution, the masses put forward immediately the contrary solution: Nasser without the Nasserite regime.

It seemed to the people that from June [1967] to February [1968] this was the direction events were taking. The trials began to take place, the press was allowed to publish the scandals of the regime, and proclaim the slogan of change.

When it began to be apparent after the formation of the ministry, the return of the youth organizations to their activity, the reconstitution of the branches of the Arab Socialist Union, the interference in the elections to the journalists' [union], the refusal to allow the formation of a students' union, the coming forward of the old faces on the pretext of continuity, the coming into prominence of new forces, and the swelling of the old forces which escaped the liquidation, then the students came out in February, reminding with a greater emphasis and sharpness [the authorities] of the demand of the people on 9 and 10 June, which was: Down with Nasserism and long live Nasser.[13]

Kishk's open letter to Sadat is even more daring in its ideas and expressions. Nasser, he tells his successor, was a President (ra'īs), but he was also a Leader (za'īm). No successor to the Presidency can, however, hope to succeed to Nasser's Leadership which the people had acknowledged and accepted. But if his successors should attempt to exercise tutelage (wiṣāya) over the Egyptian people, this will end in a dictatorship such as that which ravages Iraq or that of Papa Duvalier in Haiti. There must be an end to minutely organized demonstrations, with rigidly prescribed slogans; an end to elections without a plurality of candidates. He congratulates Sadat on welcoming the fact that three-quarters of a million voters had rejected his candidature; Sadat, however, had declared that in saying no to him, these voters did not oppose the Revolution of 1952 or its continuation. Kishk for his part would like to ensure that even if they did oppose the Revolution and all its works, they would still be free to express their opinions, and to organize themselves politically in order to do so.[14]

Kishk, then, proposes an alternative regime for Egypt. Organizations such as the Arab Socialist Union have to go. Under the Leader, they were a harmless mockery; without him, they become dangerous instruments in the struggle for power, opening the door to endless civil war. An end has likewise to be made of these parliaments which "have been elected by nomination, or nominated by election" (*untukhibat bi'l-ta'yīn aw 'uyyinat bi'l-intikhāb*), and to which Egyptians have never conceded the quality of representativeness. If there has to be a Pharaoh, he must be accessible to the people:

> The ugliest regime is that in which Pharaoh has the sole preroga-
> tive in deciding on peace and war, and in confiscating the
> peasants' donkeys, and where the people are prevented from
> approaching him, the right of speaking to him being reserved
> to the priests and the guardians of the temple of Dandara.[15]

In his 1968 pamphlet, Kishk points out that the students were shouting Islamic slogans in their demonstrations, and that their leaders insisted, in their speeches, on religious education and religious values. This, he points out, is in great contrast to the tepid attitude of the official representatives of Islam to their religion: shaykh Bāqūrī, the rector of the University of al-Azhar, omits the invocation to God (the *basmala*) at the beginning of his speeches, while the student leaders invoked not only God but his Prophet as well. In this they were more representative of the Egyptians than Bāqūrī, for it is not to be denied that interest in Islam, and the desire for a return to Islam are very strong in Egypt. How else can one explain the great opposition which arose when it was proposed— before June 1967—to omit the provision that Islam is the official religion of the state when an official committee was considering a draft constitu-tion? How otherwise to account for the steadily increasing popularity of religious books among the Egyptians? In short, Islam in Egypt is not the result of a plot by the Muslim Brothers; the Egyptians are loyal Muslims, and nothing can shake their loyalty. Therefore to belittle or repress Islam in Egypt is to go against the desires of the Egyptian people. It is also to harm Egypt's international position by isolating it from the Arab world and the world of Islam where its true strength lies, and where it has a fundamental role to play.[16] In his open letter to Sadat, Kishk reiterates that Egypt's safety and salvation lie in cultivating relations with the Muslim and the Arab world. Under his predecessor, these relations worsened considerably. Egypt became known as a center of subversion where every conspirator or fugitive or intriguer found a ready welcome at the Voice of the Arabs. The result was a remarkable diminution of Egyptian influence and almost total Egyptian isolation. Egyptians were expelled from every country. Arab capital ceased flowing into Egypt. Egyptian industrial, commercial, and cultural presence has almost disappeared from every Arab country. Compare the Lebanese Middle East Airlines and Misr Airlines: which is the larger, and which earns more revenue from the Arab countries? And this "in spite of the fact that the Egyptian air force has roamed freely (ṣāla wa jāla) in almost all Arab skies 'hitting the bases of the enemy,' extirpating the supports of imperialism and reaction, defending 'Arab unity' and its 'vanguard,' while it is impossible to record a single instance of the Lebanese air force going beyond its frontiers." Again, what kind of Egyptians are now chiefly to be seen in Arab countries? They are domestics. Socialist Egypt and revolutionary socialist Syria are the two main suppliers of domestics to the capitalist Arab countries.[17]

Egypt, then, is isolated in the Arab and Muslim worlds. Such is the outcome of Nasserite policies which have thus made even more disastrous the Soviet connections, which are again the outcome of the same policies. Egypt has become a Soviet satellite: Kosygin's intervention in the affair of Nasser's succession, the way in which they had earlier imposed 'Alī Ṣabrī on him are the outward signs of this state of affairs. The Soviet position in Egypt is now reminiscent of the earlier British domination, when British advice had the force of an order. How did this come to pass? It is true that the Soviets do not use their soldiers in Egypt as an army of occupation like the British—they make use of another army of occupation to effect their purpose, namely the Israeli army. The first arms deal in 1955 was represented both as necessary in the circumstances, and as delivering Egypt from a Western monopoly in arms. This may have been the case then, but, in fact "the purchase of Soviet arms has delivered us into the power of an absolute monopoly. The Western arms market, with its competition and contradictions, with its smugglers even, allows room for maneuver and bargaining, in contrast to Russian arms where the grip of the state is absolute and undisputed." Taking Soviet arms has in effect disarmed Egypt, and delivered her into the hands of the Great Powers. The proper answer to the Israeli threat would have been to develop an Egyptian arms industry as China had shown it possible to do. Since this was not done, Egypt has become a pawn in a Great-Power game. It is an illusion to think that Egypt can play off the U.S.S.R. against the U.S.A. The latter Power would prefer to see Egypt a Soviet protectorate and settle matters directly with the U.S.S.R.[18]

In sum, then, Egypt's security lies in cultivating and strengthening ties with the Arab and the Muslim world. It is only Arab and Islamic solidarity which can save Egypt from enslavement to the Great Powers, from the stultification of its foreign policy (the overriding aim of which is the removal of the Israeli threat), from its Islamic traits disappearing, and from a repressive and divisive police regime at home. Egypt must "practise a dynamic Islamic policy." This is Kishk's prescription, and he ends his 1970 pamphlet on an uncompromising and defiant note. He implores God "to make use of those who straighten the crookedness of the rulers by means of their swords" (*min al-ladhīn yuqawwimūn i'wijāj al-ḥākimīn bī-suyūfihim*).[19]

It is, of course, impossible to say what "a dynamic Islamic policy" really means. Nor are Kishk's pamphlets best seen as a blueprint for a practical policy. Rather, they constitute a criticism, at once reasoned and biting, of the 18 years of Nasserism. The pamphlets, as has been said, were published outside Egypt, and it is doubtful whether their importation would have been allowed. But their author is an Egyptian, and apparently still living in Egypt. The incisiveness and originality with which he formulates the grievances and discontents of his fellow-Egyptians must not lead us to think that he is an isolated eccentric. On the contrary, we may suspect that Kishk is giving body and shape to widespread fears and dislikes, and that what he has to say would find a wide audience in a country where so many had so recently sympathized with the doctrine of the Muslim Brothers. And this for two reasons: first, he speaks a familiar and acceptable Islamic idiom; and second, his frank and commonsensical discussion of burning political issues has a concreteness and a solidity which would make it immediately intelligible to his fellow-citizens, in contrast to the alembicated disquisitions of Cairo progressive intellectuals. These would fall on deaf ears, or be rejected with suspicion as officially inspired. The fate of the European-inspired idioms of politics which the ruling classes adopted under the monarchy, and which have now dissappeared without trace shows how little attractive such importations are.

But popular as Kishk's themes might be, this does not mean that they would have the slightest effect on a regime which does not have to reckon very much with public opinion, or at all with representative assemblies. Certain circumstances might make it advantageous for the present regime, or a succeeding one, to make its own some or all of Kishk's themes, just as other circumstances might make more advantageous the continued suppression of such views. But these would have little or nothing to do with the wishes of the public. The reason why this is so is not likely to give pleasure to Kishk: for it is precisely because Egypt is Islamic, and because the most persistent political tradition of Islam is oriental despotism, that his plea for a "dynamic Islamic policy" is likely to go unheeded.

NOTES

1 For an example, see Elie Kedourie, *The Chatham House Version* (London 1970), p. 140.
2 On which see James P. Jankowski, "The Young Egypt Party and Egyptian Nationalism 1933–1945," unpublished Ph.D. dissertation, University of Michigan 1967.
3 The distinction between tradition and traditionalism has been worked out in exemplary fashion for modern China by the late J. R. Levenson in his *Confucian China and its Modern Fate*. What he has to say of China is, *mutatis mutandis*, equally true of Islam. For the impregnation of modern Islamic thought by European modes and categories see Wilfred Cantwell Smith, *Islam in Modern History* (Princeton 1957), particularly pp. 115–56; Hamid Enayat, "Islam and Socialism in Egypt," *Middle Eastern Studies,* Vol. IV, no. 2 (January 1968); G. E. von Grunebaum, "Approaching Islam: a Digression," *Middle Eastern Studies,* Vol. VI, no. 2 (May 1970); and *Idem* "Some Recent Constructions and Reconstructions of Islam," in Carl Leiden (ed.), *The Conflict of Traditionalism and Modernism in the Muslim Middle East* (Austin 1969).
4 Richard P. Mitchell, *The Society of the Muslim Brothers* (London 1969), p. 80.
5 Mitchell, *op. cit.,* p. 328.
6 Mitchell, *op. cit.,* p. 129.
7 *Ma'ālim fī ṭariq al-khiyāna,* pp. 63, 37–8.
8 *Ma'ālim fī'l-ṭariq* [1964], n.p., n.d., p. 66.
9 *Ibid.,* p. 110.
10 *Ibid.,* pp. 117–8, 21, 177.
11 *Māhdā yurid al-ṭalaba . . .,* pp. 28, 36, 55–9.
12 *Ibid.,* pp. 52. 77 ff.
13 *Ibid.,* pp. 70–1.
14 *Mādhā yurid al-sha'b . . .,* pp. 7, 9, 26–8, 32, 91.
15 *Ibid.,* pp. 33, 29, 6.
16 *Mādhā yurid al-ṭalaba . . .,* pp. 25–29.
17 *Mādhā yurid al-sha'b . . .,* pp. 45–59.
18 *Ibid.,* pp. 65–69.
19 *Ibid.,* pp. 83–4, 93.

HAIM SHAKED, ESTHER SOUERY, and GABRIEL WARBURG

THE COMMUNIST PARTY IN THE SUDAN, 1946–1971

The purpose of this paper is to trace the major developments of the Sudanese Communist Party (C.P.) from its early beginnings in 1946 until the abortive, so-called Communist, *coup* in July 1971. Emphasis is laid upon the relationship between the C.P. and the different governments and regimes which ruled the Sudan during that period. An attempt is also made to analyze the position of the C.P. against the background of Sudanese society and party politics.

Each of the three parts of this paper deals with a specific period; the first describes the initial phase of the history of the C.P. until independence in 1956. It also traces the development of trade unionism during that period and attempts to assess Communist penetration, especially into the railway workers' union and the tenants' associations. Landmarks in Communist history are discussed in the second part, with special reference to Communist involvement in the October 1964 civilian uprising and to government attempts to fight Communism in the years 1965–9. The more recent period, commencing with Ja'far al-Numeiri's military *coup* in May 1969, is discussed in more detail in the last part.

It will be only fair to state those of this paper's shortcomings of which the authors are aware. Neither Sudanese Communist ideology (which is the subject of a separate study in preparation, by Miss E. Souery) nor the C.P.'s external relations with other Communist parties or with the Communist bloc, have been dealt with. Furthermore, it is impossible to draw a distinctive line between C.P. members, leftists, revolutionary socialists, progressives, or other fellow-travelers in the Sudan. Like many clandestine organizations, the Sudanese C.P. has volunteered little information on its membership and only a handful of first-ranking activists can be definitely identified as party members. This holds true even for the relatively short periods when the C.P. became legal. Another major disadvantage is the scarcity of reliable sources, which has forced us to sift through crumbs of information in order to attempt a reconstruction of the history of the

335

C.P. As in many Middle Eastern jigsaw puzzles, some crucial pieces are still missing while others do not fit together. Consequently, this paper is only a partial and incomplete account which will require further amplification and elaboration as more information comes to light. (A study of Sudanese politics, with special reference to popular Islam, nationalism, and Communism, by Dr. G. Warburg, is in preparation.)

The International Setting

The history of the C.P. of the Sudan begins in the year 1946 when the Sudan Movement for National Liberation was founded as an offshoot of the Egyptian Communist movement. As elsewhere in the Middle East, this development was a direct outcome of the post-Stalingrad period and its impact on the Sudanese intelligentsia.[1]

British imperialism was folding its flag and for the first time since the establishment of the Anglo-Egyptian administration in the Sudan half a century earlier, prospects of Sudanese independence seemed real. In Egypt, the Ṣidqī-Bevin protocol, which promised the evacuation of British troops from Egypt within three years, was published in October 1946. The future of the Sudan was defined in the protocol in rather ambiguous terms. On the one hand, it reiterated the terminology favorable to Egyptian interests, namely, the "unity between the Sudan and Egypt under the common Crown of Egypt . . . ." On the other hand, the protocol insisted on the continuation of the Condominium until the Sudanese would be able to exercise their right ". . . to choose the future status of the Sudan. . . ."[2]

It seemed therefore that Britain was at last on her way out of the Sudan. However, 1946 was rather a bad year for the Soviet Union too. Its primary aims, based on traditional Russian policy, were to secure its southern borders with Turkey and Iran. Yet Soviet demands for bases in the Turkish Straits and the attempt to set up a Soviet-controlled People's Democracy in northern Iran had both ended in a fiasco. Thus it seemed for a short while that the course was set for real independence in the Middle East. It was this turn of events which led to the Truman doctrine and to increasing American involvement in the area.

For nearly ten years, Soviet interests were diverted elsewhere except for a short-lived support of Israel, in 1947–8. The Korean War had been fought and lost, and Stalin had passed away when, in 1954–5,

Soviet penetration into the Arab countries started in earnest. For the first time Communists, left-wingers, and others in the Middle East, who had regarded the Soviets as their saviors from imperialism, had a chance to observe their benefactors at close quarters.

This also applied to the Sudan which, at that time, had just achieved her independence. As elsewhere in the Middle East, Soviet penetration into the Sudan can only be understood in the context of wider Soviet strategic interests. Following the U.S.S.R.'s failure in Turkey and Iran, where resistance to the Soviets remained strong, the Arab world provided an alternative, especially after the military *coups* in Syria and Egypt. The Soviet position was further strengthened by the failure of the Baghdad Pact, by the toppling of the pro-British regime in Iraq in 1958, and by the Arab-Israel conflict. Positive Neutralism, which had been branded during the Stalin era as a pro-imperialist policy, was regarded by his successors as a framework suitable for Soviet penetration. The influence of the Soviets in Egypt, Syria, and Iraq provided them not only with a means to exert pressure on Turkey and Iran, but also enabled the U.S.S.R. to threaten N.A.T.O. from the flank and to disrupt European oil supplies should this become advantageous.

Soviet interests in the Sudan emerged during the next stage, in the early 1960s. With their growing involvement and presence in Egypt, the Soviets, like the British before them, realized the Sudan's strategic importance. Furthermore, a presence in East Africa and in the Indian Ocean became vital for the U.S.S.R. as her interests extended to the Indian subcontinent and to Southeast Asia; the Sudan could provide some of the necessary ports and bases on the western shore of the Red Sea.

The Soviets, however, made little headway in the Sudan in the years 1956–8. Ismā'īl al-Azharī, the first prime minister of the independent Sudan, had traveled to Bandung in April 1955 but, unlike President Nasser, had returned disillusioned both with his northern neighbor and with the prospects of neutrality. Under his successor, 'Abdallah Khalīl, the policy of the Sudan government became outspokenly pro-Western and anti-Communist.

It was only after Ibrāhīm 'Abbūd's military *coup* in November 1958 that Sudanese relations with the U.S.S.R. improved and that Soviet economic aid started to flow to the Sudan, despite the anti-Communist measures taken by the Sudanese military dictatorship.

Communism in the Sudan was outlawed, the military and civil service were purged of Communist sympathizers, and leading Communists were imprisoned. Yet, in the Sudan, as elsewhere, the C.P.'s well-being seemed immaterial to the Kremlin whenever the U.S.S.R.'s interests as a superpower clashed with those of the local Communists. From the point of view of Soviet strategy and interests in the Sudan, the C.P. was merely one of a series of local factors and, ostensibly, not the most important one. While 'Abbūd imprisoned leading Communists and harassed their supporters, Soviet and Chinese leaders proclaimed the everlasting friendship between their countries and the Sudan. 'Abbūd was a welcome guest in the Soviet Union and the Soviet leaders who visited the Sudan promised their aid for agricultural and industrial development projects. *Pravda* said that it was only under 'Abbūd that the Sudan achieved her independence,[3] and Chou En-lai, during his visit to the Sudan in 1964, proclaimed 'Abbūd as the man who had finally rid the Sudan of imperialism, and promised eternal co-operation between the two progressive regimes.[4]

Soviet military and economic aid to the Sudan continued to increase throughout the 1960s, unaffected by the ups and downs of local Communism. The accelerated flow of Soviet arms to the Sudan in the wake of the 1967 Six-Day War continued despite the anti-Communist measures during the Sudanese 1968 elections. Finally, the Soviet Union sacrificed the C.P. in order to maintain her ties with Numeiri's military regime.[5] It appears that even in the wake of the so-called Communist *coup* of 1971, when 'Abd al-Khāliq Mahjūb (secretary-general of the C.P.) and other Communist leaders were executed, the Soviets, though compelled by the circumstances to protest strongly and denounce Numeiri's action, gave in when faced with an ultimatum by Numeiri to stop their campaign or else face a rupture of diplomatic relations.

The Sudanese Setting

The emergence of Sudanese nationalism in the 1920s was influenced and probably instigated mainly by events in Egypt. Thus, from the outset, nationalism in the Sudan was not allowed to follow its own course. On the one hand, Great Britain, the predominant of the Sudan's two rulers, regarded the emerging Sudanese nationalism as an artificial by-product of Egyptian propaganda in the Sudan, and hence was set on curbing it. On the other hand, the two dominant centers of

Sudanese society—the tribal notables and the leaders of popular Islam—observed the attempt of the young intelligentsia to assert itself with mistrust bordering on hostility.

During her first 20 years of governing the Sudan Britain had two primary aims: first, to pacify the country following the Mahdist upheaval, and second, to develop the economy of the Sudan so that the country would be able to pay its way without Egyptian aid. In order to achieve these aims the British rulers of the Sudan sought the aid of the indigenous Sudanese leadership, namely the tribal and religious leaders. By the early 1920s, these aims had been largely realized: Egyptian financial aid to the Sudan had been discontinued except for a yearly subsidy to the army; the country had been pacified and both tribal and religious leaders had proved their loyalty to their British patrons and had sided with them in their attempt to diminish Egyptian influence in the Sudan to the utmost.

During World War I a further development took place. Ever since the conquest of the Sudan the British authorities had viewed popular Islam with certain misgivings and had done their utmost to cultivate the authority of what is called 'orthodox' Muslim leadership. By 1914 it became quite evident that this attempt had failed and that religious leadership had remained vested in the leaders of popular Islam, especially in the so-called two *sayyids*, i.e., Sayyid 'Alī al-Mīrghanī—leader of the Khatmiyya *ṣūfī* order, and Sayyid 'Abd al-Raḥmān al-Mahdī—leader of the *Anṣār*.[6] Consequently, British attitudes toward popular Islam were modified and in the inter-war period the two *sayyids* emerged as the most influential leaders in the Sudan. The tribal leadership, the young intelligentsia, and its Congress of Graduates founded in 1938, all came to be linked to either one or the other of these two main religious orders, which have exercised a continuing influence on the political scene in the Sudan. Even the emergence of political parties during and after World War II did not change this pattern. The *Ashiqqā'*, the *Umma*, the National Unionists, and the Muslim Brothers realized that without the patronage and blessing of either Sayyid 'Alī al-Mīrghanī or Sayyid 'Abd al-Raḥmān al-Mahdī their attempt at playing politics was doomed to failure.[7]

To attempt an analysis of this phenomenon within the framework of a short paper would be presumptuous. However, certain dominant factors may be singled out. Ever since the Islamization of the Sudan—a slow process which started in the seventh century and reached its zenith during the Fūnj Sultanate, between the 16th and 18th centuries—the role of the holy families was paramount. Thus, Islam in the Sudan was strongly tainted with ṣūfī beliefs and institutions, and the loyalty of Sudanese Muslims belonged to their ṣūfī leaders, blessed with baraka, rather than to abstract religious ideas or to an 'orthodox' code of behavior.[8] The tribal structure of Sudanese society was especially suited to this type of Islam which required little, if any, education and, furthermore, did not undermine the authority of the tribal leadership. The standing and authority of the popular Muslim leadership was further enhanced through the setting up of centralized government by the Condominium. Since the turn of the century, government attempts to strengthen tribal authority had failed. Despite the introduction of indirect rule and constant government support for the indigenous tribal leaders, it soon became clear that the latter could not function as government agents and at the same time maintain their independent authority. Hence the field was left wide open for the leaders of popular Islam, whose functions and standing remained unaffected by this development. Their political strength lay in their spiritual leadership and was thus unhampered by the centralized administration of the Condominium. Moreover, until the early 1950s, the Mahdist Anṣār and other traditional elements were regarded by the British administration as a major anti-Egyptian bulwark, which should be encouraged. Far from undermining the authority of popular Islam, government policy thus increased its impact.

The decade prior to independence witnessed the development of two additional forces on the Sudanese political scene—the C.P. and the Muslim Brothers; both arising from the young Sudanese intelligentsia. The appearance of the Communists coincided with the beginning of trade unionism.[9] As early as the 1920s, the Sudanese intelligentsia had tried in vain to break away from sectarian politics. Even al-Azharī's attempt in 1943 to found an independent political party, the Ashiqqā', on modern lines, proved premature. The intelligentsia was not yet strong enough to fend for itself and when the Anṣār extended their patronage over the Umma Party in 1945, it was only a matter of time before the Ashiqqā' had to seek the support of the Khatmiyya, thus weakening its own independence. The appearance of a C.P., whose ideology and loyalties were diametrically opposed to the traditional concepts of popular Islam, created a new situation. Even more important was the foundation of the trade unions, whose members' loyalty was bound to clash with their adherence to their religious orders. The question whether the tutelage of popular Islam could be extended over these new forces too, was a matter of grave concern to the traditional leadership. It soon appeared, however, that Islam retained its paramount importance even among the rank and file of the C.P. and the trade unions.[10]

THE COMMUNIST PARTY PRIOR TO INDEPENDENCE

Beginnings

The story of the C.P. in the Sudan begins in Egypt toward the end of World War II, when Sudanese students in Cairo published their first paper, *Ummdurmān,* in conjunction with the *Mouvement Démocratique de Libération Nationale* (M.D.L.N.)—one of the factions of the Egyptian Communist Party. There had been earlier attempts to organize Communism in the Sudan, after World War I, but these were thwarted by the authorities as part of their drive against the White Flag League and other nationalist organizations.[11]

According to Communist sources, their party in the Sudan was founded in 1946, under the name *al-ḥaraka al-sūdāniyya lil-taḥarrur al-waṭani* (S.M.N.L.). Its founders were students and members of the intelligentsia who in March of that year held their first anti-imperialist demonstration in Khartoum.[12] As in many Communist parties, harmony within the S.M.N.L. did not last long. 'Opportunist' elements had infiltrated into the Central Committee, some of whom supported the unity of Egypt and the Sudan under the Egyptian crown.[13] It was only in the summer of 1947 that the 'Royalist Communists' were expelled and a new Central Committee was set up, this time with a stronger representation of workers.[14] The next crisis arose in 1949, when many of the educated members of the party left, ". . . owing to the revisionist policies adopted by its then secretary 'Awaḍ 'Abd al-Rāziq. . . ." It lasted well into 1951, when the Second Congress of the C.P. decided to expel the so-called revisionist wing.[15] The party now launched several front organizations of women and students and for the first time succeeded in gaining support among peasants[16]—the largest segment of Sudanese society. Thus, within a relatively short period, it seemed that the Sudanese C.P. had succeeded where most of the Communist parties in the Arab world had failed, namely, in expanding beyond the small group of intelligentsia into the wider strata of Sudanese society.

After the Anglo-Egyptian agreement of 1953, the first general elections in the Sudan, held later in that year, were contested by all registered political parties in the country. The clandestine C.P. fought the elections under the banner of the Anti-Imperialist Front (al-jabha al-mu'ādiya lil-isti'mār), and won one seat in the House of Representatives. According to Communist sources, the newly founded Front and its election experience enabled the party, for the first time since 1946, to come into the open and thus establish contacts with party branches throughout the Sudan.[17]

Trade Unions and Tenants' Associations

In July 1946 the Workers' Affairs Association (W.A.A.) was founded as the spokesman for the Sudan's railway workers. The fact that the Sudan Railways were chosen as the center of the trade unions was a good omen for the young movement. In a country that stretches over a million square miles, the smooth running of the railways is of crucial importance to the administration and the security, as well as to the economy and the well-being of the public. Moreover, at that time in the Sudan, with industry in its initial stages of development, the railways presented the largest concentration of labor which could be organized in the new unions. It was not merely by chance that the first attempts at trade unionism in the Sudan took place in 'Aṭbarā, a fairly new town exposed to European influence from the outset, which had developed as the center of the expanding Sudan Railways. Out of a population of some 40,000, over 90 percent were railway employees and their dependents. Owing to the town's special character its traditional centers of loyalty—tribe, family, and religious leadership—were all weakened by new forms of solidarity.[18]

Appreciating the importance of the railways and the potential strength of a railway union, if properly organized, the British management refused to recognize the W.A.A. despite its moderate demands. It was only after a mass demonstration on August 8, 1947, followed by a general strike and the arrest of the union's leaders, that the government at last gave in. By that time, however, the leadership of the union was already in Communist hands. The C.P.'s position was further enhanced by the refusal of the railway management to negotiate with the workers on wages and working conditions. The railways, it was stated, were a branch of the Sudan civil service and hence any negotiations had to be conducted directly with the government. In this way the workers' struggle for better wages and better conditions of employment became part and parcel of their nationalist struggle against a British-controlled government,[19] and the Sudanese trade unions became a militant political force.

From 1950, the trade unions were linked together in the Sudan Workers' Trade Union Federation (S.W.T.U.F.) in which the railway workers played a predominant role. In December 1951, the S.W.T.U.F. decided to take an active part in Sudanese politics. Prompted by the unilateral abrogation by Egypt of the Anglo-Egyptian treaty of 1936, the S.W.T.U.F. declared that its objective was to defeat imperialism and to attain for the Sudan the right of self-determination. To achieve this end the United Front for the Liberation of the Sudan was established and all workers' and peasants' unions were called upon to form 'national committees' in order to function within the Front which, in fact, was initiated and run by Communists.[20] The year 1952 saw the first attempts of the S.W.T.U.F. at organizing peasant cultivators and agricultural workers. First, existing organizations, such as the Gezira Tenants' Association, were branded as fake organizations imposed by the authorities. Secondly, in August 1952 the Northern province tenants held their first conference at 'Aṭbarā, under the auspices of the railway workers. This was followed by the Nuba Mountains cotton cultivators, whose congress, in May 1953, was attended and addressed by the president of the S.W.T.U.F. Finally, the Gezira cotton growers joined the ranks of the newly founded United Front for the Liberation of the Sudan.[21]

It is difficult to assess the extent of Communist influence on, or control of either the trade unions or the tenants' associations. The Sudanese C.P. claimed, during the 1953 elections, to be the spokesman of an Anti-Imperialist Front (consisting of workers, peasants, and intelligentsia) applying in the Sudan "the successful tactics of the Chinese Communist Party. . . ."[22] It is known, however, that Communist attempts to use the trade unions for political aims failed in many instances. In April 1952, the S.W.T.U.F. threatened a general strike for an unlimited period unless its chief officers were released from jail within 48 hours. However, the strike had to be called off as some of the most powerful unions were not willing to support what they regarded as a political protest.[23] The declining prestige of the S.W.T.U.F. and of the C.P. within the Federation became even more evident in 1953. When the Anglo-Egyptian agreement was signed in February 1953, it was hailed by the major political parties as a victory for Sudanese nationalism. The C.P., and following it the S.W.T.U.F., condemned the agreement as an Anglo-Egyptian imperialist plot and called for a three-day general strike in protest. The strike had to be called off due to lack of support and the S.W.T.U.F. executives had to announce that every worker had the right to hold his own political views.[24]

These few examples, as well as the close links between S.W.T.U.F. and the World Federation of Trade Unions in Prague, appear to indicate that while the C.P. was well established within the S.W.T.U.F. and its cadre, it lacked influence within the trade unions themselves.

THE COMMUNIST PARTY FROM 1956 TO 1968

Under the 'Abbūd Regime

During the two and a half years between independence and 'Abbūd's military *coup,* the C.P. could not boast of many achievements. In January 1957 a National Front was founded in opposition to 'Abdallah Khalīl's pro-Western government; it consisted of al-Azharī's National Unionist Party (N.U.P.), the National Union of Students, and the Communist-dominated Anti-Imperialist Front.[25] Prior to the 1958 general elections, the Communists, probably fearing their own weakness, suggested a merger between the National Front parties.[26] When this suggestion went unheeded the Anti-Imperialist Front ordered its supporters to vote for the N.U.P. candidates.[27] It is therefore hard to assess the true strength of the C.P. during that period. However, it seems clear that the Communists were better equipped to face 'Abbūd's military dictatorship than any other party; his order of November 17, 1958, banning all political parties and newspapers, found the Communists with well over ten years' experience in underground activities and a well-organized clandestine press. Many Communist and trade union leaders were imprisoned during the five years of 'Abbūd's rule. However, the established leadership continued to function while in prison, where the history of the party and its political program for the future were written. It also succeeded in establishing regular contact with a new generation of leaders who organized the party activities outside.[28]

From 1961–2 onward, the C.P. spoke quite openly about the impending revolution. The June 1961 strike of 27,000 railway workers was proclaimed by the C.P. as a Communist victory, while the S.W.T.U.F. with its 200,000 members was regarded by the party as a united anti-'Abbūd force, which could be led to revolution once the C.P. was ready.[29] The same became true of the tenants, whose standard of living had constantly declined since the 1958 *coup*. At the beginning of 1964 a well-known Communist, Shaykh al-Amīn Muḥammad al-Amīn, was elected president of the Gezira Tenants' Association.[30] Toward the end of 1963, the C.P. was already planning a general political strike as a decisive step in its revolutionary action against the government.[31]

Opposition to the military regime had been mounting since October 1959. The uncrowned leader of this opposition was, until his death in October 1961, al-Ṣiddīq al-Mahdī, who in 1959 replaced Sayyid 'Abd al-Raḥmān al-Mahdī as leader of the *Anṣār*.[32] However, except for the demand of a return to constitutional democratic government, the opposition lacked a coherent political program. From the beginning of 1962 onward, the main fermentors of opposition were the Communists and, to a lesser degree, the Muslim Brothers. The trade unions, the tenants' associations, movements of women and students, and the professional associations became the pressure groups through which the Communists and the Muslim Brothers continually harassed the government.

The October 1964 Uprising and the Civilian Regime

Matters came to a head in September 1964, when the government realized that its 'strong-arm' policy in the South had failed, and invited the citizens to express their views freely and offer possible solutions to this problem. Addressing himself to this task, at a meeting in the university, Dr. Ḥasan al-Turābī, a leading Muslim Brother, stated that the problem of the South could be solved only by democratic means. Despite government attempts to reverse its previous decisions and to ban further meetings, discussions at the university continued, including far-reaching criticism of the military regime. On October 21, 1964, a student gathering at the university, having refused to disperse, was fired upon by the army, and one of the students was killed. His funeral was attended by tens of thousands of citizens and turned into a mass anti-government demonstration heralding the beginning of a civilian uprising—an outstanding exception in contemporary Middle Eastern politics. The composition of the Committee of Public Safety, which was set up on October 23 in order to seek the restoration of civilian government, was a clear victory for Communist tactics. While the large political parties such as the *Umma*, the N.U.P., and the pro-Khatmiyya People's Democratic Party (P.D.P.) had one representative each on the committee and subsequently in the caretaker government, the Communists had three members in the government and were supported by two left-wing fellow-travelers.[33] The role played by the Communists in the three months following the October uprising was out of all proportion to their real strength, as subsequent events were to prove.[34] The leaders of the N.U.P. and the *Umma* demanded immediate general elections or, failing that, a newly constituted caretaker government in which they would be represented according to their real strength.

Whether or not the part actually played by the Communists in the October 1964 uprising was as predominant as they later claimed, is immaterial. What is quite clear is that, paradoxically, they thrived under persecution. On February 18, 1965, the government resigned and the Communist heyday came to an end, since in the new government only one Communist remained. A Communist attempt to save the revolution by declaring a general strike and by rushing armed peasants from the Gezira to Khartoum failed to produce the hoped-for results and proved once again that the C.P. was weak even in its so-called strongholds: the trade unions and the tenants' associations.[35] In an interview published in *l'Humanité* on May 10, 1965, 'Abd al-Khalīq Maḥjūb admitted the shortcomings of the caretaker government which, according to him, was out of touch with the people. He emphasized the weakness of the democratic movement and of the Communists themselves, which had enabled the revisionist parties, aided by imperialism, to overthrow the revolution.

Under these circumstances, the Communist decision to participate in the May 1965 elections was probably prompted more by a desire to test their strength than by their belief that the majority of their candidates stood any real chance of being elected. The results of the elections could therefore be regarded as a relative Communist success. Out of 15 special Graduates' Constituencies,[36] Communist-supported candidates gained 11 seats in the new assembly, including the first woman M.P. ever to be elected in the Sudan.[37] According to Communist sources, their victory was even greater, as Communist-supported candidates received 73,103 votes or 17.3 percent of all the votes cast.[38] This result was mainly due, on the one hand, to the fact that the elections were boycotted by the Khatmiyya-supported P.D.P. and, on the other hand, to the prominent role attributed to the Communists in the October 1964 uprising.[39]

Countermoves against the C.P.

The reaction of the other parties to the Communist success became clear on the morrow of the elections. In an interview with the Lebanese press, al-Ṣādiq al-Mahdī (who in 1961 succeeded al-Ṣiddīq as leader of the Umma) stated that his party would refuse to cooperate with the Communists in the future. He defined the differences of opinion between the Communists and other political parties in the Sudan as embracing both foreign policy and internal affairs. His main criticism was directed against the Communist attempt to politicize the trade unions and against their attitude toward Islam.[40] The special link between politics and religion in the Sudan was, however, regarded by al-Ṣādiq as an effective barrier against Communist success.[41]

Indeed, it was religion that provided the pretext for one of the biggest anti-Communist drives which started a few months later. On November 8, 1965, the Muslim Brothers organized a mass demonstration against the C.P. and its affiliated organizations, and petitioned the government to declare Communism illegal. The immediate cause for the upheaval was a speech delivered in Omdurman by a Syrian Communist student, who declared that belief in God and the Prophet was an outdated superstition.[42] Despite denials by the Central Committee of the C.P., claiming that the Syrian student was not a member of the Communist Party, the Supreme Shari'a Council devoted a special session to a discussion of the case. It then issued a statement to the people of the Sudan, stressing the dangers of Communism to Islam and requesting a full-scale investigation of Communist propaganda and study courses in the Sudan.[43] The political leaders followed suit and both the Umma and the N.U.P. demanded a ban on Communist activities.[44] On November 15, 1965, several members of the Constituent Assembly proposed that the Assembly urge the government to outlaw the C.P. and to confiscate all its property. The motion was passed by 161 votes against 12, with nine abstentions. While the debate in the house went on, thousands demonstrated outside under anti-Communist slogans.[45] Sayyid 'Alī al-Mīrghanī, head of the Khatmiyya, took the opportunity to propose an Islamic state based on the *shari'a*, which he regarded as the only effective antidote to Communism.[46] On November 24, the Constituent Assembly passed an amendment to the constitution which outlawed any Communist or atheist propaganda in the Sudan.[47] At the second reading of the amendment (December 1965) it was further ruled that no Communists could remain members of the Assembly and that the C.P. would be henceforth dissolved and its property confiscated.[48] The government was quick to act: it confiscated the passports of the leading Communists and forbade them to engage in any political activities.[49]

The reason for the anti-Communist drive was clearly political and the anti-religious utterances of the Syrian student had only provided a convenient pretext. Al-Ṣādiq al-Mahdī's statement, delivered at a radio and television press conference shortly after the event, expressed the opinion of his fellow religio-political leaders. He stressed the two dangers confronting the Sudan: first, provincialism or, in other words, the Southern problem which could lead to secession and affect other regions such as Darfur in the West, the Nuba Mountains in Kordofan, or the Beja tribes of the Red Sea; secondly, the danger of Communism, which, as al-Ṣādiq pointed out, was rejected by the Sudanese because of "its contradiction of belief [sic] and the existence of God, its binding of Sudan sovereignty with an international creed and tie, and its dependence on the basis of a class dictatorship which would undoubtedly supply the need for the establishment of other political movements and groupings."[50] The fear was therefore not of Communism becoming a major political force but rather of its potential danger as another dividing factor within Sudanese society. Communism could utilize the problem of the South and sectarian politics in order to buttress its own prestige.

The Communists tried to fight back and on 24 December the hearing of their case against the government and the Constituent Assembly started in the Supreme Court. After endless postponements, lasting a whole year, the court finally decided that the government's action was illegal and that the C.P. had as much right to function as any other political party.[51] In the meantime, however, leading Communists had been imprisoned, the C.P. and its front organizations were disbanded, and Communists were expelled from the army and dismissed from the railways and other vital public services.[52] The government was therefore in no mood to give in, and a day after the Supreme Court gave its verdict, the Constituent Assembly decided to uphold its former decision, thereby overruling the Supreme Court.[53]

Prior to the court's ruling, in October 1966, the C.P. and its supporters had led an anti-government demonstration of some 30,000 participants through the streets of Khartoum.[54] In December the government hit back when it accused the C.P. of having been behind an abortive military *coup* led by Lieutenant Khālid Ḥusayn 'Uthmān. This provided the pretext for the arrest of 'Abd al-Khāliq Maḥjūb and several other leading Communists, although no substantial link between the two groups was ever proved.[55]

In the meantime, the Communists split into two factions. The first, whose spokesman was al-Shafī' Aḥmad al-Shaykh, president of the S.W.T.U.F., advocated the foundation of a broadly based socialist party, which would enable the C.P. to function unhampered by the new law. The second faction was for continuing underground activities within the framework of the outlawed Communist Party.[56] While at least part of the Communists was regrouping for clandestine activities, the fight between the government and the judiciary continued throughout 1967. On 18 March the Supreme Court ruled once again that the outlawing of the C.P. was illegal and that Communist deputies were entitled to keep their seats in the Constituent Assembly.[57] The government, however, reiterated its former decision, stressing once more that the Communists were not fighting for democracy but against Islam.[58] At the same time the Constituent Assembly denied the right of the Supreme Court to interfere in the interpretation of the Constitution.[59]

The constitutional crisis was tantamount to a victory for the C.P.; all the major political parties were united in their attempt to outlaw Communist activities and yet the Communists succeeded in fighting back without being isolated. The judiciary, substantial sections of the intelligentsia, the professionals, and the trade unions, as well as several tenants' organizations were fighting under the banner of democracy in order to legalize the C.P. The protracted constitutional battle, culminating in the resignation of the Chief Justice, Bābikr 'Awaḍallāh, was one of the factors leading to the government crisis in May 1967, and prompting the realignment of political forces in the Sudan during the following period.[60]

Matters came to a head with the approach of the 1968 general elections. The new election law suggested that Communists and members of other illegal organizations would not be able to fight the elections.[61] There were additional ways of keeping the Communists out, such as canceling the special Graduates' Constituencies, where the Communists had gained their seats in the previous elections. Another proviso, favored by other parties, especially the *Umma*, was to allocate more seats in the new parliament to the provinces and thus to strengthen the traditionalist and tribal elements.[62]

The merger between al-Azhari's N.U.P. and the P.D.P. in December 1967, thereby establishing the Democratic Unionist Party (D.U.P.), created a new political situation in the Sudan. For the first time since the 1953 elections, al-Azhari stood a chance of winning the elections single-handed. The new alignment reestablished the authority of the leadership of popular Islam in Sudanese politics. It merged all the pro-Khatmiyya elements into one political party and thus made it quite clear that the *Anṣār* would lose their leading role in the political sphere as long as the *Umma*, which in the summer of 1966 had split into two factions (that of al-Ṣiddīq's brother, al-Hādī al-Mahdī, and that of al-Ṣiddīq's son, al-Ṣādiq), remained divided.[63]

The Communists and their left-wing allies had in the meantime not been idle, and on January 21, 1967, the founding of the Socialist Party of the Sudan was announced in Khartoum. Its central preparatory committee comprised 60 members, representing workers, peasants, and national intellectuals. They announced their adherence to scientific socialism and stressed their respect for religion as a dominant factor in Sudanese society.[64] Nearly a year passed before the first congress of the new party took place in Khartoum, just in time for the coming elections. The party's leadership included such well-known names as Shaykh Amīn Muḥammad al-Amīn, representing the Gezira tenants, al-Shafīʿ Aḥmad al-Shaykh of the trade unions, and Amīn al-Shiblī, a prominent member of the lawyers' association.[65]

When the last general elections before the Numeiri *coup* were held in April 1968, sectarianism was as strong in the Sudan as during the pre-independence elections of 1953. Out of 218 seats in parliament, the D.U.P. won 101, and the two factions of the *Umma* 72, thus proving once again the predominance of popular Islam. The Southern parties— S.A.N.U. and the Southern Front—won 15 and 10 seats, respectively. Five M.P.s represented the Beja and Nuba tribes in the new parliament, and three the Islamic Charter Front—thus bringing the number of M.P.s representing traditionalist forces to about 200 and leaving a very small number of seats to all the others. The latter included 'Abd al-Khalīq Maḥjūb, the only representative of the Socialist Front.[66] If the Communists ever had any illusions regarding their political prospects in a democratic Sudan, these must have been shattered following the 1968 elections.

The ensuing student demonstrations in Khartoum and other towns during November 1968 were reminiscent of the atmosphere before the October 1964 *coup*. Again one of the demonstrating students was killed, and molotov cocktails were thrown at the House of Parliament. Ismā'īl al-Azharī asked the Constituent Assembly to expel 'Abd al-Khāliq Maḥjūb, accusing the Communists of trying to bring about the downfall of Muḥammad Aḥmad Maḥjūb's government.[67] According to Communist sources, in March 1968 the party's Central Committee was in fact discussing the advisability of a military *coup* and, despite 'Abd al-Khāliq Maḥjūb's opposition, the majority decided to support the Free Officers and the National Democratic Front in order to overthrow the parliamentary regime.[68] The reunification of the *Umma* Party on April 11, 1969, must have caused the Communists and their allies in the army some anxiety.[69] However, the talks aimed at a broad coalition between the D.U.P. and the united *Umma,* which started on May 1, were cut short by the Numeiri military *coup* of May 25, 1969.[70]

THE COMMUNIST PARTY AND THE NUMEIRI REGIME

The Numeiri *coup* marked a new, and perhaps crucial, phase in the history of the C.P. During the years 1964–9, and particularly after the May 1965 elections, the C.P. was but one factor—of relatively minor importance—on the Sudan political scene. It was the 1969 *coup* and the new constellation of internal forces which pushed the C.P. to the forefront of political activity and enabled it to gain influence out of all proportion to its real strength. Thus, the situation in mid-1969 resembled that of the first few months after the 1964 civilian uprising.

An analysis of Numeiri's regime from the date of his own *coup* until immediately after the so-called Communist *coup* of July 1971, reveals a consistent attempt, on Numeiri's part, to overcome two extreme factors in Northern Sudanese politics—the traditionalist forces on the one hand, and the extreme leftist forces on the other. Accordingly, the political power-struggle reached its zenith first in March 1970, when the *Anṣār* in Abā island were crushed; and next, when following the July 1971 abortive *coup* the leftist opposition was annihilated. In both cases, the Numeiri regime gained the upper hand and emerged, at least superficially and temporarily, stronger than it had been before. The first period of Numeiri's rule, until March 1970, can thus be characterized as a rather successful attempt to act in conjunction with radical, leftist elements against what he regarded as his traditionalist foes. During the following period, he was free to act against his former allies — the leftists who had served their purpose and now had to be stopped from accumulating excessive power.

It was only natural that the veteran C.P. played a leading role in this political game. From the point of view of the relationship between Numeiri's circle of close supporters and the C.P., the period between the Abā affair of March 1970 and the July 1971 abortive *coup* can be divided into three phases: March–November 1970—a continuation of the temporary alliance, though on a rather shakier basis; November 1970–February 1971—the first symptoms of an open struggle; February–July 1971—attempts on Numeiri's part to isolate the C.P. from its supporters and to destroy its influence, driving it into open resistance and finally culminating in the July 1971 abortive *coup* (or, "Revolution of Correction") in the wake of which a severe blow was dealt by Numeiri to the C.P. and its declared supporters.

The May 1969 Coup

The Numeiri *coup* of May 25, 1969, was the beginning of a temporary alliance between civilian-leftist forces and radical elements in the military who may have seen in the political confusion an opportunity to seize power. It cannot be stated decisively which of the two forces initiated the series of actions which developed into the *coup*. It is quite clear, however, that the respective positions of Numeiri as chairman of the Revolutionary Command Council (R.C.C.) and of Bābikr 'Awaḍallāh, the former Chief Justice, as Prime Minister, vice-chairman of the R.C.C., and its only civilian member, were a true reflection of the relative strength of the two partners within the coalition.

There is little doubt that Numeiri realized, from the outset, that he would have need of the support or, at least, the goodwill of the

C.P. and the leftists. There were several reasons for this: first, he needed them to counterbalance the might of conservative, traditionalist, religious, and pro-Western forces; secondly, several of the officers who were, at that stage, among Numeiri's important supporters, were themselves of leftist inclination, some of them probably members of the C.P.; thirdly, through cooperation with the C.P. Numeiri hoped to secure the support of the trade unions as well as that of the students and the intelligentsia. An additional factor, of no lesser importance, may have been Numeiri's wish to mobilize the good offices of veteran members of the C.P., whose organizational experience and skills were an important asset to the new, inexperienced regime. It might be added— with some reservation—that Numeiri found it quite convenient to collaborate with the leftist and Communist elements knowing that they were not strong enough to constitute an immediate threat to his own superiority. The ideological platform of the R.C.C. officers was expressed in terms which were conducive to a partnership with leftist elements. In the first statement issued by the new regime the Sudan was declared a Democratic Republic and the main aims of the Revolution were defined as follows: in foreign relations, support of national liberation movements against imperialism; an extension of the economic, military, and cultural ties with the Arab and socialist countries and active support of the "Palestine struggle"; internally, the main aims of the Revolution were stated to be the development of national capital, finding a solution to the Southern problem on the basis of regional autonomy in a united Sudan, and the formation of a single party which would consist of workers, peasants, soldiers, the national bourgeoisie, and the progressive intelligentsia.[71] This program, in many of its facets, was identical with the Communist political, economic, and social policy as outlined in 1966.[72]

In this context it should be noted that, firstly, in 1969 the C.P. had already been divided for a relatively long period.[73] Secondly, it is impossible to determine the attitude of its leading personalities to the new regime. However, it can be assumed with a fair amount of certainty that even at this early stage there were serious debates within the C.P. regarding the extent of its integration in the new regime. On the other hand, it is likely that, at this juncture, different shades of Communist opinion were still united in their belief that through cooperation with the new regime they could gain key positions which were unattainable by ordinary democratic procedures. An unholy alliance was thus forged between two centers of political gravity: the military regime and the leftists. This partnership comprised two hetero-geneous forces; its common denominator was negative, that is, each side regarded cooperation with the other as a means to serve and promote its own interests. The officers, however, could retain their power without Communist support while the latter were, in fact, dependent on the military's goodwill.

Taken at face value, the positions held by the C.P. immediately after the May *coup* were impressive. Out of the 10 members of the R.C.C., four were either Communists or leftists.[74] On the other hand, a careful analysis of the circumstances immediately following the May *coup* reveals the stresses and strains which were inherent even then in this partnership. When, after the *coup*, political parties were suspended, the C.P., which had already been disbanded by the previous regime, was not excepted.[75] While some of the Communist ministers in the newly formed government—like Joseph Garang—were known sup-porters of 'Abd al-Khāliq Maḥjūb, others, like Fārūq Abū 'Īsā and Mak-kāwi Muṣṭafā, were known as his rivals.[76] An additional factor adding to the tension within the partnership was, paradoxically, the pro-Com-munist image of the new regime, which provoked a series of unequivocal denials by Numeiri and other leaders. A good example in point is Numeiri's statement, immediately following his *coup*: "I reaffirm that our revolution stems from the hopes and aspirations of the people. . . . There is no chance for a Communist government . . . we want to make it quite clear that all the ministers were selected for their educational qualifica-tions and their continuous devotion to the people. Their party affiliations were not considered."[77] It is not surprising, therefore, that 'Abd al-Khāliq Maḥjūb's support for the new regime was expressed in rather ambivalent terms. In an interview with the Russian weekly *Za Rubezhom*, he said that the Communists "believe that the present government is a progressive one, and that the May 25 movement has created the best circumstances for continuing our people's struggle for realizing the tasks of the national democratic revolution. Therefore, the Com-munist Party sincerely supports the new government's policy . . . our party struggles in the new circumstances for widening the masses' democratic movement and granting the people their political rights and for solving all the pending social and economic problems."[78] On another occasion he stressed that more revolutionary violence was required in order to fulfill the task of strengthening progressive au-thority![79]

June 1969–November 1970: A Realignment of Forces

The tension within the forces which formed the new political framework of the Sudan was further heightened by the fact that neither the military nor the civilian participants in the power-game were united in their respective tactics. It is reasonable to assume that even within the close circle of Numeiri's supporters there were conflicting attitudes: on the one hand, advocation to use the backing of the C.P. and other leftists for the consolidation of the regime; and on the other, an apprehension lest the C.P. might attempt to take over key positions in the administration. As stated above, the C.P. itself was also divided into two factions. One, headed by 'Abd al-Khāliq Maḥjūb, wished to preserve its identity as a party and retain an ideological as well as a political independence. While the other group, headed by Aḥmad Sulaymān and Mu'āwiyah Ibrāhīm, tried to integrate in the administration so as to use it as a launching pad for further consolidation of Communist power within the state.[80] This complex struggle was revealed by several events in the period between June 1969 and November 1970.

1) On June 19, 1969, the R.C.C. announced several new appointments as well as a reshuffle of the government. Portfolios which had not been occupied since the May *coup* were now filled and a new Ministry for Southern Affairs was added. (This portfolio was given to Joseph Garang—a Communist from the South and one of Maḥjūb's supporters.)[81] In fact, the changes amounted to a widening of the regime's political base. The new members of the government were, with the exception of Garang, mainly moderates of the right or center.

2) Another important stage was reached in October 1969 and was preceded by several significant events. A statement attributed to Bābikr 'Awaḍallāh, during his visit to East Germany, in which he asserted that the Sudanese revolution could not progress without the Sudanese Communists,[82] aroused strong feelings and reactions in the Sudan. Immediately on his return to Khartoum a joint session of the government and the R.C.C. was held in order to iron out the differences.[83] Those Sudanese leaders who so firmly reacted to 'Awaḍallāh's statement were probably motivated or, at least, encouraged by several anti-Communist demonstrations which had taken place in 'Aṭbara and Khartoum in July and October, respectively.[84] On October 28 another reshuffle in the government took place, probably prompted

by the above-mentioned events. Numeiri became Prime Minister instead of 'Awaḍallāh, who became deputy P.M. and Minister of Justice, while also retaining his Foreign Ministry portfolio. Important additions to the government were Aḥmad Sulaymān as Minister of Economics and Foreign Commerce; and Hāshim al-'Aṭā' as Minister of Animal Resources.[85] A more detailed study of the allocation of portfolios in the new government shows a relative neutralization of Bābikr 'Awaḍallāh, a further strengthening of the hold of the military over the government, and a tipping of the balance in favor of the non-Communist members of the R.C.C. and the government. A significant move in this direction—as future events were to prove—was the appointment of R.C.C. member Khālid Ḥasan 'Abbās as Minister of Defense. Nevertheless, a thorough analysis of the political inclinations of the higher echelons of power at this stage, including the R.C.C. and the government, leads to the conclusion that Numeiri's circle, though fully aware of Communist tactics, estimated at the time that the main potential threat to its power was posed by the traditionalist, and not by the leftist, forces.

3) The period between October 1969 and November 1970 was marked by a growing tension between Maḥjūb's faction of the C.P. and Numeiri's circle. This friction was a natural outcome of the basic factors mentioned above, but was nourished by substantial differences regarding both internal and external policies. For obvious reasons, Maḥjūb's faction strongly objected to the Sudan's joining the proposed Federation with the United Arab Republic (U.A.R.) and Libya. It also opposed the planned formation of a Sudanese Socialist Union, that was announced by Numeiri in January 1970.[86] These differences reached a climax in April 1970 with the arrest of Maḥjūb and his banishment (on the same plane as al-Ṣādiq al-Mahdī . . .) to the U.A.R. It is quite certain that the significance of this step, taken only a few weeks after the crushing of the Anṣār, could not have escaped political observers within and without the Sudan.[87] The deportation of Maḥjūb strengthened, to some extent, the faction of Aḥmad Sulaymān and Mu'āwiyah Ibrāhīm, who remained within the government. However, it did not ease the tension between Numeiri's circle and the C.P.

Retrospectively, a string of events can be reconstructed which exemplify the realignment of forces after the blow dealt to the traditionalists in March 1970: the delay in the publication of the National Charter[88]; the Sudanization—in June—of several foreign firms; at the beginning of July—an alleged attempt at a coup, reportedly backed by Maḥjūb[89]; the government reshuffle on July 21, 1970[90]; and finally the return of Maḥjūb to the Sudan in the same month. In August the C.P. held a congress at which the future of the relations between the party and the regime was debated. The decision not to dissolve the C.P. was in fact a victory for Maḥjūb's faction.[91] There could be little doubt, therefore, that at least one of the main tasks of the Russian delegation headed by Politbureau member Poliansky, which visited the Sudan in October, was to try to mediate or at least ease the tension between the C.P. and the regime,[92] before the relations between them deteriorated to a point of no return.

November 1970–July 1971: From Tension to Struggle

The next month—November 1970—became a crucial one in the relations between the Numeiri regime and the C.P. On 16 November, three members of the R.C.C., who later on became the main actors in the July 1971 abortive *coup*, were ousted: Lt. Col. Bābikr al-Nūr 'Uthmān, Maj. Hāshim al-'Aṭā', and Maj. Fārūq 'Uthmān Ḥamdallāh.[93] Their portfolios in the cabinet were taken by Numeiri (Planning) and by two other officers of the R.C.C. Consequently, all the remaining members of the R.C.C. were now also ministers. In addition, a purge was carried out in the army and at the same time members of the Central Committee of the C.P. were arrested—including 'Abd al-Khāliq Maḥjūb, who had been under house arrest since his return from the U.A.R. in July.[94] Explaining the reasons for the dismissal of the three R.C.C. members, Numeiri stated that they had cooperated with elements which had pretensions of being progressive but in fact stood in the way of the revolution and tried to weaken it.[95] On a later occasion he said that "They did not adhere to one collective decision in the R.C.C. but were operating outside the framework of the R.C.C. and fighting against the council's decisions. . . . I regret to say that these ideas were inspired and schemed by 'Abd al-Khāliq Maḥjūb . . . who won over them [sic], indoctrinated them with his subversive ideas, and fed them his intentions. The first and last aim was to attain power."[96]

Numeiri's action was probably prompted and made possible by a combination of three important factors: the reassurance he gained from the relatively long period of time which had lapsed since the Abā affair in March 1970, during which the *Anṣar* had shown no sign of recovery from the blow dealt to them; the growing pressure of radical, though not necessarily pro-Communist, circles within the R.C.C. (there is strong reason to believe that Khālid Ḥasan 'Abbās was a central figure within these circles); also, it is quite possible that in the aftermath of President Nasser's death Numeiri assumed that the U.A.R. and, in particular, Libya would support him, should an internal struggle ensue.

The dismissal of the three R.C.C. members led to a series of protests, in particular among students, and clashes at the University of Cairo branch in Khartoum between supporters of the C.P. and their opponents were reported.[97]

At the beginning of December 1970 the Lebanese newspaper *al-Kifāḥ* reported that the Sudanese C.P. had issued, on November 16, a statement in Khartoum calling for the reinstatement of the three members of the R.C.C. and of the "Free Officers" who had been discharged from military service during the anti-leftist purge. They also demanded the release of 'Abd al-Khāliq Maḥjūb.[98]

It was only in February, however, that the mounting tension became a publicly declared struggle. On February 12, Numeiri made clear his intentions to fight and destroy the C.P. Listing the "crimes" of the Communists he said that:

They regard anyone outside the party as unworthy of responsibility and a reactionary . . . to attain power they would trample upon all our people's values and morals, which are the morals of free citizens . . . they oppose any noble cause so long as it was not initiated by them. For instance, they opposed government programs on education and drought and also the Tripoli state charter . . . they sabotaged government work by turning trade unions against government action in ministries, departments, and establishments . . . they exercised personality cults just like the reactionaries . . . they have been traitorous at this critical stage, when our people are fighting imperialism, by printing intriguing, venomous, false, and rancorous statements and dropping these outside embassies so the latter can convey the contents to their countries. They also send hostile reports and leaflets to some embassies and governments abroad, giving the impression that the situation in the Sudan is disturbed and that these governments should freeze all interest and agreements with Sudan. . . ."

He added that there was "no room for the Communists in the Sudanese revolution" and warned: "I repeat today that the revolution is for all the masses of people. Anyone who opposes it will be immediately isolated . . . it is your responsibility to destroy anyone who claims that there is a Sudanese Communist Party."[99] Indeed, shortly after his February speech, Numeiri took a series of steps, the main aim of which was to uproot the C.P. from its strongholds.[100]

At this stage, attempts at mediation were made, apparently both by President Sadat[101] and by a Soviet delegation (which arrived in Khartoum on March 24),[102] but to no avail. Toward the end of March, there were again purges of high-ranking officials in the Ministry of Interior, in the security services, and in the military.[103]

Numeiri's speech of April 20, a short while after his return from the Cairo talks on the Federation,[104] signaled yet another wave of attacks on Communists. He made it clear that the Sudan was not at present joining the Federation, the formation of which had been announced on April 17. In the Sudan, however, the preparations for the establishment of a Sudanese Socialist Union were under way,[105] and these certainly added fuel to the fire. Any doubts regarding the intentions of the Sudanese regime to follow the Egyptian pattern of political organization were removed by the decisions, in April and May, to dissolve the Youth, Women's and Students' Unions[106]—all three of them established strongholds of the C.P. On top of these measures came Numeiri's speech, on the second anniversary of the 1969 revolution, in which he emphasized, *inter alia,* the need for national unity and a plan to change the structure of the trade unions through general elections.[107] Now it became clear that Numeiri was following a well-planned strategy for the gradual elimination of the C.P.'s influence even in its traditional strongholds.

The July Abortive Coup and Its Aftermath

On June 29 'Abd al-Khāliq Maḥjūb escaped from prison.[108] This escape marked the beginning of a series of events which would make July 1971 a critical month both for Numeiri's regime and the C.P. At this point two mutually exclusive forces collided. The Numeiri circle, which at first had tried to guard itself against Communist penetration, was now fighting aggressively against the leftists and the C.P., while the latter attempted to regain their lost positions and, hopefully, to strengthen them. This head-on collision led, in July, to what might be termed a Communist-inspired "counter revolution."[109]

The bloodless, but abortive *coup* took place on July 19, and Decree No. 1 declared the Sudan an independent democratic republic.[110] The first act of the new regime was the abrogation of the laws promulgated by Numeiri's regime and the dissolution of the organizations it had established.[111] The program of the new regime included the establishment of a "democratic political system" based on mass participation, in which all the organizations of the people would be represented; the granting of regional autonomy to the South; an "industrial and agricultural revolution" which would "pursue a noncapital path for development, which approaches the horizon of socialism"; an agrarian reform; support of the Palestinian cause and of national liberation movements; and a struggle against colonialism and neocolonialism together with the Third World and the friendly socialist countries headed by the U.S.S.R.[112]

The leaders of the *coup* were, at least ostensibly, the three members of the May 1969 R.C.C. who had been deposed in November 1970—Hāshim al-'Aṭā', Bābikr al-Nūr 'Uthmān, and Fārūq 'Uthmān Ḥamdallāh. All three were, at that time, identified by Western observers as Communists.[113] On their orders Numeiri and his close supporters, including two Communists—Fārūq Abū 'Īsā and Mu'āwiyah Ibrāhīm—were imprisoned.[114] The arrest proved to be a fatal tactical mistake of the new revolutionaries since, on July 22, a successful "counter-counter-*coup*" was launched by Numeiri.[115]

The quick recovery of Numeiri's supporters as well as the lack of serious resistance to the extreme measures he took after he had regained power are in themselves ample proof of the C.P.'s lack of deep roots and wide support in the Sudan. In contrast with the leniency which the leaders of the so-called Communist *coup* had shown to their opponents, Numeiri did not hesitate to execute his prisoners—the three officers who had carried out the July *coup,* and also 'Abd al-Khāliq Maḥjūb, al-Shāfī' Aḥmad al-Shaykh, and Joseph Garang.[116]

Thus came to an end a chapter in the recent history of the Sudanese C.P. The party lost the cream of its active leadership and, despite subsequent attempts at reorganization,[117] the present position of the C.P. is a far cry from its former strength. Muḥammad Ḥasanayn Haykal, in his *al-Ahrām* weekly article, provides a very interesting *post mortem* analysis of the Sudanese C.P. (B.B.C. translation):

. . . .Disregarding the tales, stories, adventures, plots, and so forth, what has happened in Sudan can be summed up— or more exactly, deduced—as follows: (1) The Sudanese Communist Party, which was one of the best and cleanest Arab Communist parties, slipped terribly in its analysis and action. (2) This in turn has caused repercussions, the effects of which must be contained by every means. We begin with (1). In its analysis, the party failed to realize that the Communist parties in the developing states, particularly in the Arab world, cannot assume the principal role of leading the popular struggle for several considerations. Among these considerations is the fact that the Communist organizations, because of the circumstances of their growth and work in the region and because of the values and convictions at the root of this region, cannot lead the great majority of the masses. At best they could lead small groups and in the simplest form—and I am not saying at worst—they could represent the leadership of a group of intellectuals influenced by world currents which are definitely powerful but do not automatically fit into the national (Arabic: wataniyah) reality to which they bring these currents. Accordingly, their ideologies might become one of the fertility elements in the national (Arabic: wataniyah) experiment but they surely cannot be the seed or the tree itself. As I have said, through interaction it could become a fertility element with a role and a vital effect.

Another consideration is that the Sudanese Communist Party is unable to comprehend that in developing societies in general social polarization cannot be so sharp as to make possible domination by any class. A party, any party, is ultimately nothing but an organized political vanguard of a class. When the social structure of any country is weak it is difficult to think that a leading dominant political organization can emerge. Sudan, as any other developing country, has not reached the degree of development which would make it possible for a strong working class to emerge and for a workers' party—even hypothetically—to lead it, call for the dictatorship of this class, impose this dictatorship even by force on the other classes, and say that regardless of numerous considerations introduced by the modern world, dictatorship of the majority is democracy. Accordingly, in view of Sudan's position, the Marxist Left had no right to hope to consider itself more than a part of the forces of the national (Arabic: *watani*) alliance. . . .

. . . So much for the analysis error. Now for the action error. The error in action after the error in the analysis led the Sudanese Communist Party to something like a complete Greek tragedy. There has been a split in the Party and its Central Committee. Some cooperated with the patriotic authority in Sudan under the leadership of Ja'far al-Numeiri on the basis that this was the only possible arrangement leading to social development historically, while others erred in their analysis and by hot emotions in Khartoum's atmosphere antagonized the patriotic authority in Sudan led by Ja'far al-Numeiri. It would have been sufficient if they had disagreed, if they wished, with the authority but they couldn't afford to antagonize it. The Party then turned to strange alliances including elements in contact with the Iraqi Ba'th Party which is a suspect Party all round. . . .

The great disaster came when the Sudanese Communist Party supported and participated in the 19th July *coup* led by Maj. Hāshim al-'Aṭā'. It was baffling that a Communist Party should participate in a *coup* with tanks, armored cars and machine-guns which definitely cannot possibly be called a democratic expression of the interests of the toiling classes, especially if directed against a patriotic authority. Communist parties in particular are absolutely against military *coups*. They have an opinion on military *coups* which sometimes seems rigid and overlooks the special circumstances of the developing world. They believe that the army is by nature a means of oppression in the hands of the ruling class, and that it or any vanguard in it cannot possibly play a revolutionary role in the social transformation. . . .

. . .The *coup* failed. Nevertheless, the complications of this situation and its effect on the Arab situation in general continue. The pits created by the same mistakes committed by the Sudanese Communist Party are still open. No one else should fall into them not even by reacting which is human, natural, and legitimate. . . .[118]

CONCLUSION

In the 25 years which have elapsed between the foundation of the C.P. in 1946 and the anti-Numeiri *coup* in July 1971, the C.P. of the Sudan has emerged as one of the strongest and best-organized Communist parties in the Arab world. To any observer, aware of the socio-economic structure of the Sudan and of its religio-sectarian policies, this Communist achievement might seem contradictory to its socio-political setting. However, a more careful examination of the various strata of society from which the Communists derived their support will disclose that the very nature of this society and its politics were a major reason for Communist success.

The first and most natural ally of the emerging C.P. was the Sudanese intelligentsia. This is probably true of certain sections of the intelligentsia wherever Communism thrives, but in the case of the Sudan the impact of Communism on the relatively small and weak educated sector was even stronger due to the sectarian nature of Sudanese politics. During the inter-war period, the young Sudanese intelligentsia had made several attempts to assert itself as an independent political force. These attempts, culminating in the foundation of the Graduates' General Congress in 1938, had failed due to the predominance of the religio-political sects, namely the *Anṣār* and the Khatmiyya, in Sudanese society and politics. The patronage of these sects was sought by every new political grouping, including the young intelligentsia, due to the latter's inherent weakness. Therefore the Communists and the Muslim Brothers, both of whom founded their parties in 1946, seemed the only available escape from sectarianism. The Muslim Brothers provided the answer to those of the educated class who regarded Islam as the mainstay of Sudanese, as well as of any other Arab, society, but saw in its sectarian manifestation a corruption of the true religion. The Communists attracted those who had either broken away from religion altogether, regarded Islam as a religious framework which should be devoid of any political expression, or were dissatisfied with the performance of the administration.[119] Proof of Communist strength within this sector may be seen in the 1965 general elections, when out of the 15 special Graduates' Constituencies the Communists won 11 seats and the Muslim Brothers two, while of the major political parties, the N.U.P. gained only three seats.

Another stratum of Sudanese society which proved conducive

to Communist influence, though within certain limits, was the working class and especially its trade unions. 'Aṭbarā, the center of the Sudan's railways, provided excellent openings for Communist penetration. The very beginnings of Communism in the Sudan in the 1920s can be traced to European railway officials at 'Aṭbarā. Later, when the trade union of the railway workers was founded, it had strong links with the international labor movement and regarded its struggle with the British management for improved working conditions as part and parcel of the Sudanese struggle for independence. There were, however, certain limits to Communist influence within the trade unions even at their center in 'Aṭbarā. While many of the trade union leaders became full-fledged Communists, the rank and file backed Communist policies mainly in matters regarding their own welfare but were not attracted by Communist ideology. Also, they shirked from supporting Communist-sponsored strikes when these appeared to be moving into the sphere of party politics. Thus the Communist attempt, in February 1965, to topple the sectarian government by declaring a general strike, failed to gain the general support of the rank-and-file trade unionists and ended in a fiasco.

Communist infiltration into the tenants' organizations, especially in the Gezira, was faced with even greater hazards. Peasants are generally regarded as one of the most conservative sectors of society. The Sudanese Gezira was an exception to this rule as the traditional tribal setup had been undermined by the Gezira development project which had created a new form of relationship between the cotton growers and the Sudan Plantation Syndicate (since 1950 the Gezira was managed by the Gezira Board, on behalf of the Sudan government). Hence relations between tenants and employers tended to create frictions not dissimilar to those in industry or public services. The C.P. was able to benefit from this state of affairs when in the early 1950s it became one of the sponsors of cotton growers' associations in the Gezira, the Nuba Mountains, and elsewhere. The C.P. utilized the real and imaginary economic grievances of the cultivators in order to gain their support for the wider issues of anti-imperialism and Sudanese independence. Again, during the 'Abbūd regime, and especially toward its end, the Communists manipulated the tenants' dissatisfaction with government economic policies, and succeeded in getting a Communist nominee elected as president of the tenants' association. However, the cotton growers were interested in their own welfare and not in party politics. As "gentlemen farmers," dependent on hired agricultural labor, they were more akin in their outlook to the *Umma* Party than to Communist ideology. Their support of Communist candidates and policies was thus a marriage of convenience to be dissolved once the situation changed. The failure of the Communist-sponsored March 1965 general strike, when the tenants continued to cultivate the land despite their president's support of the strike, provides adequate proof of the inherent Communist weakness, outside the relatively small circle of its true members and adherents.

Since 1965 the Communists tried to gain a foothold within the army and especially within the officers' corps. This was due to the realization that the C.P. could not hope to assert itself and become an influential political factor within the factional framework of a democratic Sudan. Their alliance with Numeiri throughout his struggle with the *Anṣār* (until March 1970) was largely responsible for the misleading impression that the 1969 *coup* was inspired by the C.P. When Numeiri turned against his Communist allies, they did not shirk from supporting army officers, known as Communist sympathizers, who attempted a *coup d'état* against Numeiri.

Communist success in the Sudan may also be ascribed to a very able leadership. One of the most prestigious of African and Middle Eastern Communist leaders, 'Abd al-Khāliq Maḥjūb, and his colleagues, were less doctrinaire in their policies than most of the leading Communists in other Arab countries. This enabled the Sudanese C.P. to gain support in the trade unions, the tenants' associations, and in the military, despite the fact that Communist ideology remained alien to many of their sympathizers. Even more revealing is their flexible attitude toward Islam, based on their awareness of its paramount position in the Sudan. In many other Muslim countries Communist leaders were either openly hostile to religion or tried to ignore it. The Central Committee of the Sudanese C.P. opened its meetings with prayers and readings from the Quran. Praying carpets were spread out in the party's headquarters, to enable members and visitors to say their prayers at the prescribed times. Organizational efficiency and political flexibility characterized Communist branches throughout the Sudan and thus made possible Communist domination of several front organizations.

Flexibility bordering on opportunism also had its disadvantages. At times of crisis the C.P. could rely only on the support of its full-fledged members, while the rank-and-file wavered in their loyalties, more often than not preferring old loyalties to new ones, and deserted the C.P. when its policies clashed with the line adopted by traditional Islamic leadership. Furthermore, flexibility with regard to fellow-travelers and would-be supporters was in many cases overshadowed by the rather rigid attitude of the party's leadership toward other political parties or the ruling power. In recent years this was clearly demonstrated during both the civilian regime from 1964–9 and after the Numeiri *coup*, when the C.P.'s leadership was divided on the question of cooperation with other political forces, a division which in 1970 caused a final split between a group which tried to cooperate with the Numeiri regime and 'Abd al-Khāliq Mahjūb's faction.

One of the crucial questions relating to the C.P. has never been answered properly: what was its real strength? The difficulty of assessing the numerical strength of the C.P. has been noted above. Members of clandestine organizations do not tend to proclaim their affiliation and prefer to be identified as members of trade unions, professional associations, and the like. Communist strength should therefore not be judged according to numbers but rather by taking into account the quality of its leaders and members, and by its impact on Sudanese politics. It has been noted that the Communists flourished under persecution and were regarded by observers as a dominant factor in any uprising and many *coups* that were attempted or took place in the Sudan from 1964 onward. The reasons for this misconception lie in the inherent weakness of the other political parties on the one hand, and in Communist skill at organizing clandestine activities on the other. Moreover, the Communists, more than any other political party in the Sudan, were quite willing to back the use of force (not necessarily their own) as a means to achieve their end, as they had little to lose in the eventuality of failure but stood to gain in the case of success. The real part played by the C.P., as such, in the 1964 civilian uprising and in the military *coups* of 1969 and 1971 was, in fact, rather modest, especially when compared to the predominant role ascribed to it.

Finally, the question may be asked whether the C.P. has been crushed in the wake of the abortive July 1971 *coup*, when it lost its leadership and when many of its first-rank members were put behind bars. To attempt a clear-cut answer would be presumptuous. However, certain alternatives may be suggested. Firstly, the Communist faction which collaborated with Numeiri and his Socialist Union may emerge as a new center of Communist activity. Secondly, the surviving members of Maḥjūb's faction, many of whom had successfully masked their Communist affiliation from the outset, may reestablish their party as an illegal organization and even attract pro-Communist or dissatisfied "progressive" elements which have become disillusioned with the Numeiri regime. Whatever the case, it would be unwise and premature to regard the present chapter in the history of the Sudanese C.P. as an epilogue.

NOTES

1 The following is based primarily on: *Hearings before the Subcommittee on National Security and International Operations of the Committee on Government Operations,* U.S. Senate, First Session, pt. 4, with Bernard Lewis (Washington 1971), and W.Z. Laqueur, *The Struggle for the Middle East* (London 1969).

2 Egypt No. 2 (1947) C.M.D. 7179, *Papers regarding the Negotiations for a Revision of the Anglo-Egyptian Treaty of 1936.*

3 *Pravda,* 17 November, 1960.

4 *New China News Agency,* 28 January, 1964—B.B.C., Summary of World Broadcasts: The Middle East and Africa, 29 January, 1964.

5 See A. Sylvester, "Muhammad Versus Lenin in Revolutionary Sudan," *New Middle East,* 34, July 1971, pp. 26–8.

6 For details see G. Warburg, "Religious Policy in the Northern Sudan: 'Ulamā' and Ṣūfism 1899–1918," *Asian and African Studies,* Vol. 7, 1971.

7 See G. Warburg, "Popular Islam and Tribal Leadership in Sudanese Society," Van-Leer Colloquium on Arab Society, June 1971 (in Hebrew, mimeographed, to be published). See also P. K. Bechtold, "Renewed Intervention by the Military in Sudanese Politics," paper prepared for the Annual Meeting of M.E.S.A., Toronto, Canada, 14–15 November, 1968 (mimeographed).

8 For details see P. M. Holt, *Holy Families and Islam in the Sudan,* Princeton Near East Papers, No. 4 (Princeton 1967); J. S. Trimingham, *Islam in the Sudan* (London 1949).

9 For details see p. 342ff.

10 It should be noted that the majority of Sudanese Communists and left-wingers have a non-Mahdist, mainly Khatmiyya, background. The explanation to this lies partly in the fact that the Khatmiyya's followers are concentrated mainly in the Northern and Eastern Sudan and especially among the more sophisticated urban population. See Muddathir 'Abd al-Raḥīm, *Imperialism and Nationalism in the Sudan* (London 1969), pp. 133–4.

11 See Jaafar Muhammad Ali Bakheit, "Communist Activities in the Middle East between 1918–1927 with Special Reference to Egypt and the Sudan," African Studies Seminar Paper No. 3, University of Khartoum, October 1968 (mimeographed). It is interesting to note that according to British intelligence sources, Communist activities in the Sudan, as elsewhere

in the Middle East, were directed at that time from the Soviet Embassy in Jidda. On later developments see W. Z. Laqueur, *Communism and Nationalism in the Middle East* (London 1956), pp. 63–9.

[12] See *Lamḥāt min ta'rīkh al-ḥizb al-shuyū'ī al-sūdānī* (Dār al-fikr al-ishtirākī 1960), pp. 24–5. This chronicle, according to the introduction, was written in 1959–60 by 'Abd al-Khāliq Maḥjūb, while in prison.

[13] *Ibid.*, pp. 26–7.

[14] *Ibid.*, pp. 27–9.

[15] *Ibid.*, pp. 31–2.

[16] *Ibid.*, pp. 40–1.

[17] *Ibid.*, pp. 55–7.

[18] Saad Ed Din Fawzi, *The Labour Movement in the Sudan 1946–1955* (London 1957), pp. 36–7.

[19] *Ibid.*, pp. 67–70.

[20] *Ibid.*, pp. 113–5.

[21] *Ibid.*; see also *Allies for Freedom, Report of the Second Conference of Communist and Workers' Parties within the Sphere of British Imperialism,* Caxton Hall (London 1954), pp. 107–8.

[22] *Ibid.*, p.108.

[23] Fawzi, p. 116. The Communists ascribed the failure of this strike to the internal strife within the C.P.

[24] Fawzi, p. 118. The strong influence of the Khatmiyya was probably a contributing factor to the failure of the strike.

[25] *Al-Sūdān al-Jadīd*, 26 January, 1957.

[26] *Ibid.*, 15 October, 1957.

[27] *Weekly Review* (Khartoum), 8 February, 1958.

[28] *Lamaḥāt*, pp. 3–4.

[29] A. Muṣṭafā, "Al-ḥizb al-shuyū'ī al-sūdānī yunāḍil fī sabīl istiqlāl wa-dimuqrāṭiyyat bilādihi," *al-Waqt*, August 1962.

[30] K. D. D. Henderson, *Sudan Republic* (London 1965), p.149.

[31] *Al-Waqt*, July 1963.

[32] For details see Henderson, pp. 129–51; I. Rabinovich, "Sudan Akhulat Ha-Nigudim," *Ma'arachot* 171, December 1965, pp. 13–18; T. E. Nyquist, "The Sudan: Prelude to Elections," *M.E.J.*, 19, 1965, pp. 263–72; Y. F. Hasan, "The Sudanese Revolution of October 1964," *Journal of Modern African Studies,* 5, 1967, pp. 491–509.

[33] Henderson, pp. 205–7; the three were Aḥmad Sulaymān, al-Shafī' Aḥmad al-Shaykh and Aḥmad al-Sayyid Ḥamad. According to Communist sources, only the first of these was a Communist, while the others belonged to the "democratic forces." See S. R. Smirnov, *A History of Africa 1918–1967* (Moscow 1968), p. 173.

[34] There is little reliable information regarding Communist members either

in 1964 or since then. The C.P.'s opponents claimed in 1964 that there were no more than 700 party members (Henderson, p. 206); *al-Jumhūriyya*, 2 November, 1964, stated that there were not less than 10,000 members at the time; the anti-Maḥjūb Communist faction claimed that the C.P. reached the climax of its strength in 1964–5 and has been on the decline ever since. At that time it had about 100 members at each of its two major branches: Omdurman and Khartoum University (*al-Nahār*, 1 April, 1971). The U.S. Dept. of State, Bureau of Intelligence and Research, in its *World Strength of the Communist Party Organizations*, 23rd Annual Report, 1971, p. 187, estimated the C.P. membership as "5,000–10,000 active members and several thousand sympathizers among professional groups, students, and railway workers."

[35] Smirnov, pp. 174–5. He claims that the Communist-attempted general strike was blocked by the police and the army. According to Henderson, p. 216, the strike failed as it was denounced by the railway and motor transport unions for political reasons while the Gezira cotton growers refused to be involved. The negative attitude of the Khatmiyya leaders to Communist tactics may also explain their failure, especially among the railway workers.

[36] These were first established in the 1953 elections in order to provide for greater representation of the intelligentsia.

[37] Henderson, p. 225.

[38] Ḥasan 'Abdallah, "Ma'rakat al-dimuqrāṭiyya lā tazāl mustamirra," *al-Waqt*, 1966.

[39] *Al-Anwār*, 4 December, 1964. In an article on the forthcoming elections in the Sudan, the paper's correspondent there pointed out that public opinion identified the anti-military *coup* with the C.P. and hence its large following.

[40] *Ibid.*, 15 May, 1965; *al-Nahār*, 16 May, 1965.

[41] *Al-Nahār*, 12 May, 1965.

[42] *Al-Ḥayāt*, 13 November, 1965.

[43] R. Omdurman, 14 November, 1965 — B.B.C., 16 November, 1965.

[44] *Al-Jumhūriyya*, 14 November, 1965.

[45] *Al-Ahrām*, 16 November, 1965.

[46] R. Omdurman, 21 November, 1965—B.B.C., 23 November, 1965.

[47] *Ibid.*, 22 November, 1965—B.B.C., 24 November, 1965.

[48] *Ibid.*, 8 December, 1965—B.B.C., 11 December, 1965.

[49] *Al-Akhbār*, 13 December, 1965; *al-Ḥayāt*, 15 December, 1965.

[50] R. Omdurman, 17 December, 1965—B.B.C., 20 December, 1965.

[51] The case was first brought to the court on December 23 (*al-Thawra*, 24 December, 1965). On December 29 the hearing was postponed to January 5, 1966 (*al-Ahrām*, 30 December, 1965); a decision was finally reached on

December 22, 1966 (*al-Ahrām,* 23 December, 1966). The government, however, refused to yield despite a warning by the Supreme Court that the judges would resign (*al-Akhbār,* 3 January, 1967).

52 *Al-Anwār,* 19 January, 1966; *al-Akhbār,* 1, 10 June, 1966.

53 *Falasṭin,* 24 December, 1966.

54 *Le Monde,* 4 October, 1966.

55 *The Morning News,* 10 January, 1967; *Le Monde,* 30 December, 1966.

56 *Rūz al-Yūsuf,* 22 August, 1966; *al-Aḥrār,* 17 December, 1966. According to the anti-Maḥjūb faction, Maḥjūb himself advocated the liquidation of the C.P. and the setting up of a socialist union such as existed in Egypt and Algeria. They further accused him of plotting to form a coalition with al-Ṣādiq al-Mahdī, the Muslim Brothers, and Deng's faction of S.A.N.U. (*al-Nahār,* 29 March, 1971).

57 *Al-Akhbār,* 10 March, 1967.

58 *Al-Dustūr,* 7 April, 1967.

59 *Al-Ahrām,* 21 April, 1967.

60 One of the best articles describing the situation is by Ahmad Ḥamrūsh in *Rūz al-Yūsuf,* 1 May, 1967. See also *al-Ahrām,* 19 May, 1967.

61 *Al-Ḥayāt,* 4 October, 1967.

62 *Rūz al-Yūsuf,* 4 December, 1967.

63 *Ibid.,* 15 January, 1968.

64 *Al-Akhbār,* 22 January, 1967. According to *Rūz al-Yūsuf,* 13 February, 1967, the Communists refused to join the new party. Apparently only one faction of the Communists joined it. See *al-Muṣawwar,* 10 March, 1967; see also Abdel A. El-Ghannam, "Die Kommunistische Partei im Sudan," *Afrika Heute,* 15 June, 1967.

65 *Rūz al-Yūsuf,* 8 January, 1968.

66 *Al-Ḥayāt, Le Monde,* 8 May, 1968.

67 *Al-Safā',* 5 December, 1968; *al-Ḥayāt,* 26 December, 1968. Maḥjūb, whose marriage without the permission of the party had generated a crisis within the C.P., was at the time on a tour of Eastern Europe (*al-Ḥayāt,* 11 October, 1968).

68 *Al-Nahār,* 26 March 1971; although *al-Nahār* quotes the anti-Maḥjūb faction of the C.P., there could be little doubt as to the validity of its report.

69 *Rūz al-Yūsuf,* 11 April, 1969.

70 *Middle East News Agency (M.E.N.A.),* 30 April, 1969—*Daily Report (D.R.),* 1 May, 1969; *al-Ḥayāt,* 26 May, 1969.

71 R. Omdurman, 25 May, 1969—*D.R.,* 26 May, 1969.

72 *Cf.,* "Barnāmij al-ḥizb al-shuyū'ī al-sūdānī," *al-Waqt,* 1966, pp. 1–9.

73 See "The Struggle in the Sudanese Communist Party" (Translation of a series of articles by Fu'ād Maṭar in *al-Nahār,* 26–31 March, 1–3 April, 1971), *Translations on Near East, No. 647,* Joint Publications Research

Service No. 53946, 31 August, 1971, U.S. Dept. of Commerce. See also Fu'ād Maṭar, *Al-Ḥizb al-shuyū'ī al-sūdānī naharūhu am intaḥara?* (Beirut, [1971]).

74 Among them Hāshim Muḥammad al-'Aṭā', Fārūq 'Uthmān Ḥamdallāh, Bābikr al-Nūr 'Uthmān, and Bābikr 'Awaḍallāh. Similarly, at least eight out of the 23 cabinet ministers were either Communists or leftists. Among these—Fārūq Abū 'Īsā, Joseph Garang, al-Amīn al-Shiblī, and Makkāwī Muṣṭafā. See *Africa Confidential*, 20 June, 1969; P. Rondot, "L'Expérience politique du Soudan," *Revue de Défense National*, June, 1969, p. 1208. Immediately after the *coup*, a purge took place in the military forces and new officers were appointed to key positions. See R. Omdurman, 25 May, 1969—*D.R.*, 26 May, 1969; *al-Ḥayāt*, 26 May, 1969.

75 R. Omdurman, 25 May, 1969—*D.R.*, 26 May, 1969.

76 *Observer*, 1 June, 1969; *Africa Confidential*, 15 January, 1971.

77 R. Omdurman, 31 May, 1969—*D.R.*, 2 June, 1969. See also Bābikr 'Awaḍallah's interview in *al-Nahār*, 21 June, 1969, and *al-Ṣayyad*, 8 August, 1969.

78 R. Moscow in Arabic, 11 August, 1969—*D.R.* 13 August, 1969.

79 *Al-Sūdān al-Jadīd*, 3 August, 1969.

80 See *al-Nahār*, 26 March, 1971; *al-Ḥayāt*, 4 May, 1971.

81 *M.E.N.A.*, 19 June, 1969—*Itim Mizrah News Agency Bulletin (I.M.B.)*, 19 June, 1969; *al-Ḥayāt*, 20 June, 1969.

82 R. Kol Yisrael in Arabic, 9 October, 1969—B.B.C., 11 October, 1969; *M.E.N.A.*, 11 October, 1969—*I.M.B.*, 11 October, 1969; *al-Ḥayāt*, 13 October, 1969; *New York Times*, 29 October, 1969.

83 *M.E.N.A.*, 11 October, 1969—*I.M.B.*, 11 October, 1969; *al-Ahrām*, 12 October, 1969; *al-Ḥayāt*, 18 October, 1969.

84 *Al-Ḥayāt*, 7 July, 1969; *Nidā' al-Waṭan*, 10 July, 1969. At the University of Khartoum, Maḥjūb reacted strongly to attacks on the Communists. See *M.E.N.A.*, 11 October, 1969—*D.R.*, 13 October, 1969; *al-Ahrām*, 14 October, 1969; *al-Jadīd*, 24 October, 1969.

85 *M.E.N.A.*, 28, 29, 30 October, 1969—*I.M.B.*, 29, 30, 31 October, 1969.

86 *Ibid.*, 5 January, 1970—*D.R.*, 7 January, 1970. For Maḥjūb's views see *al-Ṣayyād*, 5 February, 1970; *al-Nahār*, 10 June, 1970.

87 The Central Committee of the Sudanese C.P. distributed leaflets denouncing the deportation of Maḥjūb. See *al-Nidā'*, 16 April, 1970; *Le Monde*, 25 April, 1970.

88 R. Omdurman, 25 May, 1970—*D.R.*, 26 May, 1970.

89 See *Nidā' al-Waṭan*, 2 July, 1970.

90 Numeiri remained Prime Minister and became Foreign Minister—instead of Bābikr 'Awadallāh, who retained his posts as deputy P.M. and Minister of Justice. This reshuffle can perhaps be attributed to a growing pressure

on Numeiri to weaken the C.P.'s influence. See *Nidā' al-Waṭan*, 26 July, 1970.

91 *Al-Kifāḥ*, 12 September, 1970.

92 See the joint communiqué announced over R. Omdurman, 20 October, 1970—*D.R.*, 21 October, 1970.

93 The three were also ministers in several cabinets. Fārūq 'Uthmān Ḥamdallāh —Minister of the Interior in all cabinets from May 1969; Hashim al-'Aṭā'— Minister of Animal Resources from October 1969 and, from July 1970, P.M.'s assistant for Agriculture; Bābikr al-Nūr 'Uthmān—Minister of Planning and P.M.'s assistant for Economics in the July 1970 cabinet.

94 R. Omdurman, 16, 17 November, 1970—*D.R.*, 17, 18 November, 1970; R. Baghdad, 16, 17, 18 November, 1970—*D.R.*, 17, 19 November, 1970; *Morning Star*, 1, 8 November, 1970; *Times*, 17, 18 November, 1970; *Le Monde*, 18 November, 1970.

95 *M.E.N.A.*, 16 November, 1970—*I.M.B.*, 17 November, 1970.

96 *Al-Akhbār*, 13 April, 1971.

97 *Iraq News Agency (I.N.A.)*, 26 November, 1970—*D.R.*, 2 December, 1970; *Ha'aretz*, 27 November, 1970; *Washington Post*, 30 November, 1970.

98 *Al-Kifāḥ*, 1 December, 1970.

99 R. Omduram, 12 February, 1971—*D.R.*, 12 February 1971. It should be noted that the motif of Islam—later on elaborated upon by Numeiri— was not mentioned at this stage.

100 On 20 February the Peasants' Union was dissolved (*I.N.A.*, 23 February, 1971—*I.M.B.*, 26 February, 1971). In March, clashes between students and the police were reported (*M.E.N.A.*, 13 March, 1971—*D.R.*, 19 March, 1971; *I.N.A.*, 19 March, 1971—*I.M.B.*, 21 March, 1971).

101 *Kull Shay'*, 4 March, 1971.

102 *Al-Ḥayāt*, 20 March, 1971; *al-Nahār*, 26 March, 1971.

103 *Al-Ḥayāt*, 20 March, 5 May, 1971; *Africa Confidential*, 11 June, 1971; *I.N.A.*, 1 June, 1971—*I.M.B.*, 4 June, 1971.

104 *I.N.A.*, 20 April, 1971—*D.R.*, 22 April, 1971.

105 R. Omdurman, 30 April, 1971—*D.R.*, 10 May, 1971; *I.N.A.*, 29 May, 1971—*I.M.B.*, 8 June, 1971; *M.E.N.A.*, 8 September, 1971—*I.M.B.*, 12 September, 1971.

106 *I.N.A.*, 24 April, 1971—*D.R.*, 27 April, 1971; *Morning Star*, 30 April, 1971; R. Omdurman, 11 May, 1971—*D.R.*, 14 May, 1971; *Washington Post*, 6 June, 1971.

107 R.Omdurman, 26 May, 1971—*D.R.*, 28 May, 1971.

108 *Ibid.*, 30 June, 1971—B.B.C., 2 July, 1971.

109 As Collin Legum put it in "Africa's Contending Revolutionaries," *Problems of Communism*, Washington, March-April, 1971, p. 6: "Everywhere in Africa today one finds revolutionaries who are challenging the estab-

lished authorities' claims to power. Even in the few states under the rule of 'revolutionary governments'—e.g., Libya, Egypt . . . and the Sudan— there are revolutionaries contesting the right of these regimes to be considered 'genuinely revolutionary.'"

110 R. Omdurman, 20 July, 1971—B.B.C., 22 July, 1971.

111 *Ibid.*

112 *Ibid.*, 19 July, 1971—B.B.C., 21 July, 1971.

113 *The Scotsman, Davar, Los Angeles Times*, 21 July, 1971; *The Times*, 22 July, 1971; *Washington Post*, 23 July, 1971; *Newsweek*, 2 August, 1971.

114 R. Omdurman, R. Baghdad, 20 July, 1971—B.B.C., 22 July, 1971.

115 For a detailed description of the *coup* see Fu'ād Maṭar's articles and book mentioned above, n. 73.

116 *Ibid.*, 24–28 July, 1971—B.B.C., 25–30 July, 1971.

117 Reportedly, after the execution of Maḥjūb, the Central Committee of the C.P. in Khartoum elected Muḥammad Ibrāhīm Nuqud as secretary-general of the party. See *al-Nidā'*, 12 August, 1971.

118 Haykal's weekly article broadcast by R. Cairo, 30 July, 1971—B.B.C., 2 August, 1971.

119 See G. N. Sanderson, "Traditional Attitudes and Political Objectives in the Contemporary Sudan: A Study in Contradictions" [1972, mimeographed].

7. COMMUNISM IN THE FERTILE CRESCENT

Uriel Dann

THE COMMUNIST MOVEMENT IN IRAQ SINCE 1963

The Iraqi Communist Party (I.C.P.) owes its peculiar vitality to the following circumstances:

a) The ethno-religious and social heterogeneity of Iraq fosters a state of latent rebellion, or rebelliousness, and puts a premium on any movement preaching revolution as a first principle.
b) Iraq has no tradition of intercommunal coexistence, like Lebanon for example.
c) Agrarian misery has for long been particularly acute.
d) The early growth of the oil industry gave rise to a working class, geographically concentrated, which accumulated an unusual degree —for Arab countries—of general knowledge, class consciousness, and organizational experience.
e) The monarchy aligned itself with the highly unpopular West during the politically formative years of the Arab Middle East in our generation.
f) The timely appearance of a personality cult: the founder of the I.C.P.—Yūsuf Salmān Yūsuf, alias "Fahd"—was a leader whose death at the hands of the government provided the party with a myth and an inspiration which are prevalent to the present day.

In the first year after the 1958 revolution the I.C.P. emerged from its underground existence and became a serious contender for the leadership of the republic—or so it seemed to both outside observers and party members. During its subsequent confrontation with Qassem, the I.C.P. retreated step by step (without, however, being subjected in the main to physical persecution).

The Ba'th regime which put an end to Qassem on 9 February, 1963, made every effort to finish off the I.C.P. as well. In revenge for the Red Terror of 1959, thousands of Communists were hunted down and killed, including the party's secretary-general Ḥusayn al-Raḍī ("Salām 'Ādil"). All who could, fled abroad or into the Kurdish-held mountain recesses of the north. The Soviet Union and several of her allies were driven to open protest against a regime which was, after all, "non-aligned" and "anti-imperialist." In Iraq itself the party was paralyzed in a way never known before or since. Thus, any change could only be for the better.

The most important phenomenon in the history of the I.C.P. since 1963 is the instant reactivization it manifested after the overturn of the Ba'th regime on 18 November, 1963. Within days the party bodies had convened, communications were reestablished, resolutions distributed, contacts made with potential allies and collaborators. Though underground conditions were preserved, there was no major effort to remain under cover.

The change of strategy was evidently based on the appraisal that the murderous all-out persecution under the previous regime had been an anomaly, and that the takeover by even such declared enemies of the Communist cause as 'Abd al-Salām 'Ārif and his fellow officers meant a return to a tolerable state of "normal" underground status. The Central Committee (C.C.) put the matter concisely: "Never in the history of Iraq has there been such savage terror as that which took place during the Ba'th regime. . . . The C.C. meeting regarded the action of 18 November, 1963, as an action which ended the nightmare of fascist rule and created more favorable conditions for the struggle of the anti-imperialist forces. . . ."[1]

At the time, there were valid reasons for the practical optimism shown by the I.C.P. Public opinion—a factor to which Iraqi regimes are more sensitive than is often supposed—had had its fill of bloodshed; the desire to repay the Communists for the outrages of 1959 – once quite prevalent – had long since subsided. The new rulers considered their regime legitimized by the overturn of one which had "committed crimes worse than the Mongols," in the words of the military governor-general and minister of the interior, Rashīd Muṣliḥ.[2] They realized that the supposed indifference of Moscow to the fate of local Communists had limits which could only be overstepped at a price, and the fruits of positive neutralism were a heavy price to pay. Thus, during the last weeks of 1963, Communists were released from jail in considerable numbers, a few prominent party members returned from abroad and the north more or less openly and, above all, the life of any Communist was no longer at the mercy of armlet-wearing hooligans like the Ba'thi Nationalist Guard.

However, this was the sum total of concessions. The new rulers were anti-Communist by conviction, class interest, and personal background. They were conscious of being "officers" rather than "politicians" —another sore point. They had certainly not forgotten their humiliation during the Communist heyday. 'Ārif's Muslim piety made him especially averse to any communication with professed atheists, even for tactical purposes. In consequence, as long as the brothers 'Ārif ruled, the I.C.P. was treated with unrelieved hostility. Although the 'Ārifs attempted at various times to establish contact with many diverse groupings, the Communists stayed outside the pale. They continued to suffer persecution which did not, however, ever reach the hysterical intensity of the preceding regime; but mass arrests, deportations, raids, and occasional executions continued to be perennial risks.

In this situation, the I.C.P. could not maintain the stance that the 'Ārif regime, whatever its faults, was fundamentally "positive." The party leaders had long ago forsaken the hope that striving for a Communist takeover or, in party jargon, "a people's regime led by the working classes," was practical politics in the foreseeable future.[3] But even its substitute, a Popular Front government ("an alliance of all the patriotic forces working for complete liberation and social progress") could obviously not accommodate men like the 'Ārifs or Ṭāhir Yahyā. Within a year of their accession, a Communist observer defined their rule as "military, non-democratic, petit-bourgeois, nationalist . . . governed by men of despotic temperament"; yet even this observer still found it necessary to add: "The choice of the non-capitalist path need not necessarily hinge on the removal of the present government. . . . Our attitude to the present regime is a tactful problem."[4] But a few months later—in April 1965—the C.C. came out with the seditious slogan, "For the overthrow of the dictatorial-military regime of Aref-Yahya, for a provisional government of national coalition."[5] The I.C.P. did not swerve from this line of total opposition until the surviving 'Ārif was turned out on 17 July, 1968. The party had indeed no option but to welcome such measures as the Federation agreement with the U.A.R. and the nationalization decrees, both in 1964, and Bazzāz's agreement with Barzani in 1966; but it gave the regime as little credit as possible, and noted with bitter satisfaction every retreat or delay in fulfillment.

On the operational side, the I.C.P. was much tamer than its declarations would suggest. This was to a large extent a question of personalities. Ever since its reemergence at the end of 1963, the I.C.P. has been headed by a closely knit body of stalwarts, most of whom led the party under the monarchy and shared the wild hopes and subsequent disappointments of the Qassem era. These are the men who survived the Ba'th holocaust—for to them it was nothing less. Others stayed abroad, in Moscow or other Eastern European capitals, without waiving their share of decision-making in I.C.P. politics. The latter group, which was of course especially susceptible to Soviet influence, included the secretary-general, 'Azīz Muḥammad ("Nāẓim 'Alī"), a Kurd, who had taken the place of the murdered Ḥusayn al-Raḍī. Control of the party in Iraq passed into the hands of Bāhā ad-Dīn Nūrī, also a Kurd and secretary-general in the 1950s, and of the Sunni-Arab 'Āmir 'Abdallah, equally an old hand. These were joined at the top by two younger men (though already prominent in Communist politics under Qassem), Dr. Raḥīm 'Ajīna and Makram Ṭālabānī.[6] As a body, these men confined their opposition to the 'Ārif regime to resolutions and propaganda—though not always. Occasionally, they sponsored strikes which gained a measure of local support but did not affect society as a whole. In 1964 they were said to have conspired with Shī'ī circles —the shadowy Fāṭimi Party—and liberal politicians surrounding Chaderchi for the overthrow of the regime; but nothing came of it. At the start of 1968, when the prestige of the regime was already at its lowest ebb, the I.C.P. held talks with General Aḥmad Ḥasan al-Bakr, clearly the destined successor, and his political friends. These talks came to naught, probably because Bakr did not wish to become indebted to the I.C.P. for the success of what would essentially be a military operation; the antecedents of the 1958 *coup* provide a parallel

The rationalization offered for this inaction was that even so evil a regime as that of the 'Ārifs "objectively" served the anti-imperialist cause, in the Middle East and beyond. This line was energetically encouraged by Moscow. Soviet commentators repeatedly warned the I.C.P. against "enmity inertia" with regard to the regime, and "political prejudices."[7] In February 1968, the Bulgarian authorities shut down the program which purported to be the underground broadcasting station of the I.C.P. ("Voice of the Iraqi People"), "since it interfered with the friendly relations between Baghdad and the Soviet Union"; as the announcer put it, "We say good-bye for good reasons."[8] And yet it is difficult to escape the conclusion that the lack of initiative was also based on instinctive reactions—the dislike of taking great risks, which had been a conspicuous trait of these same men under the far more auspicious circumstances of the Qassem regime.

Whatever the reasons, this essentially passive line had since its inception met with opposition from a minority at all levels of the party. This minority demanded war on the regime *sans phrase*. It gave this struggle priority over every other objective and consideration. If the party majority differed, it could only be motivated by revisionist deviation, or treachery, or cowardice. If Soviet comrades counseled restraint, they were in error, regrettably, and if they could not be persuaded, they would have to be ignored until better times. Personal rivalries and antipathies within the I.C.P. played their part, without doubt. The historical proclivity of the Iraqi Communist movement to split, and split again, must be borne in mind. It is certain that there was no "Chinese" wing. "Guevarist" comes somewhat closer to the mark; but Iraqi realities are so different from those of Latin America that this label does not fit well either.

In the summer of 1964, there was talk of a *coup d'état* among Communist officers and former officers led by ex-Colonel Salīm al-Fakhrī, a veteran party member who had survived the Ba'th regime in the Kurdish mountains and returned south after its fall. The plot was uncovered before it was ripe, and Fakhrī and his friends were sentenced to long terms in prison. The I.C.P. leadership was not involved.

Incomparably more significant was an activist section of the I.C.P. whose beginnings can also be traced to 1964, but which definitely broke with the established leadership only after the Six-Day War. The I.C.P. was obviously not affected directly by the war, but it shared in the general shock. The helplessness of the Soviet Union and the Iraqi regime in the face of unparalleled military disaster drove the party opposition into open confrontation with the majority. After a long line of clashes, smear campaigns, mutual expulsions, and attempts at reconciliation, the C.C. convened a "Conference" in December 1967 (the third ever to be held). This event, a highly important meeting of delegates, was intended for circumstances where a National Congress would be impractical. The Conference ended with the final expulsion of the activists from the party. It seems certain that the moderate bloc constituted an overwhelming majority in the C.C., with a tight grip on the organizational establishment in all its ramifications. The expelled minority immediately set up its own "Iraqi Communist Party," styled the I.C.P./Central Command *(al-qiyāda al-markaziyya)* to highlight its independence and proclaim its militancy. Its secretary-general and spokesman was 'Azīz al-Ḥājj 'Alī Ḥaydar ("Ramzī Walīd"), the only prominent C.C. member who had represented the activists at the Conference. The majority party has been known since as the I.C.P./Central Committee *(al-lajna al-markaziyya)*, even in its own publications.[9]

The I.C.P./*Qiyāda* proceeded to declare and organize an "armed popular struggle" in the south of Iraq. The rising was headed by Khālid Aḥmad Zakī, once on the staff of the Bertrand Russell Peace Foundation, with "wide responsibility for Middle Eastern Affairs."[10] He was killed in an encounter with government forces in June 1968. The movement asserted itself in ambushes of police patrols, the temporary seizure of isolated police posts, the mining of bridges and railway culverts, in mail and stores robberies, and proclamations of land distributions to peasants. It was much less than a civil war, or even a general peasants' rising. The disturbances were essentially another outbreak of *fawdā*—"anarchy"—endemic in those parts of agrarian misery and dislocation. They do not compare in scope and intensity with the tribally organized insurrection of 1935. Ḥājj's command never controlled anything like a compact territory as did Barzani in the north. On the other hand, there can be little doubt that the Armed Popular Struggle enjoyed wide, if passive, sympathy among the peasants.

'Abd al-Raḥmān 'Ārif, ineffective in everything else, was also unsuccessful in combating the disturbances in the south. When he fell, they were still at their peak.

On the political front, the I.C.P./*Qiyāda* contacted various leftist-nationalist groups—Fu'ād al-Rikābī's Arab Socialist Movement and others. Nothing developed, and the contacts should not be regarded as an alliance or a bid for cooperation in any real sense. They were mere whisperings among conspirators who stood outside the political community of Iraq. The only group of any consequence, with a following, rudiments of organization, and capacity for action, was that of Ḥājj.[11]

The present regime came to power in July 1968 without the aid or foreknowledge of either Communist faction. Bakr's group—in part army officers, in part civilians—ousted the elder 'Ārif with the help of senior officers of the General Staff and the Republican Guard. After a fortnight, Bakr rid himself of his politically inexperienced allies and rivals. Since then, he and his collaborators, among whom

Ṣadām Ḥusayn al-Tikrītī soon stood out as the new "strong man," have established a pseudo-party regime purporting to be in accord with the Baʻth "national command" of ʻAflaq, which was driven out of Syria in 1966. "Rightist-Baʻth" connotes the new rulers' lack of interest, for practical purposes, in social reform; otherwise it means little. Here, however, the term will be used to avoid confusion with the Saʻdī-Windāwī faction which ruled Iraq in 1963, and with the "Neo-Baʻth" in Syria since 1966.

What has characterized the I.C.P. since July 1968 is the extent to which its record reflects the initiatives of the regime. Unlike the ʻĀrif regime, the Rightist-Baʻth has been nimble and imaginative at the tactical level, notwithstanding its determination to retain power exclusively in its own hands. On the other hand, the I.C.P. has remained frozen in that immobility which had been its distinctive trait since 1960—and, basically, long before then. Without that latent strength described below, the Communist movement would have withered away during the last three years and disappeared for all practical purposes from the Iraqi scene.

Immediately after their effective takeover on 30 July, 1968, the Rightist-Baʻth leaders opened negotiations with the I.C.P. on Communist participation in the cabinet. It is not necessary to assume that they saw these talks as a deliberate ruse from the outset. Then, as today, they were quite isolated within the political community of Iraq; then, unlike today, they lacked any efficient machinery for the control and subjugation of that community. They certainly did not entertain the idea of a proper coalition, or "National Front" in Communist parlance; in any case, the cabinet has never been more than the executive of the "Revolutionary Command Council," composed of whoever were the Baʻth's top men of the hour.[12] But the Communist response killed whatever readiness there was initially to grant the I.C.P. representation in the cabinet. ʻAzīz Muḥammad, the secretary-general, was at the time in Eastern Europe. Responsibility for the talks devolved on Makram Ṭālabānī. He, and the I.C.P. organs, warmly welcomed the offer. They defined the future cooperation as a National Front of equal partners. They demanded the immediate licensing of an I.C.P. daily, the reinstatement of all Communist army officers retired since 1959, and apparently the Ministry of Defense. That ended the negotiations. In historical perspective, it is interesting to note the recurring blindness which made the I.C.P. submit demands which could only be interpreted as bids for ultimate power, without any means of enforcing them.

Since about September 1968, there have been ups and downs in the relations between the regime and the I.C.P. defying clear rational explanation. What is clear, however, is that the pace was set by the regime.

Fundamentally, the Rightist-Ba'th has granted the I.C.P. basic, if limited, toleration. This has meant the general absence of persecution, and freedom of movement for I.C.P. politicians within Iraq and abroad. It has meant the toleration of I.C.P. conventions at high level, decently discreet and presumably closely watched, but without risk to the life and liberty of participants. Communist-inspired lists appeared at elections for professional organizations and were discussed as such. (This liberality has the advantage of pinpointing Communist sympathizers in a simple and fool-proof manner.) The distribution of clandestine publications has been winked at—with many exceptions. In 1969, *al-Thaqāfa al-Jadīda* reappeared legally for the first time since Qassem's day. This was a leftist monthly with a tradition of intellectual respectability, which now became a sort of recognized organ of the I.C.P., with Makram Ṭālabānī as editor. At least one senior I.C.P. member is known to have been appointed to high office (without political power). On the other hand, the much-publicized inclusion of the "Communist" 'Azīz Sharīf in the cabinet in December 1969— as Minister of Justice—was a tongue-in-cheek fraud of sorts, and has been denounced as such by the I.C.P. ever since: Sharīf is neither a Communist nor even an active fellow-traveler. He is an elderly lawyer whose leftist politics in the nineteen-forties and early fifties have quite undeservedly given him the perpetual public image of a Communist; in the past he had served Qassem as a convenience for the display of official goodwill when a meaningless token seemed called for. At the same level of significance, members of the regime occasionally protest their lack of malice toward the I.C.P., its leaders, and its "true" principles, and a show of readiness for negotiations is made quite regularly.

The price for this toleration has never been stated in so many words, but its essence is clear. The I.C.P. is expected to adhere to the role of a loyal opposition, somewhat along the lines of the situation during Qassem's last two years. The party need not express submission to or full support of the regime, but must recognize it as "essentially progressive." It must give full credit and unstinted praise to any measures which ostensibly fit into a "National Front" image, even though no such Front exists—e.g., fresh ties with the Soviet Union, the recognition of the German Democratic Republic, gestures of reconciliation with Barzani. The party must certainly steer clear of any plot, however embryonic. It is required to limit its criticism to expressions of pain at the regime's insufficient fervor for realizing the ideal of an alliance of all patriotic and anti-imperialist forces. At the most, outrages against individual Communists can be denounced. The official expectation which has been the hardest to live up to was that the party impose this restraint on the rank and file; that it abstain from disrupting the public peace, shaky enough in all conscience; that it prevent strikes and abstain from labor agitation.

The penalties for the infringement of any of these conditions have become well known in the history of the I.C.P. It is, however, interesting that the regime has occasionally conducted local anti-Communist campaigns of quite savage character, without known Communist provocation. The outstanding example is that of Basra in early January 1970. The authorities there—aided by army, security branches, and an ad-hoc militia of toughs—shattered within a fortnight the framework of the I.C.P., scattered cells, demolished semi-tolerated meeting places, and herded hundreds of members and sympathizers into the concentration camps of Baghdad and Nuqrat Salman. The most plausible explanation is that in such cases the authorities act in response to a sudden increase of local Communist influence, activity, or prestige.

The murder of well-known Communists is rare. That of the C.C. member Muḥammad al-Khuḍayrī in March 1970 caused much commotion and led to the appointment of an official commission of enquiry, and to hostile comments from the Communist bloc. (It is not clear whether Khuḍayrī was killed on orders from above, or "by accident"; it was certainly a case of political murder.)

The sustained interest Iraq and the Soviet Union show in close relations raises the question of how the latter views the policy just described. It appears that the Soviet attitude is a continuation of that adopted in the spring of 1960 when it first became obvious—dashing the hopes of the preceding 18 months—that the I.C.P. stood no chance of attaining any position of executive power in the foreseeable future. The Soviet Union has, in the light of her wider interests, put up with the hostility which the I.C.P. drew from successive regimes in Baghdad. Moreover, led by experience, Soviet theoreticians have enunciated the thesis that for countries at a level of political development comparable to that of Iraq, a National Front regime is no *sine qua non* for peace and progress. Even an anti-Communist one-party regime may qualify, provided it is non-aligned and "objectively anti-imperialist."[13] Obviously, the Rightist-Ba'th falls under this heading. However, one must not assume total Soviet indifference. There is a line which an anti-Communist regime in Baghdad crosses only at the risk of an immediate worsening of relations, usually demonstrated through the party press and organizations rather than government agencies. This line would be the change from controlled harassment of local Communists to all-out persecution, with at least an attempt at physical liquidation. It seems that the regime is well aware of these subtleties. Observers, particularly in Lebanon, have repeatedly pointed out that gestures in favor of the I.C.P.—of little consequence to the authorities, though not perhaps to the I.C.P.—occurred whenever the regime stood in special need of Soviet goodwill.

This being so, the "policy" of the I.C.P. under the Rightist-Ba'th regime is not very illuminating. The party accepts by implication the conditions attached to its quasi-toleration—as a rule, at any rate. It has explicitly renounced violence as a means of attaining its objectives.[14] This line is all the more natural since the I.C.P. today lacks an energetic leadership. 'Azīz Muḥammad, the uncontested secretary-general, is often abroad and has the reputation of being weak. Among the other presumed members of the politbureau (see above p. 380), 'Āmir 'Abdallah and Bāhā ad-Dīn Nūrī are ageing, after a lifetime of underground work and severe suffering; the younger men, Dr. 'Ajīna and Makram Ṭālabānī, have not yet made their mark with the party membership at large. A few points are worthy of note, however:

a) The I.C.P. is unreservedly loyal to Moscow in its confrontation with Peking;

b) In the Palestine conflict, too, the I.C.P. has adopted the Moscow line of a "political settlement." After much calumny and prodding from various quarters coordinated by the regime, the party declared its support for the Fidayeen organizations about two years ago and even sent a delegation to al-Fatḥ headquarters in Jordan, when the Palestinians were at the peak of their prestige. But the party proceeds warily and, without expressly admitting Israel's right to existence, formulates its slogans on the Soviet pattern ("restoration of Palestinian rights"; "return of occupied territories" without further qualification, etc).

c) The I.C.P. attitude toward the Kurds is interesting. On principle, the line has been fixed for many years: autonomy for the Kurdish people, in administrative and cultural matters, within the Iraqi state. Since the 1958 revolution this line has been subordinated to a higher interest, the "war against imperialism." In practice, this has meant that whenever the Kurdish struggle seemed to weaken an anti-Western regime in Baghdad, it became a liability and was condemned as "chauvinist separatism," or in similar terms. During the 'Ārif regime, the I.C.P. was generally friendly to Barzani, and hostile to his rival Jalāl Ṭālabānī who cooperated with the government; relations with the regime had deteriorated beyond the point of repair, and the Kurdish mountains served as a refuge to many Communists. The more sophisticated Rightist-Ba'th confronted the I.C.P. with a dilemma. The I.C.P. accepted, or saw fit to recognize, the claim that the new regime sought a settlement with the Kurds. Since Barzani did not trouble to hide his aversion for the I.C.P. and suppressed the attempts of Kurdish Communists to form separate units within the Pesh-Merga, the I.C.P. found it easy to blame him for his intransigence which delayed agreement and turned him into a tool of imperialism. The I.C.P. welcomed the "peace treaty" of 11 March, 1970, with enthusiasm, at any rate officially. In any event, party pronouncements on Barzani continued to be cool, perhaps because a real rapprochement between the regime and the Kurds might still further isolate the I.C.P.

However, the I.C.P. manifests itself in yet another aspect, differing from those apparent so far in this study. It is that of the only political party in Iraq worthy of the name, according to the criteria of organization, tradition and continuity, ideology, public support, and the existence of a committed cadre. We shall now examine the implications of these criteria over the last years.

· The organization of the party is unshaken. The hierarchy of secretary-general, politbureau, and Central Committee works according to rule. In September 1970 the Second National Congress convened in Baghdad—the first having been convened in 1945. The sessions were spread over eight days and 102 delegates participated. The National Congress is the highest party authority, the seat of sovereignty as it were, and it inspires more than perfunctory respect. Though the

Second Congress did not, as far as is known, adopt resolutions which amounted to important changes of policy, it was conducted with decorum and even ceremony. 'Azīz Muḥammad was reaffirmed as secretary-general. A new C.C. was elected—apparently similar in composition to the former which was naturally based on co-option. What has transpired of the discussions reflects party policies as described above.[15]

The territorial organization of the I.C.P. is based on about a half-dozen districts—a more manageable division than the 16 provinces of the state. There is a Kurdish "branch" *(far')* dealing with Kurdish affairs—not with the Kurdish countryside. There is a network of sub-divisions down to the local cell—fundamentally unchanged since the monarchy. On the other hand, there is no room for front organizations —as distinct from professional organizations—under the Rightist-Ba'th. The Iraqi Partisans of Peace had their license renewed at the beginning of 1970 under a slightly different name ("National Council for the Peace Movement and Solidarity with the Peoples of Iraq"); the council included such known leftists as 'Azīz Sharīf, Muḥammaḍ Mahdī al-Jawāhirī, and 'Abd al-Wahhāb Maḥmūd, along with a sprinkling of identified Communists.[16] The council has since come out with a number of resolutions, and sent delegations abroad. It has abstained from commenting on controversial issues affecting Iraq.

By far the most significant index of Communist influence among the educated public is to be found in the elections to professional and student bodies—in this respect nothing has changed since the Qassem regime. The following instances stand out:

a) *The Bar Association*. Elections to the council took place in February 1968 and January 1970. In both cases the first place was won by a "united list" headed by 'Abd al-Wahhāb Maḥmūd, long known as a leftist who can be fairly described as a Communist fellow-traveler. In 1970 the list was a "progressive" coalition supported by the regime. But the prominent place taken by Communists among the successful candidates (Nājī Yūsuf, 'Āmir 'Abdallah, Tawfīq al-Alūsī) points to the strength of the I.C.P.[17] A list representing the traditional Right placed a good second. It is worth recalling that 'Abd al-Wahhāb Maḥmūd's vacation of the presidency in the summer of 1959 was the first sign that the I.C.P. was losing its grip on the public, after its high-tide under Qassem.

b) *The Economists Society.* In the elections of December 1969 a "progressive" list included seven Ba'this, two Communists, one representative of the Kurdish Democratic Party, and one "independent nationalist."[18] Since the list was drawn up under the auspices of the regime, the relative strength of the Communist representation is worth noting.

c) *Student bodies.* Elections took place in March 1967 and in November 1969. On the former occasion, under the feeble rule of 'Abd al-Raḥmān 'Ārif, the "General Federation of Iraqi Students" reestablished its domination of student committees. The "General Federation" was the Communist-led organization established at the end of 1958 which, despite the Communist decline after 1959, officially represented the secondary-school and university students of Iraq until Qassem's fall. Under the Ba'th regime of 1963 it was proscribed like all other Communist organizations. Afterwards it made a comeback, though with some circumspection. The elections of 1969 were preceded by an intense campaign culminating in bloody clashes. The "General Federation" was confronted by the "National Federation of Iraqi Students," its Ba'thi rival founded as an underground body in 1961, and the acknowledged representative of the student body in 1963. After the fall of the Ba'th regime it was dispersed, but was reestablished by the Rightist-Ba'th soon after its accession. At the elections, the "National Federation" was energetically supported—in Iraqi fashion—by the authorities. Its list, the "United Students Front," won a 2:1 victory over its Communist-leftist rival, the "Progressive-Democratic Front," at all colleges save one. The exception was the College of Agriculture where the Communists gained a clear victory.[19] Considering the circumstances, the elections as a whole must be considered proof of Communist strength among the student population.

It is not easy to gauge the strength of the I.C.P. among that vast majority of the population which does not participate in politically-oriented elections—"the masses" of Communist jargon. Undoubtedly, the party is a known entity throughout Iraq, evoking friendly rather than hostile reactions. When the I.C.P. called the industrial workers out on strike at the end of 1968, in its first sharp disappointment over the new regime, the response was good. The "armed popular struggle" in the agrarian south during that year has been mentioned; its very nature would assure the Communists of fame and sympathy among the peasants, though little else. Lebanese observers persistently report that the I.C.P. has members and active supporters in the army, particularly among non-commissioned officers; such was certainly the case during the late nineteen-fifties.

This presumed popularity gives an extra dimension to the party's vitality. In terms of practical politics it means little. The fate of independent Iraq has always been determined in clashes between small groups near the center of power, victory going to the camp which united a modicum of physical means with a maximum of determination. The phenomenon is deeply rooted in the past, and there are no signs that its relevance has diminished.

Ever since the party's birth, the collective consciousness of its members has been one of the greatest assets of the I.C.P., perhaps the greatest. The party has traditionally inspired its members with a loyalty unto death which is unique in the body politic of Iraq and which commands the respect of the otherwise unsympathetic observer. As significantly, if less dramatically, this loyalty has held good in the face of bloodless attrition: the endless succession of hopes deferred, impulses suppressed, of chicanery and humiliation which make up the larger part of the party's history in the last decade. The stoical resilience of the leaders who know what they fight for, and love what they know, is shared by the rank and file—a very few thousand indeed, but as such an important segment of the political public. The ultimate "why" is a matter of guesswork. It may fundamentally be a *camaraderie* of men and women who have evolved a continuity of shared ideals and sacrifices, secured upon an organizational structure well suited to the times. Iraqi society has produced such phenomena in the remote past; at present the I.C.P. stands alone—hence its prominence. If this speculation is correct it also explains why splinter groups have not shared the high immunity of the main party body to despondency, desertion, and treachery.

The I.C.P./*Qiyāda* was uncompromisingly hostile to the Rightist-Ba'th regime from the start. The new rulers, more energetic than their predecessors, stamped out the "armed popular struggle" within a matter of months. 'Azīz al-Ḥājj and his command took cover in Baghdad where they were ferreted out by the authorities in February 1969. An official spokesman assured worried leftists abroad that the captives would be treated "as political prisoners"—and so they undoubtedly were, according to the grim tradition of the land. They soon broke down, and confessed in public. ʿAzīz al-Ḥājj seems to have reformed for good, and since the summer of 1971 he is said to be representing Iraq at U.N.E.S.C.O. headquarters in Paris. His movement has survived his defection. Subsisting in true underground conditions—as distinct from the semi-underground status of the I.C.P./*Lajna*—it calls for the destruction of the "fascist" regime, self-determination for the Kurdish people—a demand which Barzani himself has not made in public—and the liquidation of Israel. The Soviet Union is criticized for its opportunistic support of the regime, though here some restraint is shown; clearly, the movement does not wish to burn its bridges with Moscow. The command has been transferred to the safer south —probably in the region of Hilla. For about a year, the heir of ʿAzīz al-Ḥājj was Ibrāhīm al-ʿIllāwī; he too is said to have been captured some time ago. The organ of the movement is *Ṭarīq al-Shaʿb*, a name sacred in Communist tradition and shared, for that reason, with the organ of the I.C.P./*Lajna*. The I.C.P./*Qiyāda* maintains a propaganda network of sorts in several European capitals. Lately, Comrade "Najm" gave a highly interesting interview in London.[20] Contacts are with the New Left rather than with established Communist parties which tend to regard the I.C.P./*Qiyāda* as a leftist deviation. The movement has not been able to go beyond propaganda and agitation. An attempt to rekindle the "armed popular struggle" broke down immediately.

The question of which I.C.P. branch enjoys greater popularity among "the masses" is difficult to answer. The extremist movement might be expected to excite higher hopes, and this is certainly the claim of the I.C.P./*Qiyāda*. At the operational and organizing levels the matter is of no importance. It is doubtful whether the peasant or urban unemployed who feels vaguely grateful to the Communists for taking an interest in his misery has noted the split. Its ideological and political implications can mean nothing to him.

NOTE ON SOURCES

Lebanese dailies like *al-Ḥayāt* and *al-Anwār* provide reasonably detached coverage of the subject under investigation here. The weekly *al-Ṣayyād* has been especially informative on Iraq over the last few years. The Lebanese Communist press—the daily *al-Nidā'* and the weekly *al-Akhbār*—are important when used with discrimination; the same goes for the communication media of the Communist bloc. The *World Marxist Review* is indispensable as the mouthpiece of Iraqi Communists on questions of principle or major tactics. Samples of Communist clandestine literature from Iraq are not particularly difficult to come by, and tell their tale. Interviews of Iraqi Communists with Western observers are useful windfalls—the Russell Foundation paper quoted in the text is an outstanding example. Last but not least, the much maligned Iraqi press—censored, guided, terrorized—yields valuable results provided the nuts are properly cracked.

I have had at my disposal the interesting note "History of the Iraqi Communist Party until 1968" by the late Mr. Yaakov Poserson (Hebrew, unpublished). I am grateful to the director and staff of the Research Division of the Israel Foreign Ministry for their helpfulness. Finally, the Iraq section of the Shiloah Center's documentation system, managed by my colleague Mrs. Ofra Bengio, has afforded me the greatest assistance.

NOTES

[1] *World Marxist Review*, November 1964, p. 85.

[2] *Al-Jumhūriyya*, Baghdad, 18 December, 1963, quoted in *W.M.R.*, February 1964, p. 87.

[3] They had definitely entertained this hope for a brief period in the spring of 1959.

[4] Mounir Ahmid, *W.M.R.*, December 1964, pp. 37–41, an Iraqi, to go by internal evidence.

[5] *W.M.R.*, June 1965, p. 80.

[6] His name points to a Kurdish descent. Other "prominent members of the C. C." at the end of 1969 were Ārā Khāchādūr, Mājid 'Abd al-Riḍā, Nūrī 'Abd ar-Razzāq Ḥusayn, Dr. Nazīha al-Dulaymī, Dr. Safā al-Ḥāfiẓ, Bishrī Bartū, 'Abd al-Razzāq al-Ṣāfi, and 'Abd al-Amīr 'Abbās (*al-Ṣayyād*, Beirut, 20 November, 1969, copied from the signatures to a party declaration in *al-Thaqāfa al-Jadīda*, Baghdad). New elections since have not apparently greatly altered the composition of the C.C. The five names mentioned in the text seem to be those of the members of the politbureau.

[7] E.g., *Mizan*, London, April 1965, p. 7.

[8] R. V.o.I.P., B.B.C./S.W.B./IV, 26 (28) February, 1968; *al-Hayāt*, Beirut, 20 March, 1968.

[9] The secessionists will hereafter be referred to as I.C.P./*Qiyāda*; the majority group will appear as I.C.P., except when the context makes I.C.P./*Lajna* desirable.

According to an official communiqué, the Conference delegates were 62% Arabs, 31% Kurds, and 7% "minorities" (V.o.I.P., B.B.C./S.W.B., IV, 6 (9) January, 1969). This moderate preponderance of Kurds over Arabs (who are about 20% versus 75% of the population) is fairly representative of the I.C.P. as a whole.

[10] I am obliged to Mr. Christopher Farley, director of the Foundation, for this information.

[11] For a brief description of these splinters, see *al-Ṣayyād*, Beirut, 13 March, 1969.

[12] Iraqi Communists have occasionally stated that alone among his hypocritic colleagues, R.C.C. member 'Abdallah Sallūm al-Sāmarrā'ī "sincerely" strove for a National Front.

[13] E.g., M. Kremnyev, "The Non-Aligned Countries and World Politics," *W.M.R.*, April 1963, pp. 29–35.

393

[14] *Al-Anwār*, Beirut, 4 April, 1969, quoting an I.C.P. document which appears to be genuine.

[15] The proceedings were covered by the Arabic broadcasts from R. Moscow at the end of September, and in *al-Akhbār*, Beirut, 4 October, 1970. As usual much is left unsaid, but a reasonably coherent picture emerges.

[16] *Al-Jumhūriyya*, Baghdad, 8 January, 1970.

[17] *Ibid.*, 10 January, 1970.

[18] *Al-Ṣayyād,* Beirut, 11 December, 1969.

[19] *Al-Jumhūriyya*, Baghdad, 25 November, 1969. The Communist returned was Kamāl Muṣṭafā; he may yet leave his mark.

[20] *Oil, Oppression and Resistance in Iraq.* The Bertrand Russell Peace Foundation, London 1970. I am indebted to Mr. Yossi Amitay for this publication.

AVIGDOR LEVY

THE SYRIAN COMMUNISTS AND THE BA'TH POWER STRUGGLE, 1966–1970

CHARACTERISTICS OF THE PROBLEM AND DEFINITION

The Arab Socialist Resurrection (*Ba'th*) Party was formed in 1953 by a merger between two political groups: the Arab Resurrection Party, led by Michel 'Aflaq and Ṣalāḥ ad-Dīn al-Bīṭār, and the Arab Socialist Party, led by Akram Ḥawrānī. Though the political organizations of these two groups were integrated, two distinct ideological trends still remained. These, however, cut across the former party lines to some extent. 'Aflaq's "revival" wing continued to lay greater stress on nationalist, or pan-Arab, objectives, while Ḥawrānī's socialist wing persisted in following a more radical line on social issues.

The differences within the Ba'th Party became sharper in 1955 when the party made an attempt to play a larger role in Syrian politics and began cooperating with the Communists. The nationalist wing objected to such an alliance with the Communists, though this policy was espoused by the party's leftists and finally adopted as party practice until 1957.[1] Thereafter the Ba'th and the Communists have enjoyed a checkered relationship of alternating cooperation and bitter struggle.[2] During this period, the Ba'th Party underwent profound changes in composition, outlook, and political objectives. On the whole, it moved to the left. Nevertheless, the party has retained its "traditional" ideological duality—nationalist and socialist—and the issue of relations with the Communist Party (C.P.) often served as a kind of political roadfork at which these two ideological currents diverged. Predictably, relations with the Communists have tended to accentuate differences within the Ba'th Party in times of cooperation more than during confrontation. On such occasions, the extent of collaboration has become not only a criterion for radicalism but a factor generating a momentum of its own in the Ba'th's internal politics.

The Ba'th's rise to power in March 1963 heightened the importance of two additional factors pertaining to the issue of Ba'th-Communist relations. Government responsibilities made the Ba'th more sensitive to the position of the Soviet Union as a world power with considerable and

395

growing interests in the Middle East and as patron of the worldwide Communist movement. The other consideration was that of relations between the party and the Syrian military. This second factor was exclusively a feature of the Syrian scene and as such requires more elaboration.

The Ba'th Party attained a large measure of its political influence in the fifties by virtue of its connections with the officer corps. Its rise to power in March 1963 was also due to the eminence of its military supporters.[3] It was natural that the officers who had played a dominant role in the party's rise to power, and in Syrian politics generally, would hesitate to withdraw from government completely. Aside from motives of self-interest, the officers could advance several good reasons why the army should remain part of the decision-making elite. Syria had a tradition of political instability under civilian governments; the Ba'th Party itself suffered from numerous schisms of a personal and ideological nature. These proclivities among Syria's politicians have always tended to infect the armed forces and have threatened their cohesion. Finally, the Syrian army felt militarily insecure because of the proximity of Israel and unfriendly neighbors on all sides. The officers could therefore point to the fact that, given the general conditions of Syria's security, it was their duty to maintain the preparedness and unity of the armed forces by participating in the country's governing process. Hafiz al-Asad retrospectively explained that he had supported the February 1966 *coup* because of his determination to maintain the unity of the armed forces which had been threatened by the machinations of the previous regime.[4] On the other hand, Communist-Soviet principles of party-military relations call for subordination of the armed forces to the party. A close relationship with the Communists and the establishment of a state structure on the Soviet model must clearly have had some bearing on this all-important issue.

The purpose of this paper is to examine the dynamics of the Ba'th's internal politics with regard to the Communist position in Syria and to Soviet-Syrian attitudes. From this point of view, as well as in several other respects, the Syrian *coup d'état* of 23 February 1966, appears to have constituted a point of departure. The *coup* ended the first phase of Ba'thi rule in Syria and brought to power a radical and weak regime which, more than ever, needed and wanted Soviet aid and Communist support.

BA'TH-COMMUNIST COOPERATION, 1966–7

Following its rise to power in March 1963, the Ba'th formed a regime of minority support and depended on military backers to safeguard its rule against a largely hostile population. The bitterness of the internal party struggle in 1965–6 prompted the victorious radicals to oust the more acceptable moderate leaders, and thus they further narrowed the Ba'th's popular base.[5] Syria's new rulers also appeared completely isolated in the Arab world—the conservative regimes feared their radicalism while Egypt suspected their anti-Nasserism. Though acutely aware of the frailty of their position, Syria's new rulers were, however, in no immediate danger in view of their control of the army and the exhaustion of all other political forces. Under these circumstances, they sought Soviet aid and support as well as cooperation with the Syrian Communists. Such cooperation was designed both to bolster the expected alliance with the Soviets and to broaden the regime's support at home. These moves stemmed from pragmatism but were undoubtedly promoted also by the radical proclivities of Syria's new rulers.

The Soviet decision to come to the aid of the new regime was, it seems, primarily due to the latter's very weakness. A rightist comeback in Syria seemed quite possible if the new regime were to remain unaided. Such a reversion would have been a severe blow to the Soviet Union which had been developing more intimate relations with Syria since the end of 1964 when the Ba'th regime had begun to grow more radical.[6] The Soviets may have been moved by other considerations as well, such as the prospects of Communist infiltration into the weakened Ba'th Party or the fear of seeing China gain a foothold among the desperate Ba'th firebrands; such considerations, however, do not seem to have played more than a secondary role.

The Soviets promised the regime massive economic aid and, most notably, rendered them surprisingly far-reaching diplomatic support. For their part, the Ba'thists co-opted at least one registered Communist and several fellow-travelers in their new cabinet. A short while later, Khalid Bakdāsh, the leader of the Syrian Communists, was allowed to return after eight years of exile. Other noted Communists were permitted to re-emerge from private life and assume important public offices.

In order to highlight the new relationship with the Soviet Union, Prime Minister Zu'ayyin visited Moscow in April 1966 and returned with a Soviet loan of $120 million as well as a promise to construct the Euphrates Dam. Relations were not, however, limited to economic and international contacts. A series of visits by senior party delegations to Communist countries followed. In November and December 1966, Ba'th delegations held talks with leaders of the Communist parties of East

Germany, Bulgaria, Czechoslovakia, and Yugoslavia. These were culminated in January 1967 with a week-long visit to Moscow by a top-level Ba'th delegation which came for talks with the leadership of the Soviet Communist Party. The Syrian delegation included Ṣalāḥ Jadīd, Deputy Secretary-General of the Syrian Ba'th and the acknowledged strongman of the regime, Foreign Minister Ibrāhīm Mākhūs, and other Ba'thi leaders. Soviet representatives at the discussions included K. Mazurov, member of the Politburo and First Deputy Prime Minister, B. Ponomarev, Secretary of the General Committee of the Soviet Communist Party and Head of the Central Committee's International Department, and other prominent Communist officials.

The purpose of this visit to Moscow was reported by the Syrian press as "talks on ideology and party organization."[7] Further references to the visit also spoke of the instructive value of the trip for the Syrian Ba'th. A joint communiqué issued on 11 February, 1967, stated that "the experience of the Communist Party of the Soviet Union had provided important lessons for other nations on the path to Socialism,"[8] while an internal Ba'th Party circular declared that among the reasons for the visit was the necessity "to learn from the theoretical and practical experience of the Communist Party of the Soviet Union."[9] The party circular indicated that the Soviet Communist leaders had pressed the Ba'th to increase its collaboration with the Syrian C.P. through a "front of progressive groups," i.e., to allow Communist participation in government as a political party. The Ba'th leaders, however, rejected the proposition. Deliberations over this issue led to a delay in the distribution of the communiqué of over two weeks.[10]

Soviet demands for increased Communist participation in the Syrian regime were probably part of a concerted action. Taking advantage of the regime's declared radicalism as well as its growing political, economic, and military dependence on the Soviet Union, Communist elements were quick to penetrate government and public bodies. Some of the more vital development projects, especially those dependent on Soviet aid (the Euphrates Dam Authority, the petrochemical industry), enlisted the services of several Communists.[11] Echoing in March 1967 the Soviet demand of January, the Syrian Communists started pressing for the formation of a "progressive national front" and criticized the regime for its failure to do so up until then.[12]

However, Soviet-Communist pressure had been applied somewhat prematurely. From the outset, Communist activity had roused suspicions of a Communist scheme to take over the country. Fears of this nature had less than ten years earlier pushed Syria toward an unsuccessful union with Egypt, and in the spring and early summer of 1966 they were at the root of the unrest and incidents reported within the Syrian armed forces.[13] But at the beginning of spring 1967, new circumstances more seriously militating against Communist demands were unfolding.

The Syrian regime's adoption of al-Fatḥ's call for a "popular liberation war" as its declared policy and the material aid it gave to al-Fatḥ's military activities, in addition to Syria's own hardline position toward Israel, led in 1966 to a rapid escalation of hostilities along the Israeli-Syrian frontier, reaching a climax in January 1967. After a relative lull in February and March, tension mounted again at the beginning of the following month. On 7 April the border flared up in a major military engagement involving artillery and aircraft. The tensions on the Israeli frontier in early spring were not such as to cause the military to panic and seek the protection of some outside power, but they were serious enough to give military circles a reason for a general reappraisal of the suitability of radical Ba'th ideology in the Israel-Arab conflict. Furthermore, it had now become a matter of vital importance that Syria's military leadership have greater control in matters relating to the country's defense. This included supervision of the activities of al-Fatḥ and the various popular military organizations that had mushroomed during 1966. The latter included the Workers' Companies, a para-military organization set up under the auspices of the Workers' Federation and the National Guard, the Armed Peasants and the Futuwwa which were under the supervision of the Ministry of the Interior. Under military pressure in April-May 1967, these para-military bodies were grouped together under a roof organization called the Popular Defense Army (*jaysh al-difā' al-sha'bī*) which was placed under the control of the Defense Ministry.[14]

The measures listed above were taken as a growing nationalist feeling apparently began to pervade significant sections of the regime and, in particular, the new military leadership. This development must have adversely affected the Communists' drive for a voice in the regime. The fact is that in April *al-Ḥayāt* noted a deterioration in the relations between the Ba'th Party and the Communists. The newspaper reported that certain circles within the Ba'th were against an enlargement of Communist representation in the government. *Al-Ḥayāt* added that more than 250 pro-Communist officials had been dismissed, many of them from the Ministries of Education and Information.[15]

The Ḥabanka affair of May 1967 is indicative of the greater rightist assertiveness at this stage. The affair was sparked by the publication on 25 April of a strongly anti-religious article in the Syrian army weekly *Jaysh al-Shaʻb*. Its author associated God and religion with feudalism, capitalism, imperialism, etc. As "values which had dominated the older society," these had to be considered "mummies in the Museum of History." He added that "death meant the end of life and not a journey to paradise or hell."[16]

Religious circles reacted strongly to this article. Leading personalities from several Syrian towns met in Damascus at the beginning of May to concert their actions. On Friday, 5 May, religious elements staged demonstrations in several Syrian towns with the major protest taking place in Damascus. At the Manjak mosque Shaykh Ḥasan Ḥabanka, the prestigious spiritual leader of Damascus, unleashed an attack on the regime's anti-religious policies and its Marxist and Communist inclinations. Following his sermon, some 20,000 of the faithful demonstrated against the regime and clashed with police. There were a few casualties and on the following day Ḥabanka and some 40 other religious leaders were arrested.[17]

The article in the army weekly had certainly been no small provocation. However, in view of the fact that it expressed nothing more than official views current for over a year, the timing of the religious reaction may indicate that the politically astute Muslim leaders deliberately chose this particular opportunity to attack official "Marxist-Communist proclivities" because they believed that significant segments of the regime itself were in sympathy with them.

However, the incidents of May 1967 in Syria were eclipsed by the Middle East crisis which eventually developed into the June War and temporarily left internal relations in abeyance.

LEFT WING, RIGHT WING, AND THE COMMUNISTS, 1967–9

The June War elicited some muffled criticism of the Soviet role and Moscow's limited assistance to the Arabs.[18] But this was quickly hushed up and the Syrian press in general praised the Soviet Union for its assistance to the Arabs. No doubt the Syrian regime has now become more dependent on Soviet military and political aid and this has also blocked the process of erosion in Baʻth-Communist relations.

Nevertheless, as the summer of 1967 progressed the pressures within the Ba'th to curb Communist activities, temporarily suspended by the war, were once again mounting. The government reshuffle of 28 September represented a slight shift to the right by the regime for it added three pro-Nasserites to the cabinet and dropped an equal number of Communist sympathizers. This undoubtedly represented a loss to Communist influence in the government, although one registered Communist (Ṣamīḥ 'Aṭiyya) still was included in the new cabinet.[19] At the end of October, further steps were taken to bring the Popular Defense Army under the control of the Syrian Armed Forces.[20] In addition, there were growing disagreements between the U.S.S.R. and the Syrian regime regarding the strategy to be adopted in solving the Middle East crisis. The Syrians, having opposed any political approach, rejected the Security Council Resolution of 22 November. This attitude evoked a rare public reprimand from the Soviet press when, on 27 November, *Pravda* referred to those Arab governments repudiating the Security Council Resolution as "hotheads."[21]

On 29 November, a high-level Syrian delegation (including Prime Minister Zu'ayyin, Foreign Minister Mākhūs, and Chief of Staff Suwaydānī) paid a "surprise visit" to Moscow (Mākhūs having been there less than four weeks earlier) and met with such top Communist and Soviet leaders as Communist Party Secretary-General L. Brezhnev, Prime Minister A. Kosygin, Defense Minister A. Grechko, and others. In the opinion of Western observers, the Syrian delegation had been invited to straighten out differences over the approach to a solution of the Middle East crisis.[22] But Syrian government sources maintained that the visit was the outcome of a Syrian initiative to secure more Soviet arms and economic assistance.[23]

It was against this background of growing estrangement between important segments of the Ba'th regime and the Communist Party on the one hand, and the tensions created by the Middle East crisis between Syria and the U.S.S.R. on the other, that Khālid Bakdāsh, Secretary-General of the Syrian C.P., published a rather critical assessment of the Ba'th-Communist relationship in the November 1967 issue of the Soviet theoretical organ *Kommunist*. He complained that the C.P. in Syria did not enjoy "all the democratic freedoms" despite its cooperation with the regime; he alluded to "certain deficiencies" of the Syrian regime in the political, economic, and social spheres. He promised, however, that the C.P. would "continue to support the left wing of the Ba'th Party. . . ."[24] It was the first time, as far as may be ascertained, that a spokesman of the

C.P. had publicly voiced such criticism of the new regime and confirmed: a) the existence of a "left wing" within the Ba'th Party; and b) that the Communists were not cooperating with the party's "other wing."

During 1967 two conflicting schools of political thought did indeed seem once again to have crystallized within the Ba'th Party along the now "traditional" lines of "radical" and "nationalist" orientations. The radicals were bent on assigning top priority to the policy of "socialist transformation" (*taḥwīl ishtirākī*) and its achievement in the fastest possible way. For this purpose, the radicals were striving to reorganize the regime on the Soviet model, increase economic and political dependence on the U.S.S.R., and "pay" for it by allowing the Syrian Communists a larger share in government affairs and aligning the country more closely with the Communist bloc. They rejected any cooperation with "reactionary" Arab regimes, gave paramountcy to the principle of a "popular liberation war," and supported the Fidayeen. The nationalist tendency, on the other hand, wanted to accord top priority to the "armed struggle" against Israel. It demanded the adjustment of socialist ideology to the requirements of the defense effort, and more reliance on Arab strength than on the Socialist countries. Domestically, the nationalists were prepared to collaborate with what they called "national-progressive" forces further to the right, and in the struggle against Israel they were urging cooperation with the neighboring regimes of Iraq and Jordan. The radical wing was not only particularly dominant within the party's central apparatus but also claimed the support of some officers, whereas the nationalist wing enjoyed the backing of many army officers as well as a considerable following among the party rank and file. Thus, these two schools of thought again came increasingly to represent two interest groupings within the party, but in a constellation the reverse of that of 1965–6: a radical-civilian wing confronted by a nationalist-military wing.

However, it soon became apparent that these groupings were not of equal internal solidarity, let alone power. For, while the more rigid military organization and hierarchy made the nationalist-military wing more monolithic, the radical civilians were split into several factions centered around key personalities, motivated by personal (and sometimes confessional) rivalries.

In 1966–7 three major radical-civilian factions coalesced. The first faction, known as the Hawrān group, was headed by Minister of Information Muḥammad Zu'bī and by the Chief of Staff Aḥmad as-

Suwaydānī. The second faction consisted of the Dayr al-Zūr group headed by Prime Minister Zu'ayyin and Foreign Minister Mākhūs, and strongly supported by the extreme leftist 'Abd al-Karīm al-Jundī, Chief of the General Intelligence in 1967. The third and strongest civilian faction was that headed by Ṣalāḥ Jadīd who, as Deputy Secretary-General of the Ba'th Party, controlled much of the party organization. The leader of the nationalist-military faction was Defense Minister and Air Force Commander Ḥāfiẓ al-Asad, who was also a member of the Party Regional (Syrian) Command.

The first two civilian factions lost most of their influence during the latter part of 1967 and in 1968. Minister of Information Zu'bi was dropped from the government in September 1967 and Chief of Staff Suwaydānī was replaced in February 1968 by Muṣṭafā Talās, a supporter of Asad.[25] The Dayr al-Zūr group managed to stay in power until October 1968.

Now that internal Ba'th differences had been publicly aired by the Communists, the former's military wing began an anti-Communist campaign in order to discredit the radical wing and thus help to consolidate its own position within the army and at the party grassroots level. Under their pressure it seems that government offices and trade union organizations were indeed being purged of Communists. At one point in September-October 1968, 10 Communists were retired from key positions in the Euphrates Dam Authority, and Ṣamīḥ 'Aṭiyya, the Communist Minister of Communications, threatened to resign.[26] As the Party Regional (i.e., Syrian) and National (all-Arab) Congresses (held on 26 September–10 October, 1968) drew near, the question of cooperation with the Communists became one of the key issues in party politics.

The Communists themselves did not remain idle, and launched a propaganda campaign. On the one hand, they stressed the points of agreement between themselves and the Ba'th regarding economic matters, i.e., planned economy, large-scale agrarian reform, establishment of agricultural cooperatives and state farms. Like the Ba'th, they stressed the importance of the big national projects (the Euphrates Dam, the petrochemical industry, the extension of the railway network—all of which were carried out with the assistance of the Soviet bloc) and the expansion of economic relations with the Socialist countries. On the other hand, they insisted on cooperating only with the "left wing" of the ruling party. Moreover, the C.P. organ called for a purge of "reactionary elements" in the administration.[27]

At the same time, the Communists continued to exert pressure on the Ba'th Party to form a "progressive front," hold free elections for a constituent assembly, and establish a coalition government.[28] The Communists, furthermore, took steps to realize their objectives and were the initiators of talks held in Lebanon between several Syrian political groups (Arab Nationalists, Arab Socialists, and Socialist Unionists). However, in view of the Ba'th's unremitting opposition, the Communists withdrew from the talks, even though the other groups set up a "front" in May 1968.[29]

Toward the fall of 1968, with the anti-Communist campaign mounting, the Communists launched on all-out attack on the Ba'th right wing and approached the radical wing with offers for "closer cooperation of all progressive forces."[30] Moreover, when the Ba'th Party Congresses convened in September-October, the Communists submitted demands for greater participation in the government. In addition to the one portfolio they already held, they demanded two more.[31] Al-Nahār added that the Communists had specifically asked for the Ministry of Health and the Ministry of Labor and Social Affairs. The same source remarked that the Communists had presented their demands as a kind of ultimatum. They insisted on a reply within ten days and in the meanwhile Communist Communications Minister Ṣamīḥ 'Aṭiyya suspended his participation in government. The Ba'th Regional Command asked the Communists to continue cooperating on the former basis and to leave any future changes to the new Regional Command which would be elected by the Party Congress.[32]

Communist attacks on the powerful nationalist wing and their demands for increased government representation had an effect the reverse of that anticipated. At the Party Congresses Defense Minister Asad accused the radical Ba'thists of collusion with the Communists. In particular, he denounced the Dayr al-Zūr group as outright collaborators. He charged Prime Minister Zu'ayyin with having "appointed registered Communist Party members . . . as his advisers and special secretaries in the Office of the Prime Minister." Moreover, Zu'ayyin had "turned over to Communists the board chairmanship of all [government] companies in Syria. Especially, he had filled vital agencies with Communist employees, [e.g.] the information services and government departments, particularly in the Ministry of National Economy. Some government agencies, including the Euphrates Dam [Authority], the National Company for Import and Export, and the Syrian Petroleum Authority, were completely controlled by Communists." Furthermore, Asad accused Zu'ayyin of improper contacts with the Soviet embassy. Zu'ayyin, he contended, "had contacted for some time and behind the back of the Regional [i.e., Syrian] Command and the Government, the Soviet Union through the Soviet Ambassador in Damascus." Asad termed this conduct "an intolerable violation and excess" and demanded "an end to Zu'ayyin's behavior." Asad went on to call for the curbing of Communist infiltration into the government. This was his only recommendation to be accepted by the Congress, apparently because Jadīd's faction realized the danger of supporting the Communists and dissociated itself from any position which might be construed as favorable to them. Other proposals by Asad, in particular those regarding reconciliation with the Iraqi Ba'thists, were rejected by the Congress.[33]

Although the Ba'th Regional and National Congresses were held in secrecy at the party's Institute for Political Guidance in Ya'fūr near Damascus, the Communists were apparently well informed of the proceedings. While the Congresses were still in session, the Communists launched a virulent propaganda campaign against Asad, openly charging that he had "deviated from the revolutionary line." At the same time, the Communists praised "the wisdom of Ṣalāḥ Jadīd and his fine behavior." Concurrently, there were claims that the Soviet embassy in Damascus "threw all its weight behind and did everything possible" for the leftist wing of Zu'ayyin.[34]

Communist activity, if anything, must have undermined the radicals' position at the Congress, and it is questionable whether the involvement of the Soviet embassy was of any assistance either. Yet, mainly because of Jadīd's control of the party apparatus, the radical-civilian wing was able to hold its own at the Congress. The resolutions adopted by the Congress and the elections to the Regional Command and the National Command did not reflect any significant changes in the party's balance of power, despite the fact that the military wing was gaining strength and popularity and had emerged as the foremost element within the regime. Asad, who was not satisfied with the proceedings at the Congress and especially not with the election results, withdrew to his air force headquarters before the Congress had officially concluded. From there, he presented the Congress with demands amounting to an ultimatum. His principal demand was the dismissal of Jadīd from his party post and new elections to the Regional Command.[35] To press the point, Asad ordered air force planes to fly over Damascus.[36] Meanwhile, the Soviet embassy was again

reported to have been active in the attempt to prevent a further deterioration of the situation.[37] Either because the intervention of the Soviet
embassy was effective or for other reasons, the Congress did not yield to
Asad's demands. The latter tried to force the issue outside the party
framework. He completed the consolidation of his mastery over the
armed forces by the transfer of officers loyal to Jadīd to insignificant positions.[38] Thus, he defied the party's Military Bureau, controlled by Jadīd,
in which the authority to confirm significant changes in command posts
was vested. During the last week of October, the confrontation reached
crisis proportions and Asad was preparing, or pretending to prepare, for
a military *coup*.[39] Army units loyal to him occupied the General Staff
buildings and radio and television centers. According to al-*Hayāt*, these
final steps caused the government to topple and, on 28 October, a compromise solution was reached when "neutral" President Nūr al-Dīn al-
Atāsī agreed to form a new cabinet without former Prime Minister
Zu'ayyin and former Foreign Minister Mākhūs.[40]

Most other Lebanese newspapers, however, analyzed the situation
somewhat differently. They claimed that open confrontation within the
party had been averted by virtue of a compromise that had been worked
out between Jadīd and Asad. According to this, Jadīd had consented to
"sacrifice" Zu'ayyin and Mākhūs, but only if this were done by a decision
of the new Regional Command and not through the "unilateral act"
forced by Asad and the army. This would entail Asad's recognition of the
legality and authority of the new Regional Command in which Jadīd
continued to retain the post of Deputy Secretary-General.[41]

The outcome of the October power struggle was at the time considered a compromise, for the changes in party leadership and in the government brought Asad's military wing only minor gains. In fact, however,
Asad's position improved considerably because he was finally able to
shake off the remnants of party apparatus supervision over the army and
to fully consolidate his own position within it.[42] To underline this new
party-military relationship, he issued an order forbidding military units
to receive visits by party civilian leaders.[43] He thus effectively blocked
any support which his rivals might have sought within the armed forces
and could now press more freely for the implementation of the policies
advocated by the nationalists.

Nevertheless, except for the ouster of Zu'ayyin and Mākhūs, there
were no dramatic changes in the new government following the Congress.
The balance between Jadīd's radical wing and Asad's nationalist wing was

maintained and the Communists also retained their single portfolio though their previous representative, Ṣamīḥ ʻAṭiyya, was replaced by Wāṣil Fayṣal. The new cabinet also took great pains to stress the continuity of the regime and its policies.[44] On 8 December, 1968, Mālik al-Amīn, a member of the Baʻth National Command and head of its Publications and Information Bureau, read a statement over Radio Damascus and television summing up the Congress. Among passages of the broadcast were the following:

> [The Congress had] received with appreciation the role of the Soviet Union and all other Socialist states in its battle of destiny [and] . . . in reinforcing our military powers . . . [the Congress] emphasized its eagerness to promote friendly relations at party, government and popular organizations level between us and the Soviet Union and other Socialist countries.[45]

These steps were undoubtedly taken, *inter alia,* to allay Soviet suspicions. Nevertheless, Asad's ascendancy heralded a deterioration of relations with the Communists. The Baʻth leadership set up a special committee to study the files of all party members in order to flush out individuals characterized as "concealed Marxists."[46]

During the last third of 1968, the C.P. was also experiencing a leadership crisis. Khālid Bakdāsh, "Communist Number One in the Arab World" and Secretary-General of the Syrian C.P. since 1936, suffered a heart attack in August and was flown to Moscow in a Soviet plane. When it became apparent that his stay would be an extended one, the C.P. held elections for a new Central Committee which, in its turn, was to nominate a new Secretary-General. At the end of September, Maurice Ṣalībī, a Christian lawyer, was elected to this post. The new Central Committee held several meetings attended by Soviet Ambassador Noureddin Mohieddinov, but early in October it decided to declare the previous elections null and void. During the first week of October, new elections were held and Yūsuf Fayṣal was nominated as the new Secretary-General.[47] Bakdāsh returned to Damascus in December after his health had improved.[48] Meanwhile, the lack of effective leadership within the Syrian C.P. and the crass meddling of the Soviet embassy in its internal affairs undoubtedly heightened the general disrepute of both the C.P. and the Soviet Union.

At the end of 1968 and the beginning of 1969, relations between the Baʻth regime and the Soviet Union were plumbing new depths. At the

center of the controversy stood the question of the general orientation of
the regime, which the Soviets must have felt was leaning further to the
right. The Syrians, for their part, maintained that the degree of military
assistance which the Soviets were giving them was not sufficient, and in
November they sent a military mission to France to study the possibilities
of alternate arms purchases.[49] At the beginning of 1969, there were reports that the Syrian government had stopped granting exit permits to
Syrian citizens wishing to visit the U.S.S.R.[50]

The general deterioration of relations between the Syrian government
and the U.S.S.R. on the one hand, and the regime's continued pressure
against Syrian Communists on the other, came against the background of
a growing crisis within the Syrian Ba'th between the two remaining factions respectively headed by Jadīd and Asad. Since the last Party Congress,
the radical wing had attempted to regain its lost strength, particularly some
control of the armed forces, through propaganda activity within the party
apparatus, and had prepared itself for the next Party Congress where it
hoped to strip the military wing of its excess authority. The already tense
situation was even further aggravated when, on 24 February, Israeli air
force jets staged a reprisal attack on two Fidayeen camps at al-Ḥamma
and Maysalūn, some fifty kilometers inside Syria, and shot down two
Syrian MiGs. This incident provided the civilian wing with additional
grounds to criticize the military for ineffectiveness against the enemy. The
military wing reacted sharply, accusing the radicals of preparing to stage a
coup in collusion with the Communists and the Soviet Union, and also
leveled an attack at the latter for "failing to honor its commitments to
the Syrian army."[51]

Reports from Syria filtering through the Lebanese press gave the
impression that by the beginning of March the country was on the verge of
civil war, with both wings—civilian and military—actually preparing for
such an eventuality. The Beirut newspaper *al-Nahār* carried an announcement made public in Damascus on 3 March by a group of organizations
styling themselves "national bodies working toward the reestablishment
of democratic life in Syria." This announcement called on the population
of Syria to "unite around Hafiẓ al-Asad who had undertaken to free the
people of Syria from the ruling rabble whose sole ambition in the past six
years had been personal gain . . . and who maintain that the armed forces'
duty is to protect the regime of the Ba'th Party and its rulers and not the
homeland and the nation's honor."[52] That same day, another Beirut
paper, *al-Sayyād*, reported that the Syrian C.P. had called upon its mem-

bers to prepare themselves to take up arms in support of Jadīd's faction against Asad in the eventuality of a civil war which the Communists regarded as imminent.[53] A few days earlier, *al-Anwār* had published the text of a communiqué circulated in Beirut on 1 March by the Syrian Communists. It reported the resolutions of the Central Committee of the Syrian C.P., which had met in Damascus on 15 February. It attacked in the strongest terms the "reactionary elements" in the Ba'th and pledged Communist support to the "progressives."[54]

Soviet bloc embassies in Damascus were also reported to be active. *Al-Ḥayāt* reported the meeting in Damascus on 8 March of Communist ambassadors who wished "to join efforts to save Jadīd's faction" and that the Soviets had threatened to discontinue arms shipments to Syria altogether.[55]

In the midst of the crisis, on 20 March, Bakdāsh left Damascus for Moscow. *Al-Ḥayāt,* which reported Bakdāsh's departure, linked it to the current crisis within the Ba'th, but did not elaborate further.[56] Was it possible that Bakdāsh was not satisfied with the degree of pressure the Soviet embassy was applying on the military wing? Or, which is more likely, was Bakdāsh called to Moscow and asked to curb Communist interference in Ba'th internal politics because it was a course of action proving counterproductive to the interests of the Soviet Union?

The crisis within the Ba'th Party was ultimately referred to an emergency Party Congress convened between 20–31 March, 1969, in Damascus. At the time, the real issues with which the Congress dealt were shrouded in secrecy. But in November 1970, following the *coup* which ousted Jadīd's faction from power, Mālik al-Amīn, spokesman of the deposed faction, disclosed that the issues under dispute were:

a) The duality in government represented by the fact that the Defense Minister has set himself up as equal to the Command of the Party and the Revolution.
b) [The Defense Minister] had deviated from Party strategy.
c) [The Defense Minister] attempted to quash the Ideological Army experiment and incite the army against the Party and the popular organizations.[57]

However, notwithstanding the fact that the important issues with which the Congress was convened to deal concerned party-military relations, the question of the party's attitude toward the Communists and the Soviet Union was high on the agenda. Jadīd, realizing how unpopular cooperation with the Communists had become with the party's rank and file, uncharacteristically launched an attack against "Communist infiltration into the government" and tried to dissociate his group from any collusion with the Communists. The Congress again concluded without having resolved the basic impasse, but continuing to maintain the existing balance within the party. Defense Minister Asad continued to enjoy a free hand in all matters pertaining to defense and particularly relating to cooperation on the Eastern Front with "reactionary" Jordan and Iraq. Jadīd maintained control over the party apparatus. A U.P.I. report dated 12 April attributed "diplomatic sources" with the view that it had only been due to Soviet intervention that a compromise had been reached and the civilian wing had remained in power. The Soviet ambassador, according to the report, had handed Asad an ultimatum threatening a break of relations, a halt in arms deliveries, and a demand for immediate repayment of all loans unless he made some "act of loyalty" to Moscow.[58] It is doubtful whether events actually developed according to this pattern. More probably, all parties involved realized their own limitations and were aware that going to extremes would lead to greater loss and perhaps even disaster. The radical wing of the Ba'th must have sensed that the scales had tipped against it, probably not only because of the loss of influence over the armed forces, but also because the mood within the party itself, not to mention that of the public, had become more "nationalist." It realized that its image as the chief exponent of cooperation with the Communists and the Soviet Union had undermined its position among the rank and file of even Ba'th members.

The nationalist-military wing must have accepted its dependence on Soviet goodwill to obtain the arms which by its own admission it needed to prepare for the battle against Israel. In fact, the declared political theory of the nationalist-military wing, which stressed the role of the regular armed forces over that of the "popular organizations," dictated even greater dependence on the Soviet Union.

The Soviets too have become aware of the dangers inherent in pressing the regime too hard. Of course, they would have preferred to see the group with greater affinities to Communism strengthened, but to push further would have constituted gross interference with all the attendant risks. Furthermore, the ascendancy of the less extreme military wing had its advantages—mainly Syria's closer approach to the political position of the U.A.R. and a cooling effect on the Middle East situation which was then reaching one of the worst stages in the "war of attrition" along the Suez Canal. They therefore played the role of mediator in the internal Syrian dispute. They warned Asad not to go too far and at the same time restrained both the Ba'th radicals and the Communists.

COMMUNIST NEUTRALITY, 1969–70

Throughout April, the Soviets and Syrian Communists attempted to lower the level of tension. On 23 April, Soviet correspondents interviewed Syria's President and Prime Minister, Dr. Nūr al-Dīn al-Atāsī, who spoke of the significance of the last Party Congress and called it "a victory for the people and a serious defeat for counterrevolution." *Inter alia,* he also refuted any allegations of "Soviet interference in domestic affairs of Syria."[59]

The Syrian C.P. organ *Niḍāl al-Sha'b* also discussed the Ba'th Party Congress in positive terms. In an apparent attempt to be conciliatory, the paper justified the Congress' decision to strengthen its cooperation with the Arab countries, a policy demanded by the military wing. It stated: "There is no doubt that Syria is in need of a more flexible and positive Arab policy. It also should stop its extremist policy and its constant adoption of a position more to the left than anyone else. Suspicions toward Arab regimes that are royalist, or reactionary, or dependent [on Western Powers] are justified; but these suspicions have reached such proportions that they have isolated Syria itself and caused setbacks in the struggle against Israel."[60]

Relations between the regime and the Communists remained correct despite the fact that in May President Atāsī cancelled his visit to Moscow while Muṣṭafā Ṭalās, the Chief of Staff and a close supporter of Defense Minister Asad, paid a visit to Peking. The Lebanese press as well as several Western newspapers viewed this act as a sign of the beginning of Soviet-Chinese rivalry in Damascus or the renewal of inter-Ba'th strife.[61] In all probability, Asad must have known that Peking was unable to replace the Soviets as Syria's major arms supplier. His journey there was more a symbolic gesture to underline the regime's—and primarily the military wing's—independent posture *vis-à-vis* Moscow. It was this policy which impelled the Syrian government to announce on 27 May that it would establish full diplomatic relations with Albania, and to balance this step on 5 June by doing the same with East Germany.

The C.P. also reduced its partisanship. In June, *Niḍāl al-Sha'b* voiced disapproval of the new Provisional Constitution (issued on 1

May), but this criticism was mild by the paper's previous standards. The Communist organ seized the opportunity to renew the call to the regime to legalize the activities of other parties and establish a "progressive front."[62]

It was against this background of improved relations and the Ba'th regime's self-assertion that President Atāsī paid a much-publicized state visit to Moscow in the first half of July; its declared purpose was to "consolidate the friendly relations between the Arab and Soviet peoples."[63]

The consolidation of "friendly relations" was indeed uppermost in the minds of Syrian Communists as well. Interviewed by the Hungarian Communist Party paper *Népszabadság*, Bakdāsh referred to the Ba'th regime with the highest respect and caution. Asked "what prerequisites would make economic and social developments in Syria even more rapid and consistent?" Bakdāsh answered: " . . . to enable us to pursue the progressive road in the country, the road which was envisaged by the latest Congress of the Ba'th Party and the government, cooperation should be consistently strengthened among all progressive forces." To the question "what do the Communists think of the country's foreign policy?" Bakdāsh replied: "Our Party supports the government's foreign policy. It regards as necessary, first of all, a continued strengthening of co-operation in every respect with the Soviet Union and all Socialist countries." Bakdāsh went on to say that the Communists favored increasing the army's striking power and that "coordination and reconciliation of the positions of the Arab states offer better prospects for us in opposing the interventions of large imperialist powers." Toward the end of the interview, Bakdāsh added: "It is known that our Party has helped solve the winter and spring [Ba'th] crises. Since then, it has also been trying to ensure that the unity of the Ba'th Party on the basis of the policy proclaimed on 23 February, 1966, is upheld."[64]

This last statement doubtlessly offers the key to an understanding of Communist behavior since April 1969. Communist agitation and infiltration into government bodies had had an unsettling effect on the Ba'th regime. It tended to exacerbate differences within the Ba'th Party and weaken the radical faction which was more sympathetic to the local Communists and the Soviet Union. To be sure, the main causes of the radicals' defeat lay elsewhere—in their failure to curb the armed forces and in their own extremism which produced a misreading of the mood of the party's rank and file, let alone the public at large. But the radicals' known or alleged sympathy with the Communists became a weapon used by their antagonists against them. Thus, Communist meddling in Ba'th internal politics ultimately worked against the interests of the C.P. and those of the Soviet Union. Under Soviet pressure, therefore, the Syrian Communists restrained themselves so as not to polarize the Ba'th Party and from April 1969 stopped being a destabilizing factor in the intra-party power struggle.

One serious incident marred the "correct" relations finally established between the Communists and the regime. In May 1970, the Syrian authorities arrested many Communists. This was a "retaliatory" act which took place in the wake of the Lenin centenary celebrations. Apparently, the Syrian Communists had used the occasion to illegally post numerous placards in Damascus and other Syrian towns. These were taken down by Syrian security forces. In addition, the Syrian regime might have been "insulted" by the fact that the head of their delegation to Moscow to participate in the centenary celebrations, Minister of the Interior Rabbāḥ Ṭawīl, was not allowed to speak.[65] The incident was certainly incomprehensible in view of the long-improved Ba'th-Communist relations.

The next round in the conflict between the Ba'th civilian and military wings was purely an internal party affair. Its origins lay in the unresolved issues of the party-army relations, aggravated by a sequence of events beginning with a devastating Israeli air strike on Syrian military bases in June 1970 and culminating in Syria's military failure in Jordan and Nasser's death in September. Relations with the Communists or the Soviet Union do not seem to have been involved. Essentially, it was the radical-civilian wing which moved matters toward a crisis. It was on this group's initiative that the Ba'th Party convened its 10th Extraordinary National Congress (30 October–12 November, 1970). During the Congress radical leaders tried to force the issue by pushing through a decision calling for the resignation of Defense Minister Asad and his Chief of Staff Ṭalās. It was only when mediation attempts, including those by the Soviet embassy, proved futile that Defense Minister Asad carried out a bloodless *coup* on 13 November.

During this last crisis, the C.P., undoubtedly under orders from Moscow, not only did not side with the radical wing, but, in fact, acted to preserve Ba'th Party unity. The Syrian C.P. Central Committee met on 25 October, 1970, and issued the following communiqué regarding "developments in the Arab situation and the domestic situation in Syria." In this long document several phrases stand out:

... Our Party ... [is] seeking to preserve the present regime in Syria and consolidate [its] achievements with a minimum of mistakes.

... The Central Committee ... stressed that the nationalist and progressive forces are capable of overcoming the [present Ba'th] crisis and standing in the way of all attempts to destroy or shake the nationalist progressive regime. The Central Committee, in stressing the inevitability of victory ... insisted that the crisis be overcome by adhering to the progressive nationalist line adopted by the 23 February movement.

... In the light of these vital national and progressive missions, every nationalist progressive hopes that the meetings of the special sessions of the Arab Ba'th Party will be devoted to tackling the crisis inside the Ba'th Party and regime. The Central Committee believes that opportunities are available for the triumph and consolidation of the nationalist progressive line in Arab Syria.[66]

When the Ba'th National Congress began its deliberations, the C.P. Central Committee sent a message to the Congress referring to the bonds of cooperation uniting the two parties, the common enemies outside Syria and within, and the duties ahead. It ended on the hopeful note that the Ba'th Party would manage to solve its crisis on its own.[67]

By adopting such a stand, the C.P.—and the Soviet embassy behind it—emerged as a factor working for the maintenance of the existing balance of power within the Ba'th Party. In practice, however, their weight was thrown behind the nationalist-military wing against the radical civilians who wanted to redress that balance. By extricating themselves from the crucible of the Ba'th's internal issues, the Communists have, first of all, facilitated Asad's decision to execute the *coup,* and, secondly, gained for themselves the right to continue being represented in government on the same basis as previously.

NOTES

[1] *Cf.* Walter Laqueur, *The Soviet Union and the Middle East* (London 1959), pp. 167–8; Ilyās Murqūṣ, *Ta'rikh al-aḥzāb al-shuyū'iyya fi'l-waṭan al-'arabī* (Beirut 1964), p. 86 ff.; Ibrāhīm Salāma, *Al-ba'th min al-madāris ila al-thuknāt* (Beirut 1969), p. 7; Gordon H. Torrey, "The Ba'th—Ideology and Practice," *The Middle East Journal*, Vol. XXIII (1969), pp. 455–7.

[2] *Cf.* Walter Laqueur, *The Struggle for the Middle East* (London 1969), pp. 84–94; Aryeh Yodfat, "The Soviet Union between Communists and Ba'thists in Syria," *Hamizrah Hehadash*, Vol. XXII (1972), pp. 1–25 (Hebrew).

[3] *Cf.* Sāmī al-Jundī, *al-Ba'th*, Beirut 1969, pp. 70, 73, 153–54.

[4] *Al-Anwār*, Beirut, 15 November, 1970.

[5] Ba'th internal politics from the *coup* of March 1963 to that of February 1966 were characterized by a growing cleavage and eventual conflict between veteran party leaders Michel 'Aflaq and Ṣalāḥ al-Dīn al-Bīṭār and their moderate followers on the one hand, and the Ba'th military leaders and their radical civilian supporters on the other. The latter group had predominated since the early days of the new regime, but due to a succession of crises it could not assert its hegemony until the summer of 1964. In December 1965, however, the group headed by 'Aflaq and Bīṭār and now supported by General Amīn al-Ḥāfiẓ (who had earlier broken with his radical colleagues in the army) staged a bloodless *coup d'état* against the radical faction. The triumph of the moderates, however, remained partial and short-lived, for on 23 February, 1966, the radicals led by General Ṣalāḥ Jadīd mounted a bloody counter-*coup* and seized power in Syria.

[6] *Cf.* Yodfat, pp. 13–17.

[7] *Al-Ba'th*, Damascus, 27 January, 1967; also *cf. al-Sayyād*, Beirut, 2 February, 1967; *al-Jadīd*, Beirut, 10 February, 1967.

[8] *Al-Ba'th*, Damascus, 12 February, 1967.

[9] Cited in D. Dishon (ed.), *Middle East Record, 1967*, Jerusalem 1971, p. 26.

[10] *Ibid.*, pp. 26–7.

[11] *Al-Thawra*, Damascus, 22 April, 1968; *al-Anwār*, Beirut, 29 October, 1968.

[12] *Niḍāl al-Sha'b*, quoted by *al-Nahār*, Beirut, 5 April, 1967.

[13] *Ha'aretz*, Tel Aviv, 17, 27 May, 5 June, 29 July, 1966; *Ma'ariv*, Tel Aviv, 8, 27 May, 9 June, 1 August, 1966.

[14] *M.E.R. 1967*, p. 493.

[15] *Al-Ḥayāt*, Beirut, 2, 7, 15 April, 1967. *Al-Ḥayāt* adopts an anti-Communist line and should be read critically.

[16] *Jaysh al-Sha'b*, Damascus, 25 April, 1967–quoted by *al-Ḥayāt*, Beirut, 5 May, 1967.

[17] *M.E.R. 1967*, p. 499.

[18] *Al-Thawra*, Damascus, 16 June, 1967.

[19] *M.E.R. 1967*, p. 497.

[20] *Ibid.*, p. 493

[21] *Ibid.*, p. 27.

[22] *The Christian Science Monitor*, Boston, 2 December, 1967; *Le Monde*, 3–4 December, 1967.

[23] *M.E.R. 1967*, p. 27.

[24] Cited in *M.E.R. 1967*, p. 497.

[25] *M.E.R. 1967*, p. 494; *al-Ba'th*, Damascus, 16 February, 1968.

[26] *Al-Nahār*, Beirut, 8 October, 1968.

[27] *Niḍāl al-Sha'b* quoted in *al-Ḥayāt*, Beirut, 17 March, 1968.

[28] *L'Orient*, Beirut, 8 February, 1968.

[29] *Al-Ḥayāt*, Beirut, 4 March, 1968; *al-Ḥurriyya*, Beirut, 16 June, 1968; *al-Ḥawādith*, Beirut, 5 July, 1968. The anti-Communist newspaper *al-Ḥayāt* even claimed that the Communists disclosed various details about the proposed "front" to the Syrian authorities who arrested the followers of the other participating groups in order to prevent its formation (*al-Ḥayāt*, Beirut, 17 March, 1968).

[30] *Niḍāl al-Sha'b*, quoted by *al-Jarīda*, Beirut, 9 October, 1968; see also *al-Anwār*, Beirut, 29 October, 1968.

[31] *Al-Ṣayyād*, Beirut, 10 October, 1968.

[32] *Al-Nahār*, Beirut, 8 October, 1968.

[33] *Al-Ḥayāt*, Beirut, 13 October, 1968.

[34] *Ibid.*, 19 October, 1968.

[35] *Al-Jarīda*, Beirut, 18 October, 1968; *al-Anwār*, Beirut, 29 October, 1968.

[36] *Al-Ḥayāt*, Beirut, 26 October, 1968.

[37] *Al-Nahār*, Beirut, 29 October, 1968.

[38] *Al-Anwār*, Beirut, 26 October, 1968; *al-Ḥayāt*, Beirut, 29 October, 1968; *al-Ḥawādith*, Beirut, 1 November, 1968.

[39] *Al-Ḥayāt*, Beirut, 26 October, 1968.

[40] *Ibid.*, 29 October, 1968.

[41] *Al-Anwār*, Beirut, 31 October, 1968; *al-Ḥawādith*, Beirut, 1 November, 1968; *al-Jadīd*, Beirut, 15 November, 1968.

[42] *Al-Ḥayāt*, Beirut, 7 November, 1968.

[43] *Al-Jadīd*, Beirut, 15 November, 1968.

[44] *Al-Ba'th*, Damascus, 31 October, 1968; *al-Ḥayāt*, Beirut, 2 November, 1968.

[45] Radio Damascus, 8 December, 1968—B.B.C., 12 December, 1968.

[46] *Al-Jarīda*, Beirut, 8 November, 1968.

[47] *Al-Nahār*, Beirut, 8 October, 1968.

⁴⁸ *Niḍāl al-Sha'b* quoted in *al-Jarīda*, Beirut, 18 December, 1968.

⁴⁹ *Al-Anwār*, Beirut, 16 November, 1968.

⁵⁰ *Al-Jarīda*, Beirut, 4 January, 1969.

⁵¹ *Al-Ḥayāt*, Beirut, 22 March, 1969; also see *ar-Ra'y al-Amm*, Kuwait, 16 March, 1969; *al-Ḥayāt*, Beirut, 23 March, 1969.

⁵² *Al-Nahār*, Beirut, 6 March, 1969.

⁵³ *Al-Sayyād*, Beirut, 6 March, 1969.

⁵⁴ *Al-Anwār*, Beirut, 2 March, 1969.

⁵⁵ *Al-Ḥayāt*, Beirut, 9 March, 1969.

⁵⁶ *Ibid.*, 22 March, 1969.

⁵⁷ *Al-Nahār*, Beirut, 14 November, 1970.

⁵⁸ U.P.I. quoted by *Arab Report and Record*, London, 1–15 April, 1969.

⁵⁹ *TASS* in English, 23 April, 1969—*Daily Report* (Middle East and Africa), Washington, 23 April, 1969.

⁶⁰ *Niḍāl al-Sha'b*, quoted by *al-Nahār*, Beirut, 1 May, 1969.

⁶¹ *Al-Ṣayyād*, Beirut, 15 May, 1969; *al-Ḥawādith*, Beirut, 16 May, 1969; *al-Ḥayāt*, Beirut, 22 May, 1969; *Le Monde*, Paris, 22 May, 1969.

⁶² *Niḍāl al-Sha'b* quoted in *al-Anwār*, Beirut, 25 June, 1969.

⁶³ *Middle East News Agency—Daily Report*, Washington, 14 July, 1969.

⁶⁴ *Népszabadság*, Budapest, 2 November, 1969—*Daily Record*, Washington, 6 November, 1969.

⁶⁵ *Al-Ḥayāt*, Beirut, 7 May, 1970; *al-Kifāḥ*, Beirut, 21 May, 1970; *Le Monde*, Paris, 23 June, 1970.

⁶⁶ *Al-Nidā'*, Beirut, 1 November, 1970.

⁶⁷ *Al-Akhbār*, Beirut, 15 November, 1970.

AMNON COHEN

THE JORDANIAN COMMUNIST PARTY IN THE WEST BANK, 1950–1960

BASIC TRENDS IN THE ACTIVITIES OF THE PARTY

The Jordanian Communist Party (C.P.) was officially founded in June 1951. In point of fact, it developed from the League for National Liberation, which had engaged in political and other activities in the West Bank for some years past. Between 1949 and 1951, several Palestinian C.P. members, now on territory under King Abdullah's rule, began to reorganize a few West Bank branches of the League. The center of their efforts was in Nablus and the surrounding areas, and there was also some preliminary organizational activity in Jerusalem. After a year of organization and attempts at gaining popular support by distributing leaflets, the first demonstration was held in Nablus on 31 March, 1950. This resulted in the arrest of about 30 party members and their exile to the East Bank. Nevertheless, these setbacks did not halt the continuing development of the League in the two cities mentioned above nor did they prevent the establishment of a strong branch in Ramallah.

The party did not limit itself to action at local branch level, but created a country-wide apparatus. Secretary-General Riḍwān al-Ḥilū, one of the central figures of the Palestine C.P., was ousted and Fu'ād Naṣṣār took his place. A policy of recruiting members and supporters from among the intelligentsia, and not from among the workers as some demanded, was adopted. In the political sphere, the League formulated a policy of hostility and opposition to the "Hashemite

* This paper constitutes a part of a wider research project on "Political Parties in the West Bank under the Hashemite Rule," mainly based on the Archives of the Jordanian Security Services. I would like to thank the Israel Defense Ministry and especially Aluf Sh. Gazit for enabling me to utilize this rich and instructive source. Another source consisted of interviews held during 1971 with some leaders of the Communist Party, the names of whom are not cited for obvious reasons.

army of occupation," and demanded the evacuation of all foreign Arab armies from Palestine along with the implementation of the U.N. Palestine Partition Plan of 1947. Subscribing to these basic tenets, the League opposed all steps taken by the Hashemite regime aimed at annexing the West Bank. But very soon the social and organizational decisions of the party were coupled with a change in its hitherto deep-rooted and declared attitude of opposition to Jordanian rule in the West Bank. When it became clear that Abdullah would not be satisfied with less than full annexation of the West Bank, when the parliamentary elections made the annexation a *fait accompli,* and in response to the increasing Ba'th challenge, the League finalized all these changes by renaming itself; beginning with the second half of 1951, it became known as the Jordanian Communist Party.

Despite unceasing persecution by the regime, the party did manage to grow, albeit slowly, in the first half of the 1950s. Its activities were concentrated in two concentric spheres. The inner sphere involved cells and branches of the party which trained cadres and attempted to reach areas where the party had previously not existed (Mount Hebron, especially). The outer one was concerned with public activity on a wider scale within the framework of a front organization—the Partisans of Peace *(anṣār al-salām).*

The authorities tried incessantly to interfere with these attempts to establish front organizations: several Communist organizers were arrested and/or prevented from traveling to international conferences outside Jordan.[1] At the beginning of 1952, leading members of the Muslim Brethren and other religious figures were recruited by the government in order to denounce Communism in the mosques. They also served as police informers against individual C.P. members.[2] Many members were jailed and consigned to al-Jafar prison camp. Parliament approved a law ("War on Communism," 1 December, 1953) authorizing a campaign against Communism and instituting heavy punishments for any Communist activity (such as contributions to the party, distribution of leaflets, or even possession of such).[3]

In 1954, after continuous success in establishing new branches, front organizations (such as the Union of Democratic Youth), and trade unions, the party turned to the task of acquiring more legitimacy in the eyes of both the government and the public. The National Front, in which party members played a considerable role, was set up in preparation for the October 1954 parliamentary elections. Despite persecution by the regime, the imprisonment of a substantial portion of the Communist candidates, and manipulations of the elections, 'Abd al-Qādir al-Ṣāliḥ, a representative of the C.P. in the Front, was elected in Nablus.[4]

In point of fact, al-Ṣāliḥ, a prominent landowner in the Nablus area, had never been a Communist. However, from the moment the party decided to support him, he became its spokesman in the eyes of the public. Despite substantial organizational success in the Jerusalem area and considerable progress in the Hebron area, Nablus and its vicinity continued to be of prime importance for the party at this stage because of this city's longer history as a center of party activity.

The peak of activity and achievement was reached in 1956–7. The success of the 1954 National Front in Nablus led the C.P. once again to organize a National Front, but this time the main efforts were concentrated in the central Jerusalem-Ramallah area. Attempts to include the Ba'th Party in the Front failed, as they had in the past, mainly because of the Ba'th's intransigent opposition to the idea of cooperation. But this did not prevent the establishment of the Front to contest the parliamentary elections (in the second half of 1956). Demonstrations of support for Front members, public gatherings in the major cities, mass signing of petitions, meetings in villages—all these characterized the public activity of the party. During the large demonstrations which erupted in the major cities throughout the West Bank at the time of the nationalization of the Suez Canal, the Communists stood out as a united group carrying their own slogans and at times leading these demonstrations themselves. The organized activity and intensive propaganda campaign bore fruit.[5]

In the elections held on 21 October, 1956, three candidates of the Front who were completely identified with the party—Fā'iq Warrād, Dr. Ya'qūb Ziyādīn and 'Abd al-Qādir al-Ṣāliḥ—were elected to the Chamber of Deputies. When the Suleyman an-Nabulsi government took office, 'Abd al-Qādir al-Ṣāliḥ was appointed Minister of Agriculture (the first C.P. member to receive a portfolio in the Arab world). Subsequently, the party began to operate openly and publish its manifestos in the press. In January 1957, a newspaper (al-Jamāhir) began to appear under the editorship of Rushdi Shāhīn, one of the party leaders. The Communist representatives in parliament presented demands for closer ties with the Eastern Bloc and the repeal of the 1953 law against Communism, which was still in effect. Party leaders continued to maintain contact with the electorate by visiting the cities and villages, explaining their political positions and promising to continue the struggle for the national issues.[6] The speeches of these parliamentary representatives, as well as the communiqués of the T.A.S.S. news agency, mainly disseminated from Damascus, were distributed to the public.[7] All these activities contravened the "War on Communism Law" but they remained unchallenged by the authorities. Furthermore, the party turned to more daring methods. Attempts were made to infiltrate the army and carry out ideological indoctrination. For the first time in its history in Jordan, the C.P. began to hoard weapons secretly.[8]

The constant increase in the power of the party resulted finally in the government's taking decisive action against it. In January 1957 King Hussein declared his opposition to "the adherents of materialism and those principles opposed to the principles of our religion."[9] In February, distribution of T.A.S.S. communiqués was banned in the Kingdom.

Prime Minister an-Nabulsi, who had not agreed with the King on the necessity of taking measures against the C.P., was accused upon his dismissal of having aided, together with his government, the C.P. by "sowing dissension in the state."[10] The law disbanding all political parties (25 April, 1957) declared the C.P., as well as all others, illegal. But in his broadcast to the nation upon the announcement of the law, the King referred directly and explicitly only to the C.P. He accused it of maintaining contacts with Israel, damaging the unity of the nation and the country, and contravening the principles of the faith. Hundreds of Communists, members as well as supporters, were arrested and tried. The parliamentary immunity of the party's representatives was revoked and they were sentenced to long prison terms (Fā'iq Warrād to 16 years and Dr. Ya'qūb Ziyādīn to 19 years).[11]

Heavy public pressure was brought to bear on the party. The press and radio accused its leadership of maintaining ties with Israel and of treason. Religious leaders published a manifesto against the C.P. and its principles and called on the public to hunt down its adherents without letup.[12] King Hussein himself publicly attacked the party several times.[13] Large show trials were held and long jail sentences meted out to party members at the end of 1957 and the beginning of 1958; in addition, public denunciations of party ex-members were aimed at deterring citizens from further supporting the Communists.

The C.P., although suffering serious setbacks from all these activities, adjusted to the new conditions and continued to operate underground. By signing a manifesto presented by 61 Communist parties on the occasion of the 40th anniversary of the Soviet October Revolution, the party flaunted its continued existence in the face of the regime.[14] In 1958, members were instructed to refrain from engaging in any public discussions with followers of other parties as a precaution against provocateurs. Members were forbidden to leave the country and those who had already left were ordered to return.[15] These steps were directed at preserving the clandestine existence of the party. At the same time, the C.P. was attentive to public issues and did not hesitate to express itself, mainly through leaflets, on all important issues, both international and domestic. Its chief activity was the recruitment of high school students: cells were organized, an indoctrination campaign was conducted, leaflets were distributed, and participation in demonstrations was encouraged.[16] This took place in various cities (Jericho, Jerusalem, Jenin, Qalqilya, Nablus, etc.). However, the students and teachers were not always a source of effective support and at times they proved to be a hazard to the party. In one case, for instance, the attempt of a teacher from the village of Dir Astia to recruit one of his students led to the exposure of a considerable number of the cells in the Nablus area and to the arrest of their members.[17]

By the end of 1950s, the Jordanian regime could boast that it had dealt the C.P. a severe blow. The party's expansion and development had been stopped. Its first attempts to organize for the use of force were nipped in the bud. Many of its cells were uncovered, their members being either imprisoned or prevented from continuing their political activity. Public party activity was almost completely halted and the C.P. was forced to focus its efforts on internal matters. After 1960, the party no longer took to the streets, and it reduced most of its overt and public activities. Instead, the C.P. dedicated itself to reorganization and establishing disciplined cadres which, despite their small numbers, were trained for infiltration of schools and workers' organizations at the appropriate time.[18] Unique and symbolic of Communist tenacity was the party organ al-Muqāwama al-Sha'biyya ("The Popular Struggle") which, printed underground, continued to appear regularly in the face of unsuccessful attempts by the regime to discover the location of its presses and methods of distribution.[19]

ORGANIZATION AND STRUCTURE

Structure and Delegation of Authority

The structure of the party was hierarchical and did not change in essence during the period under review. The supreme body was the Central Committee (al-lajna al-markaziyya), occasionally called the General (al-'āmma) Central Committee. It was responsible for activities in all of Jordan and therefore comprised members from both banks, although the majority of its outstanding personalities came from the West Bank. The head of the Central Committee was Fu'ād Naṣṣār. There were seven to nine members during most of the period and each represented his own region. The Central Committee appointed three or four of its members to act as the Politburo (al-maktab al-siyāsī) which actually led the party.

The second echelon consisted of the Central (markaziyya) or Regional (manṭiqiyya) Committees of three to five members with a Secretary at the head of each. There were approximately ten Regional Committees (in 1953—Jerusalem, Nablus, Jericho, Bethlehem, Ramallah, Irbid, Amman, Karak, Hebron, and Tulkarm). Their members performed various tasks—secretarial duties, communications, supervision of student affairs as well as of workers and fellahin.

In the third rank were Local (maḥalliyya) Committees which extended to large cities and sometimes even to villages. Each comprised three to four members—secretary, treasurer, an ideological mentor, and an officer responsible for leaflet distribution.

The lowest organizational level was the cell (khaliyya). There were sometimes cells with up to ten members, but the average cell had four members and was headed by a secretary.

The Central Committee led the party, determined its policy, activities, and its means of finance. It was also responsible for propaganda and published the party organ and its leaflets. Regional Committees saw to matters of party organization and were responsible for distribution of leaflets (and sometimes even for their printing in their own bailiwick); they received instructions from the Central Committee and transferred them to the Local Committees which in turn passed them on to the cells. Another important task of the Local Committees was to organize the activities of the cells, to coordinate, and, when necessary, rebuild the network of cells. Conversely, information, membership dues, and requests for guidance flowed from the cells upward.

The members of a cell knew one another by their full names. The cell held regular weekly meetings which were only partially devoted to organizational questions, being mainly intended for self-criticism, ideological guidance, and discussion of topical issues. The cell leader would explain the stance of the party on different matters, as he had received it from the Local or Regional Committee. Afterwards, in his report to those committees, he might request their comments on various topics which the periodical publications or general guidelines had not discussed. Members were obliged to submit to complete discipline not only in political questions, but also in questions of daily life. A member who wished to reside in another city had to receive authorization; conversely, the C.P. sometimes requested him to change his place of residence or work. A member who refused was tried by the cell or the Local Committee and if found guilty was expelled from the ranks of the party. To maintain security and discipline, such matters were publicized in the party organ.

Clandestinity[20]

The link between the various levels was always vertical. There was no contact between cells or between one Local Committee and another. The links were maintained by permanent emissaries *(murāsil)*, loyal and few in number. These people were in charge of passing leaflets and instructions from the Regional Committees to the Local Committees which were responsible for their distribution to the cells. In each cell, one member had the duty of receiving the material and disseminating it among his comrades and the wider circles of sympathizers. In the opposite direction, the emissaries delivered letters and money from the branches to the center. The principal emissaries traveled once every week or two, concealing the material they had received in various ways (in food baskets, generally). For maximum security, the names of individuals and villages mentioned in various documents and pamphlets were written either in code or numbers which were changed from time to time. Specific instructions were given to members never to mention real names in their reports or meet with members outside their own cell. It is clear that in the traditional village society, or even in the towns, it was not possible to maintain this practice to the full, but apparently in this field, as in others, party discipline achieved notable success. On numerous occasions, Jordanian security service personnel complained to their superiors that when a cell was uncovered, it did not lead to the discovery of others. [21]

As an illegal party continually persecuted by the regime, the Jordanian C.P. found it necessary to take various steps in order to maximize internal security. In large cities it was customary to rent apartments or rooms which were to serve as hiding places for members on the run. Key members were usually supplied with forged identity cards and passports to be kept on their persons in case of need. During periods of intense persecution by the police (1957–8, for example), it was common, especially in the Nablus area, for wanted party functionaries to flee to unsettled areas and to hide in caves for several months. At such times even ordinary meetings were cancelled and material was passed on to the cells not from hand to hand as was usual, but from agreed hiding places where it had been left by the emissaries. Notwithstanding all these precautionary measures, there was always the possibility of arrest. In the course of his training, every member was instructed both orally and in writing how to act when placed under arrest. In a pamphlet of instructions distributed among the members in 1954, two phases of behavior were prescribed. In the first stage, during arrest and interrogation, the ruling was refusal to admit party membership, and refrainment from defending its principles or revealing the identity of its members. Later, at the trial, the member was instructed to confess, employ the services of a lawyer, and, especially, to exploit the situation and turn the courtroom into a political arena to preach party principles. Of course, it was not always possible to maintain secrecy and there were instances of large networks collapsing after the capture of several people. But in the majority of cases, and in all those relating to the arrest of important members, it appeared that these rules were carefully observed and thus the party was able to continue operating despite the regime's counter-measures.

Recruiting

Despite this secrecy, every member saw himself responsible for spreading the party message as widely as possible. A party member would discuss his ideas with a close friend and when it appeared that the response was positive, would give the name of the potential member to the head of his cell who would pass it on to the Local Committee for authorization. After an appropriate investigation of the candidate's suitability and his potential as a future active member, approval would be granted to recruit him. He would then be approached and the matter presented to him. Recruiting was done by an agent from among his acquaintances, not necessarily by the party member who proposed him. However, the recommender of the candidate was held responsible for him for a long time after his recruitment and this constituted a check against the natural inclination to expand the framework rashly. The new member was required to prove his loyalty in two ways—payment of membership dues and distribution of leaflets. For a few months he would engage in distribution and thus was assessed not only in terms of efficiency but also of loyalty and reliability. At the same time, the recruiter would continue the candidate's indoctrination in preparation for his admission to the cell.

Finances

The readiness to pay membership dues *(ishtirāk)* was one of the first manifestations of intent to join the party. Membership dues were paid monthly according to changing rates of 150 fils to half a dinar. The cell secretary would transfer all the dues to the Local Committee, which in turn would forward them to the Regional Committee. Despite the general order against members having written material in their possession, because of the fear that it might fall into the hands of the authorities, treasurers had standing orders to keep a record of income and expenditures and to report on them in writing to the Center. In addition to the monthly dues, members and supporters were from time to time requested to make additional contributions, usually to help the families of imprisoned members. Contributions of supporters served as one of the principal sources of party finances for unspecified purposes. Even people expelled from the party sometimes continued to maintain connections with it by contributing in this way. The payments for the party paper, which were collected immediately upon its delivery, were another source of income.

Despite all this, the party was in a chronic state of financial difficulties, especially in the first years of its activity. At the end of 1951, when Fu'ād Naṣṣār was imprisoned, the printing presses of the C.P. were confiscated.[22] Only two years later did the party organ reappear in its original format; by the party's own admission, it was forced to wait such a long time because of the difficulty of obtaining from its members the amount needed to replace the equipment. In the second half of the 1950s, however, there were rumors that the resurgence in party activity was due to financial aid of considerable proportions which it had received from its sister party in Syria.

Publications

The Communist Party was the only one which, since 1948, had consistently attempted to spread its message to the Jordanian public, unlike other parties for which ideology and propaganda were of secondary importance. Hence, the party strove to ensure that political vicissitudes and persecution by the regime would not disrupt the constant flow of printed material. In addition to the desire to stir up support and encouragement in the widest possible circles, and especially among the intelligentsia, this activity also played an important role in the process of molding new party members, since the preparation of the publications, their transfer, and, especially, distribution were considered one of the main indices of the loyalty, diligence, and dedication of the members. However, in view of the concerted efforts of the regime to seize the typewriters and printing presses, to disrupt the distribution network, and to forbid the possession of the various publications, this became almost the principal arena of the struggle between the party and the regime. Indisputably, even when the efforts of the regime to halt or disrupt the publications of the party increased, the latter succeeded in proving that in this sphere it maintained superiority.

The principal and permanent publication (since the second half of 1949) was the party organ *al-Muqāwama al-Sha'biyya* ("The Popular Struggle"). Generally, it appeared as a monthly, although sometimes two issues were published in a single month. The banner carried the symbol of a hammer and sickle—beginning with the second year of its appearance—and the inscription "Organ of the League for National Liberation in Palestine." From the second half of 1951, it bore the inscription "Published by the Central Committee of the Jordanian Communist Party." The paper was initially priced at 5 mils, then went up to 10 mils from August 1949 and 15 mils from the middle of 1951 onward. Its format changed according to circumstances: at first two printed pages with two columns, and from 1951 six printed pages with five columns. In the years 1952–3 (after the printing house in Amman had been confiscated) it was mimeographed—first handwritten and later typewritten. From 1954, it again appeared printed, but in small format—two pages with five columns—and it remained in this form throughout the 1950s (except for 1956 when it appeared in double format).

The editorial represented, generally, the position of the party on the major political events of the day and took up 15–40% of the entire issue. The major portion of the issue usually dealt with problems of Jordanian domestic and foreign policy. At least 10%, but sometimes 20–30%, were translations from the Soviet press—speeches by the leaders of the Soviet Union, or articles marking important events in the international Communist movement. There was little reference to events in Communist countries, other than the Soviet Union, but there were many quotations from the manifestos of nearly all Communist parties, including those of Israel (at the end of the 1940s and beginning of the 1950s) and the countries of the Arab world (with an increasing intensity during the 1950s). Local economic problems, employment, and salary conditions were given little coverage—not exceeding 10% of all the articles—and were presented as factual reports without doctrinal scrutiny or analysis. Comparatively little space was devoted to events in the Arab world and in the Gaza Strip.[23] Only in the second half of the 1950s did the coverage of these topics increase.

The party organ was aimed at the politically conscious public. The primary allegiance was Arab-Jordanian (and sometimes Palestinian), but care was taken to constantly remind the reader of the party's adherence to the Soviet Union in the sphere of international relations. Appeals to the masses to rise against exploitation were of secondary importance, but occasionally the readers' attention was directed to the problems of various sectors of the population—workers, fellahin, government officials, teachers, and refugees.

The actual problems of daily life were given much greater coverage in the organs that began to appear in the main cities in the middle of the 1950s. These were: Niḍāl al-Sha'b ("The People's Struggle") in Jerusalem, Kifāḥ al-Sha'b ("The People's Struggle") in Amman, Ṣawt Jabal al-Nār ("The Voice of the Fire Mountain") in Nablus, and al-Wathba ("The Take-off") in Irbid. These organs appeared in mimeographed form from the middle of 1955, attained wide distribution in 1956 and continued to appear (at least the first two) irregularly and reduced in size until 1959. They purported to represent the Regional Committee of the party in each city, yet their character was also local, detailing events and protesting issues relevant to the local public. These organs were intended to appeal to broad strata of the public, whose level of political awareness was lower than that of the readers of the central *al-Muqāwama al-Sha'biyya*. In order to gain the attention of these readers, the rule was to deal with problems which were familiar and close to them and at the same time to conduct political indoctrination through editorials which were usually variations on themes sounded by *al-Muqāwama al-Sha'biyya*.

While the permanent organs were primarily intended for members and supporters, leaflets were used to maintain contact with the general public. Every important event in Jordan or the Middle East as a whole was given Communist comment in leaflets which were distributed in the main cities. Leaflets were also circulated on the occasions of important holidays (especially May Day, but also on the anniversary of the October Revolution and even on some religious holidays). They consisted of one or two printed and datemarked pages, signed by the League for the National Liberation and later the Jordanian C.P. Occasionally they were mimeographed—typewritten or even handwritten especially when they were issued by one of the branches and dealt with local problems. (Nablus, for example, was very active in this sphere at the beginning of the 1950s.) The leaflets were usually couched more simply than the official line of the party presented in *al-Muqāwama al-Sha'biyya*.

The distribution apparatus of *al-Muqāwama al-Sha'biyya* also undertook distribution of the local organs and the party leaflets.[24] While the organs were handed out by the actual membership, the leaflets were often distributed by children and youths (for small payment and often in ignorance of their contents). One of the accepted methods was to scatter the sheets in the streets at night or leave them at the doorsteps of schools in the hope that at least some of them would reach the public before the police could confiscate them. A method used to a lesser extent was to send the leaflets through the mail to intellectuals, senior officials, or even political leaders. At the beginning of 1956, in an effort to infiltrate the army, leaflets were sent in this manner to various military officers as well. Toward the end of 1955, it was decided to make the distribution of publications more efficient and switch to hand-to-hand distribution.[25] This change was motivated not merely by the desire to increase efficiency, but also as part of the campaign (which was especially notable in 1956) to arouse the political awareness of the public at large. Police officers and detectives were increasingly criticized by their superiors for their inability to prevent this type of distribution of C.P. publications. In later years the party continued to use the same method.

Most of the publications were distributed from one center and were apparently also printed at a single location, though not necessarily at the distribution point. With only one exception—at the end of 1951—the regime never succeeded in pinpointing the printing house of the party. The Jordanian security service files tell of repeated attempts to locate the writers, typewriters, mimeograph machines, or the printing house itself—all in vain. It was no surprise, then, that on several occasions (e.g., at the end of the 1940s and in 1956) internal reports of the security services attempted to explain this inadequacy by the fact that the leaflets were printed in Israel, while the Jordanian General Staff attributed their origin to Syria.[26]

Evidence indicates that the flow of distribution was from Jerusalem to Nablus in the north and Hebron in the south. In the middle of 1953, in 1954, and also in the second half of the 1950s, large shipments of leaflets and newspapers were seized on the way from Jerusalem to these provincial centers. Predictably, the security service searched for the printing press with greater intensity in Jerusalem, but these attempts also ended in failure.[27] The Nablus branch was responsible for the distribution of party publications in the entire northern area of the West Bank. The material was sent from there to Tulkarm, Qalqilya, Jenin, and Salfit.

CONCLUDING REMARKS

The Communist Party was the strongest political party in Jordan during the 1950s. It is possible that there were periods when the number of members and supporters of other parties (al-Qawmiyyūn al-'Arab or the Ba'th, for example in the mid-50s) was greater, but even this conjecture has not yet been substantiated. It is a matter of record that the Communists succeeded in increasing the number of their members in parliament to three in the 1956 elections, which were, compared with the other elections, less manipulated by the regime. Another distinction which was conceded by the Communists' opponents, was that even though the number of Communists was not large, their high level of indoctrination and organization gave their party a strength completely out of proportion to its actual size.

It is difficult to determine exactly the numerical strength of the party during this period. In spite of its highly centralized structure it did not keep any central listing. This was due to the general directive forbidding (for security reasons) written records on any level. Our estimate, therefore, is based on the only two existing sources—the Jordanian security service reports and interviews with party members or those close to them. According to these sources, at the beginning of the 1950s there were about 200 members on the West Bank and about another 100 on the East Bank who were also mostly Palestinians. In 1958, their number fell to a total of between 100–200. At the pinnacle of the party's success (1956–7), its membership never reached more than 1,000 members, according to all the sources.

Party cells were formed not only in all the cities and towns of the West Bank, but also in many of the villages. The two most active and successful centers were Nablus and Jerusalem, in this order. A third center worthy of mention was the village of Salfit. Since the end of the 1940s, this village had been prominent not only as the place of residence of several leaders of the C.P. (Fahmī al-Salfītī, Ḥamza al-Zir, ʿArabī ʿAwād) but also because of its large and active branch. There were several reasons for the development of such an important branch in this village: its relative isolation and yet its proximity to the important Communist centers in Nablus and Jerusalem; the role played by the veteran Communist, Fahmī al-Salfītī, in organizing the branch upon his return to his village from Gaza at the end of the 1940s; friction between local clans (not unknown in other towns and villages) which gave additional impetus to the party's efforts. Another factor was the great influence of the Communist Dr. Abū Khajla from Nablus, whose family owned for generations a considerable portion of the lands in and around the village. This leader enjoyed traditionally great prestige in the village in addition to the respect he had won as a successful doctor with the reputation of a man "who cared for the common-folk." Each of these factors explains perhaps part of the success of Communism in Salfit, but it appears that there is a need for a systematic socio-political study of this village in order to gain full understanding of this phenomenon, exceptional in the entire West Bank. In contrast to the situation in these three centers, the party was distinctly weak in the Mount Hebron area and in the city of Hebron in particular. Because of the traditional structure of Hebronite society and the great influence of its religious leaders, the C.P. began to operate there later than in all other cities in the West Bank. Despite the efforts of developing branches in Hebron and its vicinity, the party machine remained weaker and smaller there than in the other cities of the West Bank.

The main reasons for the growth of the Jordanian C.P. were: the steadfast structure of the branches and their rigid hierarchy; the secrecy of activity on all levels; orderly and intensive (once a fortnight usually) indoctrination in all the cells; the dedication of members to their cause; and the political and underground experience of the leadership. In its first years of development, the party managed to capitalize on the very same issue that had previously been the most damaging to it, i.e., the Palestine issue. The earlier Communist support for the implementation of the U.N. Partition Plan, thereby recognizing the establishment of the State of Israel, was increasingly watered down so that by the middle of the 1950s this "stain" on the party's image was in some measure erased. In this period, after the signing of the Czech-Egyptian arms deals and because of the growing acceptance of leftist ideas in the Arab world through Egypt's closer relations with the Soviet Union the C.P. enjoyed the best of two worlds. On the one hand, it supported Nasser and therefore obtained the sympathy and encouragement of nationalist groups; on the other hand, it could emphasize its close relations with the Soviet Union and thus demonstrate the correctness of its path, vis-à-vis the nationalists, over a period of years. It was no surprise then, that the years of close relations between Nasser and the Soviet Union, and of overwhelming public enthusiasm for the Soviets resulting from those relations (1956–7), were also those of the Communists greater achievements. The Soviet agreement to finance and build the Aswan Dam in 1958 gave the party additional lift in the public's eyes, which helped it to survive despite severe persecution by the regime.

In its tactics the party was highly pragmatic. In retrospect, it appears that the principles it adopted in its public activity had already crystallized at the very beginning of its organization in the country. Workers and farmers, and social and economic problems were of secondary importance in the party's campaigns and efforts to recruit members. This is not to say that the working class was totally neglected. As mentioned above, from time to time social and economic issues were discussed in the party organs, while in some cities (Ramallah, for example) some of the cells consisted of members who were mostly workers. However, the main emphasis was placed on activity in the cities rather than in villages, and among educated sections of the population rather than among the masses. The high percentage of teachers among the party's leadership and rank and file was not only due to the need for relative sophistication in order to assimilate the movement's principles, but also a result of the party's deliberate recruiting policy. The advantages accruing to the party from stress on recruitment of teachers were numerous. First, it was the best and most efficient way to infiltrate the high schools and influence the students. It must be recalled that the main group from which members in the city were recruited consisted of students who were employed in distributing leaflets and who participated in demonstrations. This was a long-term investment in which the party was most interested (even though many of the students left the party after graduating from high school). Secondly, it was customary for teachers in Jordan to be shifted from place to place every few years, and in this way the C.P. could extend its influence to distant towns and villages in which it had no adequate local representation. Thirdly, the diffusion of Jordanian-Palestinian intellectuals in general, and teachers in particular, throughout the Arab world enabled the party to "export" a large number of activists.

The C.P. was also successful in recruiting some influential personalities to its leadership. In order to strengthen its appeal to the public, the party tried very hard to fashion a showcase of intellectuals (among them many with the title of Doctor) in the front rank of the membership. For example, Dr. Nabīh Arshidāt and Dr. Ya'qūb Ziyādīn quickly rose to the leadership of the party despite the fact that the latter's commencement of activity at the beginning of the 1950s had caused unusual friction among a segment of the existing leadership. While Ziyādīn was much admired by the people of the Jerusalem area because of his free treatment of the poor, Arshidāt was an owner of vast properties who could therefore recruit supporters through this channel. This last attribute applied also to Rushdī Shāhīn, who was a large landowner in the villages of Beit Dajan and Beit Fūrīq in the north and in the Jordan Valley. Thus, in order to gain influence in circles both broad and suited to its purpose, the party tried to advance people who, in addition to their personal abilities, also possessed other desirable qualifications, such as higher education or extensive economic power. The affluent social origin of such individuals was by no means considered a drawback to their holding high ranks in the C.P.

Outstanding among all other party office-holders was Fu'ād Naṣṣār. He was universally praised for his intelligence and honesty, his eloquence, strong personality, idealism, and sincerity. Naṣṣār, like several other leaders, lacked formal education and came from humble social origins. Nor did his being a Christian hinder his leading a party with a Muslim majority. It was he who established the general party policy which favored those who were well educated, showed political awareness (even if lacking social awareness), and were prepared for action in the cause of a predetermined program. Riḍwān al-Ḥilū, a veteran leader who disagreed with this program and opposed Naṣṣār's leadership, came under heavy attack. At the beginning of the 1950s Ḥilū's activities were suspended and in 1954 he was finally and officially expelled for "Titoist deviation."

Even in retrospect it is difficult to point out many mistakes made by the party which could be seen as having impeded its development. The factors which eroded its achievements in Jordan were: the persistent and harsh persecution by the regime; the party's stand on Palestine in 1947, which the public could not entirely forgive even after the Soviet Union had become the principal ally of the Arab states; neglect of any serious treatment of workers' problems; competition from the Ba'th which used partially similar slogans but was free from the "stain" of servitude to the Soviet Union; the deep split between Nasser and the Soviet Union at the end of the 1950s; and the popular conception of the party as anti-religious and therefore intrinsically alien and undesirable (even though the party was very careful in this matter—for example, during the fierce competition with the Ba'th in 1956, it instructed its members to show respect for religion, to refrain from drinking wine, etc.).

While it should be recalled that the C.P. was active on both banks of the Jordan simultaneously, the center of its activity and success was undoubtedly on the West Bank whence came the majority of its members and supporters. Moreover, as mentioned above, a substantial portion of the rank and file on the East Bank were also Palestinians. The historical background and the rich experience of the Palestinian C.P. under the British Mandate contributed greatly to the party's accomplishments. But even more important was the exploitation of this Palestinian character in the party's political campaigns. The general atmosphere of disenchantment with the Hashemite regime in various circles, especially among Palestinian intellectuals and Palestinians in general, served the needs of the party. This atmosphere also bred and served various other opposition groups which were emerging in the 1950s, especially the Ba'th and al-Qawmiyyūn al-'Arab. In the fierce competition for the support of the same social groups, these two parties achieved great success and sometimes even surpassed the C.P. in the numbers of their supporters and sympathizers. But there was one basic difference between them and the C.P. It took several years for the mentioned two parties to recover from the persecutions of the late 1950s and early 1960s, while the C.P., with its underground experience, superior organization, and better indoctrination, continued clandestine operations and its reduced but extremely loyal nucleus managed to carry on its political activity during the 1960s and beyond.

NOTES

1 *Al-Muqāwama al-Sha'biyya*, 4/5 (March 1952); 4/13 (July 1952).
2 There is evidence to this effect as early as the first half of 1952.
3 *Hāmizraḥ Heḥadash*, Vol. 5, p. 115.
4 *Ibid.*, p. 294; *op. cit.*, Vol. 6, p. 143.
5 Archives of Jordanian Security Services (J.S.S.), in Israel State Archives, Jerusalem, File MN/17/1, pp. 25, 28, 54, 59; MLS/18/50, pp. 11, 13, 21, 44.
6 *Al-Difā'*, 22, 23, 30 November, 1956; *Al-Ḥayāt*, 28 May, 1957; *Filasṭīn*, 17 November, 1956; *Hamizraḥ Heḥadash*, Vol. 8, p. 221.
7 J.S.S./MQM/4/9/p. 9.
8 J.S.S./7–520/p. 48; J.S.S./2703–36; *Al-Difā'*, 17 December, 1956; *Hamizraḥ Heḥadash*, Vol. 9, p. 196.
9 *Al-Ḥayāt*, 11 January, 1957
10 Amman Radio, 30 April, 1957.
11 Amman Radio, 25 April, 1957; *Hamizraḥ Heḥadash*, Vol. 9, p. 85; Vol. 10, p. 79.
12 *Filasṭīn*, 6 August, 1957.
13 *Filasṭīn*, 7 December, 1957.
14 *Al-Nūr*, 25 November, 1957.
15 J.S.S./MQM/20/1/pp. 47, 271.
16 J.S.S./707–8/pp. 973, 976, 1009, 1062.
17 J.S.S./707–8/pp. 893, 945, 960, 973, 976, 1009, 1062, 1102, 1168.
18 J.S.S./279–14/p. 114.
19 J.S.S./695–1/p. 52.
20 Based mainly on J.S.S., file 2703–36.
21 J.S.S./707–8/p. 824.
22 *Al-Muqāwama al-Sha'biyya*, 4/5 (March 1952); *Hamizraḥ Heḥadash*, Vol. 3, p. 262.
23 An exception to this rule was number 2/6 (June 1950).
24 J.S.S./MQM/13/pp. 81, 245.
25 J.S.S./MN/17/1/p. 255.
26 J.S.S./MN/17/1/pp. 179–80.
27 J.S.S./MQM/4/9/p. 291; J.S.S./695–1/p. 52.

LIST OF PARTICIPANTS

Mr. Yigal Allon
Deputy Prime Minister of Israel and Minister of Education and Culture

Prof. Yilmaz Altug
Hukuk Fakultesi, Istanbul Universitesi

Prof. Gabriel Baer
Institute of Asian and African Studies, Hebrew University of Jerusalem

Dr. Abraham S. Becker
Economics Department, The RAND Corporation

Dr. Wolfgang Berner
Bundesinstitut fur ostwissenschaftliche und internationale Studien, Köln

Prof. Leonard Binder
Department of Political Science, University of Chicago

Prof. Joseph Churba
Middle Eastern Studies, Air University, Maxwell, Alabama

Dr. Amnon Cohen
Institute of Asian and African Studies, Hebrew University of Jerusalem

Prof. Michael Confino
The Russian and East European Research Center, Tel Aviv University

Prof. Alexander Dallin
The Hoover Institution on War, Revolution, and Peace, Stanford University

Prof. Uriel Dann
The Shiloah Center for Middle Eastern and African Studies, Tel Aviv University

Prof. Herbert Dinerstein
The Johns Hopkins University, School of Advanced International Studies,
Washington D. C.

Dr. Oded Eran
The Russian and East European Research Center, Tel Aviv University

439

Dr. ZVI GITELMAN
Department of Political Science, Michigan University, and the Russian and
East European Research Center, Tel Aviv University

PROF. MANFRED HALPERN
Center of International Studies, Princeton University

Dr. ARNOLD HORELICK
The RAND Corporation

PROF. J.C. HUREWITZ
Middle Eastern Institute, Columbia University

PROF. ELIE KEDOURIE
London School of Economics and Political Science

Dr. AARON KLIEMAN
The Russian and East European Research Center, Tel Aviv University

PROF. ROMAN KOLKOWICZ
Department of Political Science, University of California, Los Angeles

PROF. W.Z. LAQUEUR
The Russian and East European Research Center, Tel Aviv University, and
Institute of Contemporary History and Wiener Library, London

Dr. AVIGDOR LEVY
The Shiloah Center for Middle Eastern and African Studies, Tel Aviv University

PROF. BERNARD LEWIS
School of Oriental and African Studies, University of London

PROF. RICHARD LÖWENTHAL
Otto-Suhr-Institut der Freien Universität, Berlin, and Visiting Professor,
Tel Aviv University

Dr. MATI MAYZEL
Russian Research Center, Harvard University, and Russian and East
European Research Center, Tel Aviv University

PROF. HANS MORGENTHAU
University of Chicago, and City University of New York

Dr. GUR OFER
Department of Economics, and the Soviet and East European Research
Center, Hebrew University of Jerusalem

Dr. BEN-CION PINCHUK
The Russian and East European Research Center, Tel Aviv University

PROF. RICHARD PIPES
Russian Research Center, Harvard University

DR. ITAMAR RABINOVICH
The Shiloah Center for Middle Eastern and African Studies, Tel Aviv University

MR. YAACOV RO'I
The Russian and East European Research Center, Tel Aviv University

DR. HAIM SHAKED
The Shiloah Center for Middle Eastern and African Studies, Tel Aviv University

PROF. SHIMON SHAMIR
The Shiloah Center for Middle Eastern and African Studies, Tel Aviv University

MISS ESTHER SOUERY
The Shiloah Center for Middle Eastern and African Studies, Tel Aviv University

PROF. P.J. VATIKIOTIS
School of Oriental and African Studies, University of London

DR. GABRIEL WARBURG
Department of the History of the Muslim Peoples, University of Haifa